THE RISE OF THE EUROPEAN ECONOMY

WORLD ECONOMIC HISTORY

GENERAL EDITOR . CHARLES WILSON

Hermann Kellenbenz

Revised and edited by Gerhard Benecke

The Rise of the European Economy

An economic history of Continental Europe from the
fifteenth to the eighteenth century

WEIDENFELD AND NICOLSON
LONDON

Weidenfeld and Nicolson
11 St John's Hill London SW11

ISBN 0 297 77062 4
Printed in Great Britain by
Cox & Wyman Ltd,
London, Fakenham and Reading

Contents

Foreword

'It is impossible for anyone living today to hear early music with the ears of those who first heard it, and it is idle to pretend otherwise.' Thus wrote the late Professor Thurston Dart in his *Interpretation of Music* (1955), a masterly essay in the art of concrete historical understanding. Changes in the nature of music, of instruments, notation, even of building acoustics – but above all the change in the expectations of the listeners, now accustomed to hear everything from Beethoven to Schoenberg – all these make it impossible to hear the music of Bach's day as Bach heard it. As T. S. Eliot has put it: 'the past is altered by the present as much as the present is directed by the past'.

Any social historian with a tincture of imagination will recognize the problem. It is especially true of the economic and social history of early modern Europe, the subject of this book. We come to its study from an industrial society. The concepts of industry, trade, agriculture etc. which form the starting point from which the modern historian must try to understand the past are inevitably those of his own world. It is immaterial whether, in the immortal words of *1066 and All That*, they seem to him a Good Thing or a Bad Thing; he cannot wholly divest himself of his place and time in history. Yet, like the musicologist, he must try; if he does not, his reconstruction of history will be a travesty. He will resemble Professor Dart's keyboard performers who 'continue to make Bull sound like Clementi and Bach like Czerny and the flow of the music [like] . . . a running tap rather than a wind-tossed fountain'.

The techniques of economic history have changed radically in the last few decades. Not all the changes are good but in general it is a gain that we talk less about 'theory' as understood by political economists, that we behave more 'scientifically' (which is not the same as merely aping the physical scientists), that we try to reconstruct the complex relationships of production and consumption, taking the fullest possible account of the social dynamics of price fluctuations and population movements. By such methods the historian *can* to some extent penetrate the realities of a long-past age and not remain content to describe a selection of its salient institutions from the outside. This is the essence of the conscious effort that must be made to combat the teleological threat that afflicted much historical writing in the past.

Along with the changing techniques goes a change in the areas and phenomena studied. Most economic history of the older kind was based on 'national' areas; to widen this into larger regions, where nation-states are grouped to allow us to understand better the functioning of the economic process, still creates great problems. Few scholars today have the personal knowledge, the linguistic ability or the mastery of European sources, primary or secondary, which Professor Kellenbenz possesses. It is as a dedicated European that he surveys Europe throughout its length and breadth, intimately yet objectively, and in its own, contemporary terms.

The picture he presents is one of astonishing variety of resources and skills – massive evidence of Europe's good fortune and superior management when compared with other continents. Yet equally he shows that it would be an illusion to infer that Europe was set safely on the road to economic stability, let alone permanent progress, in early modern times. The Atlantic seaboard might be relatively advanced; most areas of Eastern Europe were socially and economically primeval. Socially their condition was, if anything, getting worse. The cycle of fat and lean years retained much of its ancient and malevolent power over most of Europe and was to continue to do so into relatively modern times. Even in these pseudo-modern times, the gap between idea, invention, and social application and utility remained enormous. Everywhere enterprise and custom, innovation and conservation, still struggled for supremacy. The Dutch Republic, like North Italy, after performing marvels of economic ingenuity, fell into a torpor. Why England should ultimately have emerged to inaugurate the process of continuous growth remains mysterious – and beyond the horizons of Professor Kellenbenz's enquiries. What he makes plain is that once 'take-off' happened there were vast reservoirs of traditional commercial and industrial skill to be tapped when the turn of Continental Europe came for industrialization.

Professor Kellenbenz does not claim to have found definitive answers to the infinitely complex economic problems of early modern Europe – why there was growth or progress in this country and much less, or none, in that; why this half century was one of expansion and that one of stagnation or retraction. What he has done is to survey as much of the basic evidence as possible for Europe as a whole, gather it together into the broad categories which economists and economic historians nowadays concur in regarding as significant, and provide some preliminary findings based on his enquiries. His achievement certainly entitles him to claim to have laid a firm foundation for more detailed studies in a task which (as he says) 'has only just begun'.

Introduction

CONTINENTAL EUROPE AS AN ECONOMIC AREA

There is no satisfactory definition of the term 'continental Europe' that will fit the facts and events of economic history. A purely geographical definition cannot help much, for it would include the whole continent of Europe without the British Isles. A better approach seems to be to consider the continent and its economic connections with the seas surrounding it, and then to take into account the varying influences of the chief economic centres and lines of communication.

From the late fifteenth century onwards the Atlantic side of Europe became particularly important as a result of the great discoveries and changes in world trade routes. First Spain and Portugal, then the whole area from the Bay of Biscay along the French coast to the Netherlands, became the centre of gravity. In particular, the Netherlands benefited from an extremely favourable position for trade and from the effects of the revolt against the Spanish state. The North Sea area, that is the British Isles and the coast from Dutch Friesland to Jutland and Norway, should also be included in this economic centre.

The Atlantic seaboard of Europe had its own hinterland, which included parts of France, especially along the Garonne, Loire and Seine. It drew on the border region east of the Île de France along the Maas, Scheldt and Rhine, reaching deep into Germany. It also influenced parts of Westphalia and Lower Saxony, stretching along the Rivers Weser and Elbe as far as

Hesse, Saxony and Bohemia, and of Holstein, Schleswig and Jutland.

Beyond this Atlantic region, however, existed another, centring on the Mediterranean. Fernand Braudel's great work, *La Mediterranée*, shows how real this Mediterranean world was at the end of the sixteenth century. To it belonged the Levantine coast of Spain, Provence, Italy and, to the east of the Adriatic, a good part of the Balkan peninsula, from the Dalmatian coast through Bosnia and Serbia, to Greece and Macedonia and up to the Danubian principalities and the Black Sea coast. Mediterranean Europe also had a hinterland in Provence and Languedoc and up the Rhone valley to Lyons. It included Piedmont and Lombardy as well as Venice and its mainland, reaching through Friuli and Croatia to the south-eastern Alps and into the Hungarian plain.

Taking into account the areas where the Atlantic and Mediterranean regions join and overlap, it is possible to outline a third economic area – 'continental Europe' – which reaches from the Baltic Sea to the Alps, from Poland to Hungary and Transylvania, including north and east Europe as far as the Urals as well as the Scandinavian countries around the Baltic Sea. To this a good part of rural France can be added, although French commercial activity considerably overlapped the Atlantic and Mediterranean regions. Provence, the Rhone Valley and parts of Languedoc were strongly orientated towards the Mediterranean, whereas western France belonged to the Atlantic. North Europe also showed strong connections with the Atlantic via the North Sea ports, the Danish Sound between the North Sea and Baltic, and up to the Arctic via Archangel.

Economic links between 'continental Europe' as described above and the areas orientated towards the Atlantic and the Mediterranean were numerous. What is important is not to define them precisely, but, recognizing their existence, to evaluate their real significance. Such an evaluation will show how closely the economies of the newly emerging states interlocked and will also help to give the lie to notions of individual national economic histories. Of course individual parts of continental Europe were economically stronger than others and it must not be thought that the area formed an economically self-sufficient unit *vis-à-vis* Atlantic and Mediterranean Europe. None the less an analysis of our area – which comprises in addition to parts of France, Central Europe and the Alps, the Danube basin as far as the Iron Gates, the Baltic litoral with Denmark, Sweden and Finland, Poland and Russia – will show that the strength of its internal economic links has been underestimated until now.

Apart from the North Sea and Baltic coasts and the approaches to the White and Black Seas, continental Europe faces inward, away from the sea. In the centuries of overseas expansion it lagged behind western Europe and the Mediterranean. On the other hand its wealth of mineral resources and agrarian forest produce led to a varied trade with western Europe and the Mediterranean, based on river and overland communications, in France along the Seine, Loire and Garonne to the Atlantic and along the Rhône to the Mediterranean. In Germany, the Rhine, Weser and Elbe connected the hinterland with the North Sea. The Oder, Vistula, Memel and Duna gave access to the Baltic, and farther east, the Danube, Dnieper, Dniester, Don and Volga led to the Black Sea.

Much of the north of France, northern Germany, Denmark and southern Sweden, Poland, Russia and the central Danube basin is plain or lowland, but mountainous areas run from eastern France through southern and central Germany to the Carpathians. These highlands are rich in minerals and together with the ore-bearing uplands of Scandinavia they contributed to the prosperity of Central Europe in early modern times. The plains, which were relatively poor in minerals, became important for agrarian produce and timber.

CHRONOLOGICAL ARRANGEMENT OF THE SUBJECT

European economic history from the end of the fifteenth century to the middle of the eighteenth covers a period of basic change in men's modes of thought. At the beginning mental attitudes still belonged to the Middle Ages; at the end technical progress and science had advanced so far that society stood poised for the new world of industrialization.

Since this is a history of economic development, we shall try to arrange the mass of material in patterns which arise from the economic process itself and not from an inherited scheme derived from political history. None the less we must not ignore the interplay between economic and political events. For the political historian, 1492 or 1517 are convenient dates to divide this epoch from the previous one. In 1492 Columbus discovered America and opened up a new world for the European economy; in the year 1517 Luther nailed up his theses and began his open conflict with the medieval church, ushering in the great European religious schism. This influenced, albeit indirectly, the further development of commercial capitalism. In effect both Renaissance and Reformation were to lead the people of Europe away from medieval beliefs towards the values of a modern world.

In spite of the extension of the European sphere of action into the overseas world, the tensions unleashed by the Reformation and the events of the Renaissance were so great that they profoundly affected the centuries that followed. Political events were determined by the wars of Charles v, and the Habsburg Empire which supported him, against the French crown and its allies. The political powers of Europe were preoccupied by this struggle until after the middle of the sixteenth century to such an extent that their financial organization was wholly unable to keep pace. The result was seen in widespread national bankruptcies in Spain, France and elsewhere.

If these crises and the resulting political changes form the first convenient sub-division of the period, the next one falls at the beginning of the Thirty Years' War. This phase also is one of bankruptcies. These not only hide changes that were the result of political processes, but also clearly foreshadowed a long economic recession.

The next sub-division is crowded with the events of the Thirty Years' War. These upset the economy in many ways, but to the neutral powers they brought many benefits. If the signing of the Treaties of Westphalia in 1648 ushered in a more settled period for central Europe, this was not true for the west, where the struggles between England and the Dutch Republic and Spain and France continued. The sequence of events in the north was determined by the territorial rivalry of Sweden and Denmark and the Swedes' need to expand in the Baltic.

If the peace treaties in the Pyrenees (1659) and at Copenhagen (1660) and the treaty of Oliva (1660) formed an end to this sub-division, this was by no means the end of military engagements. In the east the Turkish wars of the sixteenth century broke out anew in the second half of the seventeenth century and lasted well into the eighteenth. In the west, Louis XIV began the wars of hegemony in France, which culminated in the Wars of the Spanish Succession and were paralleled by the Great Northern War. The last phase down to the middle of the eighteenth century is characterized by all the signs of an economic revival, especially after 1740 in terms of population growth.

INTELLECTUAL BACKGROUND

The Renaissance and its effect on the economy

In about 1500 men found themselves in the middle of a process of emancipation which has come to be known as the Renaissance. In so far as the Renaissance meant an emphasis upon man's individuality and rationality of thought and action, together with greater efforts to understand and control nature, its influence on the economy was crucial. A similar and earlier phase of commercial revolution had already taken place at the turn of the thirteenth and fourteenth centuries; now a process of rationalization, of economic emancipation from the structure of the high medieval world, was going forward once again.

Yet the Renaissance did not bring any complete break with the economic past. The evidence for economic change remains patchy: the first printed manual of double entry book-keeping appeared in 1494; decisive concessions with regard to the charging of interest followed, yet discussion continued throughout the sixteenth century. The complexity of the problem is shown by the fact that Jacob Fugger, a leader in economic matters in his time, did not acknowledge the revolutionary movement of the Reformation and retained an entirely medieval attitude to religion. Leonardo da Vinci had already designed a machine to polish needles and sketched a spinning device, turbines and other machines; but the work of generations of scientists, from Galileo to Newton, was needed before a store of new knowledge made possible technical innovations that actually brought about the age of industrialization.

One of the effects of the Renaissance was certainly a closer approach to nature and increased efforts to conquer it; another was the enrichment of European civilization, both in daily life and on especial occasions, by an increasing interest in the arts

and a decided taste for luxury. The Middle Ages had seen the
building of churches as one of its main duties. Its art was above
all sacred art. But now art also became more worldly. Increasingly its purpose was to decorate castle and palace and em-
bellish the elegant houses of the bourgeoisie. The luxury goods
which in former centuries were only obtainable by a limited
number of customers now became available to much wider
classes.

This process was connected with another which also had to
do with an intensive interest in nature. In the wake of the
discoveries, overseas markets were opened up for the European
economy. During the course of the fifteenth century, advances in
navigation and astronomy, the use of the compass, astrolabe
and cross staff combined with improved techniques in ship-
building to enable the Portuguese to feel their way along the
African coast and, finally, round the Cape of Good Hope. At
the beginning of the sixteenth century Vasco da Gama succeeded in reaching India via the route round South Africa and
in making direct contacts with the East Indian spice markets in
competition with the Arabs and their Mediterranean agents.
This opened up possibilities of extending European trade, in
the same way that the route to the West Indies and Brazil had
emerged from the voyages of discovery of Christopher Columbus
and Pedro Alvares Cabral. Economic considerations played a
decisive part in other undertakings overseas, including Magel-
lan's voyage to the Pacific and other Spanish ventures to the
Moluccas.

But the problem of national rivalry was not put aside. The
Spanish and Portuguese were not the only ones to lay claim to
overseas trade. French and English argued about the fisheries
in the northern Atlantic and applied themselves vigorously to
voyages of piracy and smuggling to South America. New
routes to the treasures of the East were sought via the north-
west passage, that is, by water through northern Canada, or by
the north-east passage round the North Cape to the White
Sea. Although the real goal was not reached, Richard Chancellor had found a new route to the alluring markets of Russia.
And finally the Dutch and English managed to wrest the
secret of the route to the East Indies round the Cape of Good
Hope from the Portuguese and even increase its importance.
Dangerous voyages round Cape Horn were less inviting.

With these advances in the Indian, eastern Asiatic and Pacific areas, and in the North Sea, where whaling promised profits, the first great epoch of discovery was, in general, complete. The Australian *terra incognita* still attracted explorers, though decisive advances in that direction were only undertaken in the course of the eighteenth century.

All these events affected mainly the Atlantic side of Europe, but they need to be mentioned here to indicate the wider framework within which the economy of Europe developed. There was no lack of response to these events in continental Europe: a system of trade routes, hitherto concentrated along the axis from the Netherlands to Italy, was modified by the displacement of the centre of gravity towards the west and was compelled to orientate itself ever more towards the Atlantic.

The Reformation and the new concept of the economy

Luther's initiation of the Reformation made a fact of the division in religious affairs that had been threatening for so long. A large part of central Europe, including Switzerland, the northern Netherlands, Scandinavia, parts of France, and England and Scotland, became Protestant. Altogether, about one quarter of the population of Europe was affected by these changes of belief.

The effect on economic conditions in these countries was considerable. The switch to Protestantism meant the dissolution of monasteries and the confiscation of church property, usually in favour of the crown, the nobility or a city. In Sweden, secularization helped to provide the newly independent state with a firm basis on which to build. In those areas along the Baltic which produced grain, the seizure of church property (much of which found its way into the hands of leading noble families) helped to support the development of *Gutswirtschaft* (demesne farming) already in train among the nobility. A further result of the religious changes was an increasing intolerance that finally broke out into open persecution and forced many religious minorities to flee and emigrate.

The first of these flights and emigrations was caused by the expulsion of the Sephardic Jews from Spain in 1492 and a few years later, in 1496, from Portugal. The introduction of the Inquisition into Portugal and its intensification under Philip II

led to more and more unrest among the 'New Christians', so
that individuals emigrated to places that had particular economic attractions for them. These areas were willing to accept
the *Marranos* (as they were soon to be called). As these were
often well-to-do, their emigration led to a displacement of
capital and trade links, mainly from Spain and Portugal, which
brought substantial benefit to cities like Amsterdam and Hamburg, whence the emigrants established a network of connections with continental Europe. Although considerable numbers
of Catholics emigrated from Protestant areas, the movement of
Protestants, to England, Scotland, the northern Dutch provinces and the Rhineland, and also from northern Italy to
Switzerland, was even greater from states which remained
Catholic (e.g. from northern France and the southern Netherlands).

Among the emigrant sects, one group, the Anabaptists,
formed a special section, part making for the territories belonging to the Bohemian Crown and part settling in Holstein and
western Prussia.

Among these emigrants there were many well-to-do entrepreneurs, with useful experience and knowledge in one field of
economic activity or another, who supplied a new impetus to
the economic life of the country where they settled. Such initiative was gladly received not only by England and the northern
Netherlands, but also in various German territories and
towns, especially Hamburg, as well as in some cantons of the
Swiss Confederation and in Denmark and Sweden. (The Huguenot migration, caused by the revocation of the Edict of
Nantes in 1685, belongs to a later phase, but, again, the stream
of emigrants was to flow to the British Isles, to Germany and
to Holland, and also to Switzerland.)

Sectarian conflict was to be characteristic of the areas which
became Protestant, sometimes causing great unrest, as the
upheavals in Münster showed. On the other hand, their community life often led to higher economic productivity, which
unmistakably characterized the energetic Baptists and Men-
nonites in Altona near Hamburg.

It is difficult to define with any precision the influence of
the Reformation on the development of capitalism. It can be
demonstrated that Luther still clung to a basically medieval
point of view. He condemned both usury and luxury, whereas

there were many among his Catholic contemporaries who held more advanced views about lending money at interest. Dr Eck of Ingoldstadt, who retained the old beliefs, became spokesman for the Fuggers' views on interest. Philipp Melanchthon was more practical and realistic than Luther, developing Lutheran Protestantism into dogmatic forms and thus giving the Protestant attitude to work its particular cast. Melanchthon emphasized the virtues of a life of duty, diligence and hard work. For some this meant reservations about care of the idle, poor and infirm: man must work.

In his basic views Calvin also differed little from the position of late medieval writers and Catholic publicists of the sixteenth century. He approved a low rate of interest for borrowing in business and condemned the practice whereby peasants and artisans had to pay exorbitant rates. Like the Lutherans, Calvin also believed that all activity, however simple, could be a 'calling' and would find its reward on earth. It was assumed that man should carry on his work according to the old monastic rule, diligently and temperately, that he should pray and go to church. In this way he could demonstrate that he belonged to that small group of chosen people predestined by God to eternal life. If he lived temperately and became rich his labours would not be in vain. This was a view that was bound to reassure those who devoted themselves to business and trade and thereby achieved a rich and comfortable way of life. The result was a Protestant ethic which accepted the traditional Christian *ora et labora* in a new world of commercial and industrial activity that began to develop out of a more feudal past.

It is difficult to say how far this Protestant ethic, which is doubtless more associated with Calvinism than with Lutheranism, influenced the attitude to economic activities in the countries that became Protestant. But it can be shown that in some areas, for instance Switzerland, industrialization made greater progress in the areas which had become Protestant than in those where the old beliefs were retained. In the Rhineland, too, leading entrepreneurs seem to have come from reformed circles. The matter needs to be treated with care, however, for Catholic Europe, northern Italy and the southern Netherlands, for instance, continued its own economic activity with measured success.

The Modern State

The medieval idea of the universal state had had its centre of gravity in the Holy Roman Empire, whose sphere of influence stretched across central Europe and also over the Alps into Italy. The sixteenth century, by contrast, was marked by important developments in government, the rise of national states, and the emergence of a European system of states.

The idea of the nation state gradually gained acceptance, especially in western and northern Europe. After the end of the Hundred Years' War, the French crown continued to round off its boundaries during the course of the sixteenth century. In the Iberian peninsula, the unification of Spain was prepared by the marriage of Ferdinand of Aragon and Queen Isabella of Castile. In the Scandinavian area Gustavus Vasa left the Nordic Union for good. For the time being Norway and Denmark remained under one crown, which also ruled the Duchy of Holstein within the German Empire. In the east of Europe the dynastic principle still prevailed over the national. The Polish Jagiello monarchy included Ukranians and west Russians as well as Poles and Lithuanians. The might of the Ottoman Empire, spreading from Asia Minor, ruled over the peoples of the Balkans as far as the boundary between Hungary and Croatia.

It is significant that it was in Italy, decentralized and divided, that Niccolo Machiavelli (1469–1527) lived and worked. In *The Prince* he gives an idealized picture of an autocratic petty ruler. Machiavelli's pragmatic *raison d'état* formed the basis on which ruling princes tried to organize their governments in the following centuries. Yet the absolute princedom of the sixteenth century was not as developed as that of the seventeenth or finally as that of the eighteenth-century enlightened despots. Further political theorists became necessary. Above all, the details of the form which governments took depended on the skill of the reigning dynasty in opposing the strength of existing social classes – the territorial estates of clergy, nobles, town council burghers and professionals: princely absolutism in the Spain of Philip II was different from princely absolutism in the France of Richelieu or Louis XIV. In an autocratically ruled princedom there was always the danger that economic affairs, which concerned the well-being of all subjects, would be abused by a small royal clique that was hungry for power and prestige. The situation was different in those states in which an oligarchic system of government prevailed: in the aristocratic republics of Genoa and Venice and above all in the Dutch Republic (which gained its independence in the war against Spain) and in England. Here, where trade and shipping were so important to the state, those groups which were active in economic matters could increase their influence.

Social mobility was important for the development of economic strength. In the great monarchies, such as France and Spain, the concept of an ideal nobility, based on the medieval ideal of the knight, still existed: it gained new strength at the princely Italian courts. Its quintessence is found in Castiglione's *Book of the Courtier* (1518), in which work is rejected as unbecoming and ungentlemanly. In coastal northern Europe men were more open-minded, for on the North Sea and the Baltic littoral the nobility played a considerable part in trade in the sixteenth century. In the Netherlands and in England merchant and burgher elements gained greater influence on state affairs than elsewhere.

A time-lag in economic development in the east of the continent is clearly visible, in comparison with the state of development of western Europe; this was particularly the case in Russia, whose economy was more archaic in the sixteenth century than that of Poland or the Balkans.

Those tendencies to state regulation which are grouped together under the name 'mercantilism' first became prominent in the seventeenth and part of the eighteenth century. If, however, we examine differences of time and place, we shall find that typical mercantilist attitudes are to be found in western and southern Europe earlier than in central, northern and eastern Europe. The Frenchman Jean Bodin (1530–96) was the first important exponent of bullion and the quantity theory of money. He was one of the first to see that the price rises of the sixteenth century were not only a result of debasement of the currency, monopolies and luxury, but were also caused by the influx of precious metals from America. His character was too complicated, he was too involved in both the old and the new, simply to be labelled a mercantilist, but among his many theoretical writings he left precepts on which was based the future development of mercantilism. In the sixth volume of his

Republic (1576) he demanded high export duties on goods in demand abroad and low duties on foreign raw materials, with high duties on foreign manufactured goods. The views of Barthélemy de Laffemas and Antoine de Montchrétien (1575–1621) also contributed to the shaping of mercantilist aspirations in the time of Richelieu and Colbert. For Laffemas, it was crucial to encourage manufacture. Antoine de Montchrétien invented the expression 'political economy'. For him, the main aim of all statecraft, apart from the gaining of prestige and power, was the growth and enrichment of the state. In central Europe 'mercantilism' became characteristic only after the Thirty Years' War, though Denmark had its first mercantile phase under Christian IV (1588–1648), who copied, in the main, Dutch models.

PART ONE

The Economic
Development of
Continental Europe
1500-1630

1 Population Movements

It is not possible to obtain an exact picture of population development in mainland Europe during the period between 1500 and 1630. No statistics which could form a reasonably reliable basis were kept regularly. Counts were only occasionally undertaken, and even those were incomplete. Thus we are compelled to fall back on estimates, for which birth, marriage and death registers kept by the churches are among the chief sources. Registers for land, poll and hearth taxes and lists of those able to bear arms also contain useful information. But it is a long way from such information to generally acceptable estimates of total populations. Today it is generally thought that the loss of life as a result of the plague in the late Middle Ages prevented any substantial increase in population before 1450. In some parts of Europe the increase was delayed until the end of the fifteenth century, and definite increase can only be established at the beginning of the sixteenth. The existing statistical evidence cannot of itself be taken as proof of population increase, but it does reflect increasing interest in fiscal matters by governments and improvements in census methods.

The tendency for real wages to fall and for basic food prices to rise does, however, indicate pressure on resources from an increasing population. Emigration for mercenary service, late marriage and a relatively high number of unmarried persons underline this fact. Gerhard Utterström, who has tried to demonstrate a close relationship between population changes in Europe and climatic conditions, suggests that, after the general population increase of the sixteenth century, bad weather conditions at the end of the century brought pronounced food crises. In Sweden, for instance, the population was higher in 1590 than in 1620. Apart from these unfavourable climatic periods, the first decade of the seventeenth century brought war to many parts of continental Europe – armed stalemate with the Turks in the Danube basin, conflict between Sweden, Poland and Russia, then the war of Kalmar between Denmark and Sweden and dynastic wars between Sweden and Poland, and finally Danish and Swedish involvement in the religious wars in the Holy Roman Empire over the Habsburg patrimony in general and Bohemia in particular.

For France it is difficult to form a general picture. For one thing, the whole of France as we know it today did not yet belong to the French crown. In 1532 Brittany was incorporated; in 1552 the bishoprics of Metz, Toul and Verdun became French. In 1607 the kingdom of Navarre was added, but the Franche-Comté belonged to the Habsburgs and Alsace and Lorraine remained part of the Holy Roman Empire. Because of the Hundred Years' War population increase was delayed for a long time, and even during the reign of Louis XI (1461–83) there were many hindrances to growth. Between 1517 and 1519 there were great losses from the plague, followed thereafter by continuous population increases, so that the losses had been made up by the middle of the sixteenth century. Then the pressure of population was felt both on the land and in the large towns. The population of Lyons is said to have increased by 50 per cent. The Venetian ambassador remarked on the density of the population at that time. A count of hearths around 1560 showed about twenty million persons, a number similar to the estimated population at the beginning of the fourteenth century, and suggests a density of about thirty to forty persons per square kilometre. Paris, the greatest city, had about 200,000 inhabitants by 1600. The religious wars of the second half of the sixteenth century probably reduced the population again over the next thirty years. The St Bartholomew's Day massacre (1572) and the flight of the Huguenots brought losses, for some towns had been almost totally destroyed and deserted by the time they surrendered to Henry IV.

The population rise in Germany is referred to by several contemporaries including Ulrich von Hutten (1518), the Bavarian humanist Johannes Aventinus (1477–1534) and Sebastian Franck, in his *Chronicle of Germany* published in Augsburg in 1538. The writer of the *Zimmern Chronicle* emphasized that land had to be cultivated and settled in the wildest forests and on the highest mountains; people were coming from crowded

Allgäu in the Alps to the county of Zimmern to use land which had been deserted since the late fourteenth century. In northern Germany we may point to the Bishopric of Osnabrück, where, according to Erich Keyser, population increased by about 84 per cent between 1500 and 1640. In neighbouring Sauerland an annual increase between 1576 and 1618 of four per thousand has been calculated. The increase in Hesse was probably as high, perhaps even higher. The fragmentation of small farm properties after division on inheritance (which rulers eventually tried to curb by legislation) is another indication of population increase. The Elector August 1 of Saxony found his own solution for the problem of landless peasants: he bought up property and divided it into allotments. Another way of relieving population pressure was by migration to the towns or into districts prosperous through manufacturing industry. Population increase was particularly marked in the mining districts of Saxony, Bohemia and Tyrol, and it produced further migration to the east.

Because of deaths from plague in the fourteenth and fifteenth centuries, Germany only seems to have reached the twelve million mark in about 1500. By 1600 the total population had probably risen as high as twenty million. In the German-speaking area, which comprised about 750,000 square kilometres, the population density may have been as high as twenty-seven per square kilometre, though some estimates suggest that the population was about fifteen million. The river valleys of the Rhine and Main together with Westphalia were especially densely populated; there a level of over thirty per square kilometre may have been reached. More heavily populated still was the Duchy of Württemberg, with about forty persons per square kilometre.

Between one fifth and one quarter of the total German-speaking population lived in townships, whose average size was about three thousand. Only five per cent of the towns had more than ten thousand inhabitants. Of these Cologne, long the largest, with 37,000, was overtaken by Nuremberg, Augsburg and then Hamburg. Yet urban growth was neither universal nor consistent. Many market and industrial towns reverted to agricultural settlements. There was no great capital, like London or Paris, because of the continuing tradition of political decentralization, so peculiar to the early modern German Empire.

Yet the spread of industry to the country districts and the renewed development of agriculture encouraged an increase in rural population within the territorial states of Germany. The export of mercenary soldiers was an indication of this population surplus.

In his studies of the population of Zürich and the surrounding country Werner Schnyder has calculated an increase in the country districts of over ninety per cent between 1467 and 1529. By 1585 the population had increased a further forty-five per cent. The population of the Swiss Confederation, estimated at 600,000 to 650,000 in the middle of the fifteenth century, may have reached about 800,000 in 1530. This trend came to a halt only with the great epidemic of 1611.

At this time wilder, undeveloped districts were first settled, the Jura and Canton Vaud, for instance, and enlistment in foreign service became a useful method of counteracting population pressure. This was partly organized by foreign powers, district by district. Chiefly interested in obtaining Swiss mercenaries was the French crown, and Switzerland probably lost between 250,000 and 300,000 men in this way during the sixteenth and seventeenth centuries. At least another 20,000 people emigrated during the sixteenth century and possibly twice as many in the following century. The spread of the textile industry into country areas also provided a welcome antidote to population pressure.

Bohemia, Moravia and Silesia supported about four million inhabitants in 1600. The Austrian Alpine areas may have had two millions. *Vorderösterreich*, comprising the Habsburg possessions in Alsace, Swabia and around Lake Constance and the parts of Hungary not occupied by the Turks, had a population of about one million. There are no figures for Croatia, but migrations caused by war and persecution were characteristic in many areas. After 1522, refugee Uskoks from the Turkish-occupied Balkans settled the border area between Christian and Turkish Croatia and Carniola. A Habsburg military frontier came into being. The new settlers were mainly Serbs or Adriatic populations of Latin descent who fled from Turkish rule because they were Christians. They settled in the war zones or areas which had been deliberately depopulated, altering the ethnic composition of whole areas of Croatia and Slovenia. Those who were settled to secure the border against Turkish raids received special privileges. As overlord of these border areas the Habsburg Emperor granted the new inhabitants and their descendants the right to use the land in perpetuity in return for service in the Imperial army. In Inner Austria the Counter-Reformation forced the emigration of indigenous Protestants from Styria, Upper Austria and neighbouring Salzburg.

In eastern Europe, Poland, which had a treaty with Lithuania, extended its borders to the Ukraine, White Ruthenia and Volhynia, until the Dnieper was finally reached. After Poland had taken western Prussia and Ermland and reached the Baltic, it seized Courland (1561) and placed it under Polish overlordship. Livonia was incorporated in the following year. In 1619 Russian territory was won and its Russian population emigrated to Russia. The southern parts of Poland seem to have been spared the effects of the plague so that an increase in population came sooner than in western Europe. A phase of land clearance for cultivation had already begun in the fifteenth century, and its continuation in the next century suggests increasing pressure of population. Overall figures have not yet been worked out, and the figures which Pawinski and Vielrose give for the year 1578 in the three most important provinces of the kingdom vary from 2,118,000 to 3,200,000. According to another estimate, Great Poland and Little Poland, together with Masovia and Lesser Ruthenia, had about 3,100,000 inhabitants.

According to yet another estimate for the population of Poland, with the exception of Prussia, in the time of Stephen Bathory (1575–86), Great Poland had 826,000, Little Poland 674,000, Masovia 589,000, Podlachia 233,000, Black Russia 573,000, Volhynia and Podolia 383,000 and the Ukraine 545,000. Podlachia and Masovia had the densest population, with twenty-four and eighteen persons per square kilometre respectively, and Ukraine, with three to the square kilometre, the lowest.

In the sixteenth century Russia stretched as far south as the Dnieper and almost as far west as Smolensk. On the Baltic coast it held only Narva, captured in 1558 and only retained until 1581. In the first half of the sixteenth century, the south of Russia was under the Tartar Khanate of Kazan which ruled an area from the Volga near Saratov extending to the Urals; the Khanate of Astrakhan ruled from Saratov to the Caspian and the river Ural; and the Khanate of Crimea from Perekop and Kaffa to the south-western banks of the Volga valley. The Volga Tartars of Kazan and Astrakhan were conquered by Russia between 1552 and 1557 and in a few decades the Black Earth districts of the middle Volga were opened to Russian colonization. Similarly, Cossack settlement occurred in the areas of the Don and Donets rivers taken from the Tartars. The end of the sixteenth century saw the foundation of Samara, Saratov and Zarizyn (now Stalingrad). In the north, on the White Sea, Archangel was founded in 1584.

Russia's great expansion in the sixteenth century caused considerable depopulation of the older settled areas. The greater Novgorod area lost nearly eighty per cent of its population between 1550 and 1600. The Moscow region, too, lost, but the town itself continued to attract people and boasted about 200,000 inhabitants by 1630. Yet the urban population of Russia remained tiny – only 2·5 per cent of the total. According to Pokrowski, Russia, an area of nearly one million square kilometres, had about 2,100,000 inhabitants at the beginning of the sixteenth century, or slightly more than two people per square kilometre. This may be too low a figure; other estimates suggest that Russia already had a population between ten and eleven and a half million in the middle of the sixteenth century and by 1600 may have had fifteen million. The great famines of 1601 and 1603 and the wars of succession seem to have decimated the population in some areas.

Denmark, which included the Danish islands, Jutland, Schleswig, Halland, Blekinge and Scania, had to endure the civil wars of succession that followed the expulsion of Christian II in 1523. In spite of these disturbances the upward trend in population persisted – the losses from plague had probably been made good by 1600, and immigration from the west and from Germany certainly played their part. Total population is estimated at about half a million or more in about 1600.

After 1558 Swedish rule extended as far as the southern Baltic, once Reval and Estonia had been occupied. In 1617 Ingermanland was added, in 1621 Livonia and several ports on the coast of Courland. Sweden too is presumed to have experienced a considerable increase in population in the time of Gustavus Vasa, until civil war and poor harvests in the 1590s seem to have reversed the trend. In Swedish Finland a count of hearths for 1557 and 1589 is available. The earlier one was 33,046, the later one 31,570. It is difficult to say how far Finnish immigration into central Sweden at the end of the century may be ascribed to the pressure of population in Finland.

During the later sixteenth century, a few large towns grew to striking size. Paris already had 200,000 inhabitants in about 1600 and within the next third of a century reached nearly 400,000. Marseilles had 80,000 inhabitants in 1580. Prague's population rose to about 60,000 by the end of the sixteenth century. The populations of Cologne, Nuremberg, Augsburg and Vienna lay between 30,000 and 50,000. Toulouse, Strasburg, Lübeck, Danzig and Ulm reached 20,000 or more. Administrative capitals usually attracted the highest immigration in their area, and there were few new urban foundations. In the first half of the sixteenth century the mining towns in the Harz and Erz mountains of east-central Germany grew rapidly, while between 1550 and 1625 Finland, Sweden and the Swedish areas under Danish rule began a mercantilist policy which encouraged the foundation of new towns. Helsingfors, Gothenburg, Christiansstad, Glückstadt and Friedrichstadt all date from this time. Immigration from the west likewise led to new foundations: Freudenstadt, Frankenthal, Mannheim and Neuhanau grew up in this way.

Exact details of population movements during this period are uncertain. In the fifteenth century a family might have between eight and ten children. But the high birth-rate was matched by an almost equally high death-rate, and the growth in population numbers generally remained slight. Only half the children born reached the age of ten – and in Frankfurt the death-rate from 1550 to 1800 was always higher than the birth-rate.

The cause of the high death-rate must be sought in the first place in bad health conditions. Medical knowledge was incomplete, hygiene equally lacking. Many mothers and children died at birth, for medical help was nearly always unobtainable. Hospitals existed, but largely in the shape of infirmaries. Dirt everywhere created good breeding-places for serious and prolonged epidemics, of which plague, typhus, dysentery, smallpox, leprosy and cholera were the most prominent. In the sixteenth century the worst outbreaks came in 1547 and 1548 and between 1575 and 1578. The plague, a disease carried by the black rat, was transmitted to man by the rat flea, to which butchers and bakers seem to have been especially exposed. During the epidemic in Uelzen in 1597, seventy-one per cent of the bakers and 67 per cent of the butchers died. Germany had its last great epidemics during the Thirty Years' War, in 1624, 1630, from 1634 to 1639 and between 1646 and 1648. The last great outbreak in England came in 1665. Plague lingered on in northern, central and eastern Europe until the early eighteenth century, but farther west its days as a major killer were over.

After a serious catastrophe such as the plague, which caused a sudden fall in population, there was usually a reaction – population seems to have increased especially fast, delayed marriages were solemnized, and this in turn led to 'wave movements' in population growth.

New diseases appeared as plague declined. Sweating sickness affected not only England but the Continent in 1529. Syphilis, transmitted by mercenaries and camp-followers, spread from Italy north into Europe after 1494. Typhus took more severe forms than before, one instance being in 1566 in the mainland campaign against the Turks, where it was first called the 'Hungarian sickness'. Syphilis, however, lost its earlier severity. Smallpox seems first to have become important as an epidemic disease in Europe during the course of the seventeenth century.

Apart from contagious diseases, numerous famines decimated the population again and again. Transport difficulties meant that the grain trade was poorly developed, so that a shortfall in local grain as a result of bad harvests, floods and fires would soon lead to famine. Famines, like all infections, raged in times of war. The break in population growth caused by war cannot therefore be considered in isolation – those who were killed, or murdered by marauders, were only a fraction of those who fell victim to war.

None the less, the losses caused by war must not be underestimated. The Peasants' War in Germany (1524–6) probably cost the lives of about 100,000 people. To these must be added the lives lost in the mid-sixteenth century civil war of Emperor Charles v against the Protestant League of Schmalkalden, the bloody foreign wars waged by Charles v against France, and those of Ferdinand I with the Turks.

The problem of food shortages has been studied little, partly because relevant source material is so scarce. News was slow to arrive and this, together with inadequate bulk transport, made it difficut to remedy shortages. Germany and to a lesser degree France experienced famine in 1501 and 1502; the late twenties and early thirties brought bad harvests in Europe, in Germany especially, whereas France escaped famine until 1531. Large areas of Europe were affected by famine again in 1556 and 1557, including north Germany, Denmark and parts of France. Finally, at the end of the century, there was a major grain crisis in the Mediterranean.

During the course of the sixteenth century, the large towns and the princes did make some provision to combat famine; this certainly helped to reduce the effect of food crises. In coastal areas, improvements in cargo shipping had a similar effect, especially as production on the southern coasts of the Baltic was increased with the support of Dutch finance to meet the demands of overseas markets. New opportunities for fishing off Newfoundland and the development of cattle-breeding in Denmark, Hungary, Croatia and Walachia also helped to make food supplies more secure.

Changes in infant mortality are obscure, for want of statistical material. But evidence suggests that the number of births rose; in Protestant areas, release from the vows of celibacy and the secularization of the monasteries may have contributed to this. How far the growth of guild-free industry in rural areas using unskilled or semi-skilled labour encouraged more, or earlier, marriages in the sixteenth century is still uncertain.

If Danish figures are anything to go by, the expectation of life was strikingly greater in the sixteenth than in the seventeenth century. The situation was similar in France where, according to Goubert, 70·1 per cent of the children of leading families in Beauvaisis in the sixteenth century survived; in the following century only 61·7 survived. Finally, Helleiner points out in *The Cambridge Economic History* that economic fluctuations markedly influenced death rates and fertility among employed persons. He sees connections between trade depressions and the slower population increase at the end of the sixteenth century and in the first half of the seventeenth century, and between the increase in epidemics after 1560 and the growth of large towns.

Population movements between town and country are also important. From the end of the Middle Ages onwards there was a great deal of internal population movement as large numbers of peasants moved into the city. Because of high death rates caused by bad hygiene, the towns depended on an influx from country areas, where relationships between birth and death rates were more favourable. Movement from the countryside was caused by pressure on land resulting from the division of farms on inheritance; eventually holdings would become too small to support the population. The desire to escape from dependence on landlords may also have been a motive. Towns offered opportunities, albeit often spurious, of personal freedom and economic and social advancement.

The rise of Calvinism after 1540 led to intensified persecution by the government in the Netherlands. Calvinist emigration was caused partly by the heavy load of taxation during the war against France and also by the hardships brought by the wars of independence against Spain. The routes taken by the emigrés followed natural lines of communication. East Friesland, especially Emden, then Aachen and the Rhine towns of Cologne and Wesel were the first to receive the refugees. After the accession of Queen Mary to the English throne, there was an exodus from England and Frankfurt became the favoured place for Calvinist settlers. Frankfurt did not long survive as a haven, and after the city limited the religious freedom it had granted earlier the Dutch emigrés moved on to the Palatinate. There they founded four new towns at Schönau, Frankenthal, Lambrecht and Otterberg. The Spanish conquest of the Palatinate in the 1620s led to an influx of Protestant refugees in the lower Rhine at Goch, Emmerich, Rees, Cleves and Krefeld. In Thuringia and Saxony, refugees helped to found the textile industry at Gera in 1572 and at Meuselwitz, in 1578. After the creation of the Dutch Protestant republic, however, a large proportion of these refugees returned home.

The conquest of the Southern Netherlands by Alexander Farnese (starting in 1579) and the fall of Antwerp in 1585 caused a new emigration to Germany of Walloon and Flemish members of the Reformed and Lutheran Church. Among those who left Antwerp the merchant class was strongly represented. Some went to Frankfurt and Wetzlar, others to trade centres on the north German coast such as Bremen and Stade, where a reformed community was founded in 1588. Another group went to Hamburg, which had been friendly to Calvinists since

1567, but religious and economic restrictions there explain why some of the Dutch refugees moved to nearby Altona in the lordship of Pinneberg and there laid the foundations of an independent town.

At the turn of the century various other new towns were founded, some of them by emigrants from earlier refugee settlements. In 1597 New Hanau was built on land belonging to the Counts of Hanau. In 1599 Friedrichstadt, later called Freudenstadt, was founded for Protestants driven from Austria, especially those from Styria. Five years later, in 1604, Joachimsthal was founded in Brunswick and in 1606 Mannheim, as a new residence of the Elector Palatine. Dutchmen had been settling in Kassel since 1604; in 1616 King Christian IV of Denmark founded Glückstadt on the lower Elbe and offered a welcome to all denominations. Immediately afterwards Duke Frederick III of Schleswig-Holstein-Gottorf founded Friedrichstadt on the Eider with the same aims.

How many people were involved in these migrations it is difficult to say. In Frankfurt there were over two thousand foreigners in 1561, one-seventh of the total population. In 1570 Wesel had five thousand or more, and in 1600 about ten thousand refugees were living in Hamburg.

These new settlers had an important effect on the conduct of economic affairs, especially in trade, textiles and luxury goods. Many came from the southern Netherlands, where textile-weaving centres in Tournai, Lille, Valenciennes and Verviers provided artisans who introduced new types of cloth. In Wesel they founded the first guild of mock-velvet- and say- (mixed silk and cotton) weavers in 1546 and, in 1559 a guild of bursat-weavers was set up in Frankfurt. In 1567 emigrés brought silk-weaving to Frankfurt, Frankenthal, Wesel and Hamburg, diamond-polishing to Frankfurt, gold- and silversmiths' work to Hanau, and sugar-refining (especially raw sugar imported from Brazil) to Hamburg. In some cases they were able to develop their skills unhindered by guilds. In others, they built up large-scale manufacture on a capitalist basis; particularly well known are Hans von Brüssel, who started producing felt hats in Hamburg in 1585, and the Dutch Mennonite Peter de Vos who set up his warehouse for says and serge in neighbouring Altona in 1637.

Foreign immigrants also provided an important stimulus to

the carrying trade. With their help the port of Emden had for a time the largest merchant fleet in Germany. In Danzig they made themselves felt in shipping and in foreign trade, and in Frankfurt immigrant financiers helped to make the city one of the leading banking centres. In Hamburg immigrants had a decisive influence in developing overseas connections with the Iberian peninsula as well as with colonial markets, and stimulated the introduction of newer methods in trade, credit and insurance. At their instigation the Hamburg bank was founded in 1619 on the Amsterdam model. It was in large measure because of the skills of these Calvinist and Jewish immigrants that economic life began to shift away from southern Germany towards the Protestant north. Economic losses can certainly be associated with the persecution of non-Catholic foreigners, although it is difficult to quantify the amount of damage thus done.

Apart from these closed settlements, some Dutch merchants infiltrated the economic life of Denmark, Sweden, the Baltic and Russia. They entered the mining industry in Sweden and Russia and settled in the Moscow suburb of Sloboda. Germans emigrated to Scandinavia in considerable numbers in the second half of the sixteenth century and in the first half of the seventeenth century to Copenhagen, Helsingør, the Norwegian ports and Stockholm.

Emigrés from the west who settled on the land were also important. They brought with them a knowledge of agriculture and stock-breeding which was very advanced for the time. The Dutch were experienced dyke-builders (the invention of windmills which pumped water from low-lying areas dates from the second half of the fifteenth century) and also specialized in cattle-breeding. The cattle were fattened for the urban meat markets and also formed the basis of extensive dairy, cheese and butter production. In this way important changes in land ownership were introduced; by increasing the size of some holdings through lease and purchase, and by the consolidation of parcels of fields, almost complete personal freedom could be achieved in the west. Economic growth was also reflected in the construction of town houses and hostelries; the Friesian farmhouse in which a timber frame was replaced by brickwork, was the largest in Europe. Friesland adopted a leasehold ownership system from the Dutch.

Thus the victims of over-population and religious difficulties were led to migrate to central and northern Europe. In this they followed routes taken by Dutch Baltic trade. As early as 1519 King Christian II of Denmark had founded a Dutch settlement on the island of Amager near Copenhagen and after 1527 Duke Albert of Prussia called for settlers from Zeeland, Holland and Friesland to build up his devastated villages – in this case without success, for the farmers refused to go to these remote agricultural areas. Mennonite settlers found more favourable conditions on the river Vistula, and in 1547 their first settlement was started near Danzig. Shortly after the middle of the century Polish demesne lords brought Dutch settlers as leaseholders to the southern part of Werder in Poland and to the lowlands of the Vistula. In 1606 tenant farmers settled the low-lying areas of Netze and Neumark in Brandenburg; in 1617 the Dutch arrived on the river Bug.

The success of these Dutch settlements may be partly attributed to the similarity between geographical conditions on the Vistula delta and the North Sea marshes. The Dutch were able to use their skill in building dykes and had a good market for their produce in Danzig. They were also able to secure the leaseholds and personal freedoms to which they had been used. Such factors had a strong influence not only on the Werder area but also on the Pomeranians who had been emigrating to Poland under less favourable conditions since the middle of the sixteenth century. From about 1600 the Dutch were also able to put their superior farming methods into practice in inland areas. On large estates they rented the livestock with the use of pasture and buildings and practised dairy farming in order to export butter and cheese.

The population growth and movements outlined here were in many areas of continental Europe a crucial factor in the development of production, transport and the exploitation of internal markets. They also significantly influenced the balance between this area and the expanding Atlantic world.

II *Organization of Production*

I CONTINENTAL STATES AND THE RISE OF MERCANTILISM

The efforts of the princes to increase their powers by 'absolutism' had already given impetus to political developments in the late Middle Ages. Machiavelli's concept of the state and its ruler suggested a close relationship between economic policy and the state, a relationship that had hitherto existed only in the city states. What Machiavelli wanted involved a principle of which the medieval order was ignorant. He considered that men fitted into the existing order more or less unconsciously owing to the strength of their beliefs. As his new ideas of government began to be established, Machiavelli had to take into consideration the new capitalist spirit in the economy and the new rivalries which it unleashed. If a strong economy were to benefit the sovereign and the state, there would have to be a permanent policy of state co-ordination and intervention. Thus there developed a 'voluntaristic' orientation in economic thinking. A rational economic order, useful to the power of state and ruler, would have to be brought about by the use of political authority, so curbing the potentially disturbing influence of individual entrepreneurs.

Such ideas have been seen as the beginning of the theory and policy later known as 'mercantilism'. But much theoretical work remained to be done before a breakthrough was achieved. As nation states became more and more conscious of their identity their governments turned to consider the practical problems of their situation. Just as in the political sphere, there were marked differences in the organization of the state between France, central Europe and territories within the Empire, Poland and Russia. Each had its own particular problems: each probed for an individual solution. Yet certain broad principles emerged.

In France the economic and political situation was conditioned by involvement in foreign wars for more than a century from 1450 to 1560, while peace was enjoyed at home. Louis xi secured and increased the power of the monarchy. After the fall of Charles Duc de Bourbon as Constable of France (1523), important advances were made towards unification: Bourbon, the Auvergne, the Forez, the Marche and Clermont were united with the kingdom; in 1532 Brittany was incorporated. Yet, in the first half of the sixteenth century, the king's administration lacked the necessary organization and stability to carry out an economic policy which would correspond with the needs of state in Machiavelli's sense.

Royal intervention was, however, most marked in financial affairs of state. The beginning of a state economic policy can be seen in an overt protectionism in favour of native manufacturing industries; in some cases this may have hindered the immediate development of trade. In 1539 a decree forbade the importation of woollen goods from Spain and the Roussillon and of 'says' from Flanders. A further decree (July 1540) permitted the importation of gold, silver and silk only through certain specified frontier towns and ports; from there they had to be sent to the staple at Lyons, where goods for France were charged at five per cent and transit goods two per cent of their value. A decree of 1564 compelled all goods coming from Italy to pass through customs at Lyons, and in 1585 these regulations were extended to goods from the Levant. Another decree of 1540 allowed spice imports only direct from the country of origin or from warehouses in Italy, Portugal or the Orient. From 1572 special permission had to be granted to export wool, hemp, flax and other raw materials and to import cloth, linen cloth, satin, taffeta and embroidery. 1577 saw a heavy *traite foraine* imposed on the export of grain, wine, linen, woollen goods and woad. In 1581 the protective dues on numerous articles, particularly manufactured ones, were increased.

This policy seems to have satisfied the French population. In 1576 the leather merchants demanded a prohibition on the import of manufactured goods and the export of raw materials, and the Normandy Estates reiterated this demand in 1588. At the Assembly of Rouen in 1596 the Estates also demanded that all imports of silk and woollen goods to France should be forbidden, and the Parisians suggested the same when Barthélemy de Laffemas conducted his enquiry in 1598. But this protectionism was also closely bound up with fiscal considerations. Many office-holders, such as stockbrokers, road-surveyors, customs and standards officers, set up controls in order to raise income for themselves.

New efforts were made under Henry iv, who had good technical experts on hand in Sully (especially 1598–1611) and de Laffemas. Sully believed that agriculture was the most important factor in assuring the well-being of the kingdom. De Laffemas on the other hand represented the interests of industry and trade, and their claims to attention were growing.

For Richelieu economic considerations also played an important role in general policy. The fourth objective of his *Political Testament* was to control the economic opportunities which were available in France and overseas. Richelieu drew on the ideas of de Laffemas and Montchrétien and of his faithful Joseph du Tremblais. He ordered diplomats to keep him informed about questions of trade and had their reports supplemented by those of special envoys. For this purpose, Courmenin visited Constantinople, Persia, Copenhagen and Moscow. Richelieu firmly believed that a country could enrich itself through trade in times of peace. With this in mind he formed the *surintendance*, had the navy built up in order to protect trade, redeveloped deserted ports and built new ones at Brouage and Brest. He also promoted measures to organize internal trade and concluded trading agreements with the Dutch Republic, England and Denmark, though many of his projects for trading companies remained on paper.

In contrast with the centralized France state, the Empire was divided into a large number of territories, each of which naturally attempted to further its own economic interests, often at the expense of the whole. To what extent is it possible to speak of an economic policy in the Empire? Leaving the dynastic aspirations of the House of Habsburg to one side for the moment, the Empire's economic policy consisted of measures which came from the Empire's executive. This executive was represented by the Emperor, who, however, had his freedom of action restricted by the Imperial Assembly – the permanent

representatives of the Estates of the Reich – who were themselves rulers of their own territories. The Imperial Assembly
gradually became institutionalized during the course of the
fourteenth and fifteenth centuries and became a reality as a
result of the reforms of the famous assembly held in Worms in
1495. The Electoral College, the council of ruling princes of the
Empire and the assembly of town council representatives from
the imperial towns voted separately, and if their decisions
coincided, the Emperor ratified them and published them as
decrees of the Imperial Diet. The most important functions of
the Diet related to war measures, taxes and legislation. At the
beginning of the sixteenth century and again in the 1520s an
imperial caretaker government was instituted as a temporary
organ of federal control, concerned above all with measures
against monopolies, the lowering of interest rates and other
fiscal and economic matters such as currency control.

The economic measures taken in the Empire consisted at first
of hundreds of individual enactments. They were based on
individual cases and had no systematic relationship with one
another. For the most part they were the continuation of regulations which princes and cities had made for their particular
domains. There were licences for markets, market courts,
money and customs, licences conferring privileges on corporations and craftsmen; there were measures to keep the peace in
the country, especially to ensure safety of travellers on the roads.
During the fifteenth century the reform movement in the
Empire, influenced by the spread of Roman law, led to an increasing concern by the Imperial Assembly with economic
matters. As early as 1435 imperial decrees forbade usury and
regulated rates of interest at an acceptable 5 per cent. Imperial
ordinances in 1530, 1548 and 1577 officially confirmed the
growing practice of selling annuities.

The economic debate entered a new phase when the Imperial Assembly, stung by the failure of Maximilian I's Italian
war policy in 1512 and, a few years later, influenced by Luther's
ideas, tried to introduce legislation against cartels and monopolies in an attempt to face up to the great trading companies
like Fugger and Melser at Augsburg or Imhoff at Nuremberg.
A law of 1525 gave the Attorney-General powers to start law suits
against Augsburg and Nuremberg companies which had capital
of more than 50,000 Florins. In his imperial letters of 10 and 13

March 1525, Charles v rejected this litigation, thus placing himself clearly on the side of the trading companies, who were also his chief creditors and without whose advances of bullion he could not manage. The most influential were the Fuggers, whose supply of credit and money had provided him with the imperial crown in 1519.

Disputes about monopolies recurred in 1526 and 1529 and, when further proceedings against the large companies were attempted, Charles ordered the suspension of proceedings from his court at Bologna. After 1530 the question of monopolies faded into the background and the Turkish wars and religious dissent alternately took precedence in the business of the Imperial Assembly. Then again in 1548 a *Reichspolizeiordnung*, or federal policy decree, probed the problem of economic powers and privileges. One of its provisions forbade the export of wool; this was confirmed at the Imperial Assembly in Augsburg in 1555, and repealed in 1559, when decisions on the matter were left to the new imperial regional circles, into which the Empire was now divided. Another decree of 1577 prohibited the export of leather from the German Empire. Earlier complaints by contemporaries, including Luther, about the way in which gold and silver were flowing out of the country led the Imperial Assembly to restrict the export of gold and silver coinage in 1524, 1555 and 1570. Plans to introduce an imperial customs duty were blocked by the imperial towns with the help of the Emperor in 1523. (This incident illustrates how the federal system worked in the German Empire.)

Though many of the laws promulgated by the Empire were ineffective, partly because they had to be repealed so frequently, this was not the case with one set of laws in an area of great economic sensitivity. The *Reichspolizeiordnung* of 1548 laid down standards of quality in gold- and silver-work which were strictly kept. An earlier decree, in 1530, had already acted against the guilds' and journeymen's associations' misuse of their autonomy, and in 1594 the Imperial Assembly threatened masters and journeymen with serious punishment to life and limb. The guilds lost the right to judge themselves and they were put under imperial and regional supervision. As happens in most voluntary federal systems which ultimately depend on the goodwill of territorial rulers and governments, many of these provisions were not enforced, and the respectability of many occupations subject to imperial economic supervision (such as weaver, barber, shepherd, miller, piper, kettle-maker, drummer, bath-keeper, mint-maker, currency-warder and customs official), began to be seriously questioned as a result of regular default and abuse.

Coinage regulations in 1524, 1551 and 1559 introduced general standards for gold and silver *Gulden*, to which the value of the actual coinage in circulation was securely fixed. Regional financial officials held regular testing days and noted and published deceitful deviations and abuses of accepted face values. In 1566 the imperial *Taler* was introduced, a coin which retained its value up to the eighteenth century, a tribute indeed to federal politics in the early modern Holy Roman Empire.

It was particularly difficult for Charles v to formulate a uniform policy for the Empire in foreign trade, since he ruled over an area which stretched from the Habsburg patrimonial estates to the Burgundian Netherlands, an area far too vast and varied to be governed by reference to a uniform set of economic interests. The contrasts between north and south showed in the conflict between the Fuggers and the Hanseatic cities, in which the Emperor was, as usual, on the side of the Fuggers. When the Merchant Adventurers established themselves in Hamburg in 1567, the Hanseatic League tried to regain a privileged position in English trade by closing the offices of the Adventurers in Hamburg and using this move in order to bring pressure to bear on London. The Hanseatic cities finally complained to the Imperial Assembly and demanded that the English should be expelled as monopolists. The Assembly agreed, but the Emperor did not ratify the mandate. When the Hanseatic League protested in 1587 against a new English settlement in Stade, the Electoral College vetoed strong measures against the English merchants. The southern German merchants, interested in exporting linen and fustian to England, likewise did not see eye to eye with the Hanse. Finally, however, the Emperor, basing himself on the imperial decree of 1582, signed a mandate in 1597 expelling the Merchant Adventurers from the Empire. In this case the Emperor followed a policy appropriate to the international situation and took the side of Spain. The Merchant Adventurers had to give up their 'court' at Stade; Queen Elizabeth reacted by having the Admiralty take over the Hanseatic *Stalhof* in London. But

James I gave it back in 1606 and in 1611 Hamburg granted the Merchant Adventurers a licence again.

It is difficult to judge how far imperial policy was 'mercantilist', although the Emperor's measures in 1597 against the Merchant Adventurers certainly had a protectionist character. The ban on the export of wool and leather in 1524 and 1577 was reminiscent of medieval policies, but many federal decrees can also be seen as attempts to operate a mercantilistic bullion theory by preventing precious metals leaving the Empire.

The economic policy of the imperial estates was most clearly visible in the powers exercised by the imperial towns and by the territorial governments of the Electors and ruling princes. The cities insisted on the rights of staple, markets and fairs, on control of roads, right of escort, customs, and on the right to extend their control over the neighbouring countryside. Each town, however, had its own particular set of economic interests. Lübeck was interested in securing transit trade; Hamburg was concerned with its connections with its hinterland on the other side of the Elbe and came into dispute with Lüneburg and Magdeburg. In Christian IV's time, when neighbouring Holstein was under strong Danish rule, Hamburg had to fight for its right to be directly subject to the Emperor and had to contest the Elbe customs dues which the Danish king imposed from his new town at Glückstadt. Frankfurt was concerned to secure its regional monopoly in large trading fairs. Ulm, Rothenburg, and Nuremberg had extensive control over the surrounding countryside; that of Ulm stretched as far as the Swabian Alb and was an important source of supplies for wool- and linen-weaving in the city. Nuremberg managed to extend its territory by the end of the fifteenth century and supplies the clearest example of the complicated economic relationship between imperial towns and their surrounding countryside. The rural areas supplied the raw materials for the rich metal industries of the city, and some raw materials were even made into semi-manufactured goods outside the city.

The economic policy of the cities towards the outside world can be seen most clearly in the case of the Hanseatic League in which the cities and towns all participated. The main aim of their common policy was the maintenance of privileges abroad. The development of nation states in the North Sea and Baltic coasts and in the west progressively reduced the power of the

Hanseatic cities. In 1494 the Hanseatic *comptoir* in Novgorod was forcibly closed by Muscovy. Lübeck, the chief Hanseatic city, suffered most, though the towns of Livonia were able to profit from the new conditions because they were best situated for trade with Russia. Lübeck was worst hit in its Swedish trade. The town had helped Gustavus Vasa to make Sweden independent of Christian II of Denmark and in the process had acquired such extensive rights and privileges that they prejudiced the development of a native, Swedish economic policy. Lübeck tried once more to regain her former rights in a subsequent Northern War in which she took Denmark's and Poland's role against Sweden, but with only temporary success. When King Eric XIV of Sweden took Reval in 1561, Lübeck temporarily won easier access to Russia *via* Narva, but under Charles IX Lübeck finally lost her privileged position, and the new Swedish monarchy began to extend its sphere of strategic influence to the southern Baltic coast. When Lübeck again organized a Hanseatic embassy to Russia at the beginning of the seventeenth century, the only result was a meagre concession to trade in Pskov.

In Denmark and Norway the objective was to preserve Hanseatic interests in Bergen, Oslofjord and Öresund. It was customary for these privileges to be extended by each Danish ruler on his accession. On the accession of Frederick II in 1560 the assembly at Odense restricted these rights for the first time, and subsequently King Christian IV refused to continue the privileges. He also tried unsuccessfully to turn the trade with Iceland into a monopoly for Danish merchants and to exclude the Hanseatic League completely. At the end of the sixteenth century England gave up its old policy of acquiring privileges abroad and used the conflict with the Hanseatic League as an excuse to close the London Steelyard.

The common interests of the Hanseatic cities showed themselves again more strongly at the beginning of the seventeenth century, when in 1616 in alliance with the United Provinces and Sweden they supported Brunswick against the Guelphs' efforts to annex the town, a move which was also aimed against Christian IV of Denmark. The increasing sea traffic to the west stimulated lively diplomatic activity in the leading Hanseatic cities, and they attempted to confirm their existing privileges in the Spanish Netherlands and France and to extend them to the

Iberian peninsula. An embassy was sent to the Spanish court in 1607 to obtain a suitable trade agreement, which, however, was never fully ratified.

Southern Germany had no grouping of towns comparable to the Hanseatic League of the North German towns. The Rhineland and Swabian Leagues proved to be of little value. In most cases free and imperial towns were forced into defensive positions against the neighbouring ruling princes who tried, usually with some success, to extend their power. In the north the Hanseatic League was also weakened because Rostock, Wismar, Greifswald, Stralsund and Stettin (Szczecin) belonged to particular territorial rulers, to whom they had increasingly to submit in matters of political jurisdiction.

The economic policies of the ruling princes can be seen in action in many different sectors, particularly in the mining industries of Saxony, the Harz Mountains, Thuringia and Württemberg. Mining was controlled by regulations which limited the cutting of wood for smelting and foundry works. Duke George of Albertine Saxony promoted mining vigorously and Duke Frederick of Württemberg encouraged his own mining and textile industries. A territorial ruler's economic policy was often combined with his private family enterprises, as in the cases of Elector Augustus of Albertine Saxony, Margrave John of Küstrin and Duke John the younger of Schleswig-Holstein-Sonderburg. Duke Maximilian of Bavaria was the first ruling prince in Germany to institute a commercial council, a representative body organizing trade.

Another important aspect of territorial economic policy concerned relations with the guilds. By the end of the fifteenth century it had become customary for the territorial ruler rather than his subordinate town authorities to confirm guild privileges. In spite of this, territorial towns, naturally wishing to emulate the policies of the imperial free towns, retained some economic autonomy in their own right as estates or *Landstände* at territorial assembly level. The towns applied price controls to protect the consumer from attempts by the guilds to form cartels and also wage controls, fixing minimum and maximum daily rates for labourers and craftsmen. In Munich fixed wage-rates helped to secure steadier incomes for weavers when demand for their produce was slack. Wage controls could also work in favour of employers, as was shown by a regulation in

Freiburg in 1478 which laid down a fixed maximum weekly wage for journeymen tailors, above which no employer was to go. The Nuremberg council investigated the average net earnings of bakers so as to fix a permissible profit for bakers. Since the range of earnings seemed too high, the council issued a bread regulation in 1521 to prevent higher earnings.

All the imperial towns as well as the princes of the territorial states levied indirect taxes. These tax regulations represented an element of central planning and direction at more local and immediate levels of government. Originally, price control had been an essentially urban phenomenon, but as princely territories developed into states they adopted urban forms of fiscal control. In Württemberg corn prices were fixed in 1528 and wool prices in 1536. In 1540 a uniform tax on the sale of meat was imposed in the whole of the Duchy. Baden also introduced an excise on wool which was fixed by commission; a standard price was reinforced by a ban on all wool exports for one year only, subject to an annual review. Within the wholesale trade, there was a set price for wine and corn. In the Landgraviate of Hesse measures of price control included a permanent ban on exports and a policy for building up state reserves of foodstuffs. In Bavaria, uniform meat prices were fixed by the authorities in 1528 and 1529, based on meat prices in the capital, Munich. In fixing meat prices, the authorities in Nuremberg tried to obtain accurate information about price regulation in Hungary, Austria and Poland, their chief foreign wholesale markets. During the sixteenth century they also informed themselves of price rises in neighbouring German towns as far away as Augsburg, Ulm and Donauwörth, and, occasionally Strasbourg and Cologne.

The imperial town of Rothenburg fixed official maximum prices for nearly all foodstuffs. Munich town council regularly investigated in both open and closed session the affairs of slaughter-houses, bakeries and breweries. Like all basic foodstuffs, fish was also under strict price supervision in shops and markets there. In Vienna municipal officials regularly had to inform themselves of the prices of wholesale grain, flour and cattle for slaughter. Bakers and butchers were checked by officials to ensure that they gave full measure at official prices and that they paid their sales taxes accordingly.

When, at the beginning of the sixteenth century, consumers

in Basle complained of the high cost of spices, the municipality sent a reliable buyer to the Frankfurt fair to purchase the necessary spices and undercut the town's syndicate. These goods were then prepared for re-sale by order of the town council. A price was calculated, taking into account the purchase price, the cost of transport and of preparation for sale, and in 1510 this became official. The operation resulted in a reduction of prices by up to 20 per cent.

By 1500 the formal boundaries of the Holy Roman Empire no longer coincided with areas of local dynastic power. In the north for example, the Duchy of Holstein remained attached to the Empire, whereas the Duchy of Schleswig went directly to the Danish crown. Danish dynasticism during the course of the fifteenth and sixteenth centuries dictated that these two Duchies should be ruled alternately from Copenhagen or Gottorf in Schleswig, while representation of the common interests of both duchies continued in the territorial estates. Farther west, the Duchy of Burgundy consisted of lands belonging to the French crown and to the German Empire. When the Habsburgs inherited Burgundy, they were entitled to claim Franche Comté as an imperial fief, but the Duchy of Burgundy itself belonged to the French monarchy. Equally, in Lorraine parts of both the Duchy of Lorraine and the Duchy of Bar belonged to the French king, others to the Empire. South of Burgundy the Duchy of Savoy belonged to the Empire, whose formal claim to rule reached into northern and central Italy and technically surrounded the Swiss Confederation.

The Confederation went its own way, however, both politically and economically, and conditions there mirrored the situation in the Empire on a smaller scale. Each canton had its own economic interests, reflected, for instance, in the policies of the Berne and Zürich cantons, as well as in Geneva, whose industrial policy was to subordinate the surrounding countryside to the city. When the Confederation took common measures they were usually concerned with securing the Alpine passes, though an agreement on tax-free trade between France and the Confederation made in 1516 was upheld until the end of the eighteenth century.

As Emperor Charles v soon realized when he came to power in Germany, Habsburg power created special problems. As well as the lands of the Spanish crown, Charles was the direct ruler of the Burgundian lands, the Austrian Habsburg patrimony, the lands of the Bohemian Crown and those parts of Hungary still free from the Turks. Here was a group of territories so far-flung and complex that it was very difficult for one man to govern directly, or even indirectly. This, together with the ambition of Charles's younger brother, Ferdinand, led to the Brussels agreement of 1522, which gave Charles the Burgundian lands, while Ferdinand took the Austrian lands. In spite of this division, Charles, as ruler of the whole monarchy, tried to subordinate Ferdinand's policies to his own economic and financial interests. To Ferdinand fell the particular task of securing the eastern and south-eastern border. This was a vital area, both economically and politically, because the mineral wealth of Slovakia, Carinthia and the Tyrol constituted an important part of the security for the south German financiers, such as the Fuggers, who gave credit to the Emperor. The Empire was an important source of demand for mercenaries, and from it came the subventions of South German capital as well as the federal military taxes, *Römermonate* and *Türkensteuer* taxes.

A mutual arrangement thus grew up. The rulers of the Empire were able to obtain money from both the Fuggers and the Genoese by the special *asientos* (the right to levy taxes) granted to them. As mining entrepreneurs and merchants, the Fuggers also helped to supply the Netherlands, Spain and Italy with essential silver, copper and war *matériel*.

Charles wanted to harry his French adversary from all sides – from Spain, the Netherlands and from Germany. He banned all trade with France and compelled both southern German and Genoese merchants to trade at the fairs in Habsburg Besançon, in order to counter the influence of Valois Lyons. The Genoese-governed Ligurian Republic and the Duchy of Milan (which had been taken from the French) became an important bridge between the Austrian and Spanish possessions of the Habsburgs in political, economic, naval and military affairs. There were new aspects to the problem when Charles's inheritance was divided between his brother Ferdinand and his son Philip. The Empire finally fell to Charles's brother Ferdinand, while Philip had to manage the Iberian possessions, the Netherlands, Franche Comté, Milan, the southern Italian possessions and Spanish America. Like his father, Philip was interested in the idea of a 'land bridge' between Italy and the Netherlands. Alba's troops were soon to use this route to march against the rebels who held sea power in the North Sea and English Channel and this alternative route remained important, for the transport of war materials and troops as well as precious metals from Spain to the Continent, as a substitute for the Atlantic route between Spain and the southern Netherlands, now permanently disrupted by Dutch and English seapower. Hopes raised just before the outbreak of the Thirty Years' War in 1618 by the Oñate agreement, which incorporated Alsace and the Upper Rhineland into this Habsburg land bridge, were not fulfilled.

In the Danube basin the House of Habsburg gained increasing power during this period. The Habsburg lands consisted of Vorderoesterreich with the Tyrol, Styria, Carinthia and Lower and Upper Austria, with the river Enns as a boundary between them. In 1515, after the double wedding in Vienna, the Bohemian crown lands were added (Bohemia, Moravia, Silesia and Lausitz) as well as those parts of Hungary which were won by the Habsburgs from Louis II after the battle of Mohacs in 1526. The rest of Transylvania belonged to a greater or lesser degree to the Turks.

The Emperor Maximilian I named the two groups of *Länder* Upper and Lower Austria; Upper Austria consisted of the Tyrol and the Alpine foothills (i.e. Swabia); Lower Austria included Austria below and above the Enns, Styria, Carinthia and Carniola. Maximilian tried to create a central government both for his Austrian lands and for the Empire, with a Privy Council to run the judiciary and general administration and a chancellery and exchequer for central financial administration. His failure to achieve financial solvency made success impossible. His only real success lay in developing the government of Lower Austria. Here, in addition to an audit office for the control of financial matters, there was an exchequer for crown lands, and a household exchequer for hunting and fishing, building works and artillery. There was also a supreme court of appeal under Privy Council control. But only the financial and audit offices (which were leased in Vienna) were successful, for moves towards centralization were frustrated by the Estates' determined pursuit of regional interests, as well as Maximilian's own preference for Innsbruck as the centre of his government. The estates of each Austrian province retained much power, which they refused to pass on to an Estates-General of the whole Austrian patrimony, despite the fact that an Estates-General assembly of Upper Austria held at Innsbruck in 1518 had proposed a detailed plan for social and economic centralization. Yet Maximilian I did make a start, and his grandson, Ferdinand I, the real founder of the Austrian Habsburg state, continued the process further.

Though Ferdinand I (1503–64) had been brought up in Spain, he soon became familiar with the special conditions in the Danube area and proved to be a very astute ruler, especially in his use of his power of prerogative. The death of the last Jagellonian at Mohacs in 1526 had left the way open for a new Habsburg order in central and south-east Europe. So as to secure the Habsburg succession, Ferdinand made concessions, especially over religious questions, and appointment to high state offices, to the Estates in Bohemia and Hungary, where traditional forms of government were preserved. The major effort was directed to defending the borders against the Turks, for, after the loss of Buda to the Turks in 1541, central Hungary with its fertile plains on the Tisa and the Danube came under Turkish control. The new military frontier, which now had to be maintained in the south and east, swallowed up vast sums each year; these were raised mainly by Estates' tax grants in Austria, Bohemia, Moravia, Silesia, the Lausitz and royal Hungary.

In organizing the administration, Ferdinand followed his grandfather's plans. His household regulations of 1527 set up an administrative apparatus for the future Austrian monarchy, with civil and military, judicial, diplomatic and fiscal departments of state. The exchequer was reorganized in 1537, administering only the royal demesne, extraordinary taxation remaining in the hands of the territorial Estates of each province. Deficit financing was authorized by the Estates, and subsidies and taxes were administered by their own treasury, which mainly provided for military expenditure. The system fell a long way short of providing centralized control, and it was not until Maximilian II's time (1564–76) that the exchequer began to produce annual budgets and balance accounts against its ordinary and extraordinary income.

Because of the Turkish threat the Military Council naturally played a crucial role in financial affairs, especially by liaising with territorial Estates' assemblies over the expenditure of moneys from taxes granted and collected by the Estates. And here the Estates asserted their independence of the central administration, an attitude reinforced by the Reformation, for large numbers of the Austrian nobility and influential burghers became Protestants during the course of the sixteenth century. Matters which went beyond the interests of individual provincial Estates assemblies were discussed in an Estates-General held in Prague in 1541.

The beginnings of centralization, and with it the possibility of an overall economic policy, were hampered by a division of the crown lands between Ferdinand's three sons. Maximilian, who succeeded his father as Emperor, became the ruler of Bohemia, Hungary and the archduchies of the Danube. Ferdinand received the Tyrol and the Vorlande reaching as far as Alsace. The youngest son, Charles, received Styria, Carinthia and Carniola. The divisions of the Austrian patrimony within the ruling dynasty, which lasted until 1665, strengthened the particularism of the provinces. These smaller units provided very favourable conditions for the development of Counter-Reformation absolutism, which showed itself very clearly in Styria at the end of the sixteenth century.

The Austrian authorities were particularly keen to enforce price regulation in mining and in the production of and trade in metals. The deposits of Styria and Carinthia offered opportunities for big profits, especially from iron exports, and so producers and dealers were constantly tempted to exceed fixed prices for the home market, thus starving it of raw materials. Grievances about high prices were one cause of the peasant rising in Upper Austria in 1595, although they were somewhat overshadowed by religious grievances, discontent over high levels of taxation, the conduct of the Turkish War and absentee landlordism. Peasant rebellion in the Austrian lands was endemic throughout the early modern era, whereas in the rest of the German Empire, and certainly outside the Alpine lands, it was almost totally suppressed after the vicious counter-measures of 1525. The problem of religious dissent, however, remained. The emigration of Protestant peasants, craftsmen and entrepreneurs (the Einbach and Hillebrand firms, for instance) from the iron-ore districts of Inner Austria shows how strongly Austrian economic progress suffered from the enforcement of Catholic religious uniformity.

In Hungary the most important economic area was the Slovakian mining district, to which, however, the Poles also laid claim. The attitudes of Ladislas II (1490–1516) and Louis II (1516–26) of Hungary to their more ambitious magnates were weak, although they were able to co-operate with the burghers of the northern towns, who were granted special rights and privileges. It was due to their support that the rising middle-class Thurzo family soon became the greatest industrial magnates of central Europe. Though the town of Spiš(Zips) acquired a number of privileges concerning trade, it was Košice that benefited most as a trade centre for northern Hungary. In this connection the resolutions of the Hungarian Estates assembly are worthy of note, for they now favoured the interests of merchants and trade more strongly than before. At an assembly held in 1500 on the Rakesfeld, the King ratified urban privileges and settled in detail complaints and questions of customs dues. In 1504 weights and measures for wine and fruit were standardized throughout the kingdom and all subsequent assemblies discussed the affairs of merchants and traders. Royal economic planning made itself felt when in 1507, 1512 and 1514 decrees were issued banning Polish money as legal tender for Hungarian export goods and a ban was placed on cattle exports.

After 1516, the Hungarian crown was more concerned with the Turkish threats to the kingdom than with economic planning. After the death of King Louis in battle against the Turks in 1526 it took nearly thirty years for the division of Hungary into Habsburg and Turkish spheres of interest to become a reality. Yet both powers wanted the northern Hungarian mining towns which were so important both economically and strategically. The Turks wished to take Budapest in order to be able to advance on Vienna from there. In 1552 they failed to reach Tokaj across the central basin of the Tisa. Neither at that time nor later did they aim at direct control of northern Hungary preferring to support native puppet rulers wherever possible. After the death of their ally Zapolyai in 1540, the Hungarian area was further divided. The north-eastern part with Spiš was given to Queen Isabella, the widow of Zapolyai, and her son; the central part with Buda came under Turkish rule, and the eastern part, including Transylvania, which had been friendly to the Habsburgs, was now taken over by Zapolyai's son, John Sigismund, and placed under Turkish suzerainty. Now the individual areas adopted their own economic policies which led, among other consequences, to the establishment of new customs barriers.

In Transylvania, Banat and the area of the Partium, local autonomy was purchased from the Turks in return for a yearly tribute of ten thousand florins (fifteen thousand after 1575), plus irregular *dons gratuits*. Here rulers depended on the territorial Estates of Transylvania, which comprised representatives from the three historic nations, Hungary, Saxony and Siculer, and their four officially tolerated religions, Catholicism, Protestantism, Calvinism and Unitarianism. The Greek Orthodox faith and the Rumanian people were excluded from public affairs. Meaningful economic policy was ruled out because of the political instability of the principality, which was a pawn in the game between Habsburgs and Turks. The Transylvanian Estates took up a mercantilist attitude to the economic development of local natural resources and in 1617 decreed that anyone, native or foreigner, had the right to exploit mineral resources of any kind.

In Habsburg Hungary the administration was organized in two chambers, one for Lower Hungary (*Magyarorszag*) and one for Upper Hungary (*Felsö-Magyarorszag*), with its seat at Košice. The chambers referred to the King in economic matters but acted independently in most other questions. The free cities – among them Košice, Levoča (Leutschan), Prešov (Preschau), Eperjes, Bordejov (Bartfield) – had a special position, however, for the Habsburgs continued to favour the economic development of the towns at the expense of that of the countryside.

The Habsburgs had to build up a new system of customs and excise out of the ruins of the old, united Hungary: among the first excises to be imposed with the agreement of the estates was a salt tax. Economic planning was rudimentary, however, and at first only the export of gold and silver was forbidden in an attempt to maintain the value of the coinage. The system of tax exemptions for native Hungarian traders meant that Habsburg officials tended to favour foreign merchants who paid a tax called the 'thirtieth' to the exchequer, and encourage them to settle in the old Hungarian free towns. Nevertheless, the staple rights of the northern Hungarian towns acted as a brake on foreign merchants intent on exploiting the interior of Hungary and Transylvania.

In Poland, too, power hung in the balance between Crown and Estates. The personal strength of Sigismund August (1548–72) and Stefan Bathory (1575–86) can be clearly seen in the rigorous economic measures they took to preserve the value of the currency. But even these only postponed its debasement. As in Germany, debasement led to the illegal clipping of coins of full value before they were called in by the authorities for recoining.

In Poland, as in Habsburg Austria, financial affairs were organized around a treasury with limited powers. Military expenditure needed the support of the Estates, and until 1565 the only sources of income were the taxes authorized by the General Assembly or *Sejm*. Direct taxes were only levied once, and indirect taxes such as excises were fixed for a period of between one and three years only. Obviously no steady crown income could be assured for state purposes in this way. The main problem, therefore, was to create a permanent royal exchequer independent of any hand-to-mouth tax grants that the *Sejm* cared to make. Efforts at royal reform were of very limited success against the true rulers in the *Sejm*, the *szhlachta*, or Polish nobility, who in 1562–3 only allowed regular taxation to be applied to unlawfully alienated crown lands. The main sources of income for running the Polish state continued to come from extraordinary tax grants made by the *Sejm*, against which any royal prerogative in fiscal affairs counted for very little. During the sixteenth century, the great royal estates, once vital to the maintenance of King and court, were eroded by gifts and mortgages, thus sharply decreasing the royal income.

The *Sejm* held at Lublin in 1569 marked a high-point of efforts to centralize state finances – though it also proved a flash in the pan. After Sigismund's death in August that year the *Sejm* reasserted its rights in relation to the king. At the provincial assemblies (*Sejmiki*), held successively in the regional capitals, economic measures favouring the interests of the nobility against those of burghers and merchants, who had enjoyed royal protection, were invariably introduced. Thus any hopes of establishing monarchy on a firm financial base were dashed and Poland gradually became an aristocratic state.

The great expansion of the Muscovite state by conquest after Ivan III's time (since 1505) necessarily influenced its economic and political attitudes. But there was no question as yet of a 'planned' economic policy. The capture of Novgorod was an act of power politics, and its consequences clearly damaged the country's economy: the immediate result of the deportation of experienced merchants and the closing of the Hanseatic League's *Comptoir* was to destroy trade with the west. To compensate for this, however, connections with Narva, Reval, Dorpat and Riga were later developed.

Under Vasily III the tendency towards royal absolutism increased, reaching its peak under Ivan the Terrible (1547–84). Russia lacked an economic counterweight, such as the Estates represented in many other European states. On the whole, the princes and Boyars submitted with good or bad grace to the will of the Tsar and there was no urban propertied middle class. Nor had the Church much power independent of the Tsar, who generally resisted any idea of secularizing church lands – at least until the time of Peter the Great – for administration depended heavily on the expertise and loyalty of the clergy. The abolition of the *kormlenje* system (which gave state officials a financial stake in the yields of their departments) seemed to form the basis for the development of state fiscalism. That this was not to be, was largely because Russia lacked a vigorous middle class to develop administratively this tsarist initiative. The Tsar was more successful in reorganizing the army which he rewarded with *pomestje* (estates). The conquest of Kazan (1552) certainly had an economic motive, for here the aim was to secure free passage for trade between Moscow and the Orient and to settle the middle Volga and Kama with Russian peasants. The capture of Astrakhan, which followed soon after (1556), made it possible to intensify trade with Asiatic markets via the mouth of the Volga and the Caspian sea. Similarly, the object of the war against Livonia was to provide direct access to the Baltic in order to increase trade with western Europe.

Ivan IV's creation of *oprichnina* had serious consequences. This was an area around Moscow under the direct rule of the Tsar, with its own government, financial administration and *streltsi* (lifeguards), detached from the rest of the state, or *zemshchina*,

The Tsar based his personal rule on extensive *pomestia* and built up a servitor class completely dependent on him. Landowners who were not suitable for oprichnina service were settled elsewhere, and in this way Ivan succeeded in destroying the political power of the Boyars in the area under his direct rule. At its biggest, the oprichnina stretched from Moscow to Novgorod and in the west to Lake Ladoga and the White Sea (including Vladimir and Suzdal in the south-east). A periphery was left for the zemschina, based on a more traditional redistribution of land and peasants than that envisaged under the pomestia. Both systems, however, aimed at decimating the old aristocracy and raising new classes of state servants. Districts which lay on important trade routes and brought in high incomes from customs dues were especially favoured. The lucrative fishing, hunting and salt industries of the cold north were brought under direct control at Vologda and the new port of Archangel. Communications in the Russian Baltic region were strictly controlled, as was the route via Mozhaysk to Smolensk. No wonder the oprichnina was so hated by the boyars and apenage princes in the later sixteenth century, for it represented a form of strict prerogative rule anathema to those adherents of the oligarchic traditions that were once more to appear in the 'time of troubles' in the early seventeenth century.

In the short term, the punitive expedition against Novgorod, the burning of Kalinin and the plundering of Pskov seem to have been pointless. In Novgorod the number of merchants and tradespeople fell from 2998 to 545. Ivan's reign of terror, with its destruction of fortunes, massacres and uprooting of traditional trade connections, inflicted great harm on the Russian economy. Trade and credit were hampered by the unsettled conditions. The violent acts of the *oprichniki* and population migrations resulted in the depopulation of hundreds of central Russian villages. Grain yields were greatly reduced, especially on the *pomestia* lands, and it was only in the border areas, especially in the south, that population marginally increased. None the less Ivan IV laid the foundations for a centralized Muscovite state with autocratic economic planning backed by a willing servitor class.

Attempts to tie peasants to the land were made as early as the fifteenth century. This met with the approval of all landowners, whether Boyar or *pomestia*, and the right to move or settle freely was finally abolished in 1649. It is difficult to say whether western mercantilistic ideas influenced the autocracy of Ivan the Terrible or Boris Godunov (1598–1605). Russian xenophobia combined with the jealousy of neighbours to obstruct the flow into Russian service of western experts willing to help found new branches of Russian industry in such a way that it is now possible for us to think of Muscovy as having produced its own distinct, native forms of centralized economic planning. Hans Stitte from Goslar, who recruited about 120 technical experts for Ivan IV, met with opposition from the Livonian order, was imprisoned by Lübeck for a year and a half and finally abandoned his project.

The privileges that Ivan repeatedly granted to the English nevertheless show that he wanted to develop trade with western Europe via the Dvina estuary. But his attempts, starting in 1558, to conquer Livonia were unsuccessful. Under the treaty of 1582 he had to give up Livonia and with it the vital port of Narva. It was to be a long time before Peter the Great was finally able to penetrate the Swedish–Polish barrier to the Baltic. Furthermore, the efforts of the Stroganov family to open up the Kama district and Siberia were undertaken with the consent of Ivan. Gregory Stroganov received concessions over customs dues and taxes and his family extensive military powers to protect their possessions.

Boris Godunov, who was the effective ruler under Ivan's weak successor, Fedor, also had an autocratic effect on the Russian economy. His wars and the armaments they demanded considerably increased tax loads. The state seized quarries, brickworks, brick kilns, furnaces and lime-works to fortify the border areas against the Tartars and Poland–Lithuania. Exports of wax were only allowed in exchange for saltpetre, sulphur and gunpowder. Increasing taxation encouraged emigration from central Russia towards the southern steppe areas, and many peasants joined the Cossacks to avoid the new state demands. In the short run this decreased the tax yield, and so Godunov continued his attempts to tie to the land those peasants who remained in central Russia.

Continuing Ivan IV's policy of expansion, Godunov founded Tobolsk in 1587 and made conquests at Sweden's expense in Karelia and Lappland, though he failed to reach the Baltic,

When he made himself ruler of Russia after the death of Fedor in 1597 fate gave him little time to think about economic planning. Disastrous famines from 1601 to 1604, the disturbances caused by the appearance of the false pretender to the throne and finally Godunov's death in 1605, led to the confused interregnum of the false Dimitris, and the years of the *Smuta*, or 'time of troubles', that followed, proved to be an enormous though temporary setback to Tsarist autocracy. The Boyars did not know how to run the new Russian economy, which suffered heavy damage. First the service nobility and then the peasants and Cossacks rallied to the Tsarevich and the Church against the larger landlords, and it looked for a time as if the Zemsky Zobor would oust the Duma and introduce a form of representative and consultative government. However, the choice of a Tsar from the house of Romanov (Michael Fedorovich) in 1613 signalled a victory for the autocratic faction in Russian politics.

Michael inherited a completely disorganized administration. The Zemsky Zobor that had chosen the Tsar sat continuously from 1613 to 1622, and gradually, with much difficulty and at the cost of a renewed tax burden, a measure of order was brought back into the administration. At the conclusion of a new war with Poland and Sweden, Russia recovered Novgorod under the treaty of Stolbovo in 1617 but lost the southern shores of the Finnish coast and the Neva, thus becoming entirely cut off from the Baltic. Smolensk remained in Polish hands and was only recaptured by Tsar Alexis in 1654.

The real ruler during the regime of the untalented Michael was his energetic father, the Patriarch Philaret. Under him techniques of taxation were improved and new land registers were drawn up. Where the land had suffered from war, taxation was temporarily reduced. Officials who kept estate registers and assessed taxes were more closely supervised than before, and the first guidelines for a state budget were worked out. A set procedure to be used against those who avoided taxes was developed. To rebuild the army, those liable for service were provided with pomestia lands from confiscated estates of rebellious Boyars, and in 1633 petty landowners holding fewer than fifteen sokhá were excused military or civil service. To help the pomestia or servitors with estate management and so improve tax yields, peasants were legally enserfed. Their customary labour services, which occupied one-third of their working time in the sixteenth century, were now increased to fill half their time. Peasant agriculture was not entirely backward, but though the need for good fertilization was recognized, in practice it was hindered by the shortage of cattle. High taxes and onerous labour services were major disincentives to any rise in peasant productivity.

Tsarist policy for industry and trade perhaps concentrated too much on central control. Nothing was done to improve the position of the craftsmen, whose productivity was low. The educative function of the guilds – important in other countries – was lacking. Luxury goods continued to be imported from abroad. Merchants were generally hampered by arbitrary state interference in commercial matters. The state farmed out harmful monopolies to bring revenue to the exchequer, and native merchants were held in check by high capital taxes and internal customs dues. Foreigners, on the other hand, received far-reaching privileges, so that native merchants could not compete effectively. The main aim of these privileges was to provide the ruling groups in Russian society with western luxury goods and also to supply the army with technology, weapons and *matériel*. Tsar, Boyars and Church all hoarded their wealth, thus creating unproductive areas in the economy. The Kremlin treasury had piles of gold, silver and precious stones, much of which was lost during the 'time of troubles'. Afterwards the hoarding began afresh, the Church following suit. From this dead capital only foreign merchants and jewellers profited. It was characteristic that the regime did nothing to stimulate the Russian economy by imposing western banking and credit. This was left very much to Russia's great rival, Sweden.

In the first half of the sixteenth century, Gustav Vasa's economic policies in Sweden were still largely based on a natural economy of barter. Money was important (as in Russia) only in so far as it could be hoarded as treasure. The object of foreign trade was to import as much as possible, and exports served to encourage and pay for imports. Gustavus Vasa was a skilled entrepreneur who made do with very slender resources in the European market of his day. He supervised his governors, stewards and other officials closely. Crown produce was hoarded and only released for sale when the highest possible price had been reached. Sales to foreign merchants took place at specified crown ports, where they could be easily supervised. Gustavus Vasa succeeded in taking over most of the Church lands for the crown: a minor share went to the nobility, whose proportion of the land rose slightly (from 20·7 to 21·4 per cent). The crown's share rose from 5·6 to 28·5 per cent and the tax-paying free peasants' decreased slightly (from 52·4 to 50·1 per cent). Although Gustavus Vasa forbade the peasants to trade on their own account, he deliberately did not suppress their trade completely, for he depended on their political support against the over-powerful nobility. A fully developed mercantilist policy for Sweden (based on the example of the north German towns) had to wait until the time of Gustavus Vasa's successors however.

The staple was particularly admired in the form in which it had developed in central Europe during the Middle Ages. Swedish towns were therefore divided into *stapelstäder* and *uppstäder*. Overseas trade and shipping was reserved for the former, and the uppstäder were only allowed to trade inside Sweden. At the end of the sixteenth century, Charles ix tried to confine foreign trade to Stockholm alone, but without success. By 1617 the division into stapelstäder and uppstäder had been completed. The towns on the Gulf of Bothnia were only allowed to trade as far as Stockholm and Åbo in Finland. The guilds were also organized on a German pattern, in the first place by the future Charles ix in the towns in his duchy of Södermanland. He fixed a maximum number of members for each trade so that young craftsmen could only become masters when a vacancy occurred. Charles's successors came to understand the monopolistic tendencies of the guild system, but it had become so strong that it continued to expand under government regulation to cover the whole of Swedish urban production.

The fragmentation that followed the division of the country among Gustavus Vasa's sons led to increased economic control in the Duchy of Södermanland, which became a closed economic unit. Gustavus Vasa had arranged the division of the country in such a way that incomes derived from barter trade were preserved, though, in the long term, enmity between Gustavus Vasa's sons had exactly the opposite effect. Individual principalities did not prove viable, and Charles ix returned to centralized government as soon as he had made himself sole ruler of Sweden.

At the end of his reign Gustavus Vasa founded Helsinki so as to concentrate the agrarian trade of southern Finland in an urban centre. Charles IX continued this process for the rest of Swedish Finland, founding a series of towns whose markets monopolized trade in local foodstuffs, so countering the trading and manufacturing activities of peasants and nobility in the countryside. To the thirty-three towns already founded in Sweden by the middle of the sixteenth century another thirty-one were soon added. Yet many of these failed to develop. Relatively sparsely populated, they were not economically strong enough to impose on the surrounding peasants and villages conditions for the sale of foodstuffs. The countryfolk resisted royal decrees ordering them to move into the towns as the government wished, for there was no genuine economic incentive for them to do so.

Stockholm grew faster because it was both an established trading port with excellent communications and the seat of central government. It therefore attracted peasant traders from as far afield as Norrland. Apart from Stockholm, the other staple towns were relatively unimportant, and none had more than five thousand inhabitants. Even the new port of Gothenburg failed to live up to expectations and only became prosperous when it began to export high quality iron from Värmland, so opening the way for overseas colonial trade in the eighteenth century. Foreign traders and entrepreneurs in the sixteenth and seventeenth centuries were quickly assimilated, unlike the earlier influx of Hanseatic merchants, who remained markedly German. From the beginning the state tried to integrate foreigners into Swedish society, and so it became easy for them to adopt the Swedish language and customs. Many foreigners were also ennobled, and almost half the families so honoured were of foreign descent on the father's side. A similar situation prevailed among the urban middle class, although no exact figures can be given.

Denmark's economic situation in the sixteenth century depended on the overwhelming importance of customs dues for passage through the Sound. By the middle of the century over thirteen hundred ships were passing through the Sound annually and by 1600 the figure had risen to over five thousand.

All these ships paid tolls to the Danish king in Copenhagen. This income increased royal determination to make the Sound a Danish monopoly, so provoking head-on conflict with the Hansa, centred on Lübeck, now much weaker after its defeat in the *Grafenfehde* early in the sixteenth century. Christian III (1536–59) repeatedly delayed renewing the Hanseatic privilege of 1370, which was finally conceded in Odense in 1560, under Christian's successor, when the Danes were for the first time granted reciprocal rights in the German towns of the Hanseatic League. The German ports on the Baltic in return retained rights of free passage through the Sound, but only for ships loaded with goods of their own manufacture. Ships sailing via the Great Belt had to pay their dues at Nyborg. Danish and Swedish ships went free if they carried domestic goods.

The Danish king put the war years of the early sixteenth century to good use by increasing income from the Sound. From each load of merchandise one taler was demanded, half a taler for the same carrying capacity in an unladen ship. Income from customs dues increased from 45,000 talers in 1566 to 132,000 the following year. In the face of protests from Dutch shippers (the main users of the Sound), it was agreed that only ships coming from the East would have to pay dues, and a later agreement allowed all ships in ballast to sail freely through the Sound and Belt.

Danish control of the Sound was an example of how economic power determined relations between Denmark and the German Hansa. In 1575 Frederick II annexed Bornholm, which had been mortgaged to Lübeck. Christian IV, his successor, refused altogether to renew the Hanseatic privileges and did not shrink from a trial of strength with Sweden which, however, only won him short-term success. One of the sources of disagreement was the foundation of Gothenburg at the mouth of the Göta river to counter the Danish and Norwegian control of the mouth of the Baltic. Dutch help was won and a colony was settled there to support Dutch navigation against the monopoly. The Dutch brought their goods to Gothenburg, declared them of Swedish origin and sailed tax-free through the Sound. From 1611 to 1613 the monopoly became a *casus belli*, but little was achieved. The war merely had the effect of forcing Denmark into an isolated position and of contributing to the rise of Sweden as a major power during the century.

Denmark's monopolistic attitude led those countries opposed to Sound dues to unite against her. In 1613 the Dutch Republic and Lübeck formed an alliance, which Sweden joined in 1614. Thereafter, Sweden began to build up her Baltic empire and as the centre of Baltic trade moved farther and farther eastwards the Swedes demanded payments for licences to trade in the Baltic ports, especially those in Prussia. Once he was sure of his economic position in Baltic trade, the Swedish king turned his political ambitions towards northwest Germany. First he had to overcome the rivalry of Christian IV of Denmark, who attempted to capture the Hamburg trade by setting up barriers at the mouth of the Elbe. In the 1620s Christian tried to secularize the bishoprics of Bremen and Verden and to secure them for his son, Frederick. He then became involved in the German wars, in the hope of gaining possession of the whole area between Elbe and Weser, only to be heavily defeated by Tilly and the troops of the Catholic League.

Christian's ambitious foreign policy was supported by an equally ambitious mercantilism. In 1619 senior merchants were appointed by royal prerogative to settle disagreements about trade, including insurance, before they reached the ordinary courts. A maritime commission began to operate. Paid representatives were accredited to important foreign towns and courts where merchants factors had sufficed previously. Following the example of Amsterdam, Copenhagen built its own Exchange in 1619. Postal services were extended, and after 1602 Hamburg merchants had regular communications with Copenhagen and the Danish provincial centres. Attempts were made to stimulate trade by forcing established small towns to give up their charters in favour of newly built towns such as Christianopel, in modern southern Sweden, and, of course, Glückstadt on the lower Elbe. In line with mercantilist orthodoxy, all trade was to be tied to the towns at the expense of the countryside. But these efforts to stimulate trade were generally hindered by *ad hoc* monopolies, granted out of short-term fiscal necessity, which played havoc with economic planning. The early modern state was not financially stable enough to afford consistency in this area of government activity. Christian IV's Denmark proved to be no exception to this rule.

In studying the part played by component countries in the overall continental economy, one is repeatedly struck by the conflict between centralized power and the forces of traditional particularism, which were closely connected with the ambitions of the estates. Thus the efforts of the French crown towards centralization were opposed by the Estates-General and by provincial estates assemblies (where they existed), who claimed the right to grant and levy extraordinary taxes. In the Empire the particularism of the territorial rulers who made up the Imperial Assembly showed itself clearly. Just as German territorial rulers had freed themselves from the influence of the Emperor, so the representatives of the territorial estates, the local nobles, the towns and to some extent the clergy tried to assert their autonomy in relation to their petty rulers.

During the sixteenth century the Estates made themselves so powerful that most territorial rulers were compelled to summon them to territorial assemblies, or *Landtage*, to obtain their consent to extraordinary taxes and new laws. This process has been clearly described by Francis Carsten, especially in his book *Princes and Parliaments*, which first appeared in 1959. If a territorial ruler controlled a number of territories, he would have to negotiate with members of each *Landtage* separately. As princely absolutism developed the territorial rulers increased their efforts to limit or abolish the influence of the Estates, and, by the end of the seventeenth century, this process had on the whole been successful. Many rulers succeeded in reducing their *Landstände* to the status of over-privileged gentlemen's clubs. In the limited area of the territories it was easier to carry out effective centralization related to the limited capabilities of early modern government than in the huge area of the Empire.

Where the central authorities were weak, the Estates could assert their authority more strongly as was the case in the Habsburg family lands during the second half of the sixteenth century and the beginning of the seventeenth. The provincial Estates of nobles, clergy and town council burghers forced their rulers to grant concessions especially in the fields of religion and economic affairs.

Rudolf ii's patent of religious toleration to the Bohemian protestants, made in 1606, was a classic example of Habsburg weakness. Generally, however, the Landstände in each province or territory were jealous of their own freedom of action and remained extremely suspicious of delegating power to any Estates-General.

In the kingdom of Poland, where the king was elected, the position of the Estates was very strong, for they were dominated both economically and judicially by a large and homogeneous lower nobility. In Russia, however, strict autocratic control meant the growth of a service nobility only. In Sweden, the aristocratic council under Gustavus Adolphus and the expert leadership of his Chancellor or Råd, Axel Oxenstierna, exerted a powerful influence on economic policy and was revived with a new experiment in absolutism, ushered in when Charles xi forced a *coup* in 1680. In Denmark the council of nobles played a decisive part in the government until it was replaced in 1665 by the *Kongelov*, or Royal Law, which imposed the most rigorous form of absolutism experienced by any European state after the 1660s.

2. THE MAIN AREAS OF ECONOMIC ACTIVITY

A. *Agriculture, landlords and tenants*

Economically, medieval Europe relied, with notable exceptions, chiefly on agriculture and barter; socially and politically it was committed to upholding property and land tenure, particularly the all-important relations between landlord and tenant. In central Europe a rudimentary social structure had developed, moulded both by ancient customs and by Christian precepts. Under this system, inequality was recognized and perpetuated at law. The Church's place in the economic structure of the medieval world was central, for it became the largest single institutional landlord. Trade was carried out by great landlords and their agents (both secular and lay) and by foreign merchants, privileged minorities under the protection of the rulers.

Peasant rights and duties in central Europe varied greatly from locality to locality. Totally free farmers with extensive holdings only existed in a few isolated locations and represented only a minority of tenant farmers in any area. They were most numerous in the mountain areas of Bavaria, the Tyrol, the Black Forest, parts of Switzerland, on the North Sea coast, particularly in Dithmarschen, on the island of Fehmarn and in Sweden. In these peripheral areas the free farmer could hold his own. In the newly colonized east, peasants first achieved comparably favourable rights during the thirteenth and early fourteenth centuries, when land there was cultivated for the first time. In Denmark free peasants still held between 15 and 20 per cent of the land at the beginning of the sixteenth century, but within one generation this had been reduced to a mere five per cent. In Sweden and Finland the greater part of the farming population remained free, and a special class of free peasantry developed in the south-east, on the Habsburg military border with the Ottomans. The Cossacks too claimed certain freedoms in the Ukraine.

By the fifteenth century clear distinctions between unfree and free tenant-farmers had generally become blurred by contracts to work on specific pieces of land for fixed conditions of rent and time, which landlords could regularly revise upwards. In France fixed conditions of tenure became the norm and in eastern Germany peasants were more and more affected by the efforts of their landlords to tie them to the soil and to make them into serfs by virtue of their farming contracts. A variety of social groups – noble, non-noble, ecclesiastical, secular or lay – might act as landlords. Just as fiefs had gradually become inherited family property, so peasant tenancies also tended to become the established right of families and distinctions between personal freedom or servitude gave way to property rights over land-tenure and land-use. The local landlord who held legal authority usually only exercised low jurisdiction and only had the right to judge minor crime and fulfil petty police duties, the German *Zwing und Bann*. But where subjects were unfree, his lordship extended to *Leibherrschaft*, or *Leibeigenschaft*, and the serf became literally his chattel.

The great noble estates developed differently in different parts of continental Europe. In France, tenants' labouring duties were extensively converted into payments of rent. Landlords tended to try to keep pace with economic trends – which at one moment made money more valuable, at the next labour services and, at other times, produce most desirable. Most clashes between landlord and tenant occurred when the one sought economic advantage over the other in tune with these economic fluctuations in the value of money, produce and labour. Under the customs of most peasant inheritance, tenant holdings were steadily and increasingly broken up, but this was countered by the consolidation of property as non-nobles of urban origin also began to acquire land and control over tenants. Changes in ownership reflected the development of a money economy and during the general price rise in the sixteenth century landed property rose in value too. Increasingly, merchants invested ready cash in land as a hedge against trade fluctuations. High interest rates could be manipulated so that debtor landowners and tenants had to give up their property and holdings under conditions dictated by their creditors. Much of Luther's argument against usury dealt with this abuse, and in the early sixteenth century the falling value of money meant that the money paid to established landlords became increasingly worthless in relation to the cost of produce and labour. Their sumptuous life of leisure and military exploits created serious financial difficulties, leading to increased turnover in sales of estates and country seats. Financial security now had to be underpinned by an official post at court, in the new military, judicial and financial departments of state. The early modern state first became powerful because of its monopoly of patronage. Rich townsmen and even well-to-do peasants became landowners, often starting their careers as professional lawyers advising the parliament and privy councils of their day. Intermarriage made it easy to merge with the old aristocracy.

One consequence of the growth of capitalism was an increase in different types of leasehold. From the simple tenancy the *Halbpacht* (Germany), *métayage* (France) and *mezzadria* (Italy) developed; under these the tenant paid his landlord a proportion of the harvest as a hedge against inflation. This particularly benefited the landlord in those areas where labour services had already been reduced or converted into money payments. A mixed tenurial relationship gave a higher income than a simple ground rent and also kept pace with price rises, at least to some extent. This of course was not the tenant's view, and the state directly favoured the landlord at his expense. Payments in kind and in coin were often made under short-term contracts of five, nine or twelve years. Where contracts stipulated fixed rents, essential movable items such as livestock generally belonged to the tenant, who brought them to the tenancy with him. Sheep usually belonged to both parties equally, and pigs were often disregarded in the livestock inventory of the farm. In *métayage* contracts, cattle were often shared equally by both parties.

Over large areas of France peasant holdings were seldom

larger than eight to ten hectares. Rents for arable land were not high, though meadow-land fetched higher prices. In France there were two farming classes, *laboureurs* (peasants) and *journaliers* (day-labourers). The peasants were generally able to live adequately from their land, and many even managed to acquire extra plots. Frequently they combined farming with a more or less profitable additional occupation, such as trade in corn and cattle fodder or renting seigneurial rights. Most farming was by family enterprise, supplemented only sporadically by hired labour.

Hired labour was, however, more common on larger properties. It was poorly paid and wages deteriorated after about 1550, for population pressure on existing resources meant that wages no longer kept pace with prices. But even the day labourers, poor as they were, possessed allotments or supplemented their earnings with cottage industries such as weaving linen or wool.

It is difficult to generalize about peasant living standards, partly because of the enormous regional variations and complexities within this one social group. In sixteenth-century France, meat and white bread were seldom eaten, and rye was by far the most extensively grown crop. Household possessions and clothing were generally modest, but well-to-do peasants might have a few luxuries, just as they might aspire to social and professional status for their sons as burghers, merchants, priests or lawyers. Some even managed to acquire lands from the local nobility and to intermarry with them.

In western Germany the pattern of land tenure, which was in continual flux, was to some extent influenced by the reaction to the revolts of the peasantry in favour of the increasing demands made by landlords. The freedoms which had been granted when the land was originally settled were systematically eroded. But by the early sixteenth century these freedoms were felt by peasants to be their 'natural ancient rights', and any infringement of them could lead to sporadic violence. This applied especially to enclosure of common forests and pastures, restrictions on mobility, lack of access to courts of appeal, and to curtailment of hunting and fishing rights; originally these had largely belonged to the settlers and were now replaced by ferocious game laws. There seems to have been a general central European 'levelling-down' of peasants to a uniform class of farm-labouring serfs from what had originally been a wide range of degrees of dependence. Throughout the sixteenth and seventeenth centuries peasants were generally forced to exchange old privileges for new duties.

But no serfdom in the west was comparable to that under *Gutswirtschaft*, or desmene farming, in the east. In some areas remnants of *Leibeigenschaft* (personal servitude) did survive, but only in the shape of personal restrictions on movement, marriage and family. At the end of the sixteenth century peasants in Upper Austria fought against the demands of their lords for the service of children as house-servants, which they had to render 'as if they were personally unfree'. Tenure took various local forms. In the south-west of Germany, property was often widely scattered and divided between various villages. Landlords took mixed rents in money and kind, but because they did not farm extensively themselves, they had no special interest in enforcing labour services. Most tenants had more than one landlord, and most farms had been split into more than one tenancy, because of division of land among heirs (*Realteilung*).

In those parts of Swabia, Franconia and Austria, which were settled late, *Realteilung* was not customary. This led to a much larger class of landless peasants, many of whom found themselves in a dependent position with regard to landlords and the law. The number of nobility working their own estates was relatively small and the Church was probably the most important landlord. For many a ruling prince, the main opportunity which remained open was to extend his jurisdiction by inheritance, marriage or force.

In north-west Germany *Meierrecht* (copy-holding on regularly revisable terms) prevailed. Landlords could claim rights of ownership in the land but tenants held the land in perpetuity provided they fulfilled the terms of their contract. Dutch immigrants in the marshy areas of Friesland as far east as Dithmarschen and Eiderstedt were leased land for a fixed period, without right of automatic renewal (*Zeitpacht*), a system also found in the Rhineland. However, under this system landlords usually allowed peasants either the privilege of inheritance or continued leasehold, though they were not legally compelled to do so. The so-called *Freistift*, which gave virtually unrestricted rights to the lord, was less common.

Labour services varied greatly, but the most that was demanded of the peasant in north-west Germany by this time was one or two days in the week. He would be called upon especially in the ploughing, sowing and harvest seasons. Compensation was paid for these labour services, but not at the same rates as the free wage earner would have expected, though the landlord also had to provide substantial meals for his peasants. The landlord could claim rents under numerous rights. They were paid on harvest and livestock produce; as well as the *Herrenge-fälle*, rents paid to the lord of the manor, there was the Church 'tenth', levied on grain and on household animals. Then there were taxes for special occasions: on the death of a tenant, the best clothes or the healthiest animals were paid to the landlord. When the landlord died the tenant paid the *laudemium* or *Lehnware* to his successor. There were marriage taxes and a tax payable on leaving the tenancy. Sometimes these taxes had to be paid to more than one landlord, and when a number of taxes descended on him at once, or when misfortune struck, the tenant had to borrow money at unfavourably high rates of interest.

In the Swiss Confederation feudal bonds were gradually broken and as serfdom decreased in the sixteenth century a group of poor peasants (*Tauner*) with little land came into existence. This group increased rapidly as the development of textile industries in the countryside brought additional opportunities for earning a living.

In the areas of upper Austria where *Gutswirtschaft* (demesne farming) developed tenants gradually became labourers on their 'lords' farms (*Wirtschaftsherrschaft*). Yet most of the cultivable land remained in self-contained peasant farms, although these were now more closely supervised than before, owing to more efficient state taxation and heavier demands for rents and services by landlords. Landlords sometimes rationalized farms by mutual exchange of plots of land or by outright land purchase in an attempt to arrogate sovereign rights (especially those of high jurisdiction) to themselves; in this they came into conflict with their territorial rulers, who tried with varying success to retain these rights. Landlords also tried to organize trade and industry on their country estates and in their villages; this naturally caused tension between them and the towns, which had been granted exclusive trading rights by the rulers. The replacement of taxes in kind with money payments made agricultural economics more flexible and led to a general increase in the lords' demands.

Robot, compulsory labour services, were lucrative in those areas where there were labour shortages. Sometimes payments in kind which had been changed to money payments were reversed again because of rising market prices. Alternatively, money rents would be raised to correspond with existing market prices. As estate managers began to keep better records during the sixteenth century, it became easier for landlords to wield their judicial and executive police powers and enforce tax increases, so that by the end of the century the landlord and state took as much as a third to a half of a peasant's property in an inheritance tax. Other grievances were the *Gesindezwang*, whereby peasant children had to work as the landlord's domestic servants, established by decree of the Habsburgs in 1582, and the *Anteilszwang*; according to this, peasants had to offer their surplus produce such as grain, cattle and linen to their landlord before they could sell it in the open market. Finally the *Tafernzwang* laid down that marriages and funerals should only be celebrated in specified taverns belonging to the landlord.

In these developments one detects a cruel and consciously calculating attitude on the part of landlords in cooperation with the state against the peasants. Higher productivity brought in more money as well as increasing surpluses for further investment. More money and more produce also led to increased luxury and ostentation; landowners often became absentees and left their estates in the control of rapacious managers (*Pfleger*). Landlords frequently embezzled state taxes collected by them and also acquired control over indirect taxes, first by leasing them and then by buying them from impecunious state exchequers. Lands which the nobles farmed themselves were in any case free of extraordinary taxes. Landlords would often advance money to peasants at fixed rates on the security of standing crops and future harvests, so ensuring excessive long-term profits.

In Upper Austria the *robot* was a major source of complaint during the great peasants' revolt of 1525, especially where it was imposed by petty noble landlords. Subsequent peasants' revolts were also caused by the *robot*, and in 1597 the Habsburgs finally set it at a maximum of fourteen days labour service each year for the whole of Upper Austria above the Enns. This concession was possible because major landlords had by now such abundant supplies of agricultural labour on their extensive demesnes that they could face the loss of *robot* with equanimity. They were more concerned to uphold the labour services that involved the more specialized tasks such as river transport, which were of crucial importance to their trading activities.

In Bohemia, southern Styria and Hungary similar developments to those described for Upper Austria started even earlier and went much further. Officials representing both landlords and the state tried to standardize taxation. In Upper Austria, too, demesne farming became widespread, probably because it seemed a lucrative way to raise money to pay for essentials such as frontier defence against the Turks.

In parts of east-central Germany, such as Saxony, the ruler was strong and prosperous because of his lucrative mineral rights. Thus he was less dependent on tax grants from his territorial Estates and could protect the peasantry (his chief taxpayers) from arbitrary exactions by the petty nobility and basic landlords. This process has been outlined by Friedrich Lütge in his study of land-tenures in central Germany.

B. *Gutswirtschaft* (Demesne farming)

Unlike France, the German Empire (except to the west of the Elbe and in the northern Alps, but including many parts of Denmark and east Elbia as far as Bohemia, Moravia, Hungary, Croatia, Silesia and Poland) was run as a demesne economy.

The large estates beyond the lower Elbe were in the hands of lords of differing social origins. Greater and lesser nobility, secular clergy and monasteries, town councils and individual burghers had all formed the original landlord class in the fifteenth century. Strongly entrenched in the newly settled lands in Denmark, eastern Schleswig and in Holstein as far as the Baltic, the nobility were well placed to develop demesne farming, and their early conversion to Protestantism destroyed any rivalry that might have come from the Roman Catholic church. Privileges acquired by the nobles during the Middle Ages were rapidly extended during the sixteenth century. Meanwhile the territorial rulers weakened their position through overambitious wars, family quarrels, divisions of property due to partible inheritance, luxury, ostentatious living and massive

defence expenditure. By exploiting the inadequate state financial organization, the nobility made corresponding gains.

The accession of Frederick I and Christian III helped the
nobility of Holstein as well as that of Denmark. Secularization
during the Reformation brought great gains to the nobility
who, as in Tudor England, had supported their rulers. Most
important of all was the power to levy taxes on the peasantry.
This occurred above all in Mecklenburg, Pomerania and in
Brandenburg, where the towns, despite the temporary strength
of the Hanseatic League, were never able to achieve such a
dominant position in political and economic life as did their
counterparts in the south and west of the German empire. The
right of staple (*Weichbildrecht*), the right to control the areas
surrounding a town and the other urban privileges were never
so extensively exploited in the urban centres on the German
Baltic coast, where shipping offered both noble and commoner
great business and trading opportunities.

Demesne farming by the lords themselves was more important in the newly settled areas than farther west. Improved
access by river and sea to the great markets of the Netherlands
led the Baltic lords to build up their *latifundia* estates by all possible means – buying land, exchange, and enclosure of common
land. The immigrant peasants had originally been enticed east
by granting them greater rights than those they had previously
enjoyed. By the sixteenth century these rights had been annulled
nearly everywhere. The peasant and his family now had to
serve in the lords' household and they were tied to the soil as
hereditary serfs. Parallels with Muscovite legislation in this
period suggest themselves; this process took place over a number of generations and in large areas of central Europe in the
sixteenth and seventeenth centuries. *Gutsherrschaft* continued to
spread until the eighteenth century, and thus the lord was able
to exploit the rural resources of land, labour and produce for
the very profitable export trade to the west. The main centres
of this type of agrarian economy were in Denmark, east
Schleswig, Holstein, Mecklenburg, Brandenburg, Pomerania,
Prussia and above all Poland around the Vistula.

In Denmark the crown probably owned between a fifth and
a quarter of all land at the beginning of the sixteenth century.
The secularization of church property added another third, so
that the crown now owned over half of the land. But part of this

land was granted to the nobility in lieu of political, military
and financial services and the nobles had increased their share
of the land from a quarter to well over forty per cent by the
seventeenth century, although this was a smaller increase than
in Holstein and east of the Elbe. Thus the Danish crown itself
played a vital part in depressing the status of the peasantry –
partly deliberate policy, for example, Christian III's rage against
the peasants of northern Jutland, who had supported Christian
II in the *Grafenfehde* of the earlier sixteenth century. To save
their lives, many peasants had to hand over their farms to
crown commissars in return for less favourable leases. On the
North Sea coast Frederick II established extensive stud farms.
He created *Vorwerke* (outlying demesne farms) in Zealand and
eastern Jutland out of lands confiscated from the peasants, and
his widow later held great estates on Laaland and Falster as an
annuity. Duke John the Younger of Sonderburg followed suit
by demesne farming on Alsen, Ärö and Sundewitt. There were
also extensive exchanges of land between crown and nobility to
consolidate holdings at the expense of any peasant land that
lay in between. Precisely how many peasant holdings were
annexed in this way is not certain, but it seems that whole
settlements may have been uprooted by this turning of arable
into pasture. It is thought that between 1570 and 1650 two
hundred farms were seized on the main island of Zealand alone
and that the position was similar in other parts of Denmark.
These developments were, however, to some extent offset by the
creation of new farms, by division on inheritance and by clearing unsettled land. Thus the legal rights of free peasants and
leasehold tenants were never as inviolable as has sometimes been
assumed. In Zealand, Møen and Laaland-Falster the free
peasants were as closely tied to the soil as the serfs, and even if
they were not liable for labour services they still had to do
some service by virtue of their tenant contracts. Like most
central European rulers, Christian IV used peasant labour for
his castle and palace buildings. Free peasants were also under
obligation to pay higher taxes than serfs.

The duty of crown tenants was to serve at court and perform
labour services; these were gradually increased to meet the demands for increased labour forces as demesne farms grew into
latifundia. Under Christian IV (1588–1648) the tendency to increase labour services was especially marked. When, in the early

stages of change, the peasants complained to the crown their rights were upheld, but subsequently they were heeded less and less. Worst off were the share-croppers, who often worked two or three days a week on the lord's estate. Originally those peasants who lived nearest to the estate were used, but then came demands upon those living farther away and finally upon those who rented land as freemen. The system was most fully developed on Fünen and Langeland and in Jutland and Scania, where many estates belonged to the nobility. Only the peasantry on the smaller or more remote islands such as Bornholm and Samsøe tended to escape degradation.

The crown was not always sympathetic to the destruction of peasant farms in favour of *latifundia*, because it thereby lost its chief taxpayers and its main source of revenues. The clergy frequently lost their 'tenth' in the same way. Yet the crown lived from hand to mouth and pursued contradictory policies *vis-à-vis* the peasantry. Instead of preserving ancient peasant rights the Danish crown extinguished them by tacit agreement with the land-owning nobility and the leading burghers.

Beyond the Elbe, too, labour services continued to increase during the sixteenth and seventeenth centuries. In Mecklenburg these services took up only a few days in the year in 1500, but by 1550 one day per week was demanded and by 1600 it was three days per week. In Poland the rate demanded was exactly double that of Mecklenburg. These provisions were harder on the small peasants, for duties were not tied to an individual. If the richer peasants chose not to carry out their duties themselves they could send their farmhands and maids to do their work on the appointed days.

The farther east one went in central Europe, the scarcer labour became and the more plentiful were land resources. Thus landlords and the state tied the peasant to the soil for fear of losing his services. The freedom of movement which he had enjoyed up to now was taken away, and he was allowed to move only when he had carried out all his obligations, which became increasingly difficult. Strict economic regulations were imposed to prevent the laws of supply and demand from operating in favour of peasants, tenants and labourers. Naturally, the lord of each manor tried to restrict the rights of his peasants, and in this he found the law increasingly in his favour. Wherever possible, *Erbzins* (heritable copyhold, based on oral tradition) was replaced by *Überlassung auf Zeit* (lease for a period of time) for a corresponding payment. When this ran out peasants were at the mercy of landlords who then, quite legally, reduced them to agricultural labourers (*Lassiten*). Their land could then be bought and sold, demesnes consolidated, and common land and fallow swallowed up, for there were no more peasant farmers with traditional rights of pasturage to resist such developments. With all the rights which he had now acquired the lord was able to turn himself into a small-scale sovereign prince. His peasants were his vassals and, with his judicial and police rights, he represented authority for them. Their condition of *Erbuntertan*, or hereditary servitude, was not legally the same as that of *Leibeigenschaft*, or personal unfreedom, but in practice it often meant the same thing.

Many of the Holstein nobility were not only great landowners and demesne farmers but also manufacturers, merchants and financiers in the nearby economic centres of Hamburg and Lübeck. They had a stake in the herring-fishing industry, owning their own ships, which plied between the Baltic and the western European ports. On Stormarn, near Hamburg and Lübeck, there was ample water-power and timber for flourishing paper-mills. Holstein nobles held significant investments in Kiel, Hamburg and Antwerp, and they regularly lent money to the king of Denmark and the duke of Holstein-Gottorf to cover the financial needs of court and government. In the second half of the sixteenth century the Kiel fair, held yearly in January, was the most important money market in north-west Germany. The leading figure among these noble entrepreneurs was Heinrich Rantzau, governor of Holstein, a great patron of humanism and of the Renaissance.

In Mecklenburg, Pomerania, Brandenburg and Prussia the wealth of the landed nobility tended to be more modest. Apart from the Schulenburg family no one was as rich as the Holsteiners, though the trend was towards creation of an exclusive class of nobles. Their economic position was often insecure and members of their families often had to supplement their income by service to the territorial state as civil servants or officers. Large-scale farming on the demesne system was not confined to the nobles, however. Members of the ruling dynasties also successfully emulated some of the nobility as estate managers.

Farming was practised on a grand scale in Silesia, Bohemia, Moravia, Hungary and Croatia. These magnates were divided both socially and economically from the lesser nobility and in some cases ruled over hundreds of villages which they administered through stewards; as absentee landlords these magnates spent their lives at the Austrian imperial and royal Polish courts. Although a similar state of affairs was to be found in Denmark, Holstein and Sweden, the east-central European countries practised absentee landlordism on a grand scale, reached elsewhere only in Bourbon France and Ireland.

In Moravia in 1619 over three-quarters of the land was owned by the nobility. Yet there was still a free peasantry, or *chodi*, who before the battle of the White Mountain in 1620 enjoyed the protection of the Habsburg rulers, as their immediate overlords. These chodi had their own court in Domazlice, freely disposed of their own possessions and property and exercised the right to carry on a handicraft or trade.

Poland was a classic example of the great gulf that separated the ranks and orders of early modern society in central Europe. Here the land was almost exclusively owned by nobility, crown and church, with autonomous, large estates run by fully-fledged administrations of their own. There was an elaborate hierarchy on these estates, ranging from *Revisor* (steward) and *Dvornik* (factor) down to a number of peasant overseers called *Karbovi* or *Vlodari*. Estates also employed droves of domestic servants. On the royal estates of Chernovoi Rusi about one-third of the domestics were employed in a supervisory capacity. The vast majority worked in ranching, only about 3 per cent being employed as gardeners, park-keepers and handymen. On the estates of royal (Polish) Prussia the number of domestics employed per farm varied between ten and fifty. Work in the fields was done by *Leibeigene* (serfs). Labour services took many forms: sometimes a fixed number of days in the week or in the whole year were worked, although it was more common to demand seasonal labour during ploughing, sowing, harrowing and harvesting. Labour services covered all the work necessary for running the estate, including milling the grain and transporting it to the nearest link with the Dutch international commodity market.

It was cumbersome to use compulsory labour services for animal husbandry, and here servants and day labour were used instead. Piecemeal agreements were made between herdsmen and cattle-owners, fixing for instance the amount of butter and cheese per cow to be handed over to the owner's factors. In bee-keeping a share of honey and wax was fixed, and similar agreements were made for fishing. Where labour services were insufficient, day labourers were employed from the families of craftsmen, petty traders and liveried servants who lived in the villages and townships overshadowed by the great house and its demesne. On the royal Polish estates of Red Russia the *Komorniki, Chalupniki, Sagrodniki* and the *Kmeti*, who each farmed less than a quarter *Lana* of arable land, formed thirty per cent of the total population, but in villages with no demesne they represented only 16 per cent. In the sixteenth century compulsory labour was on the whole more important to estate-managers than day labour, except in the Polish crown lands of Red Russia and in Podolia where estates were frequently smaller than elsewhere and where it was less profitable to employ compulsory labour. Instead, domestic servants and day labourers were engaged.

Serfdom in Poland, which had begun in the fifteenth century, developed during the sixteenth, encouraged by laws promulgated in the *Sejm*, and reached a high point towards 1600, stimulated by an increased demand for Polish grain on the Dutch international markets. As one of the largest agrarian entrepreneurs, the Polish crown itself took part in this process of peasant immiseration. The great weakness of the peasants was that they were not in a position to compete commercially with noble estates in scale or technique. The object of the nobility was to impose an agricultural policy on the crown which favoured the development of demesnes, and to this end a whole series of strict regulations about serfs were issued. Their characteristic feature was to deny peasants all access to the royal courts of appeal. Under King Sigismund I, for example, the *poddany* (peasants attached to a demesne) lost this right of appeal to royal judges against their lords. As the crown no longer protected peasants judicially, illegal flight became virtually the only means of escape from bondage, especially for those who now had only small allotments or no land at all. Measures, including punishment of neighbours, against those who had fled were only partly successful.

Unlike the petty nobility, the higher nobility was constantly increasing the size of its holdings, especially after the Union of Lublin in 1569. Poland's annexation of Volhynia and other parts of the Ukraine led to the formation of what were probably Europe's largest *Latifundia* by great Polish families, who used their influence at court and with the treasury to further their own ends. The properties of families like the Zamoyski, Kalinovski, Potocki and the Koniecpolski reached huge proportions. Ukranian magnates, the Ostrogski, Zaslawski and Wioniowiecki among others, acquired vast estates in return for loyalty to the Polish state. They functioned as autonomous marcher lords with fortresses to defend Poland against the Tartars and the Muscovite state.

Jan Zamoyski (1543–1605) was the most successful of these magnates. Rising from the ranks of the middle nobility, he held official posts under the Polish crown and succeeded by the end of his life in acquiring an estate of 6,445 square kilometres, including twelve townships and over two hundred villages. In addition Zamoyski administered as a senior royal official other domains for life, comprising another 11,054 square kilometres with twelve towns and 612 villages.

In 1600 Basil Ostrogski owned a hundred townships and fortresses with 1,300 villages. His yearly income was 1,200,000 *Zloty*, a sum greater than the regular income of the Polish state. In Little Poland the Lubomirski family were almost as wealthy. Although many landlords wished to consolidate and round off their estates, property was often widely scattered – this applied especially to Zamoyski's holdings – and this tended to weaken their political independence. The great ecclesiastical princes also held extensive lands. In 1581 the Church in the *Voivodeship* (county) of Krakow owned nine towns, 333 whole and 53 half villages. By 1629, as a result of a successful Catholic Counter-Reformation, this had increased to 13 towns, shared ownership in another 12 towns, 487 whole and 70 shared villages.

As these estates grew ever larger, the lesser nobility grew more dependent on the higher nobility and church. In the seventeenth century the Voivodeships Plock, 20 per cent of the petty nobility, or *szlachta*, owned no serfs and only shared ownership of an estate. In the Voivodeships Masovia and Rava up to a dozen nobles sometimes lived on one farm. In Podolia the lesser nobility numbered a third of the total population, but many of their property holdings were barely distinguishable from those of peasants. In the Voivodeship Leszyca the szlachta generally only had one or two serfs each, and it frequently happened that a serf was shared by more than one lord. Schlachta served in the administrations and private armies of the magnates. But a few free peasants, or *chelmer*, did survive; these had originally leased their property with an obligation to serve in the army, but this duty had gradually disappeared without destroying the privileges that went with it.

Agrarian conditions similar to those of east Elbia, Prussia and Poland existed in Livonia, Courland and Estonia. In the territories of the Livonian Order and Archdiocese of Riga the local nobility also increased their land holdings. As in Poland, access to overseas markets led to the growth of extensive latifundia during the early seventeenth century. Livonian society was ethnically split and peasant labour was provided by native Courlanders, Letts and Estonians on estates run by so-called German nobles of mixed north and west European origin.

By contrast, Sweden and particularly Finland retained a free peasantry who were politically represented in state assemblies as a fourth estate. True, the amount of free peasant land decreased during Sweden's expansion as a great power, because the crown alienated its rights over it. Yet serfdom as found in Denmark and in the rest of the Baltic area never developed. Not that no attempts at this were made; the Swedish nobility certainly tried to introduce the economic and social conditions they found in their German possessions into Sweden. Traditionally, Swedish peasants were separated into those paying rent to the crown and those paying rent to the nobility. Because of the concessions which the nobility secured under Gustavus Adolphus, their estates were totally free of taxes, as was the land of those peasants who lived within the boundaries of a village belonging to a manor house. The rest of their tenants paid only half the rate of taxes which free and crown peasants paid. Thus it was advantageous for nobles to retain tenant farmers, and relatively few *säterier*, or demesne estates, developed.

During the course of the sixteenth century Russia acquired an agrarian system, the basic principles of which lasted until 1861. The same shortage of labour which tied peasants to the land in many parts of central and eastern Europe was particularly marked in Russia. The status of Russian peasants in law deteriorated rapidly, although local conditions varied considerably.

The 'black earth' area, that is the land farmed communally by the free peasants, vanished almost completely during the course of the sixteenth century. Rulers gave land to their servants as part of the process of political patronage and even peasants frequently gave land to monasteries or churches, partly in order to obtain legal support and protection. Most peasants now found themselves as poor tenants, or share-croppers, on the so-called 'white land'. Until the middle of the sixteenth century rents were fixed verbally. Payment consisted of *polovnichestvo*, payment in kind of one-fifth to one-half of the gross harvest, and of *obrok*, a cash rent. Peasant labour services varied and were frequently based on contracts made at five- to ten-yearly intervals. During the sixteenth century high rates of interest (up to 20 per cent), especially on credit for purchasing items like seed, destroyed the economic well-being of many peasant farms. The only way of discharging such debts was by increased labour services. Often the peasant never managed to pay off such debts, making it easier for landowners, who were assisted by favourable tax policies of the Tsars, to dictate their own terms.

Old peasant laws and customs were exploited in new ways to tie peasants to the land. A law of 1494 for the first time forbade tenants to leave their land at any other time than the annual feast of St George (in April). Yet peasants were still formally allowed to move away according to Muscovite law, and to set out to find a better landlord and tenancy. After 1550 this was forbidden, unless the peasant could pay compensation to his lord, at a rate fixed by the lord.

In the economic difficulties of the second half of the century, Ivan iv in 1580 completely forbade, as a temporary measure, peasants to leave their community or lord. This ruling was revived by the Boyars during the 'Time of Troubles' and finally, in 1609, peasants were legally bound to the soil. The first Romanovs confirmed this law, which had important social and political consequences. For the security of his regime the Tsar needed an intermediate class of followers who would support him in political and military affairs; these he rewarded with *pomestie* lands (small estates granted by service tenure). Thus the service nobility merged with the remnants of the Boyar

class in the sixteenth and seventeenth centuries to become the
backbone of Tsarist autocracy.

Under Ivan IV, families were graded for state service according to the size of their holdings. A demesne of one hundred and
fifty *dessiatins* (1 dessiatin = 2·86 acres) brought with it the
services of a courtier. Pomestie service nobles had benefited
from estates, houses and men, but could neither sell, mortgage
nor will them away. When the eldest son of a *pomestchik* reached
legal age (fifteen), the government generally gave him his own
estate. A small landowning nobility of reliable state servants was
thus formed, totally dependent on the Tsar, especially after the
ukaz, or law code, of 1556. The long-term success of Tsarist
autocracy in Muscovy is inexplicable without recognizing the
support which the new class of landowners gave to it.

Under the ukaz of 1556, pomestchiki were recruited to defend the heart of Muscovy around Moscow itself. A line of
defence along the Oka was established with pomestia of intermediate size. Holdings became larger as their distance from
Moscow increased. In Kolomna district, near Moscow, the
pomestia formed in 1577 had an average extent of 189 dessiatins,
although in 1597 properties of the Moscow nobility officially
averaged 750 to 3000 dessiatins each.

Already in the sixteenth century the total area of granted
pomestia probably exceeded the size of all other land-tenures.
Before 1550 pomestia holdings in the Kalinin district exceeded
100,000 hectares, whereas allodial lands were less than 4000
hectares. In the Moscow district, pomestia took up 34 per cent
of the total area by the 1560s, and around Novgorod the figure
was over 75 per cent.

In general three areas could be distinguished: in the far
north and north-west, 'black land' predominated; in the centre,
around Moscow, the allodial lands of the old nobility and the
monasteries prevailed, and south of Moscow stretched the
pomestia. Frontier lands were entrusted to companies with extensive charters, especially in the south and south-east. Here
inhabitants tended to move outwards as the frontier of Muscovy
was pushed back, notably on the Volga, where they organized
themselves into bands and chose a leader. The government registered each group and gave it a particular area, which it was
allowed to cultivate, in return for defending it for the state. The
ukaz of January 1565 divided land into two major areas –

oprichnina, belonging to the Tsar, who converted all allodia into leaseholds, and zemshchina, land which continued free, where pomestchiki tried more and more to create family properties from land the state had granted them. The customary services which were attached to pomestia also began to creep into agreements made on allodial properties, so that by the seventeenth century the distinctions between the various forms of ownership had become obscure.

The Church was the largest single landowner. Its wealth had been increasing for centuries, and the property of the Metropolitan alone comprised 30,000 hectares. A hundred thousand people lived on the estates of the Holy Trinity monastery alone, which together with the monastery of St Sergius owned 200,000 hectares. In the principality of Kalinin in 1548 the Church owned 27 per cent of all the cultivated land and 24 per cent of the forests, in the Pskov area as much as 52 per cent. Contemporary foreign travellers estimated that in the sixteenth century the Russian Orthodox Church owned one-third of all Muscovy.

The Tsars must have regarded this development with mixed feelings, for the church paid no taxes and was swallowing up the black peasants. Ivan III did consider secularizing church property and to some extent succeeded when he annexed Novgorod in 1478. Ivan IV also made some efforts in this direction, albeit less effective, and in 1573 the Council finally forbade, on the Tsars orders, gifts of allodial lands to rich monasteries. In 1580 the clergy and monastic orders were forbidden to accept or buy landed property of any kind, and in 1584 their tax immunities were revoked. Nevertheless gifts to monasteries continued, and effective reforms in this sector of Tsarist autocracy had to wait until the time of Peter the Great.

Peasant communities were already established among the free peasants on the 'black earth' by the fifteenth century. The rent-paying tenants who received lands in Novgorod farmed pastures, lakes and forests communally, though at this time private ownership remained the commonest form of land ownership among the Russian peasantry. In the sixteenth century communal farming did become more frequent, for various reasons: it avoided the economic hardship and ruin entailed in divisions on inheritance, and the communal structure led to a more equitable fiscal and tax policy, for peasants acted together as an economic unit. At the beginning of the sixteenth century the commonest settlement in Russia was the small village with between one and three peasant holdings, but the development of pomestia saw small holdings gradually disappear; peasants who served their lords on demesne and in the household were gathered together in villages, where they could be more efficiently supervised. It became customary for each of the pomestia to have its own village, which was also the chief local unit of taxation.

The *mir*, or chosen assembly of village elders, and its representatives, the *starost*, apportioned taxes under the supervision of the pomestchiki. Gradually personal ownership disappeared, and the land was constantly redivided according to the numbers in each peasant family, though where new land was cleared it belonged to whoever had done the work.

c. *Craft guilds, the putting-out system and the workshop*

In the mainly agrarian Middle Ages, urban development was carefully and protectively organized. In the towns craft guilds grew up, especially where merchants and entrepreneurs were active, and town councils began to rely on guilds to organize and direct crafts in accordance with the state's economic policy.

In France, guilds never reached the commanding position that they held in the Netherlands and Germany and were usually active only in large towns; smaller urban centres retained free masters, and country trades remained important. During the sixteenth century and the mercantilist age that followed, however, the government tried to bring guilds and craftsmen under control.

The tendency towards regulation is most clearly seen in the German territorial states, in Hesse and Saxony, for example, where many crafts were subjected to strict guild statutes in the sixteenth and seventeenth centuries. State authorities tried to use guilds to encourage the controlled growth of industry and to set aside particular local restrictions and irregularities. The imperial policy decrees of 1530, 1548 and 1577 supported the mercantilist policies of territorial governments and tried to standardize economic policies throughout federal Germany.

The far-reaching changes caused by overseas expansion, the Reformation and the new spirit of the Renaissance had serious consequences for the guilds. That the organization and execution of work became increasingly separated was part of the development of capitalistic enterprises with their division into entrepreneur and wage-earner. This created the first clear distinctions in life-style between the individual and the masses. The tendency towards specialization of managerial and related functions was accentuated when, as frequently happened, the expert architect or engineer was a foreigner – Italian or Dutch, perhaps – who had freed himself from the guild system. Technical advances, and their use by entrepreneurs at the expense of craftsmen, frequently left the guilds in a defensive position, which large-scale entrepreneurs were able to circumvent because of their wealth, nobility and connections. But this was, however, offset by new opportunities for craft guilds to fit into the general manufacturing process by further specialization, by a putting-out system (*Verlag*), especially in the early metal industries where capitalist organization became widespread – particularly where technical equipment was necessary, as it was in the mining and smelting of ores to give silver, copper, mercury, tin and lead. Guilds and corporations co-operated with large trading companies, particularly those established at, Augsburg and Nuremberg. Shares (*Kuxen*) were issued in these late medieval mining ventures, which could be bought, sold and were transferable. A special type, which later led to the limited company, was the *Saigergesellschaft* (refining company). The production of half-finished iron goods was in the hands of forge-masters, or *Reide* masters, who controlled supplies. Nuremberg had strong economic links with the trade centres of the Rhineland and Westphalia, for instance in Cologne. Paper-making and printing offered new opportunities for capital investment for more money was needed than printers and stationers themselves could afford.

In the textile industry a putting-out system first grew up in the manufacture of fustian, where merchants controlled supplies of cotton. In the linen industry in east central Germany, where there were no strong, restrictive guild traditions, the putting-out system that quickly developed depended on a peculiar kind of co-operation between the putter-out, or *Verleger*, on the one hand and thousands of weavers on the other. This was really a particular form of marketing organization that incorporated the old craft forms of enterprise almost untouched rather than a novel kind of industrial undertaking.

Contracts made by a guild were not necessarily binding on all its members and rich guild-masters frequently remained independent of their guild. Guilds were not bound to a particular Verleger, and larger mining enterprises were seldom in the hands of a single Verleger. This allowed for more competition and choice and tended to avoid the hazards, to producers and consumers alike, of cartels and monopolies. Town councils acted as third parties to contracts between guilds and Verleger, as did other landlords, and thus had a say in economic regulation too. A strong city could naturally better protect its guilds against exploitation than an impoverished landlord.

New forms of industrial enterprise needed new techniques. A new division of labour came about in mining and ore-processing, in smelting and in forging, as well as in paper-milling, printing and coin-minting. The provision of capital now became important wherever technical equipment predominated. Such developments spread from the centre of the continent to the north, though much less to east Europe. In Denmark there were craft guilds in the towns; in Sweden the guilds were weaker, perhaps because the towns had a far smaller proportion of the total population than elsewhere and rural craftsmen valued their independence more highly.

The first moves towards a mercantilistic economy were often directed against the guilds. King Christian IV of Denmark even suspended them for a time. In Sweden, under Gustavus Vasa, in contrast, crafts and merchant activities were concentrated in the towns and thus came under increased supervision by the guilds. Much later, a decree passed in 1619 set the *bannmil*, an area round a town inside which no stranger might carry on a trade or business, at four miles in order to protect town craftsmen. Swedish guilds developed as a result of the immigration of craftsmen from Germany, Bohemia and the Low Countries during Sweden's period as a great power. In the towns of Poland during the Middle Ages craft guilds were introduced by German immigrants, and from then on they enjoyed the protection of the Crown.

In Russia crafts were more equally divided between town and country. Sometimes craftsmen who worked on the demesnes were released by their lords for work in the towns. There was relative freedom to carry on a craft – in Novgorod, for instance, where contacts with foreigners brought about considerable changes in the sixteenth century – there were two thousand craftsmen during the third quarter of the century. Moscow, Tula, Kolomna, Serpukhov and Mozhaysk were also flourishing centres of industry. Until the time of Peter the Great, however, there were no guilds comparable to those in the west.

D. *Entrepreneur and worker*

In the textile-producing areas of Italy and the Netherlands merchant entrepreneurs first came to the fore during the commercial revolution that had been taking place since the thirteenth century. These entrepreneurs traded both wholesale and retail. Their strength lay in diversification, and they were also bankers, occupied with exchange transactions, maritime insurance and the despatch of goods. They built up industry with the help of the putting-out system and exploited their far-ranging business connections by means of better communications and marketing (including an efficient news service). The Crusades, which demanded a more efficient system of supplies, strongly influenced the transition from barter trade to a money economy, especially in the Italian ports. The fiscal net which the Church threw over Europe centred on Italy and also helped Italian industrial and mercantile enterprise to gain access to the trade fairs in Champagne; these acted as extensive clearing centres for west central Europe. Because they needed the co-operation of business partners and agents, merchants turned existing organizations, the *commenda* and the *compagna*, into family businesses and finally built up, especially in Florence, the whole *sisteme di aziende*. They used the abacus and the memorandum, developed double-entry book-keeping and drew on the skills of the notaries who developed commercial law. International enterprises such as those of the Bardi, Alberti, Acciaioli and Medici in Florence, of Francesco di Marco Datini in Prato and Pietro Soranzo in Venice were an Italian invention.

The fall of Jacques Coeur in France, however, meant that the development of a French form of capitalism was retarded for nearly a century. Merchants and large bankers in Lyons, Paris, Rouen, the great ports of the Atlantic seaboard and in Marseilles were usually foreigners, immigrants from Italy, Germany and the Iberian peninsula. In Germany, however, in the Hanseatic cities along the coast and in the Rhineland, Westphalia and in the south, different economic patterns developed.

These regions could boast no great concentration of export industry, unlike Italy and the Netherlands. Yet they did not lack merchants of a capitalist type, nor did mercantile elements fail to influence the social structure. Fritz Rörig has analysed the Lübeck cloth trade and the growth of a large class of wholesale merchants who also traded in Swedish metals, Lüneburg salt, Baltic grain and Scandinavian fish. Trading companies on the Medici scale, however, did not exist in Lübeck. Only the Veckinckhusen Company showed signs of becoming a large-scale undertaking.

In west and south Germany a few groups of important merchants, who were both bankers and industrial Verleger, had already become significant in centres such as Cologne by the end of the fourteenth century. Subsequent early capitalist activity developed in south Germany, parts of Italy, the Low Countries and the Atlantic coast. In south Germany economic activity centred not only on places such as Augsburg and Nuremberg but also on many other towns, for instance, Ravensburg, a meeting-point for long-distance traders. During the sixteenth century financial dealings in mining and smelting became of prime importance to capital finance. The Fuggers' large-scale transactions with Emperor Maximilian, Charles v and Ferdinand i and those of the Welser's and others with the French kings formed the bulk of Augsburg's and Nuremberg's dealings in state debts. Most lucrative to the growth of modern finance was the monopolistic exploitation of mineral wealth in the central European territories, for mining had become the dominant industry of the whole area by the beginning of the sixteenth century. The influence of Fugger and Welser extended to Castile and its new overseas colonies and that of Paumgartner deep into the Balkans. Until the middle of the sixteenth century the Fuggers controlled the entire copper and silver output in the Tyrol and Slovakia, and they also processed the ore of Carinthia and much of that from Thuringia and Saxony. Output in central Germany – from Thuringia and Saxony, as far as Silesia – and in Bohemia was also partly run by Franconian entrepreneurs from Nuremberg. South German metal interests penetrated not only to Spain but also to England and Poland, where they competed with Italian consortia. In Carpathia many south German enterprises were active, among them those of Manlich, Haug, Link and Langnauer, later those of Wolfgang

Paller, David Weiss and Co., at the beginning of the seventeenth century that of Lazarus Henckel von Donnersmark from Vienna, and later still the Italians. Austrian mining was also penetrated by south German finance in the sixteenth century.

How did financial take-overs in the mining industry occur? The first step was to buy large quantities of copper, tin and silver on advance contract. In Hungary the Fugger-Thurzo Company, for example, rented silver and copper mines and finally established several industrial works. In the Tyrol Jacob Fugger first acquired mining shares (*Kuxen*) at the beginning of the 1520s and then set up major works at Schwarz and Rattenberg, thus becoming an industrialist in the full sense of the word. Further acquisitions followed in south and east Tyrol in the Lafatsch and Vomper valleys, in Gossensass, on the Schneeberg near Ridnau, at Lienz in the Puster valley, and at Klausen in the Eisack valley, where many smelting works were built. It was particularly significant that Fugger was able to make use of the technical innovations he had learnt from his work with the great engineer Johann Thurzo. Smelting and forging works were also operating after 1495 in Banska Bystrica (Neusohl), Hohenkirchen near St Georgenthal in the Thuringian Forest, near Cêský Tesin in Silesia, and at Fuggerau near Villach in Carinthia. The Höchstetter Company also operated for a while in Tyrol.

According to Jakob Strieder, in no other branch of the economy did early forms of capitalism develop so fast or entrench themselves so firmly as in the mining industry. During the later medieval period a new kind of co-operative production developed from the previous form of partnership, in which all workers had held a stake in the mine together. Gradually labour and capital separated. As mining expanded during the second half of the fifteenth century, the usual type of undertaking was financed by mining shares, negotiable bonds which entailed a strong element of speculation. By this method large-scale enterprises could be created, and inevitably many finance brokers also became industrialists, especially during the early sixteenth century in the combined smelting and forging works of south and central Germany, the Alpine region, Saxony, Bohemia, Thuringia, Hungary and Poland. By the late Middle Ages the leaders of such mining enterprises had often formed consortia, syndicates or cartels. Technical expertise was thus encouraged and in turn gave further impetus to the formation of large-scale business associations. By about 1500 the beginnings of the modern limited company and the international corporation could be discerned in the new forms of capital accumulation and in speculative investments in bonds such as Kuxen.

It is too simple to see the collapse of early capitalism in south and central Europe in the bankruptcies of about seventy great Augsburg firms between 1556 and 1584 and in the failure of other south German and Italian enterprises between those dates and the seventeenth century. That there was a serious crisis is certain, and perhaps an important phase of early capitalism did end at this time. But a revived system of putting-out enabled new forces to take over, and perhaps all that vanished was nothing more than the first glamour of capital wealth. When Anton Fugger withdrew from Slovakian copper in the middle of the century other Augsburg firms such as Manlich, Langnauer, Haug, Link, Weiss, Paller and finally Rehlinger stepped into his place; subsequently they were ousted by Italians. In the copper-mining area of Thuringia and Saxony new groups of entrepreneurs grew up at the beginning of the seventeenth century. One of the most important was the copper and brass works at Ilmenau, in which the Lebzelter firm of Leipzig and Johann Mahieu (a Dutchman, who lived in Frankfurt) were involved alongside the firms of Schwendendorfer from Nuremberg. Johann Bodeck from Frankfurt, and his Hamburg kinsman, Dominicus van Uffeln provided credit facilities. In 1619, however, Lebzelter went bankrupt. The copper mines at Schönburg near Graslich in Bohemia were run by a group which included Gaspar van Uffeln of Frankfurt, Michael Heldevir of Cologne and Frankfurt, Peter Luls from Hamburg and Peter Eulenaeus, a Leipzig town councillor – evidence that finance came from numerous sources. The Thirty Years' War brought about a decisive reduction in copper production in south and central Germany, which led to important changes in the industry.

In south Germany linen and fustian workers and town weavers (who were also guild members) worked alongside *Gäuweber* or countryside weavers, who did not belong to guilds but were labourers supplied by the Verleger. Gäuweber worked around

Ulm, Burgau, Kirchberg, Weissenhorn and Pfaffenhofen. In Weissenhorn and Kirchberg they became a separate group after 1525 under the management of the Fuggers. South of Ulm the fustian production of Biberach became increasingly important by supplying the large wholesale business of Haug and Co. in Augsburg and that of Zangmeister in Memmingen. Most of the south German merchants continued to use the putting-out system, though the Calw trading company did begin to establish a factory system. Companies like this bought raw cloth wholesale in central Europe, which was still very much dominated by the putting-out system. At the end of the sixteenth century large textile firms were the Österreicher in Augsburg; Lebzelter, Schwendendörfer, Pfintzing, Viatis and Peller in Nuremberg; and Koch in Memmingen. Inside the Swiss Confederation the most active firms were based on St Gallen, Basle and Zürich. In France the putting out system predominated in areas such as Poitou. Paper-making and printing also offered new possibilities for capital investment. These soon became lucrative export industries for the south German municipalities – the Basel paperworks are a particularly successful example.

A merchant family usually stayed in business only for two or three generations. Then, as interest or resources dwindled, they went bankrupt or were taken over. If they were successful, they retired to live as *rentiers*, bought country property and tried to emphasize their new status by acquiring titles. Some families, however, remained commercially active for longer, retaining their town council burgher status and connections. This was true of various Nuremberg families such as Imhoff and Viatis-Peller, whose activity in commerce and finance continued throughout the sixteenth, seventeenth and into the eighteenth centuries. In Augsburg the business activity of the Welser and Fugger families endured from the fifteenth century into the seventeenth, although the latter soon attained noble status.

The unsuccessful business families far outnumbered the fortunate few and were soon replaced by new consortia ready to try their hand at making profits. In the north German and Dutch area the most interesting example of a family combine is Richterghen-Schetz, who had industrial connections with the Aachen-Liège-Maastricht and Antwerp area. Between the first half of the sixteenth century and 1600 the Schetz family gradually withdrew from business to become lords of Hoboken and

Dukes of Ursel. 'New Christian' families from Spain, such as Ximenes and Rodrigues Evora, also joined the nobility; others emigrated to the Protestant communities of the north Netherlands, Hamburg, England and north Europe, where they, too, frequently entered the landed nobility. The non-noble Amsterdam regents were an exception. The Marselis were ennobled in Denmark and became landowners; the de Geers and de Besches became leading nobles in Sweden; the van Uffelns rose in Mecklenburg. It was perhaps easier for a merchant to be ennobled in the Protestant north-west and north European countries than in the Catholic countries, where a more traditional ideal of nobility prevailed.

Within Germany merchants in the imperial towns, themselves of solid burgher origin, were increasingly attracted by the title of Imperial knight or *Reichsfreiherr*. The economic success of the most active merchants and their ambitious efforts at social advancement inevitably alienated them from their own class. Like the late medieval clergy, the burghers split into a higher and lower group. The higher group belonged to the ruling class. In some cities, Nuremberg for instance, the creation of this group clearly showed the growing complexity of urban social development. Some of the new industrial and trading wealth accumulated by the large firms was also spread to the new experts, however, the managers and overseers on whom they relied for their profits. These families also saw themselves as respectably bourgeois. Fugger's head accountant, Matthäus Schwarz, was one of these. So were the numerous clerks and office boys, a very few of whom managed to become merchants on their own account. The office employees of chartered companies naturally considered that they belonged to the middle class, as did works' managers in mining. This can be seen clearly in the development of the metal industry in Sweden. Louis de Geer engaged such specialists, including many highly skilled master craftsmen, from the bishopric of Liège.

Early modern large-scale enterprise also gave new opportunities for the development of an urban working class, which had never before existed on such a scale. A division of labour, in mining especially, developed relatively rapidly during the sixteenth century. The process can be seen most clearly in Saxony and Jachymov, where a great number of skilled industrial workers and managers all specialized in specific, and different, tasks. The history of the Fuggers in Tyrol and Carinthia shows how private mines were gradually taken over by large concerns and rationalized. The large operator had a sounder knowledge of trade outlets and was better able to adapt to market conditions, which ultimately he sought to dominate, than the small man, who was at the mercy of everyone. Moreover, as profits from mining decreased sharply after the middle of the sixteenth century and ores became more difficult to find, mining became uneconomic and could only be made to pay from the profits derived from smelting and from diversification into trade and finished goods. For this activity capital, which the single mineowner generally could not raise, was needed. As mines became deeper, technical equipment and pumping works became necessary, and these too were beyond the resources of the small mining entrepreneur. Territorial administrations did try to support their own mining firms, but without lasting success.

The division of labour caused by the increasing commercialization of mining led to the creation of the first industrial workers in the modern sense. The Tyrolean *Lehenhauer* had an intermediate status between the small operator and the simple wage-earner; they worked on fixed, limited contracts in the mines in return for land and forest which other members of their family exploited. Further divisions in mining were between *Oberaufseher* (chief overseers) and *Werkmeister* (works' masters), down to *Truhenläufer* (truckers), *Stollenknechte* and *Knappen*, the underground miners. Of course, women and children also laboured in the mines. A similar industrial structure prevailed in the non-ferrous metal mines of Carinthia, Slovakia, Bohemia, Thuringia, Saxony and Poland, and in the Tyrol in 1582 there were over four thousand paid workers employed in mining at Falkenstein and Erbstollen; a similar concentration of workers was to be found in the armament factories of Suhl in central Germany.

The other area in which paid labour became common was the textile industry. The putting-out system, or *Verlag*, must be distinguished from that of the *Manufaktur* (factory). Under the Verlag system, guild labour was employed, although in parts of south Germany rural weavers developed cottage industries outside guild control This system depended on middlemen such as the Swiss *Zwischenträger* who eventually became entrepreneurs

on their own account. The *Manufaktur* was a special organization, in which part of the production was put out and fine
finishing was concentrated in the factory. A few other factories
employed significant numbers of workmen, among them the
printing works of Koberger, which numbered a hundred journeymen at the beginning of the sixteenth century.

These are only a few examples of the role of the paid worker
in early modern central European manufacturing industries.
Substantial concentrations of workers began to develop in dock-
ing, building and communications, that is those who earned
their living by carting, guarding, loading, wrapping, packing
and despatching bulk and manufactured goods by land and
water. They were usually outside guild organization. There
were also some paid agricultural workers employed on medium-
sized and larger farms, especially the traditional ploughmen
who also mowed, weeded, threshed, made dykes and did car-
pentry. In both agriculture and industry it is difficult to distinguish between paid workers and labourers who had an alternative means of making a living, such as subsistence farming, or
at the very least a garden. It is clear, however, that the new
type of wage-earner first appeared in central Europe in the
mining and manufacturing firms of the early modern era.

3. TECHNOLOGICAL DEVELOPMENTS

In the sixteenth century the Italians made notable contributions to technical literature and introduced inventions which
were of real value to metallurgy. But in mining techniques it
was central Europe that led the field, and miners from Germany, south Netherlands, Bohemia and Slovakia went abroad
as specialists to Sweden, England, Spain, Russia and the
Americas. Georg Agricola's book, *De re metallica*, was written
from wide experience of work in Jachymov and Chemnitz.
Published posthumously in 1556, it superceded the main Italian
works on the subject, such as Vanoccio Biringuccio's *Pirotechnica*.
Other publications, Georg Engelhard Löhneiss' *Bericht von Berg-
werken* (*Report on Mines*) of 1617 for instance, contained little
that was new, however, for the real advances in mechanization
were made in the sixteenth century. Galleries and shafts were
improved; winches and hoists were installed to remove the ore;
waterpower was used to work pumps, which were first installed

in the Jachymov mines in 1550, making it possible to work 400 metres underground. Furnaces were needed to obtain the ore and, when it was smelted, to turn it into alloy and cast. Non-ferrous metals had been smelted in blast-furnaces since late medieval times; these were now increased in size and converted to iron-casting. Everywhere inefficient open fires were gradually replaced by blast-ovens, a slow process that went on from the fourteenth to the seventeenth centuries.

The most important advance in the working of iron was the conversion of the high 'bloomery' furnace into the blast-furnace; also significant was the combination of smelting with forging and milling, a process that started with the use of waterpower in the fifteenth century. Wooden bellows, tilting hammers and rolling mills were standardized at Nuremberg in the 1550s under Hans Lobsinger, who produced fine sheet-iron. The process of making tempered metal was described in the manual *Stahel und Eysen kunstiglich weych und hart zu machen* (*how to make iron and steel artificially soft and hard*), which appeared in 1532. Experiments in making compound metals reached a peak in the sixteenth century and were reported in the *Probierbüchlein* published by Magdeburg town council in 1524 and in the books by Agricola and Erker. One of the first men to try to combine empirical experience with theory was Cramer.

How to make brass by alloying copper with hydrous zinc silicate and charcoal was already known in classical times, and in Nuremberg Ebner refined the process. The manufacture of brass was examined in the writings of Savot and Erker. Thus it it is clear that the refining of existing techniques was more significant than radically new inventions. By the sixteenth century gun barrels were bored with considerable precision. The alloying (*Saigern*) of copper and lead to obtain silver (perhaps the most lucrative of all contemporary technical advances) had been developed in Saxony by the middle of the fifteenth century. Heavy investments by Allenpeck in Nuremberg and Thurzo in Cracow in this method meant that it dominated sixteenth- and seventeenth-century European silver and copper production. Lead was also used to make tinplate with new techniques, invented in Nuremberg and Saxony. Though bismuth had been discovered as early as the thirteenth century it was not developed commercially until the sixteenth, when it was used for metal type. Printer's type was first made from tin and lead, later replaced by harder and cheaper alloys of lead and antimony. Lead was also used in roofing, guttering and window-framing.

The glass industry was developed in Venice, with new methods unknown north of the Alps and later copied there universally. The Venetian government tried to deter the glass workers, especially those on the island of Murano, from leaving the city on pain of death. But industrial espionage was more efficient than government control, and Venetian glass was already being blown in distant Sweden and Denmark by 1572. By 1600 Italian specialists in the Low Countries had developed new methods of making glass cheaply in bulk; these spread rapidly all over Europe. For most Europeans the era of bottles and windows had arrived. A more specialized technique of skilled engraving now utilized glass instead of stone.

The hallmark of sixteenth-century technical progress was not new invention but greater refinement of already existing knowledge by significant practical advances. This is shown in the extensive use of mill wheels of the overshot instead of the older undershot type. Instead of small, hand-operated mills which only had a screw-worm wheel, larger mills with several wheels were installed in most parishes by territorial governments and municipalities. Instead of the hand sieve used to separate flour and bran, sieving and shaking was combined in one mechanical process, publicized in the tract *Räderwerk der Beutel in Mühlen*, brought out in Zwickau in 1502; this sought to rationalize milling by planned specialization among mill-workers, who were also to be given technological training to raise them to the level of skilled operators.

Low-lying regions with no great head of water used windmills, originally an oriental invention which had spread to medieval Europe. Tower-shaped windmills could be seen along the Rhine as far as Cologne. The 'post-type' windmill, in which the whole construction turned on a spindle, was widespread in north Germany and the Netherlands. Precision tools were virtually non-existent in sixteenth-century industry. Hand tools were still made of wood and metal, usually locally produced. For the most part textiles were still produced by traditional methods, though some progress was made in spinning when the treadwheel was introduced in 1480. Some inventions did pre-date the loom, however. The ribbon loom, said to have been invented by Anton Möller of Danzig in 1586, was at first banned by the town council, because its more efficient methods threatened unemployment. Nonetheless it eventually caught on, especially in Holland, where all attempts to suppress it in the interests of traditional labour were defeated.

III Production

1. AGRARIAN PRODUCTION

A. *Farming and livestock*

In general the agricultural economy remained at the level of barter, even where it was not limited simply to subsistence farming. The requirements of individual farm and the prevailing natural environment conditioned production. Direct taxation by landlords and government did not have a dynamic effect; instead it was a burden on the land which only encouraged conservative attitudes towards farming. The most important tax, the 'great tithe', was paid by the farmer in produce. Incentives to go over to a money economy were not lacking, however, and often the 'little tithe' and ground rent were paid in cash. Increased turnover of business with traders in the towns, especially in grain, wine and cattle, compelled a greater use of currency, if only for the sake of convenience. By the sixteenth century most central European agriculture produced some surplus. This had led to the development of a network of markets in the areas of both *Gutswirtschaft* (demesne farming) and *Grundherrtschaft* (tenant farming), particularly near large metropolitan centres where the growth of non-noble landownership was especially rapid and where, as in the Île de France around Paris, intensive market gardening was particularly profitable. Opportunities for more intensive exploitation of the land were even seized by foreign entrepreneurs. Farms in Schleswig-Holstein, for example, were financed by Dutchmen experienced in dairy farming and cheese-making for the export market.

The increased demand for grain in west Europe, Iberia and the Mediterranean area drastically affected the social structure of east European countries such as Poland, as has already been shown. The great increase in meat consumption in Germany,

Italy and the Netherlands also led to massive developments in ranching in Denmark, Schleswig, Holstein, Hungary and Croatia. The demands of the transport and armaments industries led to increased stud-farming, especially in Lower Saxony. Pastoral farming, however, brought with it enclosures and reduced cereal production. This had an unfavourable influence on basic prices and must have caused increased social problems among the majority of the population. This applied for example to increases in cattle-raising in coastal areas from Friesland to Denmark.

Such developments had already become noticeable before imports of silver from America began to increase the amount of bullion in circulation. Rises in grain prices were alarming, especially since primitive conditions of transport limited the extent to which essential demand could be supplied. Yet the geography of Europe made it relatively easy to supply west and south Europe by river and sea. Transport by sea became easier as sailing-ship design was improved during the sixteenth century. Northern Holland built an efficient cargo fleet which developed bulk carrying and cut freight costs between the Baltic and the West. Grain could be transported down central European rivers (Rhine, Elbe, Oder, Vistula and Duna) with ease, thus supplying increased demand from the interior of the continent. Overland transport, however, was still so expensive that it was restricted to luxury or essential goods.

Increased demand went hand in hand with technological improvements, for which the impetus often came from the Netherlands. The growing interest in agrarian productivity expressed itself in a flow of useful almanacs, handbooks and texts. In the Netherlands land reclamation reached a peak in the first half of the seventeenth century and soon spread to German and Danish coastal areas, where the work was often supervised by Dutch hydraulic engineers attracted both by the religious freedom practised there and by other fringe benefits. Land reclamation carried out by Dutch experts backed by Dutch finance also took place in Languedoc, Provence and along the Durance. In 1607 Humphrey Bradley of Brabant formed a company to carry out the drainage of marshes in Bordeaux, Saintonage and Aunis. Such drainage projects affected many areas in Europe devoted to monoculture (the extensive rice fields of the Po valley for example) and represented the first heavy capital investments in large-scale agriculture for export as cash crops.

Improvements were also achieved in the field of animal husbandry. Specializatoin in milk production was introduced in Schleswig-Holstein by Dutchmen and such enterprises were called *Holländerei*. The transition to capitalist enterprise was in many countries signalled by the appearance of farms rented completely for cash; this development was most possible for free peasants, or where the contract to perform duties for landlords could be easily adapted to suit flexible market conditions. A further sign of rationalization was consolidation of isolated plots into extensive holdings by land exchange.

How far was modernization actually stimulated by the specialist literature which now became available? The beginnings of such literature existed already in the thirteenth century, for instance the *Ruralium commodorum libri XII* by the Bolognese town councillor, Petrus de Crescentiis, through to the *Instruktionen*, written by the domestic bursar of Reichersberg monastery in 1462-9. Two generations later appeared the tracts of the chancellor to the Counts of Schauenberg, soon followed by household books and collections of recipes. Philipp Jacob von Grünthal of Upper Austria compiled such a handbook in 1600; another was written in 1617 by Abraham von Thumbshirn, reflecting experience gained as a farm manager for the Electors of Saxony. This literature was geared to the prevailing ideals of humanism, Virgil and the *Georgics* – as well as to the traditional ideas of nobility – revived by the developing interest in estate management during the sixteenth century. Authors were frequently nobles or managers of estates, some of them university educated.

In the second half of the sixteenth century German writers on agriculture began to appear, among them Conrad Heresbach, Martin Grosser and Johann Coler. Heresbach was adviser to the Duke of Jülich and had an estate on the lower Rhine. In 1570 he published his *Rei rusticae libri IV* in which he quoted classical authors extensively alongside his own observations. The Silesian pastor Grosser published in Görlitz in 1590 a *Kurze und gar einfaltige Anlegung zu der Landwirtschaft* (*A Short and Simple Guide to Agriculture*) based on personal experience of a long farming life. Best known was the agricultural calendar of Pastor Coler from Silesia, first issued in 1591 and then annually between 1593 and 1601 as *Oeconomia ruralis et domestica*; it gave valuable hints and advice on farming. Whether such writings had any widespread effects must remain doubtful, though here and there works such as *La Maison rustique* by Liebaut and Estienne, or the *Théâtre d'agriculture* by Olivier de Serres, which appeared in 1600 and contained specific recommendations on growing maize (recently introduced from America), hops and beet, were doubtless very influential.

It took a very long time for changes to become effective. In general, the traditional three-field system was followed in Europe. It predominated in France, where it was written into the leases of tenants and even of dairy farmers. In the first year winter corn was to be sown (wheat and rye); then followed summer corn (oats and barley); while in the third year the ground lay fallow. As there was often little stable manure, and as marl and lime were barely used the soil quickly became exhausted, so that fields had to be left fallow for several years. Yields in France were probably lower than those in England and the Netherlands, usually reaching about four to six times the weight of grain sown. Pastures nearly always belonged to the landlords, so that the peasants were invariably short of fodder to feed to their livestock, which they had mainly to use as draught animals, seldom fattening them for slaughter. To increase the amount of fodder available, vetches and beet were grown by progressive farmers, but everywhere the shortage of cattle caused a shortage of stable manure. This led to poor growth and fodder supplies, which in turn led to less cattle. A vicious economic circle ensued. Rights of pasture, use of woods and rights on commonland consequently became crucial in an economy whose growth was blocked by lack of stock manure and winter feed. Specialization was only possible in areas rich in saffron, woad or flax, and because of transport difficulties produce was kept as varied as possible: vines were even planted in Picardy during the sixteenth century.

In Germany too the three-field system prevailed, though in the mountainous areas, as well as on the coast, where cattle were raised, grazing predominated. In Friesland the arable farms yielded only four times the amount of seed sown. In Denmark the three-field system was customary in the eastern part of the country, though in Jutland grassland and the single-field system were predominant. On the south Danish islands

four- and five-year rotations were practised, and up to a quarter
of the cultivated land rotated as pasture. Animal husbandry
used up more land than in arable farming. Yields on arable
lands were on average only three times the amount sown,
sometimes even less. Ranching was thus more lucrative to the
farmer who had indifferent soil and good market outlets. Rye
and barley and to a lesser extent wheat continued to be cultivated on the south Danish islands, however, and here it was
young noblemen who had gained experience abroad who first
introduced improved methods of cultivation. A good example
is Peder Oxe, who introduced *Vollbrudie* (complete fallow) on his
estates. Manuring could be most readily improved on larger
estates with mixed arable and pasturage. Yields on peasant
land may well have been less than on large estates, for the
simple reason that many peasants were prevented by the customary labour dues from giving their own land the full attention
that it deserved; incentives to improve their land were not
forthcoming.

Apart from grain, vegetables such as peas and lentils were
grown for export. Dutch-style farming gradually spread from
the coast, but inland districts concentrated on commercial
raw produce such as woad, madder and saffron, as well as flax,
hemp and even wine. In many parts of Europe crops grown to
meet the needs of the textile industries came second only to
crops needed for food. Woad, needed for blue dye, was chiefly
cultivated in south France, the chief market being at Toulouse,
near Erfurt and on the lower Rhine, west of Cologne. During
the course of the sixteenth century imports from America of
Brazil and Campèche wood, cochineal and indigo brought
serious competition for European dyes. The production of
fibrous plants, flax and hemp was essential to low-quality
textile production. A large flax-growing belt ran through north-
west France from Brittany and Normandy to Flanders, continuing into Westphalia and Lower Saxony, including the
Swabian Alb, the northern borders of the Alps, the uplands of
Saxony, Silesia and Bohemia, finally reaching the Baltic region.
Coarser hemp was also grown in various coastal areas such as
Friesland. In central Europe great linen-producing areas grew
up near Lake Constance, in Westphalia and in Bohemia. Where
cotton was easily obtainable, centres developed for the weaving
of a mixture of flax and cotton called fustian in the Lake

Constance area, along the Danube, at Augsburg, Ulm, Biberach and Milan.

In the relatively primitive social conditions of the day, wine and beer consumption accounted for a high proportion of personal expenditure. Vineyards were more extensive in 1500 than they are today. Although the most important wine area in France was around Bordeaux, there were also great vineyards in the Loire valley, Anjou and Orleans, Beaune and Burgundy and all over the south. Inferior wine was also produced in the Île de France and as far north as Picardy. In Germany the principal wine-producing regions were in Alsace, Neckar, Main, Mosel and Rhine, but vineyards extended as far as Xanten on the lower Rhine and far into the north German plain, as well as to Hesse, Silesia, East Prussia, Mecklenburg and even Holstein. Wine production in Germany was never more extensive than at the beginning of the sixteenth century. Then a decline set in, as the poorer vineyards of the north and east, hit by climate changes and by a reduction in the cost of transporting wine, no longer found themselves able to compete. That the Reformation and the secularization of the monasteries caused a decrease in consumption of local wine by the Church is probably less likely than the fact that improvements in river as well as sea transport made it easier to ship good wine from the Rhine and Main to the most distant areas of Germany and the north.

Beer consumption also increased. In Franconia at the end of the sixteenth century pedlars complained that they could not sell their wine because so much local beer was being brewed. Extensive government regulations on the subject show the importance of beer in Bavaria. In the grain-growing and hop-producing districts there were many places where beer production was of paramount importance, including Lübeck, Einbeck, Braunschweig, Hamburg, Rostock and Danzig.

In the Swiss Confederation wine-growing was subject to strict local control. Import restrictions were even imposed by one canton on another. Such a case was the prohibition on the importation of Valtelline wine into Zürich in 1645. To encourage local production the cantons Bern and Zürich freed native wine-growers from paying tithe, and when this proved to be an insufficient incentive customs and tax exemptions followed, for wine imports represented a major drain on bullion.

According to an account of 1633 a flourishing Swiss trade in wine was carried on from the Valais region.

Animal husbandry and the production of wool, skins, milk and meat was vital everywhere. The most important stimulus came from Holland, where capitalist methods of production based on a leasehold system were widespread. The emigration that followed the Dutch revolt, coupled with the growing need for agricultural and animal produce for the Dutch market, led to Dutch methods of export production being emulated in the German and Danish North Sea coast area, where fertile, marshy lowlands were extended and land reclaimed by dykes. Here commercially successful dairy farming first developed when noble landlords leased farms to experienced Dutchmen.

The landowning Danish nobility also produced for an export market. As many as thirty thousand cattle were exported in 1536; by the end of the century the number had risen to fifty thousand, and by the beginning of the seventeenth century up to eighty thousand were sold annually. A pork industry also grew up; peasants were allowed to fatten pigs in the royal forests on fixed payments to the crown. It has been calculated that Danish peasants owned one hundred thousand pigs, in addition to those reared on noble estates. The second half of the sixteenth century and the beginning of the seventeenth was the great period for cattle-droving in Denmark and north Germany: nearly 46,000 bullocks passed through customs at Rendsburg in 1565 and by 1612 tax was paid there on nearly 80,000.

A second great belt of pastureland existed in central Europe, in addition to the grazing land that extended along the North Sea coast to the Danish islands and southern Sweden. From this area, central and west Germany and north Italy were supplied with cattle for slaughter. The zone also extended across parts of Russia, Poland and, most important of all, into the plains of Hungary. Methods of production improved there – the average live weight of Hungarian oxen steadily increased from 300 to 350 kilograms per animal in 1570 to as many as 400 to 450 kilograms by 1650. In the first half of the seventeenth century the number of horned cattle owned by central European peasants was fairly high, probably averaging two draught and two dairy animals per holding. The consumption of beef in towns and villages may have reached a peak in the very early sixteenth century and was only overtaken in the later nine-teenth century. The main centres of east central European cattle trade were at Posnan, Breslau, Brieg, Vienna, Bratis-lava, Frankfurt-an-der-Oder and Buttstädt, near Weimar; there as many as twenty thousand animals were offered for sale during one day. In Nuremberg, the slaughterhouse for south Germany, the *Ochsen-Amt* was run by the town council and provided credit facilities for cattle traders. Cattle imports from the east, however, faced increasing competition after the mid-sixteenth century from Danish, north German, Dutch and Friesian produce.

In central and east Switzerland, particularly in the St Gallen and Graubünden areas, the transition to cattle-raising and dairy farming had gone so far during the second half of the sixteenth century that local agriculture could no longer supply its own cereal requirements. In canton Zürich ploughed land and vineyards gave way to pasture, and Switzerland became a net importer of grain, mainly from France, and a net exporter of cattle for slaughter, mainly to Italy. The cantons of central Switzerland, which were the most important cattle-rearing districts, established a system of quality control. A heavily built breed of brown mountain cattle was raised in the Schwyz area and was sent for stud purposes all over central Europe and into Hungary and Poland. The daily milk yield was up to twelve litres a day, the Lucerne authorities reported in 1665. On the strength of such output central Switzerland was able to sell dairy stock worth one million Gulden yearly. Despite ex-port restrictions, Swiss cheese exports grew steadily during the sixteenth century, and cheese from Glarus, including goats' cheese, could be bought in all the large towns of Germany and Italy and even as far afield as Russia. Large quantities of Fribourg cheese were sold at Lyons, and soft cheeses from the Bernese Oberland were supplied to Italian markets. Switzer-land exported so many pack-horses from the Entlebuch, Sim-menthal and Einsiedeln areas that home requirements were threatened, and dealers were taxed heavily in order to reduce the level of exports.

English wool exports were never really able to satisfy the ever-growing demand for raw materials in the expanding European textile industry. Sheep farms grew up in Provence, Languedoc and Burgundy, the west German highlands and lower Saxony, east Holstein and the coast, and in Hesse, Saxony and the Jura mountains. Sheep-rearing, a lucrative export industry, was usually on a large scale and destroyed the productivity of the soil so much that it threatened to lower the peasants' standard of living. Landgrave William of Hesse had a herd of twenty-five thousand sheep, and the Elector August of Saxony even had forty outlying farms on his estates with a total of forty thousand sheep. In Saxony, one of the most important wool-producing areas of central Europe in the sixteenth century, there were thought to have been 500,000 sheep producing 8800 *Zentner* (440,000 kilograms) of wool each year.

In Russia, as in many other parts of east and north Europe, peasants had to find supplementary means of earning a livelihood: in northern districts they hunted and fished for food and supplied furs for export; forestry was also essential, especially since arable farming techniques remained very primitive. Wooden ploughs hardly scratched the cleared land, which was cultivated year by year until it became exhausted and was then abandoned. The second half of the fifteenth century saw more fallowing and manuring, and slowly a Russian three-field system was introduced. Farms varied in size, although they generally decreased during the sixteenth century. In 1510 the average in the Kalinin district was 12·4 hectares, some farms having as many as thirty-seven hectares, others as few as two. The farms of demesne tenants varied considerably too – on the lands of the monastery of the Holy Trinity and Saint Sergius there were holdings of three to forty-seven hectares. In the southern steppes along the Oka river the average size was about nine hectares.

Until the sixteenth century the area cultivated by the demesne lord was limited by the shortage of labour. At the end of the century land actually cultivated in the north represented under 8 per cent of the total. In central Russia the percentage was greater, between 16 and 56 per cent. In the newly settled areas south of the Oka cultivation by the peasants themselves predominated. Compared with the areas bordering the Baltic, conditions farther inside Russia were less favourable. Lack of capital among owners of benefices and the division of holdings on inheritance also worked against stable landownership and profitable cultivation. Yields were only average. For rye it was five or six to one; for oats three or four to one. The peasants had also to make payments in kind and work for the state and the demesne; to the former he owed postal and communications duties, road-building, bridges and fortifications and, on the demesne, labour services, including military service.

After the second half of the fifteenth century customary dues were gradually replaced by money payments. On a tenancy of fifteen hectares, land rent came to about five roubles, land tax to about three and commutation of labour services to about one and a half roubles annually. Ecclesiastical landlords were especially successful estate managers and princes and nobles often let the Church run their farms for them. In the Moscow district 26 per cent of the Church estates were farmed directly by the Church itself. The Holy Trinity monastery in Kirjach farmed as much as 42 per cent of its lands. Churches and monasteries used agricultural labourers (*podvorniki*) for this work, whom they paid in kind. Smaller lay landlords did not prosper. The great prince Simon Bekbulatovich had twenty villages and in the middle of the sixteenth century received 253 roubles in rent, 206 in small obligations and 385 in produce each year, whereas the income of an ordinary demesne-owner was usually not more than five to eight roubles a year. Not only peasants but small landlords, too, went into debt. Debts accumulated so much that in 1557 the government permitted debtors to discharge their debts by granting them five rent-free years at interested rates fixed at 10 per cent.

Taxes, the conversion of customary dues into money payments and other obligations frequently forced peasants to sell to corn merchants at uneconomic prices in order to obtain scarce currency, with the result that seed and grain were often desperately scarce in their own households. Frequently a peasant had to borrow the seed he needed, and as his debts to the landlord grew it became more difficult for him to leave the estate. There remained for him only the possibility of flight, and this way out was often used, especially as settlers were needed in the south, in the newly conquered areas on the Volga and the Kama. The government there encouraged this migration by distributing land. The example of the Stroganovs shows how rapidly this colonization progressed. In 1558, ten years after they had received their concession, 32 per cent of the area was already settled and cultivated. At the same time central Russia became depopulated. In the Moscow area the percentage of uncultivated land increased to 90, and in Novgorod and Pskov it was as much as 97. Serfs and labourers replaced the peasantry, while Church estates were consolidated. During the 'time of troubles' the number of peasants fleeing increased, and labourers were more widely used, in some districts supplying more than half the rural workforce.

B. *Forestry*

Much of Europe in the sixteenth century consisted of large forest reserves; these occurred in parts of France and the mountainous areas of the Empire, and throughout the Carpathians, the Baltic area, Russia and Scandinavia. More wood was used in the wild mountain areas of central and north Europe, which had long winters and heavy rainfall, than in the low-lying districts of south France and the Mediterranean. Widespread though the forests were, increasing consumption of wood for house-building and fuel by a growing population and increasing demands by mining and industry forced the authorities to try to economize in the use of timber. Regulations as to the use of wood and forest were therefore introduced from the end of the Middle Ages.

In the sixteenth century the peasant farmer of south Germany could reckon on a firewood allowance of 15 *Klafter* (50 cubic metres) and the cottar 8 *Klafter* (27 cubic metres) per year. With the growth of wood consumption in industry these amounts were reduced. In the large cities economy had always been necessary. Paris was supplied with wood from Champagne and the Île de France, but there was never sufficient for the rising population in the first half of the sixteenth century. When the Morran was made navigable in 1552 it was used to bring supplies in bulk at reduced cost. In 1584, when the population of Paris had reached between 200,000 and 300,000, the demand for firewood was estimated at 300,000 to 340,000 cubic metres a year. After allowing for the needs of industry for timber and ash, this represented a mere 1 to $1\frac{1}{2}$ cubic metres of firewood per head per annum.

The consumption of wood rose particularly sharply in mining areas. Between 1387 and 1464 the number of iron foundries in the Upper Palatinate grew from 77 (producing 2000 tons per annum) to 200 (10,000 tons). At the same time timber requirements increased from 175,000 to about 400,000 cubic metres. The silver mines of Freiberg used more than 60,000 cubic metres of wood a year and the Kuttenberg mines as much. Such demands meant the steady deforestation of surrounding areas. Nor was the iron industry any better: a single blast furnace in the Nivernais producing 450 tons of raw iron per year used 1200 baskets of charcoal, the equivalent of nearly thirty hectares of mature forest. Its forge, which produced 750 tons of iron per year, used another 450 baskets of charcoal. French foundries and blast furnaces – about 500 in number – used up some 8000 hectares of tall forest, or 25,000 hectares of coppice, every year. This was one-sixth of the forest area available yearly. To produce a ton of pig iron, four cubic metres of wood were needed, for one ton of wrought iron, nine cubic metres were needed.

In the mountainous districts of the Rhine charcoal for iron production was produced by *Hauberggenossenschaften*, or felling cooperatives, found especially in the Siegen district from the beginning of the fifteenth century. The quantity of wood used in salt works was even greater than in iron-processing. The works at Hall in the Tyrol, which had existed since the end of the thirteenth century, originally used about 100,000 cubic metres of wood to produce 1,000 tons of salt. Between 1490 and 1515 annual production rose from 7,000 to 14,000 tons. Meanwhile firing techniques improved, but yearly needs for firewood were still estimated to be 1,000,000 cubic metres. However, other salt works used less wood. Hall consumed 80,000 cubic metres annually, Hallstatt 94,000 cubic metres. Other industrial processes, like glass works, also used wood, and for that reason they were often moved as forests were consumed.

This increasing consumption of wood was reflected in its rising price. In central Europe a slight upward trend begins around 1470; by 1535 the increase becomes general and during the *Kipperzeit*, or period of serious coinage debasement (1621–3), prices naturally reached a peak. Price rises were most acute in densely populated areas with no forests, like north France where timber prices had begun to rise noticeably by the beginning of the sixteenth century and had become prohibitive at the time of the Huguenot wars. In Paris official prices were only a quarter of the actual market price. Towards the end of the civil wars, prices generally sank to their pre-war level in Paris, not those of timber, however.

Transport of timber by water predominated in central Europe, from the north Alpine areas to the Danube, from the Black forest and the Rhenish mountains to the Rhine and the Netherlands, on the Weser and Elbe to the North Sea ports of Bremen and Hamburg, and on the Oder, Vistula and other Baltic rivers to the Baltic ports. Timber rafting was a significant transport industry in Germany. In 1496 Wolfratshausen received 3639 Bavarian timber rafts from the rivers Isar and Loisach. On the Lech in about 1600 some 3,500 rafts were sent down river to Augsburg. To prevent too heavy logging, territorial states issued regulations controlling forestry, water, rafts and wood from the sixteenth century onwards. The rafting of timber was a regalian right of each territorial prince.

Poland was the most important timber-exporting country of the Baltic region, although exports did not increase during the sixteenth century. However, exports of Polish woodash did increase, according to the customs registers of Wloclawek, conming up to six million cubic metres of wood a year, one-tenth of the Vistula region's wood production. Compared with this Russian export figures were relatively modest. Under Tsar Alexis (1629–76) up to 30,000 barrels or 1,500 *Last* of potash and 800 tons of woodash were exported via Archangel, corresponding to a forest area of 50,000 hectares. In coastal regions, where oak-wood was exploited for ship-building, pig farms, which had depended on acorns for fodder, decreased. Ranching, however, flourished as oak forests were reduced and scrub-land increased.

Typical of conservation methods in early modern forestry are the measures passed in 1561 at Perche in north France. They laid down a hundred-year cycle for the forest; undergrowth was to be cut back at regular intervals until the new growth of oak was assured. In south Germany, Steward Schwegelin of Memmingen recommended new methods of felling and restocking. The practice of sowing quick-growing, low-quality conifers, first adopted in the Nuremberg area, began to spread, and fast-growing willows and poplars were also recommended.

Because Roman Law gave no guidance on woods and forests, prerogative legislation at the behest of territorial governments for the 'common good' was used to justify intervention in the management of forests owned by Church, nobility, town councils and burghers in Germany. There is a clear contrast between the policy of territorial rulers and traditional common rights, particularly in Alpine areas. The movement in favour of traditional rights first started in Briançon, the original three Cantons of the Swiss Confederation, and Graubünden and then spread to the Slav Alps and to south Germany. The reasons underlying the Gottscheer revolt and the Poor Conrad conspiracy were a fundamental part of the grievances expressed in the Peasants' Revolt of 1525. Article five of the Memmingen peasants' manifesto demanded that all forest not bought fairly by territorial rulers should continue to belong to the community as a whole. The Taborites and Hussites in Bohemia had for a long time claimed divine sanctions by which forest, hunting and pasture were free to all. The fifteenth-century radical reform proposal, called the *Reformatio Sigismundi*, and the later radical peasant leader Thomas Münzer both stressed this point of view. The collapse of the Peasants' Revolt, however, allowed territorial rulers to enclose common and forest land. During the rest of the century regulations were issued in one territory after another aimed at satisfying the economic needs of state, even, if necessary, by intervention in the administration of forests belonging to the nobility and Church. The same pattern was followed in France, where centralized state laws for forestry emerged under Colbert.

2. FISHING

Population growth during the sixteenth century made fishing increasingly important as a food industry. At the same time the location of the most important catching grounds for central Europe and the Baltic area altered: herring fisheries in the Baltic off Scania greatly decreased as North Sea fishing grew in strength. The Dutch and English mostly caught herring, while cod was left to the Norwegians, based on Bergen. The ports of east Frisia, the Weser and Elbe estuaries and Jutland were centres of the early modern fishing industry. Flensburgers even fished in Limfjord and up to the Norwegian arctic coast. Fishermen settled in Husum, Eiderstedt and on the Friesian islands and dunes. During the sixteenth century herring fishing became increasingly important around Heligoland and as far away as Iceland, where the Hamburg fishermen built their own church.

The boats of Holstein, Schleswig, Hamburg and Bremen

were rivals for the Iceland catch. The herring trade suffered political disruption. During the Habsburg-Valois wars Dutch fishermen came to the mouth of the river Ems with their herring *busses* in order to fish under a neutral flag. By 1555 nineteen busses were sailing out of Emden, but the Peace of Câteau-Cambrésis (1559) ended this. Herring fishing continued from Emden, however, and eventually not only Dutch busses were used but local ones too.

Whaling began to increase in the North Sea from about 1600 as first the Dutch, then the British and the Danes, took the lead. At the same time, men from Hamburg and north Friesland sailed in whalers under other flags, especially the Danish. Inland, imported salt fish, like stock-fish, was used to supplement diets of locally caught fresh-water fish. The Rhine was known for its salmon and the Volga was particularly famous for its abundance of fish. Landlords, lay and ecclesiastical, maintained fish-ponds to supply both themselves and the market, especially with carp and trout. Fish prices were regulated by most medieval municipalities in central Europe, together with cereal and meat prices.

3. SMALL AND LARGE SCALE MANUFACTURING

From the end of the Middle Ages, industrial production slowly but steadily gained in importance over agriculture, which did however remain predominant. Population growth and overseas expansion brought increased demand for manufactured goods throughout Europe and contemporary technical innovations made it possible to supply these demands. In addition to craft work, larger-scale manufacture by 'putting out' and by factory organization developed. This occurred notably in north Italy, parts of the Netherlands, south Germany, Bohemia and Saxony, where raw materials, skilled labour, good management, easy communications and above all, banking facilities and cheap, reliable credit were readily available.

The presence of easily exploitable mineral resources was of course crucial. Continental Europe was rich in ores of many kinds. Even gold was to be found, although silver and copper predominated. Iron ore, wood and coal were especially plentiful. There was gold in Silesia, the Tyrol and Carpathians, mixed with large deposits of silver and copper ores, which were also found extensively in Thuringia and Saxony, Bohemia and Slovakia, Tyrol, the eastern Alps and Bosnia. Sweden exploited the copper mountain of Falun. Lead deposits needed to separate silver from copper ores lay to the north of the Eifel, in the south-east Alps and in Poland. Calamine, or zinc ore, used in making brass was mainly located in the highlands around Aachen; later strikes were made near Iserlohn. Tin deposits were found in the Fichtel mountains, in Saxony and Bohemia. Mercury came from the Palatinate and from Bohemia; from the end of the fifteenth century the deposits from Idria in Carniola gained in importance, challenging the production of mines in the Spanish Estremadura.

Iron deposits were widespread too. They reached from the Pyrenees to the Alps and across as far as Scandinavia and Russia. The oldest mainland centres of mining and processing were to be found in Lorraine and the Ardennes, in the Eifel and Hunsrück mountains, from the Siegerland to the Saar, and in south Westphalia, Hesse, the Harz mountains, Thuringia, the Upper Palatinate, in the alpine area from Styria to Carinthia, on the southern borders of the Alps and in the Carpathians, and in central Sweden. Most of these areas also held deposits of quartz, which was used in glass-making. Important deposits of rock salt were widely scattered in Lorraine, on the northern edges of the Alps, in north Germany, on the north slopes of the Carpathians and in Transylvania.

Conditions were also favourable for the development of textile industries. From Brittany and Normandy through to north-west Germany and the Baltic, flax and hemp cultivation provided plentiful raw materials. Flax was also cultivated for textile manufacture in Burgundy, around Lake Constance, in east Germany and in Bohemia. Sheep-farming too was widespread, though the quality of German wool from Lower Saxony and Pomerania was less fine than that from England and Spain. Finally there were numerous plants used for dyeing cloth, although they faced increasing competition from imported dyes and woods.

The geographical location of raw materials thus played an essential part in early modern industrial development. Industries flourished where basic materials could be found, where waterpower and fuel were available, and where at least the first stages of refining and processing could be done on the spot.

Only then could the high transport costs payable on half-processed goods supplied to the centres of fine craftwork be absorbed. For instance, Nuremberg was sent iron from Styria and the Upper Palatinate, copper from Bohemia and Thuringia, tin plate from the Upper Palatinate and tin from Saxony. Some of the largest furnaces and forges were near industrial centres such as Nuremberg. A favourable position helped Stormarn, a region between Lübeck and Hamburg, to become a centre for the northern metal export trade; copper and iron could be imported cheaply from Scandinavia via Lübeck and wood and water power were available nearby.

Wherever industries flourished the supply of wood for fuel became a problem. Territorial rulers in Germany soon felt compelled to limit the number of foundries and forges in order to prevent the total devastation of forests. The deforestation caused by large-scale industrial processes was the main reason not only for forestry regulations but for redoubled efforts to find other fuels; these led to the replacement of charcoal by coal in the Ruhr and in the Harz and Erz mountains of east central Germany. Absence of wood fuel explains why foundries often had to be operated far away from copper deposits.

There was no general agreement about ownership of mineral rights in Germany. Territorial rulers, land owners and successful prospectors all laid claim. In the absence of federal control, territorial authorities exercised prerogative rights over mineral resources. From the sixteenth century onwards strict mining regulations were issued by Saxony and the Upper Palatinate, Silesia and Brunswick, which most territorial rulers in the rest of the German Empire copied. The first phase of mining legislation was completed by about 1600. Subsequent regulations were no longer mainly concerned with conditions of work and wages but instead began to lay down a systematic code of mining law. Those territorial rulers who farmed out their own mining rights, took the customary ten per cent as well as other *ad hoc* taxes, leasing rights to co-operative mines held under feudal law. The operation of the mine itself was then in the hands of a miners' union, the original *Gewerkschaft*. All co-workers and co-owners of a pit held a share in the mine – the so-called *Kux*. Profits were divided according to the number of shares held, but losses and money for improvements had to be borne by all in the same proportion. *Kuxen* were precursors of modern shares, which were soon to be bought and sold freely on the European money markets.

When output decreased after the end of the sixteenth century, territoral rulers had to support mining with increasing amounts of state capital. Then, as capital investment increased, operations expanded, benefiting from the creation of a growing force of wage-earning miners employed on specialist jobs who had no share in the capital enterprise which employed them.

A. *Mining and metal-working*

France processed iron in the Dauphiné, the Loire basin and Lorraine. The Ardennes area formed a link with west Germany, where growing demands for iron led to technological advance, and a mining boom at the beginning of the sixteenth century. This boom was also felt in German silver- and copper-mining. The new blast furnaces made possible the extraction of greater quantities of crude iron, which was used to cast pots and pans and stove plates for export, especially via Antwerp, as well as to satisfy the ever-expanding armaments industries. Wrought iron was worked in forges, and rods, nails, bolts and wire were supplied to craftsmen such as nailsmiths, blacksmiths, and gunsmiths on an increasingly large scale. In the Saar valley iron was produced from open-cast mines as late as the eighteenth century. In the Rhineland forests of the Hunsrück, the Rheinboller forge was active at the end of the sixteenth century, and during the Thirty Years' War it was run in close connection with the Stromberger works in Nassau under the control of Jean Mariot from Liège. On the German lower Rhine, Düren and Nassau were important mining areas, together with the territories of Siegen, Dillenburg and Sayn. In 1563, in one of the most productive periods, thirty-two foundries were operating in the Siegen area alone.

Stimulated by the prosperity of Siegen and increased demand from West German markets, the county of Sayn began to run its own iron production. In Dillenburg seven foundries were operating by 1550, but real blast ovens were not built until the end of the century. In Nassau-Weilburg, Wittgenstein, Solms, and Hesse iron was also processed. Iron-processing spread into Waldeck and the Sauerland in southern Westphalia. Sauerland mineral deposits were less extensive than in Siegen, but there were numerous iron works between Brilon and Iserlohn.

Besides the existing refineries, blast furnaces were built and cast-iron goods produced. Thus it becomes clear that the industrial area of the Ruhr was established long before the nineteenth century.

In county Mark, Altena, Lüdenscheid and Iserlohn were centres of the wire-drawing industry. Specialization appeared early in the iron industry there: Lüdenscheid made crude iron wire, superior grades were manufactured in Altena, and Iserlohn specialized in fine, precision wires. As techniques of war were modernized chain-mail manufacture gave way to hooks and eyes, clasps, needles and finally *Kratzendhrat* (wire for carding). In the western part of county Mark, around the imperial town of Dortmund and the imperial nunnery and town of Essen, forge hammers were built. The products of the sword and dagger works at Solingen in the Duchy of Berg were known throughout Europe as early as the sixteenth century.

The Thuringian iron industry was centred on Schmalkalden, and eyes, clasps, needles and finally *Kratzendhraht* (wire for steel; the town became famous for knives and scissors. The iron of Suhl in Thuringia was used for muskets produced in factories under a systematic division of labour and based on export markets. The territorial rulers of this region of east central Germany encouraged the manufacture of metal for strategic as well as economic reasons. The ruling Counts of Stolberg and Dukes of Brunswick were able to provide the capital investment for new technological developments. As well as cannon balls, more precise guns and mortars, hand arms and heavy artillery with longer barrels were produced.

In Saxony and in the Harz mountains, the iron industry was further stimulated by silver-mining. The Elector Augustus of Saxony was interested in fostering mining and smelting industries during his long and peaceful rule at the end of the sixteenth century. Iron was found in Pirna and Königstein, Schwarzenberg and Krottendorf. In the last two places there were twenty-six forges in the second half of the sixteenth century processing the raw materials from Annaberg, Zwickau and Schneeberg. In Giesshübel iron stoves were cast. Farther east, in the princedom of Sagan, there was iron mining, and in Priebus many scythe-, sickle- and knife-makers operated.

In south Germany there were iron works on the Kocher and in the Black Forest. The most important area for production,

however, was in the Upper Palatinate near Amberg and Sulzbach. Of the 30,000 metric tons of iron produced annually in
Germany at the end of the sixteenth century, 10,000 came from
the Upper Palatinate. Here the development of the industry
was most advanced, and mines had already reached a depth of
between 100 and 200 metres. In the fifteenth century there were
two hundred iron forges in the Upper Palatinate, but by the
end of the sixteenth century the number had sunk by twenty.
Iron was produced as plates, bars, rings or rods. The business
was in the hands of patrician and merchant families in Sulzbach, Nuremberg and Regensburg. Mining organized by town
councils was less successful. Iron-processing was based on
Nuremberg, Regensburg and Ulm, where some high-quality
Styrian steel was also worked. Iron manufacture for export was
also found in Swabia, at Gmünd and Rottweil as well as
Wangen in the Allgäu. This widespread German iron-mining
and processing industry formed the backbone of German prosperity in the south and west. Germany's production was ahead
of that of Sweden, England and Spain in a Europe whose total
output had reached about sixty to a hundred thousand metric
tons by the sixteenth century. Of this Germany produced
probably a half.

The second mainstay of the German metal industry was
copper- and silver-mining. Efforts to find gold were curtailed
when American gold arrived in Europe, and the older gold
mines in Reichenstein and the Harz lost ground to the smelting
of copper, lead and tin ores, and also to arsenic pyrites. Copper
and silver were mined in the Harz around Goslar, in the county
of Mansfeld, Saxony, Bohemia, Tyrol, near Salzburg and in
north Hungary. In the upper Harz new pits were opened shortly
after 1500 in St Andreasberg alongside the old ones in Goslar
and Clausthal. Equally famous were the copper mines of
Mansfeld, where production reached a peak between 1521 and
1537. Copper was processed in the foundries of Thuringia (at
Leutenberg, Gräfenthal, Arnstadt, Ludwigstadt, Steinach), and
in neighbouring Franconia around Nuremberg at Enzendorf.
The Fuggers processed copper at Hohenkirchen. Crucial to all
these developments was the investment of south German capital. The largest single enterprise, the Arnstadt foundry, was
financed by investors from Nuremberg with a capital of 100,000
gulden.

The copper-mining industries of Kuttenberg, Schwaz in Tyrol, the Salzburg area and Banska Bystrica in northern Hungary were also largely in the hands of south German financiers. Copper was made into plates, wire, pans and utensils. Bronze made from tin alloys was used for bells and guns. Nuremberg and Innsbruck were the best-known arsenals. Brass, as an alloy of copper and calamine, was worked at Aachen and Stolberg, but also in the Harz, Nuremberg and the Alps. The Aachen copper industry continued at its peak until the end of the sixteenth century, when its problems multiplied. Guilds of braziers and tinkers prevented large-scale copper-masters from developing up-to-date factory methods, among them the raising hammer, which had existed since the beginning of the century. Protestant entrepreneurs, persecuted because of their religion, moved away to Stolberg, which belonged to the Duchy of Jülich and had no guild restrictions. It also had its own supply of calamine. Stolberg's production therefore increased greatly during the Thirty Years' War and by 1648 it had sixty-five furnaces.

Silver mining in the Erz mountains moved into its third boom period after 1470 when fifteen new towns were founded, sometimes placed very close to each other because of the rivalry for mining revenues between the neighbouring territorial rulers in the Electorate and the Duchy of Saxony. Much south German capital was invested, and Nuremberg financiers were prominent, though their hold was less monopolistic than in Tyrol, Bohemia and north Hungary. Saxony boasted local entrepreneurs from Freiberg, Leipzig, Magdeburg, Erfurt and even some from coastal Germany. The most important mining centre was Schneeberg, followed by St Annaberg, Buchholz and Marienberg. Saxon production slumped temporarily at the end of the 1520s when many miners emigrated to the Bohemian towns, especially Jachymov, where production reached its high point in 1533. The peak of mining production in Annaberg and Marienberg came between 1537 and 1540, but from the 1570s onwards demand increased considerably.

European silver production reached its peak in about 1540 at about 65,000 kilograms annually. The German share of this, mostly from the Harz, Mansfeld, the Erz mountains and Alsace, was perhaps not as great as might have been expected, although the figures are notoriously unreliable. But it should be remembered that silver produced in Tyrol, Bohemia and Hungary really only benefited the south German trading companies. From the 1540s onwards silver from Spanish America provided strong competition, and European production fell.

The silver-mining industry of the Erz mountains was closely connected with prospecting for lead, which was also found in Goslar and the Palatinate. In 1526 the lead mines near Tarnovitz in upper Silesia began operations. Elsewhere, on the northern edge of the Eifel for instance, older lead mines went out of production and entrepreneurs went over to iron ore. The production of lead in Germany as a whole was so limited, however, that it had to be imported from the Alps, England and Poland. Cologne was the largest marketing centre.

Tin production in Saxony was important. Tin was also found in the Fichtel Gebirge and used to manufacture household pots and pans and for tin plate, which had earlier been a monopoly of the Upper Palatinate at Amberg and Sulzbach. Unlike silver and copper, tin-mining did not need much working capital, because its mining was open-cast. In Saxony tin was found at Altenberg, where mining had started before the middle of the fifteenth century. It was financed by a putting-out system agreed between guilds and wholesale merchants from Leipzig and south Germany. Much crude tin plate was sent to Nuremberg for processing. Entrepreneurs from Nuremberg and the Upper Palatinate now took up the manufacture of tin plate in the Erz mountains with finance from the territorial government. Masters and journeymen for the industry were sought in the Upper Palatinate, re-employed and settled in Saxony. In Bohemia tin was mined in Horní Slavkov (Schlaggenwald). Here, too, capital from south Germany was invested.

In the first half of the sixteenth century cobalt was first used to make a blue dye and blue enamel. Dye works were opened at Schneeberg, Oberschlema and Pfannenstil; the product was marketed in Nuremberg, Hamburg and Holland and influenced the development of blue Delft ware. The connections between Nuremberg and Saxony were also important in the supply of arsenic, which was used in making mirrors. Hieronymus Zürich in Nuremberg developed a process used by the arsenic works at Ehrenfriedersdorf near Geyer. In the Alps there were important deposits of iron in Styria, Carinthia and on the southern borders of the Alps, in Carniola especially.

Styrian iron was mined in the Erzberg district, and the main Carinthian deposits were near Hüttenberg, where the high bloomery furnace had begun to replace the hearth process in the fourteenth century. To provide enough air, water-driven bellows were employed. Thus larger smelting works could be set up with a *Blahhaus*, the first example of which was recorded in 1380. The importance of water-wheels in driving the furnace was demonstrated when the name *Radwerk* (wheel works) replaced the name Blahhaus in 1439. The transition from craft industry to a large-scale industrial process came strikingly early. Simultaneously, the forge became independent of the foundry. Older forges which had separated soft iron from steel were mostly situated close to the Blahhaus. New, larger forges had, however, to be built in those districts in which communications allowed more wood to be supplied. Constructed on Italian patterns, they were called *welsch Hammer* (*welsch* meant 'foreign' in German) and used heavy or light hammers to make rods or fence iron. In some cases the owner of a forge (*Hammermeister*) might finance the extensions, but more often the money was obtained from iron merchants in Leoben and Steyr against the supply of iron goods. Iron merchants thus became Verleger, controlled production and steadily became forge-owners. By 1560 Styrian iron merchants had gained control of nearly half the forges in the province.

Encouraged by Styrian iron production, many scythe workshops came into production in the sixteenth century. Mostly situated in open country, they tended to concentrate around Kirchdorf and Micheldorf under guild control. By the early seventeenth century they began to follow the not uncommon fashion of limiting their membership to privileged entrants. As the use of scythes increased and production grew to supply buoyant markets in Nuremberg, Freistadt, Krems and Vienna, the Styrian scythe-makers enjoyed a prosperous business.

In Carinthia the iron industry remained more primitive. Peasants mined the ore with day labourers in the mountains and sold it to their local Blahhaus in the valley. Blahhaus and forge were mostly combined. Often a peasant would rise to be *Radmeister* (master of a water-wheel) and *Hammerherr* (master of a forge). In Carniola the iron deposits of Eisnern now (Lahovše) were worked by *Bergwerksgenossenschaften* (mining corporations) from the Friuli district. The Pögl family set up large-scale armaments works there, and under the Emperor Maximilian I Sebald Pögl created the Habsburg arsenal of heavy artillery. Pögl was both an industrial entrepreneur and merchant. After his death in 1528 the business was continued by his son, Sebald the second, who added even more Radwerke and forges.

Farther east, iron-mining and processing was mainly for local markets, but there were some exports from Bohemia, Moravia, Spiš (Zips) and Slovakia. In fifteenth-century Poland, iron-smelting works of an older type were in operation, their workshops, run by waterpower, containing bloomery hearth, forge and smithy. The owners were independent entrepreneurs mainly of bourgeois or peasant origin. They would buy from their lord rights to free use of land and forest and thus could build themselves a mill as well as a forge and continue to farm the land, paying rent in money and produce, iron bars and cereals. These mine- and farm-managers usually employed free wage-earning workers, who were given small allotments of land. The average forge employed twenty at the beginning of the sixteenth century, thirty at the end, and developed quite a sophisticated division of labour.

In the sixteenth century the northern part of Little Poland became the centre of the iron-smelting industry. Forges were concentrated in two areas, from Wielún to Olkusz in the hilly area around Cracow, and in the Swietokryskie mountains, north of Kielce. These areas used superior iron ores, but elsewhere small scattered works used bog ore. Iron and steel from Little Poland was traded in Cracow, in the Little Polish salt works of Wieliczka and Bochnia, in Drohobycz and other Red Russian salt works and in Warsaw. It was also exported to Silesia and Moldavia. In the sixteenth century the army was an important market for forges. The plentiful supply of wood in those areas which used the inferior bog ores enabled them to compete with the superior products of Little Poland.

It was in the towns of Little Poland, especially in Cracow, Novy Sacz and in the little towns of the Swietokryskie mountains, that the craft metal industries were most developed. Paul Kauffmann, a wealthy town councillor from Cracow, had already tried to establish a privileged factory in Starczynow in 1524. His aim was to manufacture weapons, knives, wire, plate and brass ware, using iron from Kauffmann's own Moravian smelting works. Like many early industrial enterprises, however, the factory did not survive for long. In the region of Cracow other enterprises made metal goods outside the guild organization. In Novy Sacz, the merchant Jerzy Tymowski produced agricultural implements from his forges. Capital provided by merchants also financed Danzig metal crafts, and some of the workshops established near Danzig and Oliva belonged to foreign merchants.

Imported iron from Hungary was the most serious competitor faced by the iron from Little Poland. The staple for Hungarian iron was centred in the towns of Krosno and Novy Sacz. In Novy Sacz the manufacture of agricultural implements, especially sickles, from Hungarian iron had been expanding since the fifteenth century. Swedish iron, or *Osmund*, however, took second place in imports. It was worked by Danzig forges and then re-exported as Danzig iron to England and even back to Sweden. Iron was also imported from Moravia. Steel was also imported into Poland from Hungary and Styria. The sixteenth century saw a substantial increase in imports of iron goods, knives, scythes and sickles from Silesia, Bohemia, Moravia, Styria and Nuremberg. Some of these products travelled even farther east to Moscow and the Black Sea region.

By the end of the sixteenth century Poland was producing iron in high bloomery and blast furnaces and trying to meet the ever-increasing demands of the armaments industry. In 1571 Stefan Bathory granted privileges to a forge near Stuhm (Prussia), whose owner, Georg Langner, made cannon-balls and grenades out of crude iron. In 1598 the iron works of the Italian brothers Cacci from Bergamo were founded near Kielce on land owned by the bishop of Cracow. During the first half of the seventeenth century at least two blast furnaces were in operation there, as well as a few bloomery hearths and armourers' workshops. In the 1620s Grand Marshall Mikolaj Wolski built two blast furnaces at Panki and Laziec near Czenstochowa, with bloomery furnaces, sheet-metal foundries and a wire factory. Blast furnaces were then built near Halicz in Red Russia by Andrczej Potocki; Hetman Stanislas Koniecpolski owned eighteen foundries in Teterev in the Ukraine. The production of these great works was chiefly directed to war purposes – cannon, cannon-balls and grenades – and to supplying raw material to more traditional workshops, such as smithies which manufactured blades.

In the Tyrol, mining was concentrated in the lower Inn valley near Schwaz and Rattenberg. In 1522 Jakob Fugger bought up *Kuxen* (mining shares) from the bankrupt Martin Baumgartner of Kufstein, and Fugger's mining activities began to spread throughout north and south Tyrol. The Fuggers held Kuxen in Lafatsch and Vompertal, in Gossensass and on the Schneeberg at Ridnaun, at Lienz in the Puster valley, and at Klausen in the Eisack valley. They also had widespread smelting works of their own. In 1549 their Tyrolean and Carinthian trade with Hungary was given specific tax exemptions closely linked to their mining enterprises. Carinthia had deposits of lead on the Bleiberg near Villach, necessary for obtaining silver. In 1495 the Fugger brothers had opened pits there and built a furnace near the market town of Arnoldstein. In the first decade of the sixteenth century about 50,000 hundredweight of copper and 22,000 Marks of silver were sold in Venice. Jakob Fugger regarded this industry as so important that he built himself a castle (the Fuggerau) at the foot of the Dobratsch.

The Fuggers were not the only owners of Kuxen on the Bleiberg, however. Citizens of Villach were also involved, as were the brothers Halfinger, the monastery of Milstatt, and merchants from Vienna, Augsburg and Gastein. When clashes of interest became acute the small local guilds were usually driven out by the powerful foreigners, who closed down the small pits on the grounds of rationalization. Of ninety-three pits which the Fuggers owned in 1584, only twenty-six were worked; of the eighty-six belonging to Lentner, only eighteen. When the Fuggers gave up their mining interests in northern Hungary their lead mines in Carinthia also suffered. Between 1553 and 1563 10,000 hundredweight were produced yearly, but in the last quarter of the century production averaged only 5,000 hundredweight. Exhausted deposits were only partly to blame for the decrease, although technological problems (such as those which arose in 1569 when mines sank below the water table on the valley floor near Villach and Arnoldstein) made further exploitation of ore very hazardous. Schloss Fuggerau was sold the following year as no longer profitable.

In the Ennstal in Styria, around the little town of Schladming, copper and precious metals were mined, and the citizens joined with the nobility of the Enns valley to form mining corporations. Then came a miners' revolt in 1525 which led to savage countermeasures by Count Solms, disrupting all production. The industry had to be refounded by foreign capital investment from Sitzinger of Nuremberg, Andreas Prantmayr of Augsburg, the Pernsteiner Union of south Germany, Katzbeck of Katzenstein in Tyrol and Weitmoser of Gastein. Some of these had been mining the deposits of Walchen near Öblarn to the east of Schladming since the middle of the sixteenth century.

The central Slovak mining area included the mining towns of Königsberg, Bugganz, Banska Stjavnica, Dillin, Kremnica, Banska Bystrica and Libethen. After mining rights had been obtained in 1523, the number of enterprises increased, and soon they combined to form mining unions, partly because of the lack of working capital. Wealthy mining entrepreneurs also had to merge to found financially stable companies, for which they received government aid, usually in the form of monopolies. A typical example of this was the Schemnitz *Brennergesellschaft* of 1571, in which the firms of Salius, Schall, and Sicelius had shares. This large company went on to absorb smaller enterprises. The copper-mining area of Banska Bystrica was to some extent an exception. From the end of the fifteenth century to the middle of the sixteenth century it was in the hands of the Thurzo and Fugger families and was later worked by a *Bergärar* (state mining fund). In the larger mining towns urban patriciates consisted mainly of rich owners of mines and smelting works, the so-called *Ring- und Waldbürger*. In such an atmosphere craftsmen and merchants could only play subordinate rôles. The number of craftsmen employed was large, however, as mining and manufacturing were technically complex and labour-intensive. Banska Stiavnica provided employment for nearly three thousand miners in the early sixteenth century, and of these the copper mines alone employed one thousand.

The Fuggers gave up their Hungarian mines in 1546. Thereafter copper production went through a difficult period. The new government of north Royal Hungary had to take immediate responsibility for the whole enterprise and invest considerable amounts of capital, because during the last period of their lease (1541–46) the Fuggers had aimed at maximum exploitation of the pits and had run down the plant. New capital was attracted from other south German trading companies, who in return controlled prices but left production to the Slovaks and Hungarians. Then came a slump in copper prices at the end of the 1560s and 1570s, disrupting Hungarian copper exports from Cracow to Breslau, Thorn, Danzig, Antwerp, and Amsterdam, and from there to Spain, Portugal, Italy and France and also to a small extent to Austria and south Germany. Antwerp remained the most important foreign market for Slovakian copper until the 1580s when Hamburg replaced her and a new boom began. Copper mines again came under the direct management of a trading company, and the metal was traded via Vienna, south Germany, Venice and Hamburg.

The copper mines always lacked sufficient capital investment, and high prices tended to lead to even greater exploitation as trading companies bid high for quick profits. None of this activity improved the lot of the miners, which was subject to constant deterioration. Problems were made worse by the Turkish threat and by technological difficulties as deposits were used up. In the 1590s the copper industry in Hungary was on the verge of collapse and began to show net deficits for the first time. In 1600 gross receipts by the crown were a mere 33,692 Florins. At the same time the yearly profits of the trading companies were over 80,000 Florins. After long negotiations the companies were obliged in 1603 to increase the price of first quality copper by one third and to double that of second quality. Until then prices had stayed at the level fixed in the 1570s and 1580s.

The deposits of lead containing silver found on the border between Little Poland and Upper Silesia were Poland's most important mineral resources until the eighteenth century. The first phase of exploitation finished in the fourteenth century. Deeper deposits could only be worked where water could be pumped out continuously, and that could only be done with the help of merchant capital. At first those most involved were merchants from Breslau and Cracow, though later finance was provided not only by merchants but also by the nobility, church, and territorial rulers, such as the Polish Silesian dukes and kings, and finally by the Thurzo and Fugger families.

Tarnovitz was built in Upper Silesia in the 1620s and handled three thousand tons of lead annually. Polish lead was sold at Leipzig and Nuremberg, particularly to the silver-producing areas of Bohemia and Slovakia. About a hundred tons a year went to Kutna Hora, and over two hundred to the mines of Slovakia. This trade was so lucrative that Thurzo and Fugger tried to gain a monopoly. Merchants invested capital in the putting-out system and also participated directly by dealing in Kuxen and by founding subsidiary enterprises to pump water and to process the ore. As in Tyrol and Carinthia, some of the small corporations went over to direct-wage labouring. In addition, *Lehenhauer* miners opened up deposits as lease-holders, and *Gedinghauer* worked at piece-rates, using their own equipment to obtain raw materials at their own expense and risk often employing their own workers.

Scandinavia, Sweden and Norway all had high-quality ores which were worth mining. Iron ore was found over a wide area of central Sweden centred on Närke. Silver was found at the beginning of the sixteenth century near Sala, though copper-mining near Falun had become predominant by the seventeenth century.

In the Kiev period Russia had had an important craft iron industry. Then came a decline in the Tartar era. In the fifteenth century iron was imported from the west via Novgorod where it was processed for the internal Russian market. Larger-scale manufacture for export only began to develop after the beginning of the sixteenth century, and in this immigrants played a crucial rôle. The Florentine Rodolfo Fioraventi set up the first Muscovite mint and arsenal. Miners also came from Hungary and Germany to Russia. In 1550 Ivan the Terrible asked the Danish king for printers, and at the same time English craftsmen and miners arrived. In 1554 Hans Stitte of Goslar tried to take 123 German master craftsmen to Russia, but without success. At the end of the fifteenth century German miners had started a silver mine near the Glyma, a tributary of the Pechora, and mining flourished with state support around Tula, Archangel, Olonets, Vologda, Viatka, and Kostroma on the Volga. In 1558, the Tsar granted a licence to the Stroganovs to mine ores and process metals, and in 1574 they were given the right to mine iron, copper, zinc, lead and sulphur in Siberia, although lack of expertise meant they were not able to exploit these rights to any great extent. In 1569 the English were given the right to set up works to process iron on the banks of the Vychegda, and on the banks of the Stochna they received concessions for iron and tin.

B. *Glass, stone and clay*

Glass was made in two main regions of Europe: one lay south of the Alps, around Venice and the island of Murano; the other stretched from the Ardennes to Bohemia across the uplands north of the Alps. In spite of strong measures taken by the Venetians to protect their manufacturing secrets, glass-making spread across Europe as far as Scandinavia in the course of the sixteenth century. In France there were numerous glass furnaces in wooded mountain areas, and its manufacture was widespread in the sixteenth century in Germany, where wood and quartz were plentiful. There were important glass-blowing industries in the Black Forest, Hesse, Franconia, the Bavarian forests and in the Erz mountains, where the high quality of the glass produced greatly stimulated trade. Nuremberg was the first place north of the Alps to make mirrors. Germany north of the Alps was so rich in minerals of all kinds that a lively export trade to the plains of north Germany and the Netherlands developed. Various centres of production grew up, in the middle Rhine near Andernach and in the Weser mountain area for instance. Limestone was quarried on a large scale on the Segeberg, on Heligoland and on Gotland in the Baltic.

In many parts of France, the Rhineland and central Germany slate was quarried for roofing. There were extensive brickworks on clay seams in the north German plains. There were brickworks near most of the larger towns. Pottery was mainly a village craft industry, but there were important urban centres producing for export. Jugs from Siegburg reached England, and Raeren near Aachen exported to France and the Low Countries.

C. *Wood and coal*

Wood was essential for fuel and for all branches of the construction industry, mining and various processing industries. As iron-smelting, casting, forging and other large-scale industrial processes spread, the consumption of wood rose enormously. In certain districts, in the Siegen area for instance, forestry corporations were formed to organize the planting and felling of oak for the production of charcoal, which was then sold to the Sauerland and the county of Mark in Westphalia.

Oak bark was stripped and used for tanning. Wood used in glass-making as potash was chiefly produced in the Bavarian forests and on the south coast of the Baltic. Tar and pitch from Sweden and Finland were important for ship-building and fitting. During the sixteenth century water-driven saw-mills were developed; these made it possible to saw trunks on river banks and float timber as planks ready for drying and use. Sweden and Norway both built saw-mills which produced rough timber for construction industries such as Netherlands shipping. The high consumption of wood gradually made the introduction of forest regulations necessary and encouraged the use of coal. This policy was successful in the Ruhr as far as Aachen, in Saxony and Thuringia.

D. *Textiles*

The main centres of the French textile industry were in Normandy, Picardy, Poitou and Languedoc. During the sixteenth century the putting-out system spread to the cloth-making areas of Poitou and Picardy, Orléans, Berry and Languedoc, and later to Beauce, Sologne and Gatenais. In Brittany, Normandy, the lower Maine and Burgundy, flax and hemp were woven into linen, and cotton was processed in the Lyons area. Later the cotton industry spread to Normandy, the Vosges and Orléans. Silk and lace production began in Amiens and the surrounding villages during the sixteenth century. Luxury goods such as pillow-lace were made in Bourbon, Auvergne, Velay, Alençon and Normandy. Silk was thrown and spun in Touraine, Languedoc, Nîmes, Vivarais and Provence and sent away for weaving, principally to Lyons.

In Germany the old centres of wool-weaving were at Aachen, Düren and Cologne, Brunswick, Stendal and Salzwedel, and Görlitz in Silesia. A further cloth-making area stretched from the middle Rhine to Hesse. In central Swabia various urban centres had a flourishing textile industry, as did most south German imperial towns. Starting at Ulm and Nördlingen, there was a zone which manufactured coarse outdoor cloth (*Loden*), reaching as far as Straubing in lower Bavaria. In 1620 Munich had a total of 120 *Loden* makers employing three thousand spinners in the town and surrounding country.

In addition to heavy woollen cloths, lighter, cheaper materials became fashionable; these were called *Zeuge* in Germany and 'say' elsewhere. Other products included *bursat, tripp* (mock velvet), *moquette, grosgron* or *grobgrain*, and *bombasin* or *bombazine*. Some of these were half-finished stuffs made of wool, silk, linen or cotton composites. These branches of the industry had first developed as country crafts in England and the Netherlands, partly in competition with cloth manufacture in the towns. Emigrants brought their skills to Germany, which included lace-border making (*passementerie*), pillow-lace making and embroidery, carpet-weaving, silk-weaving and stock-making. These newer industries were found in Wesel, Hamburg, Frankfurt and Frankenthal, Göttingen, Gera and Meuselwitz. In south Germany the most important enterprise of this type was the *Zeughandlungskompanie* in Calw. Here, in an area of sheep raising, cloth weaving developed from home products, and by the late sixteenth century entrepreneurs had introduced the putting-out system. These entrepreneurs came from among the dyers. At the beginning of the seventeenth century in the Calw district, there were five to six hundred weavers who were organized by 1622 under fifteen entrepreneurs, combining to form a company which survived the temporary disruptions of war-time.

The processing of flax flourished in Westphalia, Lower Saxony, Swabia, and east central Germany. The most important centres for the industry in Westphalia were Coesfeld, Münster and Bielefeld, where the bleaching floors which were important for the process were concentrated. Flax-processing was complemented by hemp-growing and manufacturing nearer the German coast. Swabian linen was produced along Lake Constance, and from the Swabian Alb as far as the Lech and Danube rivers. By the sixteenth century Constance had lost its leading position to St Gallen, and the Ravensburg trading company wound up its linen enterprise. The towns of the Allgäu kept their importance as centres of fustian manufacture, supporting large towns such as Ulm and Biberach, Augsburg, Memmingen and Kaufbeuren. Ulm had the great advantage of a relatively large territory over which it enforced a trading monopoly. Rural outworkers, or *Gäuweber*, were mostly employed in the putting-out system. When the centre of the cotton trade moved from Venice to Marseilles, Antwerp and Amsterdam, fustian-weaving lost its importance, but linen flourished once more, and Ulm won new markets in the Mediterranean and overseas. During the sixteenth century 450 linen-weavers from both town and country made deliveries to the Ulm show (*Schau*). Ulm also had an important bleaching industry based on linen from Bavaria and Silesia as well as from Swabia. Linen production in the Allgäu was considerable too, and in 1610 five thousand pieces of bleached linen came to the market from Leutkirch alone. New centres of production grew up in competition with each other as foreign demand increased. Just outside the walls of Ulm, the Fuggers developed fustian weaving on their estates at Weissenhorn, and competition also came from Württemberg. In Urach Duke Frederick I founded his own guild of weavers at the end of the sixteenth century and had a special suburb built for them. In true mercantilist fashion he then gave the Urach bleaching floor a monopoly for the whole of Württemberg. His linen trading company, founded in 1600, suffered heavy losses during the Thirty Years' War.

Linen production in east central Germany increased steadily during the sixteenth century. The medieval Saxon and Silesian towns found markets for their cloth products both at home and farther east. From the 1450s onwards south German merchants engaged in foreign trade began to develop the mineral resources of the area. The lower standards of living and wages prevailing in east Germany made it possible to produce half-finished goods at a profit despite costs of transport to south Germany, where the goods were usually bleached, dyed and finished. Between 1450 and 1550 many south Germans emigrated to Saxony and in about 1500 the south German colony at Leipzig was the largest of its sort; immigrants from Franconia and Nuremberg in particular were the most numerous. In the Saxon cloth trade south German traders particularly acted as middlemen. They initiated rapid changes in textile production and brought Swabian weavers into Saxony, who went over to coloured linens and black-dyeing was started. Yet most Saxon cloth was still finished in Nuremberg. Production was organized on the putting-out system, backed by collective delivery contracts, of which those of *Zunftkauf*, or buying by guilds, was the most common form. German clothing firms worked with a capital outlay well in excess of half a million Florins, and Viatis and Peller of Nuremberg had increased their business capital to one million Florins by 1624. In Saxony, Lausitz and part of Silesia nearly four thousand master weavers are thought to have worked the putting-out system at local levels, some however with only one weaving loom. Each guild averaged thirty-five masters, producing merchandise to the value of five to six thousand Talers a year. Taking an estimate of about 630 Bohemian masters, then yearly production was worth about 630,000 to 750,000 Talers, not including village-made (non-guild) linens, coarser types of cloth and cottons. In Thuringia and Franconia as a whole, and in Henneberg (Meiningen) and Vogtland in particular, the Nurembergers organized cotton weaving on the same putting-out system as linen weaving. There was plenty of competition from English and Dutch cloth merchants by the end of the sixteenth century: the Dutch specialized in yarn and the English in multiple cloth dealing, exchanging their own products for German linens for resale. The Thirty Years' War, however, shifted the balance of the German cloth trade away from Nuremberg towards Hamburg in the north.

In the fifteenth century Swiss linens concentrated increasingly on St Gallen. The nearby villages certainly produced as much as the town, because the municipality failed to enforce a local monopoly of production. But the town was recognized as a natural centre of trade in cloth, throughout Switzerland. Village weavers usually worked up flax they themselves had grown, and although they were sometimes employed by entrepreneurs from the town many also worked on their own account. Up to the beginning of the eighteenth century cloth production in rural areas probably exceeded that in St Gallen town itself. New centres at Herisau, Trogen, Rorschach, Arbon and Hauptwil grew up to challenge St Gallen in cloth production. They arranged their own shows and disposed of their goods more freely and economically, mainly because they paid lower wages. The Appenzell chronicle of Walser gives a vivid account of rural weavers at work. The poor span, reeled and wove, whereas the rich traded the finished product and took the profit. Yet the putting-out system had a much smaller part in the Swiss linen industry than in fustians and cottons, no doubt because raw materials like flax were produced locally, so that workers were less dependent on outside suppliers of raw materials. In about 1600 a new area of linen production opened up in the four original cantons, in Aargau, around Lucern, in Willisau and in Emmenthal. After 1550 Protestant emigrants from Locarno to the Zürich area introduced improvements in weaving, dyeing and fulling. Once the difficulties raised by the guilds had been overcome, the industry went over to the putting-out system, not only in the whole canton but also in the districts around Zug, Lucern, Schwyz, Glarus, the Free Counties, Töss valley and Thurgau. Spinning and weaving were largely carried out in the country areas, and municipalities claimed a monopoly only of combing, even so without much success. Finishing was reserved for the urban guild craftsmen, however.

During the fifteenth century the Swiss cotton industry expanded from the north-east to Zürich. At first mixed cloths, fustians (*Schürlitz*) were produced, but by 1500 pure cotton cloth was being made. Cotton now became an alternative employment to mercenary military service (*Reislaufen*). The new industry's expansion was not hampered by guild regulations and great possibilities for large urban entrepreneurs opened up. Some craft enterprises did survive to become local producers and suppliers (*Tüchler*).

After promising beginnings the Swiss silk industry collapsed and had to be re-founded in 1555 by immigrants from Locarno. It developed as a free industry outside guild supervision, although the citizens of Zürich had a trading monopoly which they built up on the putting-out system. Outside the town silk-throwing was forbidden, although rural labour was needed to reel and wind the silk. In addition, woof for filling and *Fiorett*, knub silk, were made. The spinning of Fiorett, which used up waste material, was also put out to women and children at home.

In Basle the weaving of silk bands (*passementerie*), introduced in the last quarter of the sixteenth century by French and Italian refugees, was the only industry to escape guild restrictions. In 1612 the guilds failed in their attempts to control the industry, and Basle silk-weaving flourished where the rest of the weaving trade had languished under restrictive practices by the guilds. The movement for the rights of local inhabitants grew stronger after 1600 and led to foreign labour settling outside Basle, where it was exploited by Verleger from within the town. Apprenticed and unapprenticed hosiery-knitters also operated in the Basle area after 1550, spreading out to Aargau, Schaffhausen, Zürich, Luzern and Canton Solothurn.

The linen-weaving industry of Upper Austria was founded on the putting-out system. In the country above the Enns flax-growing was widespread and flax was steeped and spun into yarn as a winter cottage industry. Weaving was organized in guilds, and sharp conflicts between town and country workers led to a great number of craft regulations. The first of these was issued at the beginning of the sixteenth century, and by 1578 they formed a centralized, standardized procedure for the linen industries in the seven royal towns of Linz, Enns, Freistadt, Gmunden, Steyr, Vöcklabruck and Wels; the surrounding villages were brought under unified pay codes and quality controls in 1581. These regulations represented the interests of town and market weavers and were aimed at restricting the activities of village outworkers by severely limiting their work quotas. They were forbidden apprentices and fine yarn and were only allowed to make flock. They were restricted to wage-earning status and might not sell their produce themselves. In this way cheap Austrian linen could outsell and undercut linen prices in neighbouring Bavaria, especially since Upper Austria also had more raw materials of its own. Kirchdorf and Vienna also had fustian weaving industries in the fifteenth century, but they could not compete with superior goods from Swabia. In 1548 the government invited fustian weavers from Augsburg to Enns, and a privileged company was founded on the putting-out system. Only two years later, however, the town had to take over its business and fustian weaving soon stopped completely.

In Bohemia, especially at Dihlava, the cloth and linen industries were of long standing. Brno was the centre of Moravian cloth-making. In the towns of Slovakia and at Sibiu in Transylvania the industry flourished and Italian experts had a stimulating effect after 1550. Poland also had its own cloth-making industry, improved by Dutch immigrants to Danzig. The same happened in Christian IV's Denmark. This shows that textiles could flourish everywhere as local industries based on local demand, although produce was very often of inferior quality, but thus much cheaper than internationally traded products. Everywhere the textile industry was the subject of early control by mercantilist state and municipal regulations.

E. Printing and Paper

The great political and educational – as well as religious – movements of the early sixteenth century are inconceivable without the spread of printing. Printing was a new branch of industry which developed rapidly after movable type had been invented in south Germany in the 1440s. Nuremberg, Augsburg, Basle and Strasbourg were the first commercially viable centres for printing in the German language area. The first large German printing works was built by Anton Koberger (died 1513), employing a hundred journeymen at twenty-five presses, and his concern survived him by ten years. The centre of German printing was Nuremberg, and Augsburg developed a considerable industry in graphics alongside its printing. Cologne had the most important printing industry in the Rhineland, whereas Lübeck dominated in the south Baltic. Book fairs at Leipzig and Frankfurt-am-Main were also crucial to the development of the industry. In France, Lyons and Paris were the main centres of printing. The Estienne family in Paris were one of the greatest printing dynasties ever known.

Paper production expanded to meet the needs of the printing industry. In France production was so well developed by the beginning of the sixteenth century that Italian paper was finally squeezed out of the market as France began to export. There were paper-mills in many areas, especially in Provence, Comtat-Venaissin, Savoy, Languedoc, Auvergne, the Île de France, Champagne, Orléans and Normandy. In 1500 there were also about fifty paper-mills in Germany. In the early sixteenth century Ravensburg, which had five and later six mills, was the most important centre of German paper-making. During the century numerous other mills were built in Upper Swabia, near Lake Constance, in Bavaria and also in west, central and north Germany. Territorial governments who supplied the capital were also often the main customers. It was Swabia that became the chief paper-making district in Germany, based on Ravensburg, Reutlingen and Kempten. The limited supply of rags for raw material meant that paper-mills were most successful near large urban centres. Only a certain number of mills, limited by the size and relative affluence of the local population, could be supported in any one area. Thus in Austria above the Enns, Steyr was never able to run more than five paper-mills for lack of cloth waste at economic prices.

F. Ship-building

In the coastal towns the ship-building industry was carried on an unscientific basis, using only practical, inherited expertise.

In the Hanseatic cities, however, it was the first craft after brewing to change from a guild organization to capitalist methods of production. Yet ship-building was so important and complicated a branch of the total economy of the sea ports that it needed town council regulation and could not be left in the hands of ship-builders.

The most important ship-building ports on the Baltic coast were Lübeck and Danzig. In medieval Danzig the *Kraweel* (round-bottomed type of ship) was especially favoured. Lübeck's ship-building flourished with the increase in voyages to Spain after 1550, although the centre of gravity in ship-building had long ago shifted to the northern Netherlands. There new types of boats, such as the *Boyer*, the *Vlieboot* and the *Fleute*, were developed, although centres like Lübeck tried to catch up with the Dutch. The first German *Fleute* (fluit) was built in Lübeck in 1615. On the North Sea coast Emden had a particularly lively ship-building industry in the early seventeenth century, but its prosperity was due to short-term political, rather than long-term economic, factors. On the east Baltic coast ships were built at Riga and Reval from the plentiful supplies of excellent, cheap timber in the hinterland. In Scandinavia small *Schuten* were built for local shipping.

G. Building

The gradual transition from wood to stone and brick gave the building trade great opportunities for technological advance. The emphasis, wherever possible, was increasingly on pomp and circumstance. Even timber-framed town houses were decorated in Renaissance and Baroque styles. Town halls were rebuilt and enlarged and churches altered to keep abreast with the new ideological rivalries of Reformation and Counter-Reformation. Instead of castles, elaborate fortresses were constructed to withstand the new ballistic weapons, and rulers and noblemen moved into more comfortable fortified country houses. Town fortifications had to be renewed continuously to keep up with the firepower of new weapons. Outstanding examples of these were the new fortifications built on the Dutch pattern at Hamburg; these had just been completed by the beginning of the Thirty Years' War. These large projects increased the power of town councils over their own guild and craft industries. The medieval *Bauhütten* (masonic lodges) lost out to individual architects and engineers, who were often trained in Italy or of Italian origin.

H. *Salt production*

Salt was panned from the sea on the north Friesian islands and on the west Atlantic coast. During the sixteenth century the north used more and more sea salt, which was produced on the coast of south France, Spain and Portugal, because it was cheaper than salt mined in Lüneburg and the Alpine regions. Its fine quality meant that Lüneburg salt continued to be sold, and most regions of central Europe had their own pans or mines where salt was produced for local consumption. In central Germany there were important salt deposits in Halle, and south Germany had the deposits at Schwäbisch-Hall, Berchtesgaden, Reichenhall and Hallein. Central Austria had salt deposits at Hall, Admont and Aussee.

In south-east Europe much salt was produced in Transylvania. In Poland the two important centres of production were at Olkusz and Wieliczka. Russia produced salt on the White Sea and the Arctic sea, and many important towns had their own salt pans, Novgorod for instance. In the sixteenth century salt production was expanded in the Perm area, thanks to the initiative of the Stroganovs. Under Anikej Stroganov the family owned one small salt pan; his sons expanded production by setting up branch offices and soon succeeded in dominating internal salt production.

I. *Alcoholic beverages*

The manufacture of beer, which kept better than fermented pure cereals or wine and other fermented fruit juices such as perry and cider, from barley and hops became more widespread during the sixteenth century. Most brewing for export had taken place in northern Germany, chiefly in Hamburg, Bremen, Brunswick, Einbeck, Rostock and Zerbst. Einbeck became less important during the sixteenth century as competition from new types of beer developed. Minden was the most important brewing city in Westphalia, but every town had its local brewery. In south Germany matured pale ale (today's white beer brewed in Berlin) became very popular. In the Hanseatic cities of Hamburg, Wismar and Brunswick brewing was carried on by merchants with their own labour, and all the beer produced went for export in barrels. In Denmark the royal brewery in Copenhagen achieved a leading position.

During the sixteenth century the manufacture of cognac developed in the higher areas behind Bordeaux, supplementing wine-pressing, and in 1513 cognac was first exported. In Poland, where beer but not wine was drunk, the manufacture of mead was important. Russia had Kvass, which was mostly made at home as in Poland. *Aqua vita* (strong alcohol distilled from burnt grain and herbs) become especially popular in Holland and spread from there to north-west Germany, but gin-type beverages were not common in the sixteenth century.

IV Service Industries

I. COMMUNICATIONS

A. *Technological development*

One of the most startling technological developments of the sixteenth century came in ship-building. Boats increased in size as trade became more lucrative, especially in bulk goods between Baltic, Atlantic and Mediterranean. Boat-building was not standardized, however, the Baltic continuing to favour Lübeck *Krawels* (carvels), which were copied farther west as *Hulks* and North Sea *Rahsegler*. Henry VIII built up his fleet mainly by buying ships from the Baltic for use as patterns by English ship-builders. In the Baltic a tonnage of 300 *Last* (600 tons) was the maximum possible, since the heavier west and south European carracks or galleons could not be used in the shallower waters of the Baltic. In 1585 the papal legate at the Polish court explained that large Spanish ships would hardly be able to enter the Baltic, because their deep draught made it difficult to pass through the Sound. Baltic harbour and river mouths were also treacherous for ships with excessive draught.

In German and Dutch waters the small tub-like *Bojer* was developed for maximum carrying on minimum draught. In the 1620s the Hamburgers used these boats to trade with Zeeland, England, Scotland, Norway and across the Baltic. Towards the end of the sixteenth century the Bojer plied to Spain. By now they were built with two masts, the second a small mizzen with lateen sail. The advantage of these ships lay in their economy. Whereas a threemaster of 100 Last needed a complement of fourteen men, a Bojer of 50 Last could manage with five or six men. A Dutch Rahsegel would usually make only one sailing to the Baltic each year, and one to Brouage. Exceptionally, it might ply the Baltic twice in a year. The Bojer, however, did three Baltic voyages a year. It was not as seaworthy as the Rahsegel, but it was quicker to load and unload and easier to dock. The Bojer was confined to the Dutch and German North Sea coast and it dominated northern sea trade. In Lübeck and the Baltic ports there was no native Bojer shipping.

In the 1570s a new type of boat, the *Vlieboot*, was developed; this had a considerable effect on the economic viability of the Bojer and the Rahsegel. Probably a Frisian invention, it was copied from the *Doggboot*, a vessel used for cod-fishing on the Dogger bank, and was first employed in herring-fishing. Ships of this type were soon built for general cargo and were first put into service on the main routes going through the island passage in Vlieland – hence their name. Whereas Bojer were usually built only up to a tonnage of 50 Last, Vlieboote from Emden sailing in the Baltic had a tonnage of up to 70 Last. On the whole the Vlieboot shared the advantages and disadvantages of the Bojer, although its draught was considerably shallower than the Rahsegel's, and it was faster than the Bojer. In 1565 a Dutch Vlieboot made four sailings in the Baltic; twenty years later, six out of a total of twenty-five did the trip nine times in the year. The increase in traffic through the Sound is very closely connected with the rise of the Dutch Vlieboot, for boats had to become smaller and faster to make Baltic bulk trade profitable. In voyages to Portugal, Spain and the Mediterranean, however, where well armed ships were needed for self-protection, the Rahsegel still predominated, though before 1600 a new type, the Dutch *Fleute* (fluit), had been developed for this trade too.

The fluit, first built in 1595, combined the advantages of the Vlieboot with those of the Rahsegel. At first fluits were built four times as long as they were wide, although later their length was often increased to five or six times their width. These boats had a low centre of gravity and thus could carry more cargo. Their rigging was also improved, with three masts to increase spread of canvas and speed. They were narrow in beam and could sail closer to the wind than their predecessors. Masts were taller and yards could be shortened considerably. Sails became smaller and easier to handle and manpower was used more economically. With these ships the Dutch dominated the north and west European cargo trade in the early seventeenth century, undercutting the freight charges of all their competitors.

As the fluit developed from 1600 onwards, the number of large ships of over 100 Last passing through the Sound again increased. In 1620 nearly four thousand Dutch ships passed through, half of which were 200-tonners (100 Last or more). By the 1650s small ships had almost entirely disappeared from the long-distance Baltic trade. The number of sailings also increased with ship size – in 1615 nine Dutch ships of over 100 Last each passed through Danish customs at the Sound between eight and twelve times in that single year. The fluit was soon bought by the Hansa and the Scandinavians. In 1615 the fluit was first built in Lübeck and sea trade soon increased at the expense of trade by land. Shipping became the most lucrative industry of the period and a yardstick of economic status.

The Baltic region had its own shipping law, though it was often disrupted by the rivalries of powers such as Sweden, Denmark and the Hansa, who all aspired to overall control. The first great general conflict was the Seven Years' War between 1563 and 1570, in which Lübeck and Poland were also involved. The Danish Crown had increased the Sound dues so much that by 1567 economic warfare, piracy and blockade dominated the Baltic trade. After 1567 the Sound tonnage due was exacted, and the navigational difficulties in the narrows meant that the Danes could take reprisals on ships for any reason they cared to think of. Political pressure on Copenhagen first from the Hague and then from Stockholm soon limited this freedom of action, however.

The catholic Vasas of Poland attempted to blockade their Swedish cousins from 1597 to 1598 by imposing embargoes on salt, hops and grain imports. German and Danish ports also supported the Polish measures. These policies were unsuccessful, as were attempts by Poles from Danzig to take Älvsborg (later Gothenburg) from the Swedes and so destroy their west coast trade. Although the War of Kalmar (1611–13) between Sweden and Denmark was fought mainly on land, the Danes soon established naval supremacy and won, an achivement which was never to be repeated.

Compared with advances in shipping, land communications remained stagnant. There were no innovations either in types of vehicles or in methods of propulsion, but land transport continued to be rationalized to cut down costs. Wheeled transport was introduced in the Alps and a number of large transport firms appeared during the sixteenth century, including Annoni of Milan, Della Faille of Antwerp and Kleinhans, Enzensperger, Lederer and other firms of Alpine origin. Frammersbacher, the carriers of Hesse, and those of Schmalkalden were well organized for the time and could reckon with greater security than sea traders who were more subject to wind and weather.

Cartography also improved, and itineraries, guides and travel booklets became very popular with the growth of printing and graphics. Early maps confined themselves to providing lists of stops and stages between main towns. A typical example was the travel map of central Europe published by Erhard Etzlaub, a compass-maker from Nuremberg, in the year 1501; in the centre of his map was Nuremberg, with all the major routes radiating outwards. Another favourite method was to make all roads lead to Rome. A really competent *itinerarium orbis christiani* was first published in 1579/80. This was a travel atlas of eighty-three pages – Europe's first road atlas. In time travel books became more and more comprehensive and popular – Sebastian Münster's *Cosmographie*, which went into 46 editions between 1543 and 1650, is a good example.

In 1632 Martin Zeiller of Ulm published an *Itinerarium Germaniae Nov-Antiquae*, to which he added an *Itinerarii Germaniae Continuatio* in 1640. On more than a thousand folios minute travel descriptions were given. Zeiller thus became the first historical geographer. Meanwhile, surveying for cartography became ever more important for in the first place maps could now be reproduced accurately by printing; Mercator's first map of Europe appeared in 1554 and in 1568 Philipp Apian's map of Bavaria appeared – far ahead of its time in central Europe because of its accuracy and skill in representation. In 1595, the year after his death, Mercator's complete works were published in atlas form. In the seventeenth century the Dutch led in cartography for sea navigation, emulated by the French, British and Germans.

Central European postal services improved markedly under the Habsburgs. In 1505 Franz von Taxis obtained a monopoly from Philip the Fair to run postal services between Spain, France, the Netherlands and Germany. Charles v confirmed this agreement in 1516. Habsburg postal services could always be disrupted and they were subject to political and economic sanctions such as those created by the Valois and Turk wars. Courts and governments still needed to make use of the news services of merchants such as the Fuggers. Unrest in Germany, the Netherlands and France in the later sixteenth century led to the collapse of the Taxis–Habsburg postal monopoly, which was reformed on a limited scale in Germany in the early seventeenth century.

Merchants' news services became increasingly important. The Venetians provided one of the best sources for sixteenth-century history, as did the Fuggers' newspapers, which were sent to south Germany. By the later sixteenth century all the European courts and governments were regularly supplied with economic and political news. Courts had postal services and newspapers were distributed from the early seventeenth century. Trading centres also kept up regular communications.

Postal services were reorganized on a government basis during the sixteenth century. In France, Henry III established *messagers royaux* in 1576 to deliver documents to all regional and local administrative centres; the expenses were recouped by carrying letters, money and goods for private persons and firms. In 1595 Leonhard von Taxis became imperial German Postmaster and two years later the postal services were made an imperial prerogative. A real reorganization was only achieved by his successor, Leonhard Taxis the second, who was created imperial German Postmaster in 1615. The Taxis were unable to maintain their claim to a monopoly, however; imperial towns and German territorial rulers set up their own local post, and Sweden and Denmark, for instance, extended their postal services as far as Hamburg.

Shortly before the outbreak of the Thirty Years' War, the first printed newspapers appeared in the lower Rhineland and Holland, supplementing handwritten letters of information and standardized *Relationen*. Their contents, when not sensational, were of practical interest to merchants, carriers and shippers interested in political and economic changes in different parts of the world. These papers first appeared weekly in 1618 in Holland, and German-, French- and English-language editions soon followed.

Shipping on inland waterways was hindered by numerous tolls, mills and weirs, and attempts by central government to abolish them, as in France, mostly had little success. Instead of irregular rafting and *ad hoc* cargo shipping, regular sailings were started, as on the Danube, Rhine and Main. The increasing importance of inland shipping in the sixteenth century is reflected in the advances made in lock and canal construction. Improvements in Brandenburg, for instance, linked the rivers Elbe, Havel, Spree and Oder by means of canals. By 1578 Berlin had been connected with the North Sea and the Baltic, although the whole network was not completed until 1669. Yet canals remained of little overall importance to bulk carrying trades until the later seventeenth century, although most European governments had started building them a century earlier. As in sea navigation and hydraulic engineering, the Dutch were the first to build canal systems for central European governments in this period.

B. *Sea routes*

During the sixteenth and seventeenth centuries, above all as a result of technical improvements in shipping, the centre of European economic and political affairs shifted decisively to the north and west. Developments centred on the United Provinces, whose most important connections were with the North Sea and above all with the Baltic, the greatest reservoir of strategic raw materials west Europe had ever known. The Sound toll archives record the ebb and flow of this great Baltic–North Sea trade in the sixteenth and seventeenth centuries. In the years after 1578, the number of Dutch ships passing through nearly always exceeded half the total traffic. The wars in the seventeenth century meant that these figures decreased considerably, and by 1645 there were only 874 sailings through the Sound, of which only 59 were Dutch ships. Grain and wood products, and especially materials for ship-building, were the chief cargoes, together with salt, fish and beer. French and Portuguese salt was brought to the Baltic and bricks were a favourite form of ballast.

The most important routes went to Danzig and other ports on the east Baltic coast. In the 1630s between four and six hundred Dutch ships plied to Danzig annually, although under Stefan Bathory the Polish grain staple had been temporarily transferred to Elbing. The peak period of Dutch trade with Danzig was between 1585 and 1620. From the 1620s the Swedes began to blockade the Danzig roadstead and to take control of the Prussian ports, exacting heavy war taxes to the detriment of long-distance trade.

The east Friesians and north Hollanders played a large part in the Baltic trade, though from the 1550s English ships sailed to the Baltic in increasing numbers. They were especially attracted to Narva, which was occupied by the Russians in 1558. The Swedish king, Eric xiv, tried to divert the English to his ports at Reval and Vyborg, and the Russians soon lost Narva in 1581. The most attractive port for the English was Danzig, however, at least until the brief revival at Elbing. When the necessary facilities were not provided there, a considerable part of the English trade was transferred to Königsberg (Kaliningrad), which became their chief entrepôt. English and Baltic trade was always at the mercy of the Dutch during this period, and it was only with the Navigation Act of 1651 that the English improved their position decisively.

It took the Danes and Swedes a long time to find the capital resources to challenge Dutch trading supremacy. They even had difficulty in suppressing Hansa monopolies based on Lübeck and Danzig and smaller ports such as Wismar and Rostock. In the sixteenth century the neutrals, Portugal and Spain, were involved in bringing grain to the Atlantic and Mediterranean coasts. A short, summer-time alternative to the Baltic route was found when Richard Chancellor sailed through the entrance to the White Sea in 1553. The Russians were now able to trade directly with the west via Archangel, which became all the more necessary once the Swedes had taken Narva from them.

c. *Land routes*

(i) Southern and Central France

For the southern and central areas of France the most important ports on the Atlantic coast were Bordeaux and Nantes. In the sixteenth century there were two main routes to the Rhône and Mediterranean from the west and Atlantic coast, one via Clermont, the other through Toulouse. The main internal waterway remained the river Loire. To avoid Spanish blockades internal French transit trade had to go via Bordeaux and Nantes. American contraband gold and silver came via Nantes to Lyons and from there across the Alps to Milan. Lyons and

Marseilles were the most important centres in the east. Fairs had flourished at the former since the time of Louis XI, and Marseilles was its chief outlet to the sea. Lyons was Europe's most important internal trade centre in the early sixteenth century, its connections with Antwerp, south Germany, Italy and Spain competing well with the system of sea and land routes controlled by the Habsburgs. Not for nothing did the Emperor Charles V try to support the fairs of Besançon in the Franche-Comté against Valois-controlled Lyons. French connections with the Levant were important in the spice trade, in which they rivalled the Venetians.

(ii) Northern France, the Netherlands and the German
      North Sea coast

The most important route out of northern France started at Rouen and went via Orléans to Lyons, or alternatively through Champagne. The route to Italy from Rouen via Lyons is well documented in the archives of the family bank of Rucellai (Rousselay), which had offices in Rouen, Lyons and Nantes. Routes out of Antwerp were particularly important until the outbreak of revolt in the Netherlands. After 1564 Middelburg, Emden, Stade and Hamburg became bases for the Merchant Adventurers, and the mouth of the Rhine gained in importance. For transit trade the route via Lyons and Marseilles remained essential, as did the traditional routes between Antwerp and the fairs of Lyons. Despite its importance, relatively little is known about the route from Antwerp to Lyons and Italy, and it is difficult to distinguish between goods meant for the Lyons fairs and those for Italian destinations. The Mont Cenis pass to Turin, from where goods were sent to Milan or Genoa, was most used; routes via the Little St Bernhard and the Simplon were of minor importance in the sixteenth century.

Relatively little is known about the Besançon route. Besançon could be reached from the valleys of the Maas and Mosel, from Nancy and via Vesoul. How much trade went via Besançon over the Jaun and Simplon passes as through traffic from the Netherlands to Italy is uncertain. Geneva was probably an important entrepôt, at times equal to Lyons and Nuremberg. Most French roads did not lead to Italian centres, and serious political difficulties occurred in the sixteenth century because of the continuous rivalry between Habsburg Spain and Valois

France over their Italian possessions, settled for a time after 1559 in favour of the former.

The neutral Swiss routes always held the advantage in Italian trade with central Europe. Transit via Basle reached a peak between 1530 and 1570, before Venice gained control of routes in the eastern Alps and before Antwerp went into decline. Among routes through Lorraine, the branch from Nancy via Baccarat and Saint-Dié over the Col du Bonhomme to Kaysersberg and Colmar was frequently used, whereas the trade route from Luxemburg via Saarbrücken to Strasbourg had lost its former importance. Routes to the lower Rhine and from there upstream also increased in importance. During the Guelderland War (1542–3) freight coming from Antwerp was diverted from the usual routes through Herenthals, the Maas and Turnhaut-Roermond to Limburg, Malines, Liège and even Malmedy. English kerseys were quoted in Lyons for the Levant trade, although Marseilles usually shipped them. In 1575 the Duke of Savoy tried in vain to route the Italy–Netherlands trade through his lands. Despite political pressure, the Netherlands route via Mont Cenis remained more economical. Only war-time emergencies could temporarily divert bulk trade along more uneconomical roads. In the 1570s, for example, goods travelled from Antwerp to Rome and Naples via Turin, using the Lyons route over Mont Cenis when the Lorraine route was obstructed by Spanish troops.

After 1585 the Cologne area came under blockade from the Spaniards and the Dutch, and German trade was diverted via Mainz, along the east-west central high road. One branch of this road went via Namur and Dinant to Luxemburg and Grevenmacher, thence to Trier and Kreuznach. The other branch led via Liège, Malmedy and Stavelot, Saint-Vith and Prüm to the Mosel. Although the Cologne routes were noticeably cheaper, those via Mainz were politically safer, despite increased transport costs through the highlands of Hunsrück, Eifel and Ardennes. From Cologne and Mainz the most convenient routes led up the Rhine to Basle and thence overland, so avoiding navigational difficulties. The two routes to Italy via Basle were of equal value: one led via the St Gotthard and the other through Zurich via Splügen and the Septimer pass. Considerable improvements were made at the beginning of the sixteenth century to the Gotthard route to Ticino and Bellinzona.

Before the Revolt of the Netherlands the most lucrative trade route went to Milan via Basle. Thereafter the centre of gravity shifted eastwards and northwards. Instead of Antwerp the north Dutch and north German towns of Middelburg, Rotterdam, Emden, Bremen, Hamburg and Lübeck came into prominence. In south Germany routes went from Mainz and Speyer, from Strasbourg and Pforzheim to Ulm, then via Lindau to the upper Rhine valley, or via Augsburg-Füssen to the Inn valley. There were the routes from Frankfurt via Donauwörth and roads via Nuremberg. The most important of the eastern routes over the Alps was the Brenner pass. The Salzburg route came into favour after 1519, when a special road was built, and although it proved to be longer it was used because customs tolls were low. This changed in 1554 when higher customs duties were introduced at Kremsbrücke, and after 1587 further taxes were added.

The importance of long-distance trade routes depended on local Alpine fiscal policies. After 1604 the Tyrol road again had a distinct advantage. Equally, the road to Venice via Verona represented a long detour but it was cheaper because waterways could be used, thus balancing out longer distance by lower costs. All the east Alpine routes declined after 1530 compared with the Swiss routes, however. It was then that Venice forced all merchants who took their goods through Venetian territories to pass through customs at Verona, which caused transporters to avoid Venetian territories whenever possible, though Venice adjusted to these changes by improving the quality of roads between Bergamo and Chiavenna. Increased tolls demanded in Tyrol and Salzburg also had their effect.

(iii) Connections between the North Sea and the Baltic

In spite of increased use of the Sound, goods still went by land between Lübeck and Hamburg throughout the sixteenth century. Traffic only decreased when Hamburg introduced new customs dues, and Lübeck priced itself out of the market by asserting the right of staple in 1607; after a long dispute Hamburg was again given transit rights. After 1600 the over-riding consideration for Lübeck was to consolidate its declining trade by monopolistic sharp practices. The town council banned all foreigners from the transit trade, and the citizens tried to rely on the staple granted them by the Agreement of Odense in 1560. The result was that many traders used the longer route via the port of Neustadt. Hamburg also tried to control the land route from Lübeck by enforcing staple rights on the lower Elbe, and Hamburg soon became the leading North German entre-pôt. For geographical reasons Lübeck was unable to compete, for the North Sea soon began to rival the Baltic in economic importance. Even so, Lübeck continued to trade in English cloth from Emden via Itzehoe and also to import half-finished goods via the Sound for as long as they were exempted from Danish duty in the Sound. Lübeck exported powder, iron, ores and steel, as well as flax, wax, tallow, butter, tar and liver oil which came from Sweden and other Baltic countries. Lübeck also used the land route via Segeberg and Neumünster to supply the Dithmarschen market. This route was monopolized by Joachim Thiessen between 1559 and 1577 through his depots at Heide; Thiessen was also the chief importer of spars and rigging through Dithmarschen. Traffic via Kiel and Eckernförde to the Eider was also lively; there the traders of Rendsburg were most active. When Christian iv increased the Sound tolls, the Eckern-förde trade became an attractive alternative to Dutchmen and Hamburgers. Danish grain came to Eckernförde and was trans-shipped to Rendsburg and the west. Part of the Baltic transit trade to the west also went via Schleswig in the sixteenth century. Fish, iron and grain from the east was unloaded there and sent overland to Heide, Husum and other towns in the West.

In the sixteenth century Husum developed a flourishing transit trade with Flensburg. By mutual agreement Husum took its Baltic goods, especially Danzig grain, via Flensburg, and the latter used Husum as its North Sea outlet. Only when Flensburg tried to extend its staple rights at the expense of Husum did the system break down. One of the difficulties was that Flensburg and Eckernförde came under different ruling princes, each of whom had economic ambitions of his own. While the disagreements with Husum continued, the Flens-burgers transshipped at the Ockholmer Siel. But this was only a temporary measure, and it shows just how much local and terri-torial state rivalries could disrupt international trade. North Germany and Denmark were probably the most sensitive areas of central European long-distance trade. Any disturbance here could mean bankruptcy to a long-distance trader such as Heinrich Rantzau, who praised the port of Husum, where many goods could be found from Holland, Zeeland and even Scotland. These goods could easily be taken to Flensburg only five miles away and so transferred from the North Sea to the Baltic.

(iv) East central Europe
The Elbe provided a waterway from Bohemia to Hamburg. Although traffic was always hindered by many local customs dues, in 1570 the Habsburgs made strenuous efforts to arrange free passage on the Elbe and Moldava for direct trade with Prague from as far away as Scandinavia and the east Baltic. East of medieval Frankfurt-am-Main, Erfurt, Halle and Leipzig were the most important centres of the transit trade between the south, the west and the North Sea, and between the Baltic and the east. Routes from Nuremberg to the Baltic coast either went via Erfurt or via Wroclaw (Breslau) and Frankfurt-an-der-Oder. During the sixteenth century Leipzig managed to gain a lead, thanks to its central position for land and river trade and to the fact that in 1497 and 1507 the Emperor Maximilian I sold it the right to hold imperial fairs four times a year; this included rights to staple and entrepôt over the surrounding countryside. The chief trade routes of central Germany now converged on Leipzig, and the town negotiated with the appropriate territorial and state governments to keep open the high road from Russia, Poland and Silesia via Lausitz to Saxony and from there through Leipzig to Nuremberg in the south and to Frankfurt in the west. At Leipzig roads branched off to Bohemia and southwards to Vienna via the growing markets of Linz. Traffic from north-east Poland via Poznan and Fraustadt also joined this high road.

Leipzig opposed free passage on the Elbe, Oder, Havel and Spree as contrary to its own interests as an international entrepôt in the heart of central Europe. The town continued to draw other routes into its network of connections via Magdeburg and Lüneburg to Lübeck, Hamburg and Bremen. Yet Leipzig was never able entirely to suppress traffic along the old trade route which led from Lübeck to Hamburg and thence via Lüneburg, Brunswick and Erfurt directly to Nuremberg.

The rise of Leipzig led to rivalry from Frankfurt-an-der-Oder and Wroclaw, which combined in an attempt to blockade Leipzig by sending their goods directly to Stettin, Stralsund, Lübeck and Lauenburg instead of via Leipzig. Their efforts were supported by Brandenburg and Bohemia but faltered in the face of political opposition from Albertine Duke George of Saxony in 1513. In the ensuing blockade, Wroclaw was supported by Brandenburg and the Habsburgs against Saxony. The result was a stalemate in 1528, since Saxon counter-measures to safeguard its monopoly on the high road were never totally successful. In 1545 Nuremberg merchandise by-passed Leipzig and went via Prague to Breslau so as to reach the Baltic via the Oder. This route went via Cham and Plzen to Prague and from there to Sadowa, using the depression between the Riesen and Sudeten mountains to reach Wroclaw via Nachod and Glatz. It is therefore understandable that Emperor Ferdinand II showed such an interest in establishing Habsburg power in the Baltic and North Sea in the 1620s. Had he been able to secure the mouths of the Elbe and Oder, he would have controlled the economic life of north-east and east-central Germany from Austria and Bohemia in the south to Hamburg, Stralsund and Stettin in the north. This was the most important economic issue behind the Edict of Restitution in 1629, for Habsburg religious and economic interests were planned in unison and were only destroyed by the entry of the Swedes into the Thirty Years' War.

Farther east Cracow exercised the same pull as Leipzig. Its connections with Hungary increased after Turkish expansion and the subsequent division of Hungary had closed routes to the south and west. Hungarian metal products exported to the west now went via the Vistula or Ceský Tesine and Wroclaw to the Oder and from there to the Baltic. As these routes developed various supply routes over the Tatra and the Carpathians also improved. The old medieval trade route, which went from Constantinople via Brasov, Sibiu and Buda up the Danube to the west was destroyed after the 1540s by military and ideo-logical enmity between the Turks and Habsburgs in the eastern Alps and on the Hungarian plains. Its decline had started after the battle of Mohacs in 1526. The route shifted farther to the east and now went along the coast of the Black Sea via Brasov, Cluj, Košice, Novy Sacz and Cracow.

Another route went from northern Hungary via Zilina, the

Jablunka pass and Ceský Tesin to Silesia. Its growing importance is shown by the fact that the Fuggers set up an agency in
Ceský Tesin. However this route was no real rival to Cracow
since the river route via Cracow to Danzig was always the
cheapest and led to the best market contacts with the west.
When the Fuggers withdrew from Hungarian copper, numerous Augsburg firms were swift to make trade agreements with
Cracow: these allowed them to continue to take profits from
the copper trade now directed through the Baltic. When con-
sidering connections between Cracow and the Adriatic it is
worth noting that there was an Italian merchant community
in the town. Connections with Venice, for instance, were also
supported by colonies in Nuremberg, Prague and Vienna. From
north Hungary it was possible to send copper via various routes
to the north, east or south. As an export market for Hungarian
copper, Venice was as important as Cracow and Ceský Tesin.
Yet the Turkish conquests in the heart of Hungary tended to
force western trade eastwards and then northwards in a wide
Baltic detour from which the Poles and Dutch chiefly profited
after the 1540s.

Baltic trading links with Russia traditionally went via Novgorod, and Vitebsk, Smolensk, Pskov and Kaunas were internal
entrepôts for Russian trade westward. This trade was disrupted
when Ivan III in 1494 closed the Novgorod *comptoir* of the Hanseatic League and trade temporarily had to go via Finland,
Sweden and Lithuania. In 1514 the Livonian order obtained a
treaty to reopen the Novgorod *comptoir*, and subsequently Baltic
trade with Russia was concentrated more and more in the
Livonian towns of Riga, Reval and Dorpat. The volume of
European transit trade was small, because routes through
Russia were uneconomical and because connections to the
Black Sea at Rostov and Feodosia were frequently disrupted by
wars with the Tartars. During the sixteenth century, however,
Turkish merchants occasionally found their way to Russia with
luxury items such as pearls and silk goods from the Orient for
trans-shipment via the Baltic to north and west Europe.

After the collapse of the Livonian order Russia took possession of Narva and made efforts to organize some Baltic trade
via this port; the resulting opportunities were seized not only
by Lübeck but also by the English, the Dutch and the French.
In 1581 the Swedes took Narva over and Russia lost all direct

contact with the Baltic. Thereafter Russian trade went indirectly through Reval to Novgorod and Pskov, and the Hansa lost its former privileged position. Their embassy to Boris Godunov brought confirmation only of Lübeck's privileges. The new route to the west via Archangel, established by Richard Chancellor's expedition, transported Russian goods via the White Sea; it was crucial to the Russians whose sailings in the Baltic were disrupted by Swedes and Poles. The English received comprehensive privileges in the Arctic and were allowed to trade in Kazan, Astrakhan and as far as Persia.

After the loss of Narva, Russia based its foreign trade on Archangel, although the port was ice-bound for two-thirds of the year. From it the most important routes into Russia went via Moscow, which dominated the Russian economy from its position at the centre of a network of inland waterways. From the surrounding agricultural areas Moscow could support a large population and trade in dairy products, cattle, tallow, skins, leather, hemp and potash. The districts to the south supplied grain, and Siberia produced furs. Luxury oriental goods reached the capital via Kazan and Astrakhan, among them cottons, silk, gold and silver brocade, steel blades and precious stones such as turquoise, rubies and pearls. Moscow was the natural collecting-point for native Russian production and for trade in export goods shipped along the Dvina to Archangel. Moscovite inland and export trade were subject to strict government regulations.

Continually changing political conditions determined routes taken by export goods all over central Europe; this was especially so with Russian goods, whether they went via the Baltic or the White Sea. Russian linen and hemp exports, for example, always had to go through the Baltic ports because of their geographical proximity to the producing areas. Until the Volga region was conquered, Russian trade with Persia was of an occasional nature, but by the seventeenth century direct routes had been established, of mutual importance to the two states. Both countries recognized common interests against the Turks, whose dominance of the Black Sea and Asia Minor could not be broken and had therefore to be circumvented. The Russians traded with north Persia through Shemakha, Ghilan, Tabriz and Kashan. Persian trade with Russia was mainly conducted by Armenians who concentrated their attentions on Astrakhan and Povolshe. Russo-Persian trade extended to west Europe via Archangel; during the seventeenth century it was shared between the English and Dutch, especially after Isaak Massa had secured favourable conditions for the latter from Moscow in 1617.

2. TRADE

A. *France*

(i) Internal trade

By the sixteenth and early seventeenth centuries the internal trade of continental Europe was based on a sophisticated network of local markets, densest in the West and fanning out to become increasingly sparser farther to the east. Each township had its own local market and circle of local suppliers and producers at village and farm level. The larger the town and the greater its economic importance the farther these circles extended and the more they overlapped each other. With the rise of territorial governments, this marketing system was incorporated into the new mercantilist state and its budding national economy. As bullion theories became fashionable and, most important of all, shipping technology made favourable export balances an essential requirement of power politics, distinctions between internal and external trade and between planned and unplanned industrial and commercial growth became more and more absurd.

If one takes the example of France, to what extent can one speak of an internal trade network in the sixteenth century? Bad roads, inadequate transport, the variety of weights and measures all made difficulties for the exchange of goods inside the country, but in spite of this trade steadily increased. Yet it also fluctuated when, in order to secure food supplies, grain movements especially could be stopped in years of bad local harvests from travelling between provinces. A Valois edict of 1559 stated explicitly that local export in times of good harvests should be allowed, but should be forbidden when the harvest was bad. During the religious wars, however, such orders were frequently unenforceable.

In France there were various markets of national importance – Lyons and Paris of course, but also towns like Toulouse, with its due trade, and Rouen, quite apart from the sea ports. The fairs at Beaucaire in southern France were also significant.

(ii) Foreign trade

Where foreign trade was concerned most internal, regional, protectionist measures were a hindrance, as for instance when in 1539 the import of woollen goods from Spain and Rousillon, and sayette from Flanders was forbidden by the Valois. Gold and silver cloths, as well as silks, were all taxed by the crown at luxury rates at Lyons after 1540. In 1564 this was extended to all goods coming from Italy, and after 1585 to all goods from the Levant. After 1540 spices could only be imported into France if they came direct from their country of origin or from specific warehouses in Italy, Portugal and the east. A regulation of 1572 forbade the export of unfinished cloth and the import of the finished version. Import and export goods could always provide revenue to cover extraordinary state budgetary needs, as in France in 1577 and 1589. That much government time was taken up with economic affairs can be seen in the mass of petitions from individuals, corporations and Estates that survive in all the European archives. Fiscalism now began to exercise a crucial influence on European life.

France's trade connections with Italy are easily reconstructed by plotting the settlements of Italian merchants on a map. More Italians traded in sixteenth-century France than Frenchmen in Italy. The same is true for the Swiss and south Germans, who had privileged depots, particularly in Lyons. On the other hand French trade with Spain increased and was helped by numerous French trading colonies on the other side of the Pyrenees. Spain needed both the agricultural and manufactured products of France. There were also active trade links with the Netherlands, especially with Antwerp. Exchanges with England were lively – France could offer wine, fruit and grain, and England wool, cloth and metals.

Trade agreements with Denmark and Sweden in 1541–2 furthered French trade with Scandinavia. Although at first only about six French ships passed the Sound every year, by the 1590s this had increased to about sixty. Francis I's policy of friendship towards the Turks, allowing them access to Marseilles, was of great importance for French trade with the Levant. The first trading arrangements, made in 1528, were expanded to a trade agreement in 1536. Colonies were set up on the north African coast, and Alexandria, Algiers and Tunis became the main depots for French trade. Connections with

Morocco were maintained from Marseilles and even from the Normandy ports.

A series of ports, stretching from Bordeaux, Brouage, La Rochelle and Nantes to Saint-Malo, Honfleur, Dieppe and Rouen whose port at Le Havre was completed in 1547, competed for sea trade on the Atlantic coast. Eleven years later Calais was taken from the English, although its trade only became important later. Sea salt was an especially valuable export from Brouage and the Bay of Bourgneuf. La Rochelle exported the wines of Poitou, while Bordeaux shipped out Garonne wines as well as wood and dye-stuffs produced near Toulouse. From Brittany and Normandy linen goods were exported, mainly to the Iberian peninsula and the Mediterranean. Saffron from south France supplied the German market.

B. *The Empire*

(i) Internal trade

The early modern German economy was subject to considerable regional diversifications. The northern coastal belt was loosely controlled by the Hansa. In the west, the lower Rhine and Westphalia were closely connected with the Netherlands. Germany south of the Main and east central Germany were also regionally distinct. There was a lively exchange of goods both within and between the regions, based on a large number of well established markets and towns. Yet there was no central direction in the exchange of goods. Large-scale economic planning was hindered by the large number of territories, each exercising their own economic policy independently within the Empire. This aided the growth of different systems of weights, measures, coinage and customs dues on waterways and roads and often made a mockery of Germany's good system of natural internal communications. A complicated set of permits and escorts had to be obtained from each territorial authority to use any local road or waterway, and it was not easy to organize effective security with so many petty jurisdictions each responsible for their own strictly limited area.

The complexity of the internal market network can be seen from the role played by the great rivers as well as the great land routes in providing the large centres with foodstuffs and raw materials and with finished and half-finished goods. Via the rivers Oder, Elbe and Weser the sea ports were able to supply a deep hinterland, receiving their exports in return. Sea salt from Hamburg was sent to Brandenburg and Saxony in the second half of the sixteenth century and even, via the Havel and Spree, as far as Silesia. Wood and grain reached Hamburg via the Weser and road links from Westphalia. The Rhine connected Cologne with the largest west German economic area, which stretched as far as Switzerland. Its trade chiefly consisted of wine, timber and grain, going downstream, and fish, textiles and finished goods, which went upstream. South Germany traded its linens and fustians across Lake Constance, down the Danube and the Lech. Ulm was connected by its iron and wine trade with the Neckar area and the Upper Palatinate. Augsburg was the most important centre of trade south of the Danube, and in Franconia Nuremberg held first place. East central German linen was dyed in Nuremberg, which also worked tin from Saxony, copper from the Harz and Bohemia and obtained calamine for making brass from the Aachen area. Regensburg was the most important trade centre on the German stretch of the Danube and acted as entrepôt for trade between south-west Germany and Austria.

Urban fairs played an important part in German internal trade. The Frankfurt fairs were the highlight of Wetterau and Hesse trade. The chief fairs in the south were at Worms, Strasbourg, Zŭrzach and Nördlingen. Yet the Nuremberg Heiltum fair never established itself, and the Allhallows fair at Würzburg was only of local importance. Like those at Frankfurt, the Leipzig fairs were the centre of a trade that extended far beyond Saxony to north-west and north Germany. Leipzig overshadowed Erfurt, Magdeburg and Halle and was in sharp rivalry with Brunswick. Only the Peter and Paul fair in Naŭmbŭrg and perhaps those at Frankfurt-an-der-Oder, Wroclaw and Danzig competed in any way with the Leipzig fairs. Rights of staple were of crucial economic importance in the sixteenth century and were increasingly used by territorial rulers as part of their mercantilist economic planning. Administrative territorial capitals such as Munich were especially favoured by rulers and became an important new element in the German economy.

(ii) Foreign trade

German foreign trade depended on a range of land, river and sea routes from the North Sea and Baltic to the Alps, the Adriatic and Ligurian Sea. Two of Europe's largest rivers, the Rhine and the Danube, played a crucial role in German north-south and east-west trade. Yet compared with west Europe, land-locked Germany had obvious geographical disadvantages, which hastened the decline of the Hanseatic League as a political as well as an economic organization. Receiving insufficient support from Emperor and Empire, the Hanseatic cities found their special economic and foreign trading policies progressively weakened by the new nation states near by. That the Hanseatic cities had become Protestant did not endear them to Habsburg politicians in Brussels, Vienna and Madrid. The Hanseatic towns had to seek alliances with neighbouring territorial rulers who had often been their greatest political and economic rivals: the towns of Mecklenburg, Wismar and Rostock turned to their ruling princes in order to survive economically, and Danzig joined forces with Poland in 1466, on the understanding that membership of the Hanseatic League would be retained.

Although Hanseatic trade declined drastically in the sixteenth century, that of certain individual towns increased. Hamburg's ascendancy began as world trade moved towards the Atlantic and North Sea coasts and as sailings to Spain and Portugal increased. Whereas Hanseatic Lübeck declined, Hanseatic Hamburg flourished – a fate determined by the geographical position of the two towns. At the end of the sixteenth century the trader Heinrich Rantzau called the town of Hamburg *florentissimum emporium totius Germaniae*. This prosperity was largely built up by immigrants who brought their trading skills from England, Holland, Spain and Portugal. Hamburg opened her own Exchange only four years after Antwerp, and the town's central position in the German money market became clear when the first Girobank was opened there with the help of the immigrant merchant community in 1619. Even so, Hamburg had local rivals in Danish-controlled Glückstadt which held customs controls on part of the lower Elbe. Conditions for Hamburg were at their most favourable during the Thirty Years' War, when it became the greatest money market in north-west Germany for the Swedes and Dutch. Trading circles in Lübeck remained strongly traditional, and as their geographical position made direct activity more difficult they diversified into underwriting and commissionary and forwarding trade, although without the same success as Hamburg.

Bremen, the second Hanseatic town to flourish amid the general decline, had trade connections all over the North Sea and also took part in Baltic trade. In the second half of the sixteenth century, Emden briefly profited from dislocations in Dutch trade caused by the revolt against Spain. For a short time Emden harboured the largest northern fleet trading with the Baltic and Spain. But increasingly the Swedes dominated the Baltic, and north Germany was the main sufferer. Though trade with Russia via the Baltic never came to a complete standstill, it depended on political considerations outside the control of German traders. At the same time, new opportunities for direct trade offered themselves via the route north of Scandinavia to Archangel, which Hamburg and Flensburg attempted to use in competition with English and Dutch traders.

Hanseatic monopolies had perhaps been strongest in Denmark and, above all, in Norway, but by the sixteenth century they were steadily being eroded. German merchants were chiefly interested in herring-fisheries off Scania and Limfjord and in Danish grain. German traders passing through the Sound paid full tax dues and no longer received favoured nation treatment, unlike Holland and later, Sweden. Even so, the Hansa retained its monopoly at Bergen up to the Thirty Years' War. From Bergen, Hanseatic merchants even traded in Icelandic fish and sulphur. Later in the seventeenth century Hamburg shared a monopoly on this trade with Glückstadt.

In England, the Tudor monarchy curtailed Hanseatic monopolies granted under Edward IV and also encouraged its own Merchant Adventurers to circumvent Hanseatic home ports whenever possible. The Hansa formally expelled the Merchant Adventurers by imperial decree, but this led to counter-measures in London and East Anglia. Groups of German merchants still welcomed contacts with English cloth merchants in various German ports, but the days when Germans dictated the terms of trade were gone. The Hansa steel-yard in London closed after losing its last privileges in 1650.

Dutch–German trade increased despite official rivalries with the Hanseatic League. More Dutch ships sailed to Danzig and

Hamburg than to any other destination. In Danzig they were attracted by Polish and Prussian raw materials, and in Hamburg a large Dutch colony kept up a lively trade. Yet German sea trade with France did not really become important until the seventeenth century, and Iberian trade only came to Germany when Spanish hostilities closed the Dutch and English ports. When in 1621 war broke out between the United Provinces and Spain, German sea ports again benefited. The occasional German boat even visited the Turkish ports. During the Mediterranean food shortages in the 1590s, grain was even taken overland via Germany and the Alps, although most of it was shipped around Europe from Poland and Amsterdam. The land routes to Milan and Venice remained vital to the south German textile and luxury trades. Strict limits were set on German sailings to Africa, America and Asia by the mercantile colonial policies of the Spaniards, Portuguese and later by those of the Dutch. Sailings from Hamburg to Brazil via Lisbon started up, half legitimate and half secret, but profits remained very much in Portuguese hands. With the consent of the Spanish Court German trade was also conducted with America via the Andalusian port of Seville. The Welsers and other Augsburg entrepreneurs were heavily committed to the opening up of America in the early sixteenth century.

(iii) The great merchant houses

The early sixteenth century, which traditional historians have called the era of early capitalism, was a great time for the merchant family firm in south Germany. This was particularly true for Augsburg, where the Fuggers, Welsers, Paumgartners and Höchstetters were all active. In Nuremberg traded the Imhoffs and Tuchers and another branch of the Welsers. The Besserers lived in Ulm, and the Zangmeisters dominated Memmingen. Until 1530 there was also the great Ravensburg Company, which had connections with Italy, especially Venice, and also with south France, Spain, the Netherlands and east Europe. When the international spice market moved from Venice to Lisbon and Antwerp, the merchants of Augsburg and Nuremberg adapted to the new conditions. For a while they were successful, and south Germans played an important part in the spice market at Antwerp until the Revolt of the Netherlands. They also succeeded in obtaining a temporary hold on

Iberian trade with America, Africa and Asia. The Fuggers had shares in the early development of mineral resources in the Spanish colonies. Yet it was trade with Italy that remained of fundamental importance to the welfare of German merchant firms. Augsburg gradually moved into banking, providing credit for ruling dynasties like the Habsburgs. The Spanish financial crises in 1557, 1575 and 1607, when payments to creditors were suspended and the bankruptcy of the French government were heavy blows to the Fugger banking concerns from which they never fully recovered. The merchant house of Welser, south Germany's second largest, went bankrupt in 1614 and left a gap that successors such as Österreicher or Koch in Memmingen could not fill adequately.

Nuremberg was less skilled than Frankfurt in utilizing immigrant labour. The vested interests of guilds hampered industrial and commercial growth, as exemplified at Cologne, which forbade Italian and Dutch expansion within its walls. In Nuremberg a branch of the Welser family was active, as were the Ebner and Fürer concerns and later the Schwendendörfer, Viatis and Peller houses; they were all interested in finance and trade in textiles and minerals. But instead of actually trading on their own account, these merchants turned more and more to commission and the forwarding trade, linking their business with the fairs of Leipzig and Frankfurt-am-Main. In 1621 Nuremberg established its own *Banco Publico* which, however, did not prosper as well as the earlier Hamburg Giro-bank.

The early seventeenth century saw the general decline of most German towns as international trade moved away from central Europe to the periphery of the Continent. The most lucrative area of trade, in minerals, had been dominated by the firms of south and west Germany. In the Aachen area the van Richterghens married into the Schetz family and took a leasehold interest in the Altenberge calamine trade which lasted until the second half of the sixteenth century. In Leipzig many firms were of south German origin, among them Pufler from Isny, Lebzelter from Ulm and Schwendendörfer from Nuremberg. On the Baltic the Loitz firm, which was based in Stettin, soon over-speculated and went bankrupt. Despite the long-term success of a few famous families, most trading firms were extremely unstable enterprises. During the century important Flemish firms, whose great strength lay in their international connections, also succeeded in building up great undertakings in Germany. The best examples are those of Uffeln in Hamburg and their kinsmen, Bodeck, in Frankfurt. Of the Italian firms in Germany, the Wertemanns from Piuro concentrated their business in Nuremberg and at the Habsburg court. The Iberian Ximenes group and Rodrigues d'Evora operated from Cologne for a time and then transferred to Hamburg.

c. *The Swiss Confederation*

The Swiss acted as intermediaries for trade from France, Germany and Italy. Their own prosperity was founded on the export of dairy products, textiles and mercenary soldiers. The most important trading centres were Basle, St Gallen and Geneva. Basle, which had colonies of Italians and Dutch, was officially an imperial town until 1648 and acted as a banking centre as well as a textile producer. Among the immigrants, Socin, Perez, Servauter, Battier, the Pellizari and the Wertemanns were most important. In St Gallen, however, the linen trade was monopolized by native townsmen, led by the Zollikofers. Hans Heinrich Lohmann of Zürich ran a textile and salt business of international standing. The refugees who had settled in Geneva also helped the town to gain an international trading position at a time when its fairs were declining. Important were the Pellizari and Turrettini from Lucca; the Diodati, Micheli, Balbani, Burlamachi, Minutoli, Calandrini and Trochin from Lyons; the Thelluson and des Gouttes from France; and the Sarasin and Delarue from Flanders.

d. *East central Europe*

Minerals, textiles and cattle were the most important exports of the eastern alpine area, Bohemia-Moravia, Slovakia and Hungary. This trade was totally reorganized by the Habsburgs as they gained control of the area in the sixteenth century. The close proximity of the Turks constantly endangered trade in their lands. Parts of Hungary and of Slovakia went their own way under Turkish suzerainty, and frontier towns which had been orientated towards the Hungarian plain, such as Wiener Neustadt, tended to lose out to less vulnerable centres such as Linz. In south Tirol the fairs at Bolzano served Italian trade, and apart from Innsbruck in the north Tirol, Hall was the centre for the salt trade and for transport between the rivers Inn and Danube and the Italian plain. On the Tauern route, Salzburg retained its trading importance. In the interior of Austria, at Graz, Judenburg, Villach, Klagenfurt, Ljubljana and Pfuj, long-distance trade was chiefly in the hands of south Germans and Italians. The Linz fairs were used by merchants from Memmingen, Isny, Augsburg, Nuremberg, Salzburg and Venice, as well as by iron merchants from Judenburg. Iron from Innerberg was an important item of trade. Scythes and sickles from Kirchdorf-Micheldorf were also exported. Much of the trade of Linz went on a north-south axis, linking Poland and Silesia with Italy, via Bohemia and Austria. Farther down the Danube trade from Krems was directed north-eastwards, linking up with Wroclaw and Cracow.

The proximity of the Turkish frontier hampered Vienna's trade in the sixteenth century. Until the 1520s merchants from Swidnica, Neisse, Olomouc, Brno, Kutna Hora and Jihlava had brought herrings, tin, leather and especially cloth to Vienna, where they sold them in exchange for Italian goods such as figs, oil, almonds, grapes, wine, glass, sulphur, alum, as well as Styrian iron and tartar, used in dyeing and textile printing. Cinnamon, pepper and other spices from Venice, however, were already by-passing Vienna, travelling due north via Salzburg or Linz and Freistadt.

During the 1520s merchants from Wiener Neustadt also enjoyed a brief but lively cloth trade with Bohemia and Silesia. Cloth from Jihlava was cheap and of low quality and much sought after. In the fifteenth century Wiener Neustadt had become an important market in competition with Vienna. The Habsburgs granted it special freedom from customs duties and gave it staple rights for all Austrian and Hungarian wines. These liberties were extended in the brief period of Matthias Corvinus' rule, and in 1487 Wiener Neustadt obtained staple rights for all Hungarian trade. The town also retained the staple for all Styrian iron sent via the Semmering pass. Wiener Neustadt trade now dominated the west Hungarian counties of Vasvar and Sopron, reaching as far as Buda and Bratislava. Hungarian trade thus did not have to depend on Vienna for its western outlet, although the Turkish conquest of the Hungarian plain destroyed Wiener Neustadt as an international trading centre.

The Turkish destruction of western Hungary in 1529 and 1532

led to many bankruptcies among trading firms in Lower Austria. The investments that were left drained out of the country, mainly to south Germany, Nuremberg and Augsburg, where Austrian patricians were assured of safer returns on their capital.

Bohemian trade, which was based on haberdashery, metals and cattle, was essential to Nuremberg in the sixteenth century. From the 1520s, however, it was increasingly concentrated on Prague. Between 1520 and 1550, forty-five Nuremberg firms had business connections with Prague, but apart from Nützel and Welser these were small concerns active in the cattle trade; however the total volume of business they generated was large. The Nurembergers controlled the flow of credit to Prague. According to an early Czech–German guidebook compiled by Andreas Klatovsky in 1544, the Nurembergers gave Prague merchants buying wholesale in Nuremberg credit at a rate of 56·3 per cent. This outbid any other foreign merchants and assured that Prague was supplied almost exclusively from Nuremberg. But when trade in Bohemian metals decreased after 1580 the hold of Nuremberg finance over Prague declined. Prague wholesale trade was so buoyant that it now began to by-pass Nuremberg without going bankrupt. Competitors began to arrive from Italy, from the Rhineland, the Netherlands and Hamburg.

Plzen shared in the rising prosperity of Prague, for most of the transit trade to south Germany went via the town. It was the cattle trade above all that led to its prosperity in the sixteenth century. Cattle were herded through Bohemia to Nuremberg from Hungary and Poland. The Primda customs tolls on cattle between 1540 and 1560 came to an average of 5,500 talers a year, corresponding to an annual transit of about 18,000 oxen. This is not the total figure, as there were also numerous smaller collecting points. In 1538 Ferdinand I imposed new taxes on cattle exported from Habsburg lands which hit the Nuremberg merchants especially hard. The customs dues at Plzen were fixed at seven Bohemian Groschen per ox in 1557 and the maximum size of single herds at 600 oxen and 1,000 pigs annually per operator for transit to Nuremberg. Five Plzen firms ran this trade in the first half of the sixteenth century and became the richest citizens, with their own factory in Nuremberg.

After the Hungarian plain was conquered by the Turks, south-west Slovakia became the most important district for the

export of cattle to the Austrian and Czech areas. Cattle merchants moved into Trnava and Bratislava and a main route
went to Stupava and via the Morava. By 1600 between 7,000
and 8,000 oxen were driven each year through customs at
Stupava towards the markets of the west, but by the second
decade of the seventeenth century the number was down to
about 2,500 to 3,000 per year. This was due to factors like the
devastation caused by Bocskay's rebellion in the years 1603–6.
Thereafter dealers from Bratislava moved into the foreground
as exporters. Cattle were moved in the summer and autumn
months, those of finest quality coming from Turkish Hungary,
the Tisa district and as far away as Transylvania. The best
drovers were Slovaks in the north and Croats in the south-west
and they serviced the most important cattle markets at Senec
and Trnava. Ranching was organized on a large scale by the
great landowners on the Hungarian plains. Their produce was
supported with western capital finance and, like the grain
growers of Poland, the Hungarians produced for export. The
Puszta was turned over to grazing, and many peasant farms and
villages disappeared. In the sixteenth century there were large
ranches with up to 10,000 oxen each. In 1646 the town of
Szeged had a herd of nearly 9,000 cattle on the *Puszta*. Although
the war between the Turks and Habsburgs of 1591–1606
resulted in great damage, the Hungarian cattle trade recovered
quickly. Ranching was particularly attractive to landlords, who
avoided land-taxes, and to tenants, who earned enough to buy
themselves free of serfdom and labour service. The total number
of fattening cattle in Hungary between 1550 and 1650 has been
estimated at several hundred thousand. The major markets
were in Austria, Moravia and south Germany through to
Vienna, Nuremberg, Frankfurt and Strasbourg. Italy and
Venice were also supplied from Hungary. Turkish wars and
cattle diseases only disrupted exports temporarily; this happened between 1549 and 1551 when south Germany received no
Hungarian meat, although nearly 200,000 Hungarian oxen
were still sold on the Viennese market. On average up to
50,000 Hungarian oxen per year were sold in the mid-sixteenth
century, and as late as 1624 Augsburgers complained that they
could no longer buy their cattle directly in Hungary as they
had always done before. For German dealers the most reliable
markets for cattle were in Moravia.

Hungarian cattle-breeders were often also dealers, although the export trade was conducted through Hungarian customs by professional drovers or *tözser*, who plied to Vienna and Hustopeče. These cattle-dealers were organized into guilds and traded either on their own account or in companies. They lived in the border towns and villages between Habsburg and Turkish Hungary at Trnava, Gjör, Magyaróvár, Debrecen and Keczkemét. Cattle-dealers were mainly of rural origin, sometimes from the lesser nobility, but were usually native Hungarians. Magnates who controlled border areas also took part in cattle-trading, often as factors. Very few burghers from Hungarian towns were actively engaged in the cattle trade. The staples in Vienna and Hustopeče benefited Hungarian cattle-traders, who thereby controlled prices and prevented any direct access by German and Italian traders to producers on the plains. Large-scale firms such as that of Sebastian Thököly, whose descendants rose high in the aristocracy, exported up to 6,000 cattle per year.

At the end of the fifteenth century Hungary exported slightly more to Italy than to Austria and south Germany. The situation changed completely in the 1530s because of the Turkish advance. Exports of copper and cattle gave the Hungarians a very favourable trade balance despite the hostilities. By 1500 a considerable number of merchants in Buda were Italians, at first mainly Florentines but later also Venetians. They monopolized luxury textile imports. Articles exported to Italy were copper and cattle and Hungarian currency. Cheaper Italian cloths, and after the 1520s more expensive ones too, were also imported by German merchants in Buda with the help of their compatriots. Unlike the German immigrants, the Italians, who retained their original citizenship, played no part in the town council politics of Buda. These were dominated by the Germans patriciate, which was composed of immigrants originally from south Germany and Austria and, after the 1550s, from native Hungary.

At the beginning of the sixteenth century Hungary's foreign trade was estimated to have been worth 1,330,000 Gulden a year. Although most of this came from trade with the west, connections with the Ottoman Empire became increasingly valuable. Textiles and finished metal goods imported from the west went farther southwards, and in return came, among other things, Turkish textiles and luxury goods. A negative balance of trade was redressed by the export of minerals and cattle. Copper exported as raw material and gold cast as gulden played a very important part. As well as cattle, wine and agricultural products were exported. Thus despite the political disaster the Turkish conquests represented, the Hungarian economy continued to flourish throughout the sixteenth and seventeenth century.

Large landowners who concentrated on the export of iron, timber and wine played an important part in Hungarian export trade, and some, like the Zrinyis, also dealt in imports. The Zrinyi lands reached from the Adriatic ports to properties north of the Danube, where they held dairy farms in the Mur-Au district to the south and east of Vienna. Most Zrinyi farms were let to peasants and the family estates were self-sufficient in grain, supplying the army and extensive mining populations. Native wine was sold in state- and family-controlled taverns, and taxes were levied on consumption. A zone almost 100 kilometres in length along the Dalmatian coast belonged to the Zrinyi family. At Chabar annual exports of 3,000 hundredweight were recorded. To these must be added Dalmatian naval products such as spars, beams, and oars. The timber stores at Bakar alone were worth 12,000 Venetian zecchini and sea salt was a major import, storage and warehousing providing a capacity of 70,000 hundredweight. There was also trade in textiles, olive oil and majolicas of Italian origin.

Serf labour services were used for dock and transport work. Peasants on the domains at Grobnik transported iron goods of 170 tons yearly from Chabar to the Adriatic. The Zrinyis alone disposed of the labour of over 4,000 serf families, and their profits from the transport industry in Dalmatia amounted to about 150,000 gulden a year. Often it was the Zrinyis and not the imperial government who defended Croatia and Slavonia from the Turks. They kept a private army fully armed against the Turks and on the majority of their properties between 20 and 30 per cent of the lord's income was devoted to military purposes. They controlled wholesale and foreign trade in their part of the country and disposed of huge sums of money. These, however, did not become trading capital, because the greater part was swallowed up by military expenses as marcher lords in Habsburg service. The Slavonian estates of Alexander Mikulich were engaged in industrial production, and profits were hoarded, eventually being spent on luxuries or used for further lending. The estate of Stephan Czaky in the Tokaj wine district was smaller than any Zrinyi tenancy, but its vineyards were sufficient to support an aristocrat. Czaky's demesne vineyards were cultivated by paid labour and the profit he made as landlord was worth nearly 25 per cent of his total income. Taxes on vineyards rented to serfs made up 58 per cent of his total stock of wine, and he bought a further 17 per cent in the local market. Of this, a quarter was exported and 40 per cent sold in the local taverns. Czaky made profits of between 600 and 1000 per cent on these transactions. Landlord Czaky only produced a fraction of the volume of wine exported from northern Hungary, but even he could count on a pure trading profit of 15,000 gulden from one good wine harvest.

The regular export of wine to Poland from northern Hungary was an important part of the export trade. According to the customs receipts of 1610 and 1611, annual exports reached to 30,000 barrels, valued at about 1,000,000 gulden, equivalent to 50,000 head of cattle. Hungarian landlords usually allowed the peasants to farm the land, and demesne farming was strictly limited to the lord's own needs, although it was extended more and more to satisfy the export industry in wine and livestock.

E. *Poland and Lithuania*

Poland and Lithuania were important suppliers of primary products to western Europe. Above all they produced grain, timber, cattle, furs, resin, tar, potash and pitch for export. In the 1550s grain, timber and cattle exports formed 90 per cent of the total and 80 per cent of all Polish exports went via Danzig. The importance of Elbing was only temporary when it was the staple of the Eastland Company. Among imports from the west, textiles made up 60 per cent, luxury goods and bullion the rest.

Most of the grain went down the Vistula to Danzig. But furs and cattle went by land routes in the interior of Poland, linking the Ukrainian-Moldavian steppes with the west, well away from Tartar hostility and warfare. The north-western trade route went from Vilna, Mogilev and Brest Litovsk to Warsaw, Gniezno, Poznan and Leipzig. Cheap furs were crucial exports on this route. The south-western trade route went via Vladimir, Lvov, Jaroslaw, Przeworski, Kazimierz near Cracow and Brzeg to Leipzig. This was the cattle route, but both routes serviced the Lublin fairs held three times every year. The merchants of Poland and Lithuania congregated at Lublin and Brzeg and delivered the export goods destined for west Europe via Danzig and Leipzig. Price differences between Danzig and Amsterdam show how large the profits from Polish trade and freight were. The wholesale price for rye on the Amsterdam Exchange between 1597 and 1647 was on average nearly 50 per cent higher than in Danzig. In retail prices there was a difference of 35 per cent. Shipping was western-owned and the Danzigers went in for warehousing and internal trade often as agents for the Dutch.

Grain exports gave Poland a positive trade balance up to the seventeenth century, but the country nonetheless had a net outflow of precious metals. Many theories were forwarded to explain this; one was that Poland lost its western bullion imports to the countries farther east. Polish economists and statesmen were convinced that from about 1600 there was a positive balance in sea trade and a negative balance in trade with Turkey. Calculations are made difficult, however, by the fact that Poland to a large extent played the part of middleman in trade overland between east and west, while at the same time losing much of the handling profits to western transporters and shippers.

F. *Russia*

From the sixteenth century onwards Russian trade increased considerably thanks to greater production and the expansion of the money economy. Taxes in money forced peasants to farm with a view to producing surpluses to sell at market. But the great expanse of Muscovy meant that its internal trade, compared with that of European countries to the west, was itself the equivalent of another export trade. Furs, salt and fish came from Siberia through Ustjiny and Vologda in return for finished metal goods and textiles. The towns of the central area, including Moscow, were important grain markets which also supplied the north and east. Trade from the south went via the towns of the Volga and through Nijni Novgorod (Gorki), Jaroslaw, and Kazan and Astrakhan, towns recently conquered by the Tartars.

During the sixteenth century Moscow became Russia's chief centre of trade, and merchants from all over the Empire had colonies there. A bazaar for foreigners operated twice weekly, and west Europeans coming via Archangel and merchants from Poland and Lithuania, Siberia and Central Asia met here. In the north-west of Muscovy there were markets in the border towns of Pskov and Novgorod, which had however lost their former glory and been partly replaced by other towns farther inland, such as Smolensk and Vijasma. After its capture, Astrakhan became the entrepôt for the south-east.

As well as the proper towns (*gorodi*), there were marketing centres called *possadi* and markets in villages near the monasteries and on large estates. Large landowners could force their peasants to bring goods to a specified market. All ranks and orders of society took part in trade – peasants, monks, clergy, Boyars and even the Tsar. But Russian townsmen did not develop the same laws and privileges over property, production and movement as the burghers of the west and centre of the continent. Craft industries were also far less developed in Russian urban centres than in those of the centre and west of Europe. At the end of the sixteenth century 44 per cent of the population at Tula were merchants and 75 per cent of the total population lived from trade including flourishing small shops. In Tula 93 per cent, and in Nijni Novgorod (Gorki) 75 per cent of the merchants only had one booth. In Tula 20 per cent of the shops were in the hands of serfs, 30 per cent in the hands of soldiers, and the proportion of soldiers rose even more during the seventeenth century. Large landowners also engaged in trade, among them Boyar Morosov and Princes Cherkassy and Pojarsky. Prince Varotinsky bought satin, silk and other costly textiles in Archangel and in return sold grain, fish, pigs, birds, butter and meat in his warehouses in Moscow. He employed more than a hundred men in his trading ventures. But the largest enterprise was that of the state, the Tsar's own *Kasna* or exchequer, which exercised the right of first purchase on all imports. Imported goods were sold under licence in state ships. On the export side, the exchequer held monopolies on furs, especially sable and salt, which was a state industry. The same applied to the export of caviar, silk and, surprisingly, rhubarb. Despite the Tsar's mercantilist controls – only licensed merchants were to engage in trade – there were many interlopers. Regulations against foreigners in the retail trade were more effective, although in the middle of the seventeenth century there were complaints that Swedes and Lübeckers were retailing in Novgorod and Dutchmen in Vologda.

The *gosti* were the chief merchants in the towns and came under strict regulation. The administration of customs tolls, fisheries and salt-pans belonging to the state was under their control, and they rented the state-owned trade of Siberia. They were the Tsar's chief agents in matters of trade, developing links with Persia, India and Sweden. Kochkin, the great iron merchant in Novgorod, set up a colony in Stockholm, but outside Russia prejudice ran high against Russian merchants, and they were considered cunning and grasping and accused of selling their wares for up to twenty times their worth. No doubt there was an element of envy in this.

The Stroganovs developed extensive trading activities on their estates, which stretched from the Kama to Siberia, and exported salt and minerals produced on their own lands. As yet there was no great specialization in trade. Butter, iron, hay, footwear and weapons were all handled by the same merchant, and wholesale and retail trade were carried on alternately. In Nijni Novgorod (Gorki) forty-eight wholesale merchants, who controlled trade on the Volga also owned fifteen small shops for retail trade in the town.

After Russia had closed the Hanseatic *comptoir* at Novgorod, connections with other western powers were developed. In 1516 a trade treaty was made with Denmark. Yet Russian trade often lacked the training and initiative needed for profit. When the Germans were driven out, the English had a great opportunity in Russian trade. In August 1553 an English ship tied up in Kholmogory, a small port on the White Sea. Richard Chancellor, the leader of the expedition, went to Moscow at the Tsar's request, where he was well received. In 1555 the English trading company on whose behalf Chancellor had undertaken the journey received privileges, which laid down certain places where these trade exchanges were to take place and specified the rights of the English merchants. Instead of Kholmogory, Archangel developed into the main port of the White Sea. This port, however, had the disadvantage of being free of ice for only three to four months each year. Yet the English were so successful in their White Sea voyages that their privileges were extended by the Tsar in 1564, and they were allowed to set up colonies in Vologda and Moscow. After 1557 they made contact along the Volga with Persia and also traded indirectly with Russia via the Baltic ports of Dorpat and Narva. But in the Baltic the Moscovy Company came into competition with the Eastland Company, winning when in 1569 its privileges were again extended. The Moscovy Company was freed from customs dues as far as the border with Persia via Astrakhan and set up craft industries, even minting English coins in Russia.

Ivan IV hoped that the English crown would ally with him against Sweden and Poland; when this did not occur, the Tsar withdrew trading privileges in 1570, only to re-issue them in 1572 under less favourable terms. From then on the English had to pay half of all customs dues and were forbidden to trade directly with Persia. Boris Godunov reinstated their previous wide-ranging privileges in 1586 and gave permission for English courts to be established in Moscow, Jaroslav, Vologda, Kholmogory and Archangel. The English built iron forges and rope works in Kholmogory and Vologda, where their profits were estimated at 20 per cent between 1566 and 1581; a trip to Persia made a profit of 108 per cent. Dutch competition soon reduced profitability however. English imports to Russia consisted mainly of linen, lead, copper, tin, sulphur and armaments, as well as luxury goods for the Tsars and Boyars. Exports consisted of wax, butter, fat, furs, hemp, flax, salted meat and fish. Some Russian goods such as wax, fats and honey were expensive as they were a state monopoly. Grain was only exported on exceptional occasions, as for instance in 1597, and was never a significant item. In 1606 the English privileges were renewed by Dimitri but also by the Swedish puppet-Tsar Shuisky, who in 1617 further granted them until 1645. The English Civil War seems to have caused the Tsar to cancel the exemptions from customs dues and in 1649 English merchants were finally banned from Russia.

The Dutch also succeeded in getting a footing in Russia and the first Dutch ship sailed round the North Cape in 1564. In Holland a company was formed for Russian trade but because of English resistance it was a long time before the Dutch obtained permission to trade directly with Russia. Various companies were formed with government support, however, and in 1647 a trading agreement was reached. The subsequent expulsion of the English gave the Dutch decisive advantages and they set up colonies in Moscow, Vologda, Kholmogory,

Archangel, Kola, Jaroslav and Pskov. German trade to Russia went indirectly, usually via the Livonian towns of Riga, Reval and Dorpat, and Lübeck profited by trading rights through Swedish-controlled Narva after 1581. Yet indirect trade always increased the ultimate price to consumers. A land route for Russian trade to Leipzig was even developed in spite of difficulties caused by the Thirty Years' War.

Russia had almost no direct trade with France, especially since the Dutch acted as middlemen. Yet Dieppe traders had already plied Russian ports by the beginning of the sixteenth century. In 1587 an association of Parisian merchants signed an agreement which allowed them to trade in Archangel, Vologda, Novgorod, Pskov, Jaroslav and Moscow at half the usual customs dues, and in 1607 a merchant from La Rochelle even loaned Tsar Dimitri three thousand roubles. The Parisian merchants soon prevailed on their government to send an embassy to Russia to obtain favourable trading conditions. The year 1629 marked the high point of Russo-French contacts, after which direct trade increasingly lapsed.

Tartar merchants dealt in oriental goods and in horses, and the main connections with the Orient were via Persia. According to Venetian accounts, there were already three hundred Russian merchants in Tabriz in 1475, and merchants from Tver were already trading in India. In Moscow Persian trade was often in Armenian hands and it increased with the conquests of Ivan the Terrible. Russian merchants also opened up trade to Walachia via the Crimea and Black Sea, and from there to Hungary and Germany, whenever relations with the Turks allowed. Russian merchants were also active in Constantinople and Bursa.

Western Europeans had tried to reach Russia by direct trade routes that were free from Scandinavian and Turkish control, and to a large extent the English and Dutch achieved this during the sixteenth century. From Boris Godunov's time onwards a number of semi-permanent foreign embassies were established at the Tsar's Court with the specific task of obtaining better facilities for trade. Yet Russia's direct participation in European trade was still very slight, and she was not politically strong enough to assert herself in the Baltic and on the Black Sea during this period. Direct access was only available for four months of the year via Archangel.

G. *Scandinavia*

Sweden's participation in the international exchange of goods was relatively limited because of its rather peripheral position isolated from the rest of Europe. Imports for Stockholm, Gävle and Söderköping in 1559 show that salt made up nearly a quarter and hops nearly 19 per cent of the total. Textiles provided the lion's share, with 35 per cent, and spices led in the luxury trade for wealthy burghers, court and nobility. Chief exports were iron (29 per cent), fats (25 per cent), skins, hides and furs (22 per cent). Among iron exports *osmund* (Swedish bar iron) was of prime importance, and other iron exports only amounted to 5 per cent of the total. Of the fats, bacon pork (17·5 per cent of the total) was the most important. Copper amounted to only 6 per cent, flour and grain took up 4 per cent and finished wood products 12 per cent.

The export trade was still mainly in the hands of foreigners, and the basic policy of Gustavus Vasa's government was that foreigners should fetch their goods and pay export duty to the crown. He was eager to encourage west European trade, especially with the Dutch and Scots, in order to break the monopoly of German merchants, especially those of Lübeck and Danzig, in the Swedish export trade. In this he was only partially successful, and Sweden's trade into the North Sea only really developed in the seventeenth century. In 1571 Stockholm's North Sea trade was only 5 per cent of the total, though it had risen to 32 per cent by 1620. The Dutch share of total Swedish exports was 27 per cent. Not until the later seventeenth century did Gothenburg begin to dominate the Swedish export trade in the North Sea.

Denmark's rôle in international trade was at first characterized by determined efforts to reduce the influence of German seaports. The Edict of Odense in 1560 was a first step in this direction; it placed restrictions on the Hansa in Danish ports and allowed the Danes reciprocal status in Hanseatic ports. Under Christian iv, the Hansa tried in vain to have their privileges restored but these finally lapsed in 1622. In 1541 a trade agreement was made with France and at the same time a convoy sailed to Russia. Salt, which had previously come from Lüneburg via Lübeck, was now brought from the Bay of Biscay. From the 1550s onwards at least twenty boats a year sailed from Denmark to France, Spain and Portugal. It was the Dutch, however, who dominated shipping between the North Sea and the Baltic. They disputed the main part of the Danish king's sound tolls, and by the treaty of Speyer in 1544 they obtained equal rights with the Hansa. The Dutch worked on a large scale and on the whole co-operated well with Danish merchants, who were loaned capital and hired as agents. In that way the Danish merchant received a basic training from the Dutch and in time began to make himself independent. Founded on Dutch and foreign expertise a class of great merchants developed in Copenhagen; these supplied the court and nobility and advanced money to the crown as agents with good international connections. The state took strong measures against resident foreigners who refused Danish citizenship, and in December 1623 they were all officially expelled.

The exchange of goods with its Norwegian dependency was a particularly important part of Danish trade. The greater part of Norway's grain came from Denmark, and the latter took timber, copper, iron, fish, liver oil, pitch and tar. Trade with Schleswig-Holstein was also lively and its merchants had special rights up to the time of Christian iv. This applied to Flensburg although Christian iv reduced these rights in order to increase the Copenhagen monopoly. The King also took measures against Hamburg by founding Glückstadt on the lower Elbe. Further conflict developed with Hamburg over the Iceland trade. Christian iii had already tried to obtain a larger share of it for Copenhagen in 1547 but Hamburg still did most of the business. Iceland had become strategically important because of its large deposits of sulphur, which were crucial to the early modern armaments industry. The Danes were quick to assert their claims to trade in this commodity, although the crown soon farmed it out to the German ports. There were about fifteen Icelandic harbours, and in good years Hamburg sent up to seventeen ships to the island. Merchants from Bremen, Stade and Lübeck also took part in this trade. The Danish share remained slight in the sixteenth century.

At the beginning of the seventeenth century Christian iv attempted to monopolize the Icelandic trade. In 1602 the merchants of Copenhagen, Malmö and Helsingör received exclusive rights to trade with Iceland for twelve years. But Danish merchants lacked the ships, the appropriate goods at reasonable prices and the sailors to carry out the task they had been set, and so they were forced to lease their rights to the Germans, who continued to send between five and ten ships yearly from Hamburg to Iceland. This changed when regulations enacted in 1623 made the newly founded Glückstadt the staple for goods from Iceland.

By decree of the Danish crown an Iceland Company based on Copenhagen was founded in 1619. Only former Iceland merchants from Copenhagen, Helsingör and Malmö were allowed to participate. The company also received a monopoly of trade with Shetland and the Faroe Islands. Its organization was modelled on the flourishing overseas companies now developing in west Europe and based on controls and price-rigging. Naturally, this hardly suited the Icelanders, who were now supplied less efficiently with goods at a higher cost and received a lower price for their own exports in return. As well as organizing trade with Iceland, Christian iv also tried to increase Danish whaling by subsidizing voyages to the Norwegian and Russian arctic islands. He also founded trading companies for the West Indies, Africa and East India, emulating the Dutch. His East India Company of 1616 was founded with the help of two Dutchmen, Jan de Willum and Hermann Rodenburg, who were given trading rights for twelve years. This was the first Danish joint stock company, raising 165,000 Reichstalers, much of it from Hamburg and Holland, the rest by forced loans imposed by the crown on its important officials, courtiers and town councillors. In fact a tax on coaches partly financed the venture. The whole enterprise was state controlled. Overseas agencies were under a royal governor or an official of the company who also represented the state. Company administration was sophisticated, with a board of directors or *bevindthebber*; all profit was paid out as dividend, with the result that the company was unable to reinvest internally. The company at first ran Tranquebar on the Coromandel coast as its main base, but fitting out expeditions often presented such difficulties that visits to the colony could not be made every year.

The export trade of central Europe depended above all on grain, cattle and minerals. It was an area that supplied raw materials to west Europe, and as such it tended to suffer from the domination of western capital finance and advanced western technology. But without this hinterland west Europe could not have been so wealthy and could not have supported such a large population in the sixteenth and seventeenth centuries.

3. MONEY CREDIT AND INSURANCE

Early modern coinage and money was above all dominated by increased silver production in central Europe, which by 1500 had given silver coinage greater importance than gold. The striking influx of silver from America after the 1540s gave gold a new rôle as a currency regulator, for its price rose considerably against that of increasingly plentiful supplies of silver. In the later sixteenth century, face-value copper coins were circulated more and more, because of the inflation that spread all over Europe from the Iberian peninsula. The problem of obtaining metal for minting, which led to metal shortages for countries without their own mineral wealth, gave way to the problem of matching money circulation against rates of general economic growth during the sixteenth century.

Each state experienced different aspects of this problem. France made do with a smaller silver coin, the *teston*, which was first minted in 1513; following the Italian example, it was worth originally 70 sols or sous. $25\frac{1}{2}$ *testons* made up the silver *Mark*. The teston remained in circulation for most of the sixteenth century (the coin had obtained its name because it carried the King's bust in true Renaissance fashion). France had over forty mints in operation. Henry II also introduced a new coin, the Henri d'or, valued at 67 to the gold Mark, and worth 50 *sous*. Under Henry III (1574–89) a new silver coin, called the *franc*, appeared in 1576; this was worth 20 sous at $17\frac{1}{4}$ to the silver Mark; half and quarter francs and half and quarter écus were also minted. Henry III had circulated the first French copper coins in 1575, the double and single deniers tournois; these were used more and more during the wars of religion. In 1574 the crown fixed the value of the écu d'or at 58 sous, but a year later it rose to 60, and on the open market it was even worth 68 sous. Not until Henry IV's time was there any improvement in the intrinsic value of small and medium-size coins.

A new generation of silver coins in central Europe was inaugurated with the Guldiner of Sigismund of the Tirol and Joachimsthal. The German Empire issued uniform coinage regulations in 1524, 1551 and 1559; under these the gold or silver

Gulden (fl.) or Taler (tlr.) at 32 Schillings was proclaimed the standard unit of account. This applied particularly to the Reichsspezietaler of 1566, reckoned at 68 Kreuzers; this was a stable coin and it held its value until the middle of the eighteenth century. Among smaller coins there were the *Groschen*, valued at 3 *Kreuzers* and used in north Germany, and the Batzen, valued at 4 Kreuzers and used in south Germany. The Thaler ran at 60 Kreuzers. Towns such as Lübeck retained their ancient mark-schilling currency, much debased but still measured according to the Flemish pound as a unit of account. It was the task of regional Münzwardein or assayers in the imperial circles to run *Probationstage*, meetings at which coins from all over the Empire were tested to counteract the regular minting of inferior coins, which led to crises of confidence and slumps in trade. Even so, these regional assayers were unable to prevent the great inflation of 1620–23, called the *Kipper and Wipperzeit*, a period of coin clipping in the German Empire.

By 1500 many of the smallest mint-houses had vanished, but all German territorial rulers had at least a theoretical right to mint their own coins, and most of them exercised this right. At the end of the century the first copper coins appeared in Germany, at first in the towns of Lower Saxony and Pomerania, and quickly spread to Brandenburg and Silesia. Coins of dubious value were struck in clandestine mints (*Heckenmünzen*, coins from the hedge-rows). These mints were then leased by unscrupulous territorial rulers to coiners, who accounted to various under-cover agents, so that the original ruler was often protected from prosecution in the imperial federal courts. In the Wettin saxon area alone there were forty-three mints of silver bullion, and in the Brunswick Guelph lands, another forty. Shortage of silver bullion led to popular outcry as well as to imperial edicts that did decrease abuses after the 1620s, but these soon rose to new heights as the Habsburgs and Swedes used debasement to pay for their war effort. By 1625 the Habsburg lands based on Prague and Vienna had experienced their first great state bankruptcy.

After this new adjustments were called for. In north Germany, a Gutegroschen of 1/24 Taler and a Silbergroschen of 1/30 Taler were established, in south Germany and Austria a Taler of 90 Kreuzer or 1½ Gulden, a goldgulden worth 1¼ Taler and a Dukat of 2 Reichstalers or 3 Gulden. In the Habsburg lands there were mints in Alsace and Swabia, the Alpine areas and upper and Lower Austria. Bohemia had mints at Prague, Jachymov and Kutna Hora. During the rising of 1617–20 the Estates of Bohemia and Moravia minted coins in Brno, Cesko Bedejovice, Mikulov and Olomouc under their own name. The Winter King and then Albrecht of Wallenstein followed suit. In Silesia the local lords or town councils occasionally minted their own coins, as did Legnica, Krosno Odrzanskie, Wroclav, the Bishop of Neisse and the lords of Münsterberg-Öls. Silesia was also affected by the inflation of the 1620s.

Currency developments in the Swiss Confederation were characterized by the economic individualism of the Cantons. In 1509 Fribourg and in 1512 Basle sought and obtained papal privileges to mint coins. Berne, Basle, Solothurn and Sitten adopted the Taler early (between 1493 and 1501), although a large number of different coins still circulated. In the German-speaking Cantons traditional names such as Batzen, Rappen and Angster were retained for new coins. In the Italian and French areas coins such as testons, called Dicken in German, were also adopted. Apart from the Cantons, other authorities minted their own coins, among them the bishops of Basle, Chur, Lausanne and Sitten, and the lords of Neuchâtel. Like the Empire, the Swiss were also involved in the great debasement of the 1620s. Typical delinquents were lords like Freiherr Thomas von Ehrenfels auf Schauenstein, who bought the right to mint his own coinage from the imperial Habsburg chancellery and exploited his privilege by coining debased money from which he took quick profits in 1612.

In Hungary the main mints were in Kremnitz, Baia Mare, Košice, Bratislava and Smolnik. However Habsburg minting in the years between 1526 and 1540 was interrupted by John Zapolyai and between 1540 and 1571 by his son John Sigismund. In Transylvania the rulers had mints in Cluj and Sibiu. In this area, the imperial Taler and the Hungarian ducat were standard currency. In Poland currency was not standardized, despite various efforts at reform. In 1526 King Sigismund decreed that only the following coins were to be minted: pennies at 540 to the Cracow silver Mark; denari at 96 to the silver Mark; and the grosz, szoslak and ducat on the Hungarian money standard. Talers were added later and efforts were made to keep them at the German equivalent rate of 60 groszy. Stefan Bathory tried to curb coinage depreciation by government regulations between 1578 and 1580 but with little real success. The Polish federal state had too little control over exports, particularly to the west, to be able to control the coinage effectively.

Until the middle of the sixteenth century the Russian economy was short of coin. Barter and roubles in bar form were common. The money economy was, however, greatly helped by Muscovites who had to pay tribute to the Khans, armies and mercenaries. Early attempts were also made to unify the currency. Towards the end of the fifteenth century the Moscow rouble was considerably debased, whereas that of Novgorod held its value. It was the Novgorod coinage that was adopted by the state, but by 1543 the rouble was only worth one-third of its value in 1500. Smaller coins were kopeks, at 100 to the rouble, and dengi. In 1535 a state mint in Moscow replaced numerous private enterprises, although individuals were encouraged to mint their own money under state supervision from silver on payment of a 2 per cent tax. Coinage debasement was rampant during the 'time of troubles'. Bad coin drove out the good, and counter-measures in 1620 came too late. Up to 1630 Russian currency steadily depreciated.

Sweden left the Nordic Union and began to strike its own coins in 1522. These were *öre* with the portrait of St Eric. During the long reign of Gustav Vasa a great variety of coins were minted. As well as the öre there were whole and half silver Gulden; from 1534 whole and half Reichstaler on the German standard; after 1540 Salvatortaler, and then double, whole and half Mark pieces. Chief mints were at Stockholm, Västerås and Åbo. Copper coins or *Klippen* were also minted at more dubious values ranging from 2 to 16 to the öre. Eric xiv and his brother John iii also minted gold and silver coins worth up to four Talers per unit. Under Gustavus Adolphus gold coins up to the five-ducat piece and silver coins worth up to four Talers were struck. The chief mints were now at Stockholm, Kalmar, Norrköping and Gothenburg. After 1625 round and square copper coins were added, struck in Avesta, Nyköping and Arboga. Sweden also minted its own coins in Germany, East Prussia and Poland during the Thirty Years' War.

In the middle of the sixteenth century a general currency stabilization took place in central Europe. The Danish Reichstaler was reckoned according to the customs in Lübeck, at 3 Marks and the Mark at 16 Schillings. But during the hostilities of the 1560s the currency inevitably depreciated, so that the old Taler was now reckoned at 4 Marks.

In Germany a new standard was introduced in 1566, according to which the Taler was now reckoned at 32 Schillings (or Groschen). Following this, in 1572 Denmark fixed its Taler at 2 Marks each of 16 Schillings. However, the old standard was not abolished, and it was typical of the early modern period that more and more systems continued to co-exist.

Under King Christian IV more debased coins were struck in order to increase state revenues in the short term. The Danes took advantage of higher silver coinage rates in trade with Hamburg, Altona and their own German staple at Glückstadt. By 1624 the rate of 32 Schillings to the Spezietaler had risen to 100 Schillings. The new debased Taler coin, now called the Krone, had a wide circulation. In 1625 there followed a serious devaluation, and the Reichstaler was now valued at 6 Marks, each worth 16 Schillings. The debased Schilling-Mark currency which bedevilled the economy of the north German hinterland in the late sixteenth century was now finally abolished. The north Germans went over to imperial Talers, and the Danes established their own national currency, the Krone.

A. *Forms of credit*

In the sixteenth century, two factors above all influenced the development of the central European economy. One was the rise of the Habsburg world empire, and the other overseas expansion, which gave the European sea-coasts increasing predominance over the hinterland. Economic advance was steered by important family banks. For a while the south Germans managed to take the lead from the Italians, among whom the Genoese remained prominent. The house of Fugger combined trade in central European minerals with credit advanced to the Habsburgs, especially to Maximilian I, Charles V and Ferdinand I. After 1496 Cardinal Melchior von Meckau, ruling bishop of Bressanone, became one of the most important secret suppliers of money to the Fuggers, and his deposits even exceeded the Fuggers' personal fortune. The death of Meckau caused the bankers considerable difficulties. The Fuggers used Meckau's standing at Rome to facilitate German remittances for benefices, indulgences and fees. Fugger connections had helped finance the Church jubilee of 1500 and also the election of Pope Pius III.

Church taxes from central Europe, Hungary, Poland and Scandinavia were transferred to Rome via Fugger. Jacob Fugger financed the benefices of Cardinal Albrecht of Hohenzollern in Mainz, Magdeburg and Halberstadt, gaining a dubious place in the early history of the Reformation by financing the sale of indulgences in Germany. The greater part of Jacob Fugger's banking business was conducted for Maximilian I and his grandson Charles V, for whose election in Frankfurt in June 1519 he raised not less than 850,000 Gulden. Repayment difficulties gave the Fuggers access to the Spanish state rents and trade, including the Maestrazgo mercury leases of 1525.

On the death of Jacob Fugger in late 1525, the family bank had assets of two million Gulden. His nephew, Anton, inherited the family business, and links with the Habsburgs grew even closer. Anton Fugger financed Ferdinand's successful bids for the thrones of Hungary and Bohemia, only to find that Ferdinand played him off against his banking rivals, the Höchstetters. The Fugger Slovakian copper business meant, however, that Anton had to accept the terms that Ferdinand I dictated, and the family received a salt monopoly in return for financial aid against the Turks. Habsburg security was above all American silver, especially after the 1540s. Fugger and Welser offered them the best returns on tax farms up to the middle of the century, but thereafter the Genoese began to offer even better terms. By mid-century the Genoese were advancing 50 per cent more credit than the Germans. Of the 9,650,000 ducats advanced to Charles V in his last years the Genoese alone supplied more than half.

Yet the Habsburgs remained the Fuggers' most important clients. The bank even did business with the Tudors via its agency in Antwerp. Financial transactions were conducted with the Medici rulers in Florence, and after 1555 the Franconian bishoprics were given war loans against one of Germany's most spectacular bandit rulers, Margrave Albrecht Alcibiades. On the death of Anton Fugger in 1560 the great banking period of the family ended. The next generation consisted of territorial rulers of small states and gentlemen of leisure, although they did still play a certain rôle alongside the Genoese in lending money to the Habsburgs, above all on the basis of their Maestrazgo rents.

The second largest bank in Augsburg was that of the Welser, up to 1517 the Welser-Vöhlin company, which was subsequently taken over by Bartholomäus Welser. Like the Fuggers, they combined trade with production on the putting-out system and high finance. The family character of the business was less rigidly maintained than in the case of the Fuggers. Kinsmen were active in the company, which drew in the patrician families of Vöhlin, Peutinger, Haintzel, Ehinger and Rembold. There were more investors; to a greater extent than in the Fugger bank the Welsers attracted money from clergy, state officials, local nobles and outsiders in return for steady rates of interest. Bartholomäus Welser boasted that his investors had faith in his trading ventures as far afield as the Spanish Empire. Welser's chief depositors in the mid-sixteenth century were Kaspar Besserer of Memmingen, who deposited nearly 33,000 Gulden, and the Habsburg Imperial Treasurer, Villinger von Schönberg (19,000). In 1614 the imperial Privy Councillor Andreas Hannewald had 74,000 Gulden deposited with Marx and Matthöus Welser. A similar system prevailed in the banks of Höchstetter, Haug, Linck and Langnauer.

Thus activities of south German companies were not only based on the capital of individual families but also, more broadly, on a *rentier* class. Official rates of interest were 5 or 6 per cent, whereas the trading companies offered up to 12–14 per cent on large transactions. Most ruling princes, high nobles and clergy used bankers such as the Fuggers and Welsers for borrowing as well as investing, and for transferring or storing assets, jewels, silver and gold plate. Because of the dangers involved in transporting cash, assets were frequently paid in at one of the many agencies so that a corresponding sum might be drawn at another agency or at a trade fair. The bill of exchange, first pioneered by the Italians, was in universal use in central Europe from the sixteenth century. Such exchange transactions increased the volume of business far beyond the actual amount of bullion deposited and brought banks into the centre of state planning. Lists of Welser clients for large loans survive from the reign of Emperor Frederick III and the number of clients reached a peak under Charles V. For his imperial election in Frankfurt in 1519 the Welsers advanced 143,000 Gulden, a modest sum only when compared with the Fugger effort.

The Welsers also took a part of the Maestrazgo lease in Spain and tax-farmed part of the *Cruzada*. Their dealings in precious metals from America, however, were not as extensive as that of their rivals, the Fuggers. In spite of Habsburg opposition, the Welsers lent to the French crown, especially via Lyons. They were financially involved with Ferdinand I, the Brussels government, England, Hungary and the papacy. When Bartholomäus Welser retired, his son Christoph took over. Parts of his account book for 1554–60 that survive show that after Augsburg his Antwerp agency had most turnover. In 1556 this agency had twenty-two debtors, who altogether owed 877,817 Gulden. Large Welser loans to the crowns of Spain, Portugal and France, and to Holland, were lost in the second half of the sixteenth century. In spite of this, the banking trade survived and Matthäus Welser was even made *Reichspfennigmeister* (imperial federal tax collector) in 1603. Yet this position brought such financial liabilities that he soon went bankrupt. Among his debtors was Emperor Rudolf II who owed 181,000 Gulden, the Archbishop Elector of Mainz (39,000 Gulden), the Spanish crown (14,000 Gulden), and the King of Poland (90,000 Gulden). Against total assets of 374,000 Gulden, Welser had debts of 600,000 Gulden, and payments were suspended in 1614. Even though Fugger and Welser were the greatest south German bankers of the sixteenth century, other firms must not be overlooked. Paumgartner, Gossembrot and Höchstetter were competitors especially in the Tirol and under Ferdinand I. Neidhard and Seiler played their part in Antwerp and Lyons, and Meuting negotiated loans to Spain.

In Nuremberg Heinrich Wolff and Christoph Scheurl the elder were the chief financiers in about 1500. After Wolff came Hans Thumer, who died in 1498, and Hans Schütz, who had a capital of 100,000 Gulden. Yet compared with Augsburg, Antwerp and Lyons, banking developed relatively slowly in Nuremberg under Endres Imhoff and Lienhard Tucher. Jacob Welser and his sons kept a tight control on financial business transacted at the large trade fairs. In 1522 Jakob Welser raised 35,000 Gulden in a lump sum for Charles V, but in 1529 he believed that Habsburg credit was not good beyond any lump sum of 25,000 Gulden. It was now that the Spanish crown came to consider Jacob Welser's company and his Antwerp and Augsburg representatives as candidates for the Maestrazgo lease. Hans Welser and the Augsburger Sebastian Neidhard also took a share in a tax-farm of the Fuggers with the Emperor for over 100,000 ducats. The Welsers loaned the French king 12,000 crowns in 1542 and in 1545, with Weikmann of Ulm, they loaned the French crown 50,000 écus. However, they decided that Francis I was only worth credit to the value of 24,000 crowns and their factor in Lyons was to ensure prompt repayment. By 1551 the Welsers had ventured into secured income bonds based on Spanish exchequer bills on sale in Augsburg. Surprisingly, assignments of gold and silver were rejected as too risky. As a result of this miscalculation Sebastian Welsers had to liquidate his firm in 1561 after suspension of payments by the Habsburgs in Spain and the Netherlands. Bad debts amounted to 72,625 Gulden net.

In the 1550s twelve Nuremberg firms took part in advances negotiated by Kleberger for the King of France. Bonaventura Furtenbach even gave overtly political loans when in 1526 he and his brothers advanced to the Habsburg imperial *Landsknechtführer* (mercenary infantry commander) Frundsberg 24,000 Gulden, which were never recovered. Among Furtenbach's customers was Archbishop Elector Albrecht of Mainz. In 1549 Margrave Albrecht Alcibiades mortgaged Erlangen and Baiersdorf for 14,000 Gulden to Furtenbach, and Ferdinand I also used him. Typical negotiations were those in 1552–4, in which the Habsburgs received 40,000 Gulden at 10 per cent interest.

In Nuremberg, according to town council estimates of 1568, 416 burghers had capital resources exceeding 5,000 Gulden, of whom 240 had more than 10,000 Gulden. But there were also regular bankruptcies after mid-century, as for instance Christoph Harsdorffer in 1564 and the brothers Neumai in 1573. Sooner or later most German family banks made risky transactions which led to their collapse. There were however so many relatively small firms that others usually stepped into the breach and rescued business confidence with further credit. The secret of the success of banking centres such as Augsburg in the sixteenth century lay in diversification: numerous smaller firms invested both regionally and at international level. Losses could then be spread. Eventually south German banking centres were worn down by the uncertain political situation, the expansion of trade away from central Europe and continuing Habsburg state bankruptcies. Thus by the 1570s Nuremberg had nearly 350,000 Gulden of bad debt owing to it. Christoph Fischer and Johann Schäufelein were owed 96,000 Gulden, Sebastian Welser the Elder nearly 60,000, the Imhoff brothers 50,000 and Förenberger-Bosch 34,000. Bartolome Viatis was at first only marginally active but loans to the Dukes of Saxony already ran at 36,300 Gulden in 1596–1602. In 1622–3 he lent to Saxony 165,000 Gulden; 240,000 to the territorial Estates of Silesia; 100,000 to the ruling bishop of Bamberg and Würzburg; and 24,000 to Adam Sebisch of Wroclav. The company was forced to buy protection in the above mentioned territories in which it operated. Nuremberg for instance was forced to lend to Henry IV in return for royal protection of its French assets.

Strasbourg stood out as a financial centre on the upper Rhine. The Strasbourg-based firm of Minckel and Obrecht was particularly active in Lyons, arranging loans for the French king on the death of financier Kleberger. In Frankfurt-am-Main the efficient firm of Josef zum Schwan was especially notable. In central Germany the Leipzig trade fair was the centre of credit business. In north Germany the house of Loitz in Stettin stands out among the great merchants with banking business. Loitz and Andreas Bundholz were chief creditors to the Electors of Brandenburg. In 1564 his debts with them amounted to 1·8 million Gulden, on which he defaulted, and in 1572 the house of Loitz went bankrupt. Lübeck had no single great merchant at this period, though Herman Iserhel was especially active in helping Gustav Vasa to the Swedish throne. In Hamburg and Bremen during most of the sixteenth century there were as yet no great specialist firms with abundant partnership capital. This situation changed for the better when immigrants arrived from the west.

South German bankers depended on their contacts in Antwerp and Lyons. One such was Lazarus Tucher from Nuremberg, a speculator and broker who took up finance in the 1520s and was for a while agent to the Brussels government. Hans Kleberger, from Nuremberg, became *valet de chambre* to the French king in 1543 and negotiated south German loans for the king, as Tucher did in Antwerp. After Kleberger's death at the end of the 1540s, Georg Obrecht and Israel Minckel from Strasbourg succeeded in carrying out important financial transactions for the French king via Lyons. The huge sums which flowed into France in the critical years 1556–64 mainly through their efforts were largely never repaid. Suspension of payment from the French and Spanish crowns had serious consequences in south Germany, and over seventy firms failed in Augsburg between 1556 and 1584. In Strasbourg Ingold suspended payments, in Memmingen Zangmeister failed to meet his debts, and in Munich Ligsalz and Fleckhamer crashed.

New stimuli to the development of exchange, insurance and particularly of international money drafts were provided by immigrants who came in the second half of the century from Antwerp to Cologne, Frankfurt and Hamburg. Thanks to the Portuguese Ximenes, Rodrigues d'Evora and Alvares Caldeira and to the Italians Navaroli Gavi, and Neri, Cologne became a centre for international bills of exchange in the 1570s and 1580s. Subsequently it lost its position to Frankfurt and its fairs, where foreign expertise was better catered for. Among the greatest exchange dealers was Bonaventura Bodeck's son Johann, domiciled in Frankfurt since 1585 and married to a daughter of the Antwerp merchant, Arnold Borman, who carried on business with his brother-in-law, Hans Scholier. In this they merged with the Augsburg firm of Rehlinger and kept close family ties with the Flemish van Uffeln family in Hamburg.

In the Habsburg lands after 1550 only a few firms stood out as bankers, having grown from local beginnings, such as Lazarus Henckel of Donnersmark; or having immigrated, like Werdemann or Vertema from Piuro in the Val Bregaglia. They helped to finance Emperor Rudolf II's war against the Turks. Before the Thirty Years' War there was also the Dutchman, Hans de Witte, who became Wallenstein's banker in the early 1620s. East Europe remained on the periphery of large-scale banking, being dependent on western credit finance, though the influence of a Jewish bank run by João Migues from Iberia, who later called himself Joseph Nasi, extended from Constantinople to Poland.

Credit facilities were badly organized in Russia, and the state had no machinery for raising loans in a western manner during the sixteenth and seventeenth centuries. The money market was still in its infancy there. Only the monasteries disposed of cash surpluses from properties and gifts. Cash scarcity sent up rates of interest, and by law it was fixed as high as 20 per cent at minimum repayment of five years. But these provisions could not be kept. Olearius mentions a rate of interest as high as $33\frac{1}{3}$ per cent in his description of Muscovy, and rates of over 150 per cent were even recorded. On small loans 1 per cent per day could be expected.

B.   *Fairs and exchanges*

Credit banking firms needed fixed centres such as Augsburg and Nuremberg as well as regular trade fairs, above all those of Lyons, Besançon, Piacenza and Novi. Their importance grew because of Spanish silver, which mainly went via Genoa after the sack of Antwerp. The Brabant fairs in Antwerp and Bergen-op-Zoom, like the Lyons fairs, were closely connected with those of Castile. However, the latter lost much business as the Spanish economy went into decline in the second half of the sixteenth century. The regular rotation of west European fairs was crucial to credit finance, since it meant the rotation of bills of exchange often issued in excess of actual bullion cover. The *Ricorsa* type of exchange led to speculative dealings. Endorsements practised in Spain and Italy in the sixteenth century soon spread to Germany. In Antwerp, however, the practice was at first forbidden.

The sixteenth century saw the rise of permanent money markets. These exchanges were securer than the old markets and fairs and also received territorial state support. In the north-west exchanges spread from Bruges. In Antwerp the town council built special premises for bankers in 1531. The system then spread to Cologne in 1553, to Hamburg in 1558 and Frankfurt in 1585. But during the seventeenth century all other banking centres were overshadowed by Amsterdam with its *Wisselbank*, its reserves of money and credit, and its share in the Dutch East India Company, with profits from the commodity and stock exchanges.

In the seventeenth century banks with 'public' backing first came into being. The first of these, the state Girobank in Venice, the Bank of Rialto, was founded in 1587. A similar bank was set up in Amsterdam in 1609. Its main purpose was to help to improve the bad state of the currency. Hamburg followed suit in 1619. Like other Girobanks, Hamburg's was first founded to check the debasement of the currency. All its transactions had to be fully covered in bullion. Merchants made credit transfers in Marks of account. The bank itself lent money against full security. In 1621 the city of Nuremberg set up a similar public bank for credit transfers and deposits.

In central Europe insurance was still in its infancy. The need to obtain compensation for the loss or damage to transport and freight was met by introducing marine insurance. A contract was made to cover the risk of the sea voyage by bringing in a third party with capital. In this business the south Germans were accepted in Spain, Portugal and the Low Countries. Hanseatic merchants developed insurance from Antwerp, where it was particularly well advanced. The first recorded insurance contract in Hamburg dates from 1588 and gave coverage for a grain shipment to Italy. At the beginning of the seventeenth century the immigrant trading community in Hamburg tried to set up a Chamber of Insurance like that in Amsterdam and London. It attracted a certain amount of outside business, above all from Lübeck, but also from the Danish East India Company in 1616.

During the Spanish–Dutch twelve-year truce (1609–21), voyages became safer, apart from the regular danger of Barbary pirates in the Mediterranean. New uncertainties arose when the truce between Spain and the United Provinces ended, and soon England was also involved in the conflict. At this time most insurances were taken out on long voyages, and more than half the Hamburg insurance brokers were Dutch and Portuguese. Appropriately qualified lawyers, especially notaries, were needed to arbitrate insurance disputes, and a whole new and lucrative branch of commercial law arose. Notary Peter van der Willigen, originally from Antwerp, specialized in this business while his brother Nikolaus ran a family trading firm, and men like Dr Rutger Ruland established themselves as specialist marine insurance lawyers. In 1630 Ruland published a text-book of marine insurance.

In other fields insurance was much more backward. Fire insurance slowly developed; in Schleswig-Holstein, for example, it grew out of community responsibilities to engage *en masse* in fire-fighting. With the rise of insurance there developed an interest in fire-prevention and regulations against naked lights were often issued by governments. Sickness and life insurance were still mainly in the hands of town councils, guilds and ecclesiastical, charitable institutions.

c. *Public credit*

From the time of Charles VII France adopted a twin system of ordinary and extraordinary budgeting. The ordinary budget consisted of demesne income of state, controlled by four treasurers. The extraordinary budget was made up of taxes such as *gabelle*, *aides* and *taille*, administered by four departments with general and special receivers. The payments were usually assigned directly without first being centrally collected; this, however, led to misappropriations and strictly illegal borrowing. Taille was levied on non-noble property. Aides were an excise sales tax, comprising one-eighth to one-quarter of the retail price of drink and one-twentieth of food and manufactures such as meat, fish and textiles. Customs dues were levied on all imported and exported goods. Finally the salt tax, or gabelle, began to play its nefarious rôle in French fiscalism.

Financial officials in the fifteenth century formed a syndicate of families connected with each other by numerous ties. The most important of these were the Berthelot, Robertet, Semblancay, Bohier and Poncher families. Coming from the merchant class, they were able to enrich themselves further by means of their position in financial administration. As well as their government duties they also carried on many varieties of banking business. A typical case was Semblancay, treasurer to Anna of Brittany, after 1495 chief financial official of Languedoc and, from 1509, of Langue d'oïl, as well as mayor of Tours. He acquired extensive property around Tours, including the noble seat of Semblencay in 1515. At first he was finance minister under Francis I and was subsequently arraigned and executed.

The new system combined all revenues, which would lead, it was hoped, to greater clarity in accounting. The heads of finance had their powers much reduced and were put under a *conseil du roi*. Sixteen districts of financial administration, called *généralités*, now took the place of the old regions. In 1493 government expenditure was 16,000,000 livres. The growing expenditure on court and army led to a further increase in the need for money. Taille on all commoners was continuously raised, from 2,400,000 livres in 1527 to double that amount by

1543. In 1588 income from taille had risen to 18,000,000 livres. – the depreciation of money must, however, be taken into account in these figures. State property above all was sold and offices, urban excises and tenths from the clergy enforced to raise additional revenue. The sale of offices led to abuses as posts were created merely for fiscal reasons. In order to obtain the necessary cash, the crown was forced to turn to *traitants* (tax-farmers), who usually banded together in companies or *partis*, thus forming financial oligarchies. An additional method of increasing income was to debase the currency. *Rentes* issued by Paris town hall started in 1522. The town hall became a tax-farmer and creditor to the king. Whereas in the 1550s bankers in Lyons took 16 per cent interest, the Paris town hall offered the crown *rentes* at $8\frac{1}{3}$ per cent. *Rentes* saved the crown from bankruptcy, especially during the religious wars, but state debt grew all the more. *Rentes* issued by the Paris town hall in 1577 totalled 3,132,000 livres. Taxes were increased by adding supplementary charges, or *taillons*, to existing rates and indirect taxes were regularly extended. On top of this *affaires extra-ordinaires* were resorted to, including sale of offices, patents and more or less forced contributions demanded from town councils and convocations of clergy. Abuses by the *partisans* (tax-farming companies) became more and more open, and in 1596 Sully was given enough state power to deal with them.

In the German tax system, distinctions must be drawn between Emperor, Empire, individual territorial rulers and imperial town councils. From the 1490s efforts to tap new sources of income began to emerge more clearly in agreed imperial taxation policies. The first uniform federal tax was the 'common penny', clearly defined at the Worms imperial assembly in 1495. Everyone over fifteen with property worth under 500 Gulden had to pay 1/24 Gulden; those over 500 Gulden, $\frac{1}{2}$ Gulden; over 1000 Gulden, 1 Gulden, with self-assessment for the really wealthy. This income tax was intended to cover the costs of federal peace-keeping entailed in setting up a court of the imperial treasury (*Reichskammergericht*), which was to function as a supreme court of appeal in the Empire. The 'common penny' was however replaced in 1507 by *Kammerzieler* which served the same purpose, but under the fiscal control of territorial rulers and their estates.

The imperial tax register was extended in 1521, and *Römermonate*, by which the imperial army was to be financed, became the most important taxes. *Römermonate* were originally levied on all imperial feudatories who had a duty to supply soldiers for the Emperor's coronation journey to Rome. The basis of calculation was an army of 4,000 cavalry and 20,000 infantry, plus money to pay the cavalryman twelve Gulden a month and the infantryman four Gulden. The total estimated cost of one *Römermonat* was 128,000 Gulden. This tax assessment was adapted for all-purpose federal finance after 1521, mainly for financing the Habsburgs' wars against the Turks. In the period between 1594 and 1598 *Römermonate* raised 3,303,823 Gulden in federal taxes. Imperial assemblies were called as necessary and authorized taxes based on multiples of up to fifty or sixty *Römermonate*.

In the 1520s the federal tax system was reformed so as to cover Charles v's financial needs as Holy Roman Emperor. Heavier taxation of clergy and imperial customs duties were proposed but not introduced. In view of this limit on federal taxes, the Emperor was thrown back on using the income of his own dynastic, territorial possessions, as well as employing a burdensome policy of borrowing. Under Maximilian i Habsburg credit finance entered a new phase of development connected with the Tirol inheritance of 1490. Tirolese copper and silver production was offered as surety for loans larger than previous Habsburg rulers had ever enjoyed. By 1523 Ferdinand estimated that Maximilian had one million Gulden in state debts. It cost Charles v that much alone to purchase electoral support to get elected Emperor in 1519. In the following decades Charles' financial resources increasingly failed to cover his political ambitions and wars. At the beginning of his reign in Spain, Charles had a yearly income of one million ducats. By the 1540s this had increased to two million. Without loans from south German and Italian merchants, in particular from Jakob and Anton Fugger, who were repaid principally from Spanish and Neapolitan assets, Charles could not have afforded to keep his extensive empire together.

There were wide discrepancies of wealth among territorial rulers in Germany. In 1500 consistent financial administration with budget and audit was largely lacking. Regular income from demesne and customs dues was administered by the

Kammer, or territorial ruler's own treasury. Alongside the Kammer there was the individual exchequer of each set of territorial Estates or *Landstände*, each with its own treasury or *Landkasse* expenditure, used above all for financing rulers' debts.

By 1450, of the annual state income of approximately 60,000 Gulden in the Electorate of Cologne, one-third was supplied by the Estates' treasury to the rulers' Kammer. In the neighbouring Duchy of Julich income was half that of Cologne, but the Kammer received nearly half its income from the Estates' treasury. The Rhine tolls were important items of territorial finance in the Palatinate, amounting to about 60 per cent of regular income, whereas only about 20 per cent came from territorial Estates, and demesne revenue was very low. During the sixteenth century extraordinary tax grants of territorial estates were necessary for running the state. One cattle tax granted by the Electoral Cologne Estates could raise as much as 200,000 Gulden. Without such taxes territorial rulers' governments and courts would have quickly become bankrupt.

Farther east, and especially beyond the lower Elbe, territorial states were run much more on demesne revenues. Even so, states such as Brandenberg with an annual income of merely 50,000 Gulden in the fifteenth century, reaching 80,000 by 1500, were run on considerably less money than the territorial states of the Rhineland. Exceptions were the Albertine Saxon territories, where mining royalties made the rulers the richest in central Europe. In the 1550s a quarter of the Saxon state revenues came from mining revenues alone. State revenues had grown to four times their size between the 1480s and 1550s, a process inaugurated by the reforms of Duke Albrecht in 1485–1500. His Estates granted him an excise and he was a skilful financier. The total income of Albertine Saxony rose to 500,000 Gulden; this territory had the highest income of any single territory in the German Empire until the middle of the sixteenth century, after which its mining industry began to show signs of exhaustion. From then on demesnes provided half the state revenue.

Some ecclesiastical rulers were also good financiers. The classic case is Melchior von Meckau, ruling bishop of Bressanone, who deposited large sums with the Fuggers. Others, such as the Archbishops of Mainz, were traditionally more spendthrift. Yet the deaths of three archbishops within a short period of ten years caused an acute financial crisis and a backlog of taxes to Rome. When Albrecht of Brandenberg was elected in 1514 he faced debts of 1,200,000 Gulden. He had been chosen mainly because he was expected to pay for the *Pallium* out of his own pocket. He then tried to get out of this difficulty by borrowing from the Fuggers and by financial expedients such as selling indulgences in Mainz and Magdeburg with which to repay Rome and the Fuggers. His most pressing debt was a mere 48,000 Gulden. Tetzel, who sold Indulgences, was a Fugger employee, and it was his activities that called forth Luther's celebrated protest in Wittenberg. Indulgences were, however, a financial success for Albrecht of Mainz, for he was able to pay off most of his Fugger debts. He also received over 100,000 Gulden in bribes from the Fuggers on behalf of Habsburg Charles, in return for his electoral vote in 1519.

Urban tax systems had basically remained unchanged since the fourteenth century. The chief source of income came from a 1 per cent capital tax, expressed as income tax, according to current rates of interest. Indirect taxes were the excises or *Ungelder* on wine, flour, meat, salt and luxury foods. The excise income of Basle represented half of its total income, and in Frankfurt at the beginning of the fifteenth century it came to over 60 per cent. In seventeenth-century Hamburg excise revenue provided up to two-thirds of total town council income, despite the great value of customs dues.

Town councils were the first to accumulate money by selling rents for life. These annuities became less important during the course of the sixteenth century as town councils, like territorial rulers, began to raise increasingly large loans from the trade-banks. When imperial towns such as Cologne also had to finance wars, as happened over Neuss, then finances were ruined for decades. In 1512 Cologne town council faced a debt of 3,243,000 Marks. This led to civic rebellion and various patricians were executed in the subsequent era of reform. In future money was only to be borrowed with the consent of the whole town's council. The great seal of Cologne could only be used with the consent of all twenty-three guilds.

If we look at the budget of one imperial town, Basle, in 1502 and 1503, we obtain the following picture. The yearly budgets closed with incomes of 27,000 pounds and 4,800 pounds (at two Marks to the pound). The servicing of debt ran at

10,000 pounds a year and thus amounted to nearly half the total annual expenditure. Building costs were a mere 710 pounds, and the town guard cost even less at 437 pounds. Representation at assemblies of the Swiss Confederation cost 381 pounds, and the town's contribution to the sieges of Bellinzona and Lugano 4,800 pounds. Thanks – among other things – to a French annuity investment of 8,500 pounds, the Basle budget in 1517/18 closed with an income of 82,628 pounds, whereas expenditure was a mere 42,716 pounds. Towns were well off when they attracted investments in annuities and life rents, and these played a more important part in town council finance than did taxation during the sixteenth century.

In Frankfurt-am-Main it is difficult to get a clear picture because important departments of the town council, dealing with grain, forestry and building, had separate budgets and particular councillors assigned to deal with them. These only communicated surpluses and deficits to the central Technei (accounts office). Religious foundations also remained outside the control of the accounts office. The war of the Schmalkaldic League in the 1540s increased public indebtedness in the territories, and when a bad speculation in Mansfeld copper was added, the town council had to pay out 40 per cent of its annual income in interest on standing debt.

Of the Habsburg provinces, the duchy of Austria, centred on Vienna, was the wealthiest. By 1438 all the Austrian provinces provided 93,000 pounds of state revenue. This was equal to 140,000 Gulden, of which Austria by itself provided half. Chief revenue at this time came from excise taxes, followed by revenue from ducal rights and jurisdictions, with demesne income coming third on the list. Extraordinary taxes granted by the territorial Estates brought in even less at this time. The Tirolean mines, although still in their earliest stage of development, already provided a net income of 48,000 Gulden, gross income totalling a mere 67,000 Gulden. In about 1500 the mines accounted for 128,000 Gulden out of a total income of 218,000. This had increased to 380,000 Gulden by 1600, still largely made up from rulers' rights and jurisdictions and demesne. Although the peak of mining prosperity had been passed, customs revenues now provided nearly one-third of total income at Innsbruck, a sign of the increase in trade between Germany and Italy. Lower and Inner Austria, however, were not as wealthy as the Tirol in the sixteenth century. Their gross income in 1520 had hardly increased since 1438, especially since Maximilian I had reduced crown revenue drastically by alienating demesne. Increases in taxes such as excises imposed by royal prerogative improved gross income again under Ferdinand I. He made 500,000 Gulden a year, of which customs dues alone made up 35 per cent of the total. But standing debt finance reduced regular income by 20 per cent. Under these conditions Ferdinand I needed revenues from Bohemia (200,000 Gulden) and Hungary (400,000 Gulden). Total exchequer income was nearly 1,000,000 Gulden. On top of this came tax grants by the territorial Estates, levied annually from the time of Ferdinand I in response to the Turkish threat to Austria. Estates' grants (excluding Tirol) represented another million Gulden a year under Ferdinand I. Against this, Habsburg state debt was nearly 7,000,000 Gulden by 1550, and Fugger alone had claims of a million Gulden. Nearly one-third of this debt was secured with assets in Tirol and Austrian Swabia, but the unsecured floating debt still amounted to three million Gulden. From 1568 onwards Austrian provincial territorial Estates took over increasingly large amounts of this debt. The Habsburgs were now bound to Estates' finance for the next century. Without the Estates' help as financiers, the Habsburgs could hardly have beaten the Turks.

In Denmark the Crown was temporarily enriched by the Reformation, for nearly half the land previously held by the medieval church was secularized. Annual revenue in kind alone rose from 100,000 to 300,000 tons of corn, to which must be added rising prices. On top of this, much property which had been granted as fiefs to the nobility was confiscated. In 1583 55 per cent of the kingdom still comprised free fiefs, but by 1600 the share was down to 12 per cent of the land. Free fiefs were replaced by service estates rendering their accounts to the Crown each year. On top of this revenue there were lucrative customs dues, especially those of the Sound, which went directly into the Danish king's privy purse. There were also dues from town councils, and Estates' extraordinary taxes. Even so, it was the Danish peasantry that paid the bulk of all taxes. Under Frederick II they paid 80 per cent, the towns 15, the clergy 4 and the nobility a mere 1 per cent of extraordinary taxes. Although broadly speaking the poorest section of the population, the peasantry were, however, by far the most numerous. Yet there was no efficient system of budgeting and accounting by the Danish Crown, and regular revenue never covered expenditure. Extraordinary taxes formed a large part of the total state revenue by the sixteenth century.

By the 1560s state debt was 1,375,000 Danish Marks, whereas annual regular revenue was a mere 60,000 Marks. Borrowing thus exceeded income by more than twenty times. Even so, by the time of Christian III's death the Crown had succeeded in funding this debt. This was achieved only by debasing the coinage and increasing revenues paid in kind at a time of rising prices, which led to considerable economic hardship and social discontent. Income at the accession of Frederick II was 100,000 Marks, representing a two-thirds increase. In the reign of Frederick II, yearly expenditure increased even more than income, although income from fiefs now stood at 80,000 Talers, three times as great as in Christian II's time; income from customs dues had also risen. Amazingly, when Frederick II died in 1588, the Danish kingdom had no interest-bearing debts and the Crown was even lending money from its privy purse. This was wholly due to the introduction of new tonnage duties at the Sound after 1567, which had made two million Talers under Frederick II alone. This favourable economic position was disrupted by the many wars waged under Christian IV. The tax burdens in early seventeenth-century Denmark were among the heaviest in Europe.

In Sweden Gustavus Vasa introduced an orderly system of state finance. Crown taxes were largely first paid in kind and wherever possible expenditure was also on this basis. Official salaries were paid in the form of clothing, housing and subsistence. Yet money was increasingly needed for military, mercantile and diplomatic purposes. To balance its budget the Crown depended on income from trade. Attempts to switch to a money economy in the 1540s were premature, for Crown trade and mercantilism were insufficiently developed to finance such economic advance. The war policy of Eric XIV against Denmark was financed by higher taxes in kind levied on his peasants; higher taxes in money were avoided. The first expenses of war were defrayed by coining silver which Gustavus Vasa had hoarded. Eric's successor, John III, was really the first to raise substantial tax revenues in cash. Despite increased revenue from trade, the resources of the sixteenth-century Swedish state were still too slender to challenge the power of Denmark and Poland in the Baltic. Experiments in the structure of administration under John III led to revenue decreases and to civil war with the high nobility as well as with Charles of Södermanland, the future Charles IX.

Muscovite state centralization led to increased tax revenue. From the early sixteenth century the former Tartar tribute was levied for the benefit of the Grand Duke. He also imposed postal service taxes, which were increasingly paid in money after the 1490s. With the creation of standing armies with artillery parks came the imposition of 'cannon money', 'powder money' and taxes for upkeep of the *Strelzi* or Tsar's bodyguard. After 1556 local officials began to receive money salaries. Up to the sixteenth century tax collection had been based on village units which assessed themselves communally. These units were subsequently regarded as too small and inefficient for the new system of taxation. New units of assessment were based on the Moscow *Sokha*, applied universally, and fixed at a certain number of *Chetvert*, varied according to district and quality of soil. In central Russia the Sokha was 800 Chetvert of black earth, and the church lands got away with 600. On the Sokha land registers were drawn up; these became the basis for Russian state taxation up to the end of the seventeenth century.

The 'time of troubles' is thought to have reduced standards of living generally in Russia. New taxes were levied in the form of food, forage and equipment to supply large numbers of soldiers. The levy of 'bread reserves for payment of the military' was soon echoed in Germany during the Thirty Years' War. As church and nobility were usually exempt, the peasantry had to bear the brunt of all these tax burdens.

Little is known about the Muscovite state budget. As well as taxes, income came from demesnes, though it decreased because of the pomestia policy of grants for state service after the sixteenth century. Revenue from trade carried on as a Crown monopoly was important. In the 1560s English traders estimated that the Tsar was worth 1,400,000 roubles a year. Of this four-fifths came from direct taxes and only one-fifth as rent from demesnes. Ivan the Terrible may have taxed his people almost four times as heavily as the English Crown taxed its subjects. Three-quarters of Muscovite state expenditure was for defence.

Having briefly surveyed state tax systems, we now turn to more internationally based credit institutions. The centre of gravity clearly lay in the north-west and south-west of Europe where international trade was probably most intensely developed. Large-scale international finance in the sixteenth century was centred on Genoa and Antwerp, Lyons and Seville. With Antwerp's decline Amsterdam took over, influencing above all the Baltic–Scandinavian region. The greatest economic growth occurred in the Netherlands, in the fifteenth century in Bruges-Sluis, in the sixteenth at Antwerp and in the seventeenth at Amsterdam. The control of Amsterdam over world credit and world commodity prices was the first of its sort. It seemed that by the early seventeenth century all the world's trade had accumulated on the streets and canals of Amsterdam. Of international importance was above all bullion traffic, and to the east of Amsterdam Hamburg became the most important money market. Through close family ties with leading merchants in Amsterdam and other Dutch merchant circles, generations of Hamburg citizens were able to profit by Dutch credit and exchange banking in north and east Europe. In central Europe the Leipzig fairs in particular functioned as clearing houses, whereas in south Germany the connections of the Nuremberg and Augsburg merchants extended not only to the Hungarian, Polish and Transylvanian area but also to the Baltic seaports. The Italians were serious rivals to the south Germans too, especially during the seventeenth century when they were chief bankers to the Habsburgs.

v *Prices and Wages*

There was a general economic boom in Europe from the end of
the fifteenth century until the 1620s. Many factors contributed
to this development, above all a larger population which neces-
sitated increased production to cover growing demands; extension of markets by overseas expansion; and widening and
intensification of marketing systems within Europe with
increased traffic in the Atlantic and Baltic. Prices moved continually upwards to meet growing demands, especially from
about 1510 onwards. A second wave of increases began in
about 1550, but this affected parts of Europe differently. Price
increases were acutest in the precious-metal-producing areas of
central Europe and in the bullion-importing regions of Iberia.
Increases in the money supply came at the same time as general
population growth, so that pressure on existing resources was
doubled. Within a hundred years of 1520 silver production had
increased fourfold, although gold production was more modest.
The economy of Spain was unable to exploit the stream of
precious metals from America, and the chief benefits went to
bankers in the low countries, north Italy and south Germany,
leaving Iberia with the greatest price rises, followed by France,
the Netherlands and Italy.

Price rises did not affect all goods equally. The greatest
increase was noticeable in grain prices, which rose well beyond
those of meat and fish. Recent research has shown that apart
from changes in the influx of bullion, other factors such as
population increases, mobility and exchange of goods, together
with displacement of population because of political, military
and religious factors all led to overall economic growth, albeit
uneven, in sixteenth-century Europe.

In 1568 Jean Bodin, in his famous reply to the arguments of
Malestroit, tackled the problem of price increases by pointing

to the rôle played by the influx of precious metals. He also stressed additional causes such as increased production of luxury goods to the detriment of basic food, which brought in less profit. The purchasing power of silver dropped considerably; in 1500 one could buy five times more with the *livre tournois* than in 1600. Land prices rose threefold in the course of the century. The first group to feel the pinch was, as always, the *rentiers*, officials and those landlords living on fixed incomes. Peasants, tradesmen, merchants and financiers had more chance to keep up with movements in prices. Salaries and wages rose far less than prices, with the result that the families of day labourers and craftsmen were the chief sufferers of sixteenth-century price rises.

Attempts by territorial state governments to act against price rises often suffered from a failure to understand their causes, although recent historians have tended to be cautious in their judgments, in view of the difficulties encountered in world trade and resources in our own age. In the sixteenth century governments thought that the best way to tackle inflation was to introduce freezes on prices and wages, to forbid excessive profits, speculative buying, cartels and monopolies, to institute measures against luxury and conspicuous consumption and to impose duties on exports and imports. Most of the measures still in use by national governments today were pioneered by their predecessors in the sixteenth century.

In Schleswig-Holstein prices rose drastically after the 1550s. By the 1570s they had already more than doubled, although the rate of increase between 1575 and 1622 slowed to 50 per cent. Similar increases occurred in Alpine areas, and in Graz not only in grain but also in those of most other goods. Wages also went up after 1550. Developments in the Tirol were similar to those in Styria and in Habsburg Silesia, emphasizing how much the grain trade and prices were linked in central Europe. Whereas prices of basic foodstuffs increased fourfold in Styria between 1460 and 1600, only masons' wages rose to the same extent, while most other wage-rates only increased by two and a half times during the same period.

In Lvov during the second half of the sixteenth century the price of rye rose steeply and despite a slump in the 1580s, it rose again to reach an all-time high in 1604 and again in 1625. The same trends can be seen in the prices of other types of grain. Wine and mead similarly increased in price in Poland after the 1550s. Textiles and manufactures rose in price in the first half of the century, reaching a peak just after 1600. Even the salaries of royal officials failed to keep up with these increases. One way of cushioning price increases was to pay labourers and craftsmen partly in coin and partly in kind. The guilds encouraged this practice for their apprentices and journeymen. Although they did lag behind, wages tended to rise when prices went up. Later in the seventeenth century, as prices fell, wages followed suit. Compared with this, land prices, leases and rents remained far more stable, despite modest increases in officially tolerated mortgage rates. The 6 per cent charged almost universally against safe securities was considered quite high before the 1580s. House prices moved even more slowly than land prices.

Price rises tended to hit different countries at different times. Thus in Poland prices tended to remain stable in mid-century, and the worst rises came with the currency crisis of 1610–30. Depreciation occurred so rapidly that prices could not follow fast enough, and the end effect was to cause an actual drop in prices once food prices had levelled out. The Polish currency crisis was partly influenced by events in Germany and Sweden, with whom Poland was at war. The influx of American silver, which was thought to have led to price rises, may have been partly offset by increased production of Polish grain and its massive export, via Amsterdam, to west European markets. Even so, in the course of the sixteenth century the price of grain rose more than fourfold; cattle and meat prices doubled; butter trebled; linseed and flax rose fivefold; and salt rose by a modest 30 per cent. The price of manufactured goods went up far less than foodstuffs, an average 150 per cent, and labour was also relatively less expensive to the employer in 1600 than in 1500.

In Sweden, according to Ingrid Hammarström, a noticeable rise in prices occurred in the first half of the sixteenth century, although silver prices remained more or less unchanged. Sweden was not directly flooded with American or European silver and so other factors must have been contributing to the rise. Hammarström sees the main cause in the depreciation of currency and coinage debasement. The silver content of coins in circulation was continually reduced in order to keep pace with the higher circulation of money required by increases in population, shifts in income and increases in government spending, especially on warfare. When Sweden became the main European exporter of copper and iron in the seventeenth century, this too led to further price increases. By this time it was realized that low prices were not necessarily a sign of a good economy and that high prices did not mean a bad economic situation. However, sixteenth-century inflation led to a prices and wages 'scissors', whereby prices rose more than wages, a drastic situation for the common people in Europe and one that led to social discontent and rebellion.

Denmark benefited by the increased price of grain and cattle, which rose 100 per cent during the first half of the century and another 50 per cent in the second half. The influx of American silver had little effect, but other factors, such as population rise, increases in transport costs and new tolls and taxes, must be taken into account. Official prices after 1600 can be calculated from the records of surviving capital tax registers; these show that prices of butter and beef rose more in Denmark than grain prices between 1600 and 1620. Grain reached a peak in the 1620s and steadily fell in price during and after the Thirty Years' War. This damaged Danish agriculture, whereas previous price rises had contributed to its prosperity.

Movements in prices and wages are only one part of total economic development. If economy as a whole is considered, it will be seen that the agrarian sector proved to be the most important branch, although the increasing influence of manufacture and foreign trade must not be overlooked. Perhaps the most important factor of all was the population increase during the sixteenth century, although it is difficult to pin-point exact effects. Geographical shifts in trade and communications as well as shipping technology were also important in shaping the sixteenth-century European economy. As Italy stagnated, so the Netherlands flourished, together with other Atlantic ports such as Lisbon and Seville, although Genoa and Venice continued to prosper. By 1600 even the remotest parts of east and central Europe had come into the orbit of the money economy. Economics had become of key importance in the policy-making of all European governments.

In the German economy as a whole, the importance of merchant houses has doubtless been over-estimated. The sixteenth-century capital market was still very new, and by the third generation large-scale entrepreneurs had usually given up their merchant activities, invested their fortunes in landed property and become aristocrats. There was a wide general increase in prosperity, especially since borrowers from all levels of society were increasingly able to contract debts; this could not have been possible without massive increases in the value of assets. South German industry in particular was able to diversify, and its merchants, having been principally interested in exports, emerged as organizers of production (such as textiles in Nuremberg), exploiting the resources of rural Saxony, Lausitz and Silesia. Similar developments occurred in north-west Germany, where the decline of Hanseatic monopolies in no way implied economic collapse. German shipping through the Sound steadily increased. Hamburg was only the most important of the newly prosperous towns. In Westphalia, prosperity moved away from the east–west trade route in the south of the province, called the *Hellweg*, to the wooded uplands, suitable for industry; towns such as Bielefeld, Iserlohn, Altena and Lüdenscheid, and later Elberfeld, Solingen and Remscheid, grew up as centres of the early modern iron armaments and textile industry with outlets along the Rhine, Ems and Weser.

How did east-central, east and north Europe fit into the general European pattern of growth? The Baltic area came to be a crucial and strategically separate region of interest to the whole of Europe because of the essential raw materials that it produced. Shipping through the Sound increased continually, and it was the west of Europe that gained from the expansion of Baltic trade. Western finance developed Polish grain, and western ships sailed to Danzig to collect it for Amsterdam warehouses. From there it was sold all over south and west Europe. Bad harvests in the west in 1561, 1565, 1586 and during most of the 1590s were relieved with Polish grain imported by the Dutch and resold as far away as north Italy. After the 1590s, shipping through the Sound decreased for a number of years, only to reach new record levels in the period between 1610 and 1620. Subsequent wars such as those between Sweden and Poland then led to a decline. East-west maritime connections also developed along interior roads and waterways, such as the Vistula. Similar economic developments occurred in the Mediterranean area, although it was the Baltic that provided the most spectacular advances in this period.

PART TWO

The Economic
Development of
Continental Europe
1630-1750

1 Intellectual Movements

The first two decades of the seventeenth century saw the end of a phase of economic growth that had started in the later fifteenth century. A period of crisis began, about which much has been written recently, notably in *Past and Present*. Wars, demographic changes, crises in society and economy, all had great influence on the early seventeenth century, an era more violent, with the Thirty Years' War in Germany, and the Eighty Years' War in the Low Countries than ever before. Only a few years later a series of wars began which continued until the Spanish War of Succession and the Great Northern War of the early eighteenth century. Warfare thus plays a crucial rôle in any assessment of the seventeenth-century European economy; after the mid-eighteenth century other conditions also combined to produce the great upheavals of industrialization.

In the seventeenth century new scientific ideas came to the fore to mingle with attitudes formed by Renaissance humanism, Reformation and Counter-Reformation. The spirit of the Baroque now shaped literary, religious and artistic endeavour. Monarchical absolutism developed into a system of rigid state control that eventually forced enlightenment by paternalism and economic planning. Yet the most important tendencies can all be identified as developments of earlier ideologies, started during the Renaissance, Reformation and Counter-Reformation, very often even as a reaction to these movements (thus the new pietism, mysticism and pragmatism). Natural science became increasingly important, society ever more secular. However devout they may have been, men like Kepler, Galileo and Newton began to make calculations that led to the formation of scientific laws about the nature of the universe; these may not have been any more rational than those of their predecessors but they did lay the foundations of a later technological and industrial society.

The power of the state also grew, and the state began to make use of an expanding bureaucratic apparatus to control subjects in their own best interests.

It was from Britain, not Holland, that the most important impulses towards industrialization and technology came. Britain developed the pragmatism necessary for the early development of economic competition. Rational or, conversely, religious motives faded in importance when faced with practical considerations of production and trade in competition for the best markets and profits. Britain was especially suited for industrial 'take-off' not only because of its geographical position away from continental involvements but also because of its natural resources of coal and iron; its internal economy could be relatively easily developed through river, canal and coastal communications. Another important factor was the British social structure which gave political power and status to men of wealth, no matter how it had been accumulated. The oligarchic system of Lords and Commons in Parliament fostered this development without a social revolution, despite the Great Rebellion of the 1640s and the subsequent Cromwellian era.

In central Europe mercantilism, based on the writings of men like Seckendorff and Becher (1625–82), was generally first adopted as government policy after the Thirty Years' War. Swedish mercantilism only became effective in the seventeenth century, especially during the regency government of young Queen Christina after 1632. In Russia it was introduced at a much later time, under Pososhkov (died 1726). But by the beginning of the eighteenth century mercantilistic thought became influenced by a new, pedagogic paternalism called the Enlightenment. Here many of the ideas of the Physiocrats and Adam Smith were anticipated, and in France, Prussia and Austria fiscalism and population policy moved into the centre of government activity.

In the first half of the seventeenth century the English economist Thomas Mun combined the idea of a balance of trade with the concept of England's 'national capital', an early form of assessing national wealth especially by trade. The later mercantilists extended this to cover national resources such as population, labour, mining and manufactures. Sectors of national economic planning were delineated in order to calculate state capital, above all in foreign trade and in industrial production,

in the interests of national policy. National economic goals
began to be set for which, however, a theoretical economic base
was still largely lacking, although in central Europe it was Justi
who first attempted to reduce the whole idea to a system.

Mercantilist economic thought remained the prevailing
orthodoxy until well into the eighteenth century in many parts
of Europe, and even beyond, as E. F. Heckscher has shown in
his monumental *Economic History of Sweden*. The later mercantilists anticipated the new ideas of the Physiocrats and even of
laissez-faire liberalism, so that the boundaries between old and
new became very blurred in the economic history of later
eighteenth-century central Europe.

In their writings the French economists Vauban and Bois-
guillebert already began to question the desirability of state
intervention. They supported a free rural economy divested of
urban, guild control. During the reign of Louis xiv the French
became the first to apply the new science of economics to any
large extent. Subsequently the Physiocrats suggested that the
wisest economic policy was not to involve oneself in arbitrary
planning but first to study the behaviour of nature and then
adapt human society to it. Of writers in the early eighteenth
century, Cantillon went farthest in this direction, an isolated
forerunner of later thought on the subject.

Questions of population, settlement and more humane taxation were the subject of discussion by German Cameralists,
especially Justi, whereas Sonnenfels spoke out for the liberty to
exercise a trade. But the view that state support was needed in
most economic planning remained fundamental. According to
the Physiocrats a natural order should prevail not only in social
life but also in economics, to correspond with the doctrine of
natural law known since antiquity. The founder of this doctrine,
Francois Quesney, was physician to Louis xv and Madame de
Pompadour, and he went deep into the philosophy behind the
national economy in *Tableau économique*, which was published in
1758. He worked out a cyclical theory of economics. The
Physiocrats start from a divinely appointed order, which was
reflected in the natural instincts of man, especially in his quest
for self-preservation, which required ownership and cultivation
of land. Property ownership was thus natural. But this natural
order conflicted with the political world of the Man-made state.
To be most harmonious, the state should correspond as closely

as possible to the natural order, and should be ruled by an enlightened despot who would achieve this aim.

According to the Physiocrats only nature was productive. Agriculture, the land and its cultivation was thought to be the source of all riches. Only in this way could goods, the intrinsic value of which was greater than their cost of production, be created. Peasants who tilled the soil as tenants for a landlord were thought to be the ideal productive class. Landowners only had a distributive rôle to play; they presided over the distribution of land, supervised work, saw to land improvements and to the payment of taxes. In contrast, craftsmen and merchants were described as a sterile (non-productive) class, because their only function was to process, improve and bring into circulation agrarian produce, and other natural raw materials.

Some of the Physiocrats had also more practical advice to give. Their theories of taxation had an important influence on the future development of government fiscalism and statistics. According to Quesnay the soil was the only source of wealth and its cultivation the only means to increase that wealth. Only in the agrarian sector could there be real surpluses of production and so net gains. Taxes could therefore be wisely assessed if based on agriculture. Every tax must be covered by agrarian production. It would therefore be best to abolish the majority of existing taxes and replace them with a single land-tax paid by all landowners. The influence of this line of thought on continental, agrarian Europe should not be underestimated, and it reached well beyond the middle of the eighteenth century.

II *Population Movements*

Records from this period begin to coincide with the infancy of the science of human statistics, or demography. Parish registers were now to be kept more thoroughly and on their basis the first total figures of births, marriages and deaths were calculated. States began to organize their first census returns during the eighteenth century, although for very pragmatic purposes, such as to calculate poll-taxes and military service. Methods were never standardized, and lack of staff invariably meant that the census was incomplete. Population policy was part of power politics, but the most powerful state of all, Britain, conducted no census before the nineteenth century. One is thus still dependent on estimates, as in the sixteenth century, athough these are now far more accurate.

Church registers of births and deaths, estate records, land tax and hearth tax registers, poll-tax lists and musters to arms provide essential population records. Interpretation is difficult but according to recent calculations, Europe had 100 million inhabitants in 1600, 140 million in 1700 and 188 million in 1800. These totals do, however, hide great regional variations in growth.

The effects of war on population in the seventeenth century are still hotly disputed. Central to the debate is the question of population loss in Thirty Years' War in Germany. Loss remains a vague term, and displacement of population by movement from one region to another is probably a more realistic approach than outright devastation. It is too early to say what overall population displacement had taken place in Germany by the 1640s. Calculations of the losses are between 30 and 40 per cent, and it is thought that it took about three generations to reach again the figure of twenty million. Industrial and commercial expansion of certain centres stimulated by the needs of warfare and armaments policies were particularly noticeable in this era of almost continual war.

The Swiss Confederation succeeded in retaining its neutrality throughout this period, although its population was hardly spared the effects of war, for the basic export of the Swiss remained mercenaries. Even so, population increased from about 1,000,000 in 1600 to 1,200,000 in 1700, despite the fact that about 300,000 Swiss mercenaries left the country during the century. The Swiss also received immigrants, such as the French Huguenots after Revocation of the Edict of Nantes. By 1789 the population of Switzerland had grown to 1,700,000.

France, whose population in 1660 is estimated at about 24,000,000, suffered greatly from famines in the second half of the seventeenth century, especially in 1660 to 1662, 1674 to 1675, 1679 and 1693 to 1694. About 200,000 Protestants left France during the later reign of Louis XIV. Despite his successful conquests, Louis XIV's continuous wars had adverse effects because of epidemics and economic disruption, so that after the 'great winter' of 1709 the French population was down to about 18,000,000. Montesquieu estimated the same number in the middle of the eighteenth century, whereas Quesnay suggested 16,000,000, surely too low a figure. In about 1770 France probably had 24,000,000 inhabitants, the same as in 1660.

Sweden underwent a population increase up to 1690; then famines and the effects of Charles XII's wars brought a period of standstill which lasted until 1720. In Swedish Finland serious famine in 1696 and 1697 brought a temporary halt to an otherwise continual population increase. Birth-rates in the Swedish empire in the 1720s, for which the records are particularly good, were 21·2 per thousand and 20·8 per thousand in Finland. At that time Finland had a population of nearly 300,000, Sweden of 1,400,000. The birth-rate was still affected by the preceding period of war, but the death-rate was always well below it, so that increases of births over deaths in Finland between 1729 and 1736 were 16·7 per thousand per year, whereas in the ten Swedish provinces where sources are available for statistical analysis the increase reached only 9·7 per thousand between 1722 and 1728. Food crises and epidemics were not as severe as before, although the years 1737 to 1743 were bad. Swedish population rose by 16·5 per cent between

1721 and 1735 to 1,703,000; then up by a more modest 4·6 per cent to reach a total of 1,780,000 inhabitants in 1750. Totals in Finland went up more, by 24·6 per cent between 1721 and 1735 to 360,000; then by 17·2 per cent to 422,000 people by 1750. Denmark's population rose from 777,000 to 806,000 between 1732 and 1750.

At first Poland experienced a sharp decrease in births, especially in the decades 1650–60, 1670–80 and 1710–20, implying population stagnation over the whole period. In the Danube basin, Habsburg–Turk wars led to considerable population movements. Some of the areas taken by the Habsburgs were almost totally depopulated and were resettled by colonists from south-west Germany and Lorraine. Serbian families, Slovaks, Wallachians, Greeks and Jews were also encouraged to settle on the Hungarian plains. The Habsburg lands officially belonging to the German Empire had about 6,500,000 inhabitants in the middle of the eighteenth century. Hungary with Transylvania and Croatia-Slovenia probably had another 10,000,000 people.

It is particularly difficult to obtain accurate details of Russian population because of her vast and fluid frontiers. A census was carried out in central Russia in 1680, when 791,018 hearths were counted. Further censuses were conducted in 1701 and during the years 1707 to 1710. In some regions population seems to have fallen considerably, in the north by over 40 per cent and even around Moscow by a quarter. The total number of hearths was 637,005. These decreases had several causes: enlistment in the army; impressment into new industrial projects; flight because of heavy burdens of taxes; and the possibility that officials were less efficient in keeping records. Yet between 1700 and 1707 Peter the Great authorized military impressment, which took away 250,000 young men from their homes. Population increase in border regions seems to have been especially high, for instance in Siberia and on the lower Volga. Peasants fled to distant, freer areas, and many others avoided the census, so that the decrease was really only a matter of shift and re-distribution.

A more efficient census followed in 1716–17, for the number of hearths counted showed a great increase, whereas the number of peasant flights remained about the same between 1710 and 1717. The government recorded increases in population despite the inadequate way in which the census was carried out. Officials in charge of the count sometimes calculated twenty persons per hearth, sometimes ten, according to whether they were drunk or not! In 1680 a Russian hearth had been estimated at seven persons. In 1719 a regulation was made that souls and not households should be counted, and subsequent instructions to censors were even more explicit. Servants were to be counted separately, since peasants liked to hide them. From the available figures, the Russian population seems to have grown steadily, although this may only be a reflection of increasing administrative efficiency. Rural population increase was crucial for agricultural improvement, but also for conscription into industries such as mining, made possible by the introduction of *obrok* labour services for peasants. Russia's population was probably 14,000,000 in 1724. By 1747 it may have been 16,000,000. Under Peter 1 population density was, however, a mere three inhabitants per square kilometre. By 1800 it had risen to eight. In central Russia density was greatest, reaching fifty per square kilometre around Moscow.

Population figures for individual states varied greatly according to urban development. In general there was continuous movement from country to town, because the countryside produced a surplus of population which villages could not support. Towns took in this surplus and also showed much higher death-rates than rural areas. In countries with highly developed manufactures industry was also conducted in rural areas, thus a higher density of population could subsist. This was true for Westphalia and parts of Switzerland and above all for Holland and south and east England. A classic example is the ship-building industry in the villages around seventeenth-century Amsterdam.

Among the towns, the capitals and residences of ruling princes grew most rapidly because they benefited from trade and government expansion. Paris grew to 550,000 inhabitants during the eighteenth century and Lyons reached the 100,000 mark. Vienna, which had 50,000 people in 1600, rose to 247,000 and Berlin, with 12,000 inhabitants in about 1600, had 172,000 by 1800. Hamburg and Danzig each provided shelter for about 60,000 inhabitants in the 1640s at the height of the Thirty Years' War. These large towns also had particularly high death-rates, above all because of the lack of hygiene, which made epidemics uncontrollable. Only constant immigration from the countryside could make good these death-rates.

Fluctuations in population growth need more detailed analysis. Population losses caused by the wars have previously been over-estimated by historians, but they still have to be taken into account. This is true for the Thirty Years' War, the wars of Louis xiv, the Spanish War of Succession and the Northern wars, which must have caused considerable loss of life. The results of epidemics which often accompanied wars were even more devastating. We know of the decimating effects of typhus, which was studied among soldiers in Schleswig and Jutland in 1659. In 1703–04 there was a particularly savage epidemic of typhus in war-torn Bavaria. Even plague reappeared in Europe as late as the early eighteenth century. In 1708 it spread from Poland to Silesia, arriving in Stockholm in 1710. In Danzig 32,600 people died of it in 1709, more than a third of the total population. The next heaviest losses came from Stockholm, Helsinki, Riga and Königsberg (Kaliningrad). Rural districts were equally hard hit. In East Prussia 11,000 farms were left deserted by the plague, which reached Germany, Bohemia and Austria in 1712–13. In Prague alone 37,000 persons are said to have perished.

In 1720 a ship from a Syrian port is said to have brought the plague to Marseilles, where 40,000 out of 90,000 inhabitants died. The epidemic spread all over Provence and various smaller towns lost a third or half of their inhabitants. Arles and La Valette even lost three-quarters. Why did plague then disappear from Europe? Most states and town councils began to set up more efficient medical boards of supervision, and although there was no advance in diagnosis and preventive medicine as such, improved quarantine and hygiene began to contain the spread of epidemics. Increases in brick and stone building over wood, plaster and thatch also gave improved protection against vermin.

1721 was the last year of plague in Europe and subsequent epidemics were never so terrifying. Years of good harvests in the 1720s also increased population again and the death-rate was lower than at any time until the 1780s. In a famous article Utterström has shown that death-rates were influenced by such factors as poor harvests and weather and climatic fluctuations, both of which affected standards of living and housing and contributed to epidemics. In eighteenth-century Sweden death-rates seem to have been higher in the east than in the west and north of the country. At that time most of the larger towns were in east Sweden. Bad housing and poor access to clean water supplies were the chief cause of high death-rates. Advances in preventive medicine did not come until the nineteenth century. Birth-rates in the seventeenth century are estimated to have been relatively high at thirty to forty births per thousand. From various church protests we have the impression that crudely effective methods of birth control were practised. During famine years birth-rates tended to fall drastically, for instance in the Beauvaisis between 1649 and 1652, 1661 and 1662, and 1693 and 1694. The same is true of the Liège district. It was not only during times of obvious crisis that birth-control was practised, however.

Population migration needs separate investigation. In the seventeenth century warfare and religious persecution caused major migrations. In the 1640s Swiss emigrated to Germany, and, later, French protestants moved into central Europe. The largest migration in the second half of the seventeenth century was caused by the Revocation of the Edict of Nantes in 1685. Protestants in Austria and Salzburg, the so-called *Exulanten*, moved into north-east Germany. Geneva, Berlin, Magdeburg and Erlangen became favourite goals for refugees. Frederick II's Prussia took in great numbers after proclaiming a policy of religious toleration.

Colonization was also encouraged in the Habsburg lands under Maria Theresa, and immigrants were brought from south-west Germany into the Danube basin and to Galicia and Bukovina. Unlike refugees, colonists were actively attracted into east and south-east Europe by being offered better prospects to escape famine and over-population caused at home by division of land on inheritance. The Palatinate was most affected by this sort of colonial emigration. In north-west Germany there were many *Hollandgänger*, men who worked in Holland, and soon Ruhr iron and coal began to attract miners from Saxony and Hesse. Apart from going to Prussia and to the Danube basin, south-west German colonists went to the Russian Black Sea region. Some emigration was accidental, as for instance the Hessian mercenary soldiers who took service in British colonial America and then remained there. The Swiss sent out about

300,000 young men as mercenaries during the period, although recruitment tended to fall off as prosperity increased at home. Thus poor and overpopulated highland regions, such as the Alps as well as the Scottish Highlands and south Ireland, provided mercenaries, because men there could find no alternative employment.

The population increase after the beginning of the eighteenth century was both cause and effect of further economic growth in agriculture, trade and industry stimulating supply through the increased demand and consumption. Although overseas trade incressed, a greater volume of trade was still handled within Europe. In addition the economic policies of absolutist dynastic states centred above all on increasing armaments ostensibly for defence of the state. Mercenaries were still used in the second half of the eighteenth century, but conscription became more and more important. Armies continually increased in size. At the battle of Malplaquet in 1709 200,000 men were involved, and by the time of the French Revolution the peace-time armies of the great continental powers were in excess of 200,000 men each. Army supply created an early form of mass production and led to standardization, technical simplification, and rationalization of methods of production. The growth of specialized navies in place of earlier types of armed merchant ships was especially striking. French advances in ship-building on a national basis came early and had spread throughout the European navies by 1800; these were an important factor in increasing ship sizes before the era of iron hulks. Freighting, especially of raw materials, became more economical and was especially helpful in Baltic and North Sea sailings to west Europe and the Levant, as well as on the transatlantic routes which became so lucrative in the eighteenth century.

The increasing demands of armies and navies were matched by consumption in the large towns and by a growth in distributive trades. The exchange of colonial goods such as tobacco, cane-sugar, cocoa, tea and coffee for textiles and manufactured goods became especially important. The fashion for *chinoiserie* led to large-scale manufacture of porcelains, with famous names such as Delft, Meissen, Nymphenburg and Copenhagen. Fashion and taste in interior decorating and furnishing arrived for all those who could afford them.

III State Planning and the Economy

Entrepreneurs and workers were strongly influenced by paternalist state supervision in continental Europe, especially in the France of the mercantilist Colbert. He formed a *conseil du commerce* in 1664 to centralize control over manufacturing industries, their workshops and marketing outlets under Bellinzani, who was named the first inspector-general of factories. Various entrepreneurs were given state development aid; Camuset, for instance, for large-scale production of knitted goods, the brothers Dalliez for foundries and mining works, Madame de la Petitière for lace and embroidery works. All workshops were expected to follow state regulations, and many undertakings were owned by the crown, among them the tapestry works of Paris (Gobelins and Savonnerie) and Beauvais and the arsenals at Brest, Toulon and Rochefort. State-backed enterprises often marked their products 'by royal appointments'. Italian specialists in glass, mirror, lace and other luxury manufacture were imported, as were miners, foundry-workers and tin-plate makers from Sweden and Germany and weavers from Holland, among them Van Robais, who built a factory for fine cloth in Abbeville on English models. The flight of French skilled workers was forbidden by severe state punishment. A regulation in 1682 threatened workers who tried to leave the country with death. In 1665 Colbert sent master-weavers to Bourges to improve the textile industry. The *intendant* had a stocking and woollen cap workshop built in Poitiers and a leather workshop in Chatellerault. Workshops were set up in poor houses and hospitals. The poverty hospital at Bordeaux made stockings, lace and carded wool.

The state often provided entrepreneurs with interest-free loans and even with land, buildings and equipment at initially low rents. Workmen were offered temporary tax-freedom from *taille* and from any obligation to billet soldiers or serve in the army themselves. Town councils and Estates' assemblies were also ordered to help. Frequently workshops were given monopolies over regional production. Such an example was late seventeenth-century Languedoc, where the workshops of Clermont l'Hérault, Saptes and Conques held a monopoly for making fine cloth.

Luxury industries were given favoured treatment. Lace manufactures were set up in Paris, Rheims and in the Bourbonnais, Auvergne and Normandy. The lace-makers who had so far worked at home were collected together in workshops, although this led to conflicts with excluded workers in Aurillac, Auxerre, Bourges and Alençon. A workshop for silk crêpe was set up in 1660 under licence in Lyons and the import of Italian crêpe was prohibited. A workshop for velvet, silver and gold cloth was opened in Paris in 1668. Nîmes became the centre of a taffeta industry and silk stockings began to be made in Lyons. Camuset employed women as milliners on the putting-out system, and there were said to have been 20,000 operatives in the Beauce area alone. The weaving loom spread so widely that by 1700 the government attempted to restrict it to Paris and seventeen other privileged towns. Amiens began to copy Brussels camlet, and Meaux took up Flanders damask. Even if some of Colbert's workshops did not last long, French industry was greatly stimulated. This was especially the case in Languedoc where industry had been almost non-existent before 1660.

Colbert set up a complicated system of state supervision with workshop chambers of commerce and a factory inspectorate. The system depended on overall direction by a solvent central authority, and this was noticeably lacking after Colbert's death. Unwise political and military measures were undertaken in the later years of Louis xiv's reign. For this Colbert cannot be blamed, and it remains an open question whether his system could have worked more successfully had Louis xiv waged fewer wars. Colbert's industrial policy had been closely linked with trade, which was to be controlled by protective customs barriers, freeing raw material imports, but taxing imported manufactures. Exports of home manufactured goods were to be encouraged with subsidies. The new tariff of 1664 was based on these ideas.

Colbert's economic policy soon led to trade war, especially with the Dutch. No matter how much success the French had in the military field, ultimately they lost at sea. Colbert certainly played an important role in the great trade wars of the 1670s but by the end of Louis xiv's reign a freer tariff policy was introduced under Pontchartrain and Desmarets; this included bi-lateral agreements with states as distant as Russia and Persia in 1708, Portugal and Prussia in 1713, and the Austrian Nether-lands in 1714. Yet Colbert had been the first to produce a practically effective French national budget, although his tax reforms were ineffective and he could never raise enough money to abolish internal tolls. He did succeed in balancing the French budget by 1670, although Louis xiv's ostentation and wars soon destroyed credit, and he did succeed in making the rôle of the absolutist state crucial to the economic well-being of all its subjects. The recognition that economic strength also meant political power remains a basic belief of both central and local government right down to our own times. Various stimuli were used in order to increase industrial production. Above all, special banks were founded to supply cheap credit, if possible at $2\frac{1}{2}$ per cent from a special state industrial budget, as well as privileges of manufacture, distribution, prices and sale. Prizes were freely given. Inventors were lionized and industrial espionage in foreign countries encouraged. Everything was done to promote technological advance for the greater glory of the state. While in France the rôle of the state predominated, in Germany economic power was more diffused and more traditionally exercised. Guilds and town councils operated at two levels. Some were responsible only to Emperor and the imperial assembly and others to territorial rulers and territorial Estates' assemblies.

The tendency of guilds to isolate themselves from economic development was already apparent by the sixteenth century, and it now developed even further, leading to economic stagna-tion. Production was often held down so much in the interest of a few guild masters that it failed to satisfy demand. This was the less creditable side of mercantilism – monopoly for the sake of restricting growth, or simply too many regulations to make production worthwhile. Seventeenth-century governments showed that the state was capable of both strangling and encouraging economic growth.

Restrictive practices cancelled out technological advances and reduced productivity to traditional, more labour-intensive levels. This could also hinder unwelcome redistributions of income, however, and therefore help to prevent social discontent. Guild incomes often remained equally distributed. Yet wage- and price-fixing, so common in early modern Europe, was usually in the interest of those with economic power not, therefore, the majority of wage-earners and peasants. Hence there were cartels fixing minimum prices, buying up raw materials, restricting access to manufacture, distribution and trade, and creating a 'closed shop' mentality. Restrictions were imposed on all aspects of economic activity right down to small-shop keeping, limitation of working hours in all jobs, restriction of advertising and sales and detailed regulations for piece-work. No one could work for anyone else in an early modern German town or village without permission from the local authorities.

The guild of mirror-makers in Nuremberg monopolized distribution of imported mirror-glass and shared profits equally among its members. Only the senior master received an extra 3 per cent as compensation for organizing the overall storage and sale of goods. The syndicate was so popular that it was extended indefinitely in 1723. Some towns even had rules for levelling incomes between different guilds.

Energetic measures could usually be taken against trades which had no guilds to protect their interests, in the town itself as well as in its suburbs, and surrounding villages. Interlopers and 'botchers' were declared enemies of the guilds who asserted, albeit sometimes spuriously, a certain quality control over production and sales. Abuses could become extreme, however, as was the case in late eighteenth-century Nuremberg, where guilds kept 'black lists' of lax customers. The difference between masters and journeymen was also strictly enforced. Wages, which failed to keep up with devaluations of currency, inflation and price rises, were pegged by guilds, and the duties of journeymen were exactly defined. A close watch was kept on apprenticeship. Moral supervision included snooping into fornication, adultery and other 'crimes', such as birth of illegitimate children, which could result in exclusion from the guilds and economic ruin.

Guilds also engaged in welfare and cultural activities for

members and dependents, though guild income was often too low to provide adequately for sick and infirm members, and they remained dependent on town council, church and state institutions, as well as private bequests. Guilds retained numerous social occasions, monthly dinners, processions, and festivals. Some defence duties remained, but they were often merely formal and festive occasions. Fire-fighting was still carried out, however. On balance, guild traditionalism seriously hindered industrial growth and prevented important technological innovations. But guilds very often had the support of their town councils as well as the territorial state government. Town councils had the duty to protect consumers and often needed guild help to supervise quality, quantity and price of retailed goods. In Nuremberg, for example, strict bye-laws regulated bakeries and slaughter houses, barbers, tanners and dyers. Town council power was based on the need of all its citizens to secure adequate food supplies and protect market outlets at all times. Minimum prices were fixed for the town's own exports and maximums for necessary imports, especially of raw materials. Each town juggled for a favoured position over its neighbour by seeking to operate numerous local regulations which ultimately interfered with the economy as a whole. Competition was thus directed towards the hunt for privileges and monopolies. There was no such thing as free trade. Measures designed to keep order in the economy were the prime responsibility of the political authorities.

The main problem of guild activity based on small town autonomy in Germany was that it led to the formation of a very narrow-minded society. Political, religious and economic uniformity were the result, and although one region varied from another local inhabitants had little chance of benefiting from variety. Social policies were strictly moral. Everything and everybody had their place in a God-given, man-controlled order. Perhaps the only real flexibility was in operating urban systems of taxation, which tended to favour increasingly high excises or indirect taxes, thus taxing the poor relatively more heavily than the rich.

There were of course advantages to be gained by paternalism, especially in the field of welfare, where most towns operated poor laws. In Nuremberg private foundations made available 20,000 Gulden a year to those decreed as needy poor by the town council. Education was also catered for and most recipients were of the urban artisan class, well below the honourable status of 'burgher'. Under the Nuremberg market superintendent Andreas Ingolstätter, public provision for the poor was reorganized to exclude street beggars. The money raised officially made it possible to help a thousand poor townsfolk yearly. Aid to the poor was minimal and only extended to the young, old or infirm. A rational view of humanity prevailed – an individual was to blame if he failed to succeed in life. In such cases the authorities regarded it as their social duty to 'correct' – that is, punish – such deviance. Eighteenth-century Nuremberg had no fewer than eight hospitals for its own townsfolk. Town council policy was always to preserve what had been achieved and the standards of those burghers who had an economic or social position to uphold; questions of further economic development were always subjected to these factors. This attitude ultimately caused the economic decline and political collapse of the town.

Territorial rulers were able to operate more imaginative economic policies. Brandenburg-Prussia gave the clearest example of this in this period. Measures to increase population were particularly important, especially in areas devastated by warfare. Productivity was thought to depend primarily on size of population, as were tax yields and military effectiveness. Immigration was encouraged, irrespective of language and creed. French Huguenots were accepted as well as Protestants from Salzburg. Among the 30,000 expelled from Salzburg 15,000 were allowed to settle in East Prussia. About 200,000 Huguenots settled in Ansbach-Bayreuth and Brandenburg-Prussia. Emigration was heavily discouraged and at times it was completely forbidden. An increased birth-rate was favoured and homes for foundlings and orphans were set up. The unmarried began to be taxed more heavily.

Agrarian policy in Prussia was aimed at making good war damage. Materials and stocks were provided to re-establish farms and tax relief was given for several years. In east Germany some demesne lords even offered land on *Lassrecht* (for a ground rent). Wasted peasant holdings were given rent-free to new settlers for limited numbers of years, and the state offered tax-free years. But these privileges only lasted as long as economic necessity required, although anyone might try his hand at farm management, and a cottar or ploughman could rise to be a

peasant. An important service carried out by territorial governments was to cancel arrears of interest especially on war debts.
Deserted farms were frequently taken over by enterprising landlords setting up their own demesnes and latifundia. State aid
was invariably needed to supervise and restore the quality of
cultivated land at times of crisis, such as during and after the
Thirty Years' War and the wars of Louis xiv, especially in the
Rhineland, northwest Germany and Saxony. The Thirty Years'
War above all encouraged the further development of demesne
and latifundia farming, leading in northeast Germany especially
to a new era of serfdom for many families of previous tenant
farmers.

There were, however, deliberate state policies of peasant
protection in northwest Germany, Thuringia and Saxony,
where governments forbade landlords from altering tenants'
contracts so as to safeguard state revenues from the land-taxes
that peasants paid. When the state attempted to alter the laws
of inheritance, peasant custom was often stronger. *Realteilung*
(the division of land on inheritance) had spread from the west
as far as Thuringia. When the rulers of Bavaria attempted to
impose Realteilung as opposed to closed inheritance, their own
peasants resisted the move. Even so, most peasantries had to
accept at least the codification of their customary rights during
the course of the seventeenth century.

The state tried to increase harvest yields by circulating handbooks and almanacs containing useful hints on farming. The
Great Elector set up show farms called *Holländereien* on Dutch
models. Frederick William i and Frederick ii were also interested
in improving farming. New crops such as turnips, beets, potatoes, flax, tobacco, lupins and hops were introduced under their
rule. Old mine workings were reclaimed for agriculture and the
cultivation of winter feed for cattle was encouraged. Frederick ii
formed regional credit banks to finance agrarian improvements.
The early eighteenth-century Cameralists made an especial
study of farming. Johann Christoph Schubart, who developed
clover-farming, was ennobled and took the name of Kleefeld.
Cameralists and Physiocrats influenced each other as the chief
economic theorists of the late mercantile era in Europe.

State industrial policy aimed at the consolidation of productive capacity into larger units, in order to achieve a positive
balance of trade. But craft industries were not neglected and

governments were often prepared to pay higher prices in order to equip their courts and armies with home manufactured goods, such as textiles, as well as luxuries – silks, porcelain and tapestries.

French immigrants with new manufacturing skills were settled in Erlangen and Magdeburg only after conflict with native guild interests. Indeed immigrants often had to find towns where for some especial reason vested interests were already weak. Such was the case of Magdeburg after the great sack of 1631. Sometimes territorial rulers used immigrants to break guild monopolies and increase the competitiveness of their subjects. A favourite government method was to withdraw the charters and privileges of town councils and reissue them without monopoly rights in trade and manufacture. The Hohenzollern rulers were particularly fond of this course of action in their west German territories.

In order to increase production privileged *Freimeister* (free masters) working outside guild restrictions were created by territorial governments. They went into larger scale *Manufaktur* and were the forerunners of industrialists. In addition to craft workers, merchants also frequently received licences to set up a Manufaktur, often with government aid to obtain raw materials and preferred marketing outlets. Territorial rulers were primarily interested in establishing native textile and luxury industries. Next in importance came more overt armaments industries, metals and chemicals, cannon, guns and munitions. In addition there were crafts producing porcelain and paper, and working in gold and silver. Industrial planning was thus the most important feature of government economic policy as the eighteenth century progressed, and such traditional areas as agrarian and trading policies began to be increasingly subordinated.

Mining and iron founding had already exhausted easily accessible resources by the sixteenth century and new workings needed more sophisticated, larger-scale operations, which could often only be financed with government backing. The state now had to intervene or even take over the whole business. In order to make it pay, technical improvements had to be introduced and became increasingly necessary for industrial survival by the eighteenth century. The increasing use of coal was especially important for continued profitability; central and east Europe were very well endowed with deposits of lignite and coal. Initiatives for state supervision of coal mining came from Prussia, with improved mining regulations for County Mark in 1737. State supervision extended to conditions of work and safety measures as well as control of leases to increase output at a rate favourable to the treasury. The revised mining regulations of 1776 introduced a *Direktionsprinzip* (unified mining administration). As coal production rose the state also turned its interest towards the conservation of timber resources. Not only did the iron and other metal industries need a great deal of wood, but glass foundries, salines, shipyards and the building and domestic industry continued to require large amounts. Older iron and glass foundries were closed in order to protect forests and game laws were now put under forestry management. No doubt Frederick ii of Prussia despised hunting as barbaric. Game control was now no longer only a pastime of the landed gentry but also a science to protect agriculture and forestry.

Workshops of the new Manufaktur type employed increasingly large numbers of semi- and un-skilled workers. At first the socially unfortunate, such as tramps, beggars, criminals, orphans and the unemployed, were put to compulsory work in workhouses, and the unemployable were often locked into lunatic asylums. The textile industry had enough extremely dull and simple operations to absorb their work. The state often farmed out so-called social misfits under its care to private enterprise.

Industry now began for complex social and fiscal reasons to reign supreme over merchants and trades. Whereas merchants needed an increasingly free-trade area, home manufacturers needed increasingly protective tariffs, and it was these that fitted better into the mercantilist ideology of sovereign state economy and power. Merchants were now only needed as exporters of home-made industrial products and as importers of foreign raw materials to feed home industries. In this subordinate but essential rôle state-regulated merchant enterprise would achieve a positive balance of trade, and the state would become a great power. In other words crass egoism towards neighbouring states was typical. The mercantilist state bequeathed a legacy of patriotism and xenophobia to its modern successors, and industry as well as trade had become another sinew of war by the later eighteenth century.

The budgets of smaller central European states were increasingly balanced by the receipt of subsidies from stronger neighbouring and foreign powers. France, Holland and Britain at most times in the later seventeenth and eighteenth centuries subsidized one or other of the German territorial states. Bullion imports were also encouraged by lowering the price of exports where necessary, for with increased population and home demand a buoyant money supply was needed to prevent a slump. Such a policy was considered all the more suitable where no native production of precious metals existed. Although experiments with paper money had been conducted since the mid-seventeenth century on a national scale, no effective way had ever been worked out whereby paper could supplant bullion.

Coinage policy thus remained the backbone of early modern economic planning. As late as the 1750s Prussia experienced an hysteria of coinage clipping reminiscent of the 1620s. In central Europe, coinage came increasingly under the supervision of the German imperial, federal circles, who renegotiated bullion rates at regular intervals. Such a meeting was that at Zinna in 1667, organized by Saxony, whose ruler was director of the Upper Saxon Circle. At Zinna north-east Germany went back to the gold standard of 1623 with a Gulden of account at 2/3 Taler or 90 Kreuzers. By 1690 most of north-west Germany, including the Brunswick dynasty, had joined in as well. A 'Leipzig standard' was created according to which 12 Talers instead of the previous 10½ went into the silver bullion Mark. But abuse of the currency was not thereby prevented. Although much publicity was made of the coinage delinquencies of small princes such as the Counts of Sayn-Wittgenstein, these states were too insignificant economically to disrupt inter-German trade with their bad coin. Instead it was the large territories, such as Austria and Prussia, who debased their coinage at times of war and caused real economic hardship and disruption in central Europe.

The Empire intervened in various ways in the coinage policies of territorial rulers. Imperial economic policy encompassed those matters of common interest to the territories, such as supervision of the guild system, and also economic measures affecting foreign countries. After the disruption of the Thirty Years' War, federal economic planning was taken up again at imperial assembly level. A brake was put on the efforts of guilds to extend their legal powers by means of boycott, and there were extensive measures to prevent the status of 'master' from becoming too exclusive. On the other hand, sumptuary laws were promulgated to prevent conspicuous consumption among the common people. These measures reached their peak in the imperial regulations for industry of 1731, issued with the especial support of Prussia and Saxony by the standing imperial assembly at Regensburg. Guilds were now state controlled and town council autonomy strictly curtailed, except in those few remaining imperial towns that exercised their own state power. Guilds no longer had legal authority over their members. Meetings could only take place under state supervision. Guild access was made easier. Enforcement of these measures, however, depended on the strength of individual territorial rulers. Needless to say, the Hohenzollerns led the way in imposing their new powers on municipalities in their territories.

In addition, measures were introduced against foreign countries. The imperial war against Louis XIV in the 1670s was also waged on the economic front by the imperial law of 7 May 1676, which outlawed trade with France. According to the Austrian economist J. J. Becher this measure cost Germany about 4,000,000 Reichstalers in lost trade. War conditions were used to encourage the growth of native industry. But these efforts only lasted a short time. The imperial towns in particular were against them. After the Treaty of Nijmegen in 1678 imperial war legislation lost its effectiveness, although it was renewed during the Palatinate War from September 1689. But whenever political conditions allowed, the imperial towns saw to it that embargoes became ineffective. Trade with France was again disrupted during the Spanish Wars of Succession after 1702, and in 1705 Joseph I incorporated the embargo into his Habsburg imperial commercial code.

Just as the Empire had been powerless to prevent coinage clipping in the early 1620s, so it could do nothing during the monetary crises of the 1670s to 1690s. This time efforts at reform came mainly from Brandenburg-Prussia and Saxony. The Leipzig standard of 1690, which allowed 12 instead of 10½ Talers to be struck to the silver bullion Mark, was finally adopted by the Empire in 1738. But the Habsburg Emperor decided on another standard of 10 Talers or 20 Gulden to the

Cologne silver bullion Mark in 1740. This standard was adopted by Bavaria in 1753, by an agreement (*Konvention*) which gave subsequent south German coins the name of Konventionstalers. Many German territorial mints followed suit and the era of the Maria Theresa Thaler had arrived.

Swiss economic policies generally followed imperial German lines. But cantonal autonomy was even stronger than that of many German territorial states and left little opportunity for federal co-operation. The Swiss Diet concerned itself with the protection of home markets. Mostly it issued warnings and recommendations. Frequently measures were only passed because they were in the interest of the most economically powerful cantons. Mercantilist ideas soon gained a foothold, especially in Berne, which as the centre of the Confederation attempted for a time to copy Colbert's ideas and encourage large-scale industry by state direction. Similar attempts were made by the administrations of Fribourg, Lucerne and the bishopric of Basle. Solothurn tried to encourage large-scale production by issuing privileges, while in Geneva, St Gallen, Zürich and Schaffhausen economic policy favoured the towns. Among the earliest measures were salt monopolies. The supply of grain, meat and butter was soon made a matter of strict cantonal supervision.

In the Austrian lands economists like Becher, Hörnigk and Schröder attempted to encourage the Habsburgs to introduce mercantilism, but with qualified success. More sustained efforts were made by Charles vi and Maria Theresa. Under the former, merchant councils were set up in Bohemia and Silesia, and in Vienna a *Kommerzkollegium* or Board of Trade was formed with supreme authority. Maria Theresa created a central commercial directorate for German-speaking Austria, with subordinate commercial offices in each province. The whole system was later reorganized but retained a two-tier structure, which was important for federalism.

During the reigns of Maria Theresa and Joseph ii, Habsburg mercantilism was stimulated by efforts first of all to regain, and then to find substitutes for, industrial production lost in Silesia to Frederick ii's Prussia. Many Austrian measures now followed Prussian examples. Two great phases of Austrian state reform were inaugurated in the 1740s and later 1760s. Settlement and agricultural policy was largely directed towards the newly won southwest. Tariffs protecting home industries especially benefited the German speaking areas of Austria. Austria had been forced to compete with Prussia, but she was still a long way from being able to compete economically with the west European powers. The Habsburgs remained weak above all in banking and credit facilities.

East Europe imported western mercantilist ideas relatively late. The beginnings can be traced to the reign of Tsar Alexis, but the real high-point came with Peter the Great, until the death of his minister, Pososkov, in 1726. Tsarist mercantilism was clearly a Russian hybrid on a western model. Peter i concentrated on mining and export industries. Customs and tariffs were manipulated in the conventional mercantilist manner to increase home production. Those of 1724 had an especially protectionist character. Bilateral trading agreements were made in support of Russian foreign policy as a whole, based whenever possible on the new town of St Petersburg (Leningrad), rather than on Archangel as before. The construction of canal systems was begun under Peter and also served this purpose. In addition to measures for foreign trade efforts were made to build up internal trade; these were of benefit to the yearly fairs of Makariev in Nisni Novgorod, as well as to the main centres, St Petersburg and Moscow. Two central offices were set up to control industry, one council or *Collegium* for industry generally and one especially for mining. Foreign experts were imported to build up industry and train necessary specialists under extremely lucrative contracts. They were supplied with abundant forced labour, and a flourishing Russian arms industry soon emerged. Peter the Great's own brand of mercantilism has a particularly violent character all of its own, linked to the traditional powers of Muscovite autocracy to a far larger extent than Peter's frantic policies of westernization would otherwise lead one to believe.

Poland too provides examples of mercantilistic ideas, but there was no central authority whatever to enforce them. From time to time the import of goods detrimental to home industry was hindered, but these were measures that on the whole served the interests of particular factions in the *szhlachta* (nobility). Measures only assumed a more mercantilist character after the middle of the eighteenth century, but by then it was too late to save the Polish state from partition and disintegration at the hands of more powerful neighbouring states.

In Sweden policies of state intervention were successful for as long as the nation remained a great power with colonial economic interests in Europe that needed expensive defence. Under Queen Christina it was feared that the forests of Bergslagen, the industrial heart of the country, were being decimated. Forging and iron finishing were thus diversified and transferred to other parts of the country in order to conserve timber. Despite the problems of transport, new manufacturing centres (*bruk*) were built throughout Sweden, especially where there was access by water, as in Södermanland, Öster – and Västergötland, Norrland and Finland and especially in Värmland. But no *bruk* might be set up without state permission after the 1650s.

Although the state's main interest was in copper and iron production, from the time of Charles xi onwards it also promoted textile factories, foreign trade and shipping. A special tax was put on salt from the Iberian peninsula and Mediterranean. The *Produktplakat* of 1724 acted like a Swedish equivalent of the English Navigation Acts – foreign ships were only allowed to import the products of their own country into Sweden. This was aimed above all at the Dutch entrepreneur. Native, privileged trading companies were now a clear expression of the state's mercantilist trade policy, and the most successful of these in Sweden was the East India Company, licensed from Gothenburg in 1731.

With the development of an extreme form of royal absolution in Denmark after 1660 the burghers began to be favoured over the nobility. Nobles had predominantly agricultural interests which were a constant hindrance to the crown's mercantilist policies. Men who had become prominent in trade and industry now became more influential, for instance the great merchants of Copenhagen and Holstein such as Irgens and Müller. Workshops were built and all industrial activity leading to economic self-sufficiency was encouraged by privileges and monopolies. Under Frederick iii the council of state set up a Board of Trade or *Kommerskollegium*, which was not, however, fully operative. But under Christian v it was presided over by the king's half-brother, Ulrik Frederick Gyldenløve, one of the most successful entrepreneurs of his time.

The new Danish customs regulations of 1672 were characteristic of state protectionism. The activity of foreign manufacturers was severely limited, and they were not accorded full religious freedom. But wherever guilds stood in the way of industrial advance, measures were taken against them. They were temporarily suspended and use was made of 'free masters', as in the German territories. Chartered companies were even established to engage in the slave trade and Danish St Thomas in the West Indies was made a depôt for colonial trade. St Croix was acquired and an Asia company created for trade with the East Indies.

To increase agricultural productivity, farming needed the same care and attention as industry. State-supported agriculture was first systematically developed in north-west Europe where easy communications and a relatively dense urban population demanded strict policies of food control and supply. These affected grain production in the Baltic area, as well as improvements in shipping and marketing, but did not amount to more logical internal agricultural policies based on any uniform principles in the states concerned. Measures were dictated by prevailing political, fiscal or economic interests.

Everywhere the consolidation of rulers' central powers of state led to disputes with their Estates and assemblies or parliaments. The absolute ruler needed a new service nobility, devoted to him personally, to carry out new military, administrative and economic tasks. In order to achieve this, and to break the political power of the old nobles, towns and clergy, there followed heavy attacks on traditional conditions of land tenure that altered agrarian production in ways that rulers had not always desired. This can be seen in the absolutist regimes of Denmark and Sweden, as well as in Russia where, in the course of the eighteenth century, serfdom took on its severest form. In contrast to more industrially advanced states, rulers of the agrarian east laboured under many disadvantages. They could not rely on the capital resources of a rich indigenous urban patriciate to underwrite their fiscal policies. Distances were greater, population sparser, and the money and market economy were at lower levels. Traditional demesne revenues did not suffice to pay for ambitious foreign policies anywhere in Europe, and east Europe tended to rationalize agrarian production by favouring the large-scale producer at the expense of the peasantry. A taxable class of townsmen and traders was also encouraged with state monopolies. The rationalization of rulers' finance from the sixteenth century onwards depended on a policy of monopolies, and this was particularly the case in the agrarian states where credit facilities were strictly limited. In Russia, for instance, state customs on alcohol produced more income than any other indirect taxes, despite frequent tax evasion.

West European industry could absorb surplus land labour, but in the more agrarian east there were fewer alternatives, and skilled workers were a rarity. Instead there was a great surplus of unskilled labour, employed in increasingly crude ways by the state and its servitors. Yet restrictions on peasant mobility were often the worst forms of labour conscription, especially in Bohemia and Moravia, where towns grew up faster than in the other east European countries.

Landowners in the east were often industrial entrepreneurs because only they had enough serfs to supply new concerns with sufficient labour. Russian industrialists were often given the right to dispose of whole village populations in this way. Foreign entrepreneurs, technicians and specialists were only of decisive importance when sufficient unskilled native labour had been mobilized. This applied to the early industries of countries such as Denmark as well as to those of Russia. The more economically advanced states were able to rely on a strong class of vigorous merchants in their mercantilistic policy, but in the agrarian countries the state had to intervene to create such a class and then to make it possible for it to accumulate wealth.

In excise policy an agrarian country such as Russia, which had strong autocratic rule from a central authority, could achieve startling economic progress. Internal customs dues, especially those with the Ukraine, were abolished more successfully and earlier (1733) in Russia than in the rest of continental Europe. Maria Theresa was only ever able to abolish a few of the Austrian internal customs dues – a customs barrier between Austria and Hungary remained, as did another division between Transylvania and the Banat.

Colbert conserved forestry reserves because he saw their importance to the French economy, especially to its naval power. He aimed to make forestry an autonomous branch of the state economy. In 1661 he replaced the king's head forester with a series of provincial commissioners. Nicolas Lallemant's national survey map was used as a basis for the forestry regulations of 1669. They included outline directions for future planting and felling, to be applied to state forests, to 3,000,000 hectares of church and common forest, and also to 4,000,000 hectares of Estate-owned woodland. Types of trees for planting were specified, as were suitable soils, and forest pasturage for pigs was closely regulated. All *servitudes* or cottage enterprises that had encroached on forest land since the 1560s had to be redeemed by a special tax. Although these measures were never fully carried out, Colbert did assure France of self-sufficiency in timber, especially for ship-building. By the 1720s his measures had been extended to cover the forests of Franche-Comté and Dauphiné. A temporary shortage of wood supply in 1723 led to the withdrawal of state permission to set up new foundries and forges. In about 1750 Chief Naval Inspector Duhamel created modern forestry science in order to assure supplies to French shipyards. During the various French military occupations of the Rhineland, Alps and north Italy, forestry regulations were introduced, but with little permanent success until the Napoleonic era.

Forestry was largely subordinated to hunting in the German territories, where game laws were often particularly harsh in the decade after the Thirty Years' War. Hunting and shooting were prerogative rights of high nobility and conferred social status. There was no place for an autonomous state forestry industry in Colbert's sense, although the Cameralists did recognize that territorial state income could be increased by efficient forestry administration, a point taken especially in the Alpine regions of states such as Bavaria. Even so, the early literature on husbandry paid only scant attention to the new science of forestry.

In the German mining districts some advances in forestry planning were made out of sheer necessity, though they often came very late. In 1713 the chief mining official of Saxony, Hans von Carlowitz, published the first German book on forestry, the *Silvicultura oeconomica*. He recommended planting of conifers which grew faster than other types and were thus the forester's equivalent of a cash crop. Such forests soon spread throughout Saxony, Silesia and Moravia. The state forests of Hesse specialized in deciduous products. Between 1720 and 1730 the chief forester of Hesse-Darmstadt, von Minnigerode, engaged in large-scale afforestation projects. In Hanau-Münzenberg chief forester Christian von Einsiedeln introduced a strict code, aimed at systematic felling for natural reseeding of beech and oak, which spread over the whole of Hesse-Kassel and was introduced in 1744 in the Electorate of Mainz. A more efficient system of taxation led to the introduction of proportional felling with mathematical formulae to calculate the volume of standing timber. J. G. von Langen worked as forester for the Brunswick Guelph family but was soon moved to the Norwegian crown forests, which he exploited as fuel especially for the metal industry, before returning to north-west Germany and to the United Provinces. Forestry became a university taught science by the later eighteenth-century Cameralists. Forestry manuals began to appear in Germany in the 1750s. A more light-hearted approach was Stilser's *Forest and Hunting-History of the Teutons*. In 1759 the first lexicon appeared in Langensalza, written by a Saxon forestry official, and a new phase began for the young science with W. G. Moser's *Grundsätze der Forstökonomie* (*Principles of Forest Economy*), published in 1757. Frederick William I of Prussia issued a combined forestry and hunting ordinance for Brandenburg in 1720, and Frederick II added romance by forming an élite corps of *Feldjäger* (chasseurs or huntsmen). He held that clearing of forest for settlement was more important than planned forestry preservation. Under Maria Theresa the Habsburg state produced new forestry regulations for the crown lands, especially under the ministry of Haugwitz for those in Bohemia, and later on for the Austrian provinces.

Peter the Great followed conventional mercantilist thought by conserving forests for naval power. After 1701 he set up a separate Russian forest administration and employed German master-foresters. In 1708 he proclaimed a forest law for shipbuilding, which monopolized oak and put the management of all forests within 55 kilometres of either bank of large rivers and 22 kilometres of small rivers in the hands of the Romanov Admiralty. Estate-owners on whose lands the *steppe* had encroached were forced to reafforest where the original woodlands had included oak.

IV *Production*

I. LANDLORDS, FARMERS AND TENANTS

In the seventeenth and early eighteenth centuries the majority of Europeans, at least those outside Holland, were engaged in agriculture. But industrial activity now formed an essential secondary sector, and a dynamic tertiary sector of service industries also emerged.

European agriculture was divided into two broad categories. *Grundherrschaft* was the system whereby the landowner received payment in kind and rent from peasant cultivators. This system, which consisted of various forms of dependence, including labour services, spread from the Mediterranean region to the British Isles, France, Netherlands and west-central Europe; there were great differences from one locality to another. In contrast, Schleswig-Holstein and the areas east of the lower Elbe, the lands of the Habsburg monarchy and east Europe generally used the system of *Gutswirtschaft*, based on the labour of serfs who could own their own little. Gutswirtschaft, demesne or latifundia farming was conducting by landlords or their managers with legal rights over their labour force. Peasants in this system had little or no status.

Free peasants formed only a small proportion of the total number and were mainly to be found in areas of cattle-ranching and in the border regions of mountain and marsh. Within the peasantry distinction must be made between those who worked a full peasant holding, or *Hufe* in the medieval sense, and those who only had a modest holding, often because of the effects of divided inheritance, they were forced to seek additional income as rural labourers. There also grew up a class of totally landless peasants and they, together with the gardeners and cottars, were by far the most numerous of all peasants. Finally there was the tenant who had no land rights of his own and who lived by his special skills, which enabled him to work in a rational and capitalist way, producing relatively high profits. Such tenants were often market-gardeners near large centres of population, like those of the Île de France, or they went in for ranching as in the marshes. But there were always substantial local and regional variations in the agrarian economy of Europe.

In pre-revolutionary France the privileged classes by no means owned the greater share of all land, although in some provinces at least a third of the area was in their hands. Church holdings were about 5 per cent of the whole land area, and the countryside around towns was often in bourgeois hands. Nobles and clergy rented out their lands and were often absentee landlords. Latifundia were almost unknown.

A great deal of land was directly farmed by peasant-proprietors in *ancien régime* France – in the western provinces it was 20 per cent, in the north, the Loire district and Burgundy it was about 30 per cent of the whole, in Dauphiné 40 per cent, and in the centre and south about 33 per cent. However, most peasants had too little land for full employment, and they had to find some additional source of income as wage-labourers, servants, inn-keepers, tradesmen or craftsmen. Some extended their farms by renting neighbouring plots. A really small number were coveted *laboureurs*, who had enough land to pay rent and to support themselves.

Rented holdings varied greatly in size. Fifteen hectares was a substantial peasant farm size. The usual peasant contract in France was under *métayage*, renting for half the produce. In his travels in France Arthur Young seems to have painted too black a picture of the French peasant. Many peasants paid fixed rents which inflation had made increasingly unrealistic. Leases were agreed for between three and nine years, predominantly in north France, where large areas of land had been acquired and farmed by rich tenants by the second half of the eighteenth century. They were able to benefit from price rises. But peasants were never free proprietors, and they all had residual feudal duties such as the *aveu*, or acknowledgment of tenure, as well as obligatory services and payments, although personal servitude had almost vanished. Serfdom still existed in Lorraine and Franche Comté, and in scattered localities in central France. Most French peasants had freedom of movement and compulsory services were often down to a few days unpaid labour a year. *Cens* was paid in money or kind, usually quite small items by the eighteenth century. Then there were customary payments to the lord when tenancies changed hands on inheritance and game laws, which caused great bitterness. Landlords acted as judges and the tenant was caught both ways. Finally tithe was exacted universally by the Gallican church. Landlords rights were most onerous in Brittany.

No doubt French peasants were relatively well off compared with the peasants of central and east Europe. They rebelled at the end of the eighteenth century partly as a reaction to landlords who were trying to make peasants pay more realistic rates of rent. The way in which most landlords attempted to do this was by dubious legal methods that increased often long-obsolete feudal dues, or destroyed custom and common rights to land-use. This led to social as well as economic conflict which destroyed the ancien régime, especially when burdensome state taxes are also taken into account. The latter consisted above all of taille, followed by capitation, and frequent *vingtièmes*. In some places these state taxes consumed up to a third of the peasant's gross production, and when other burdens such as forced labour to mend roads and bridges and billeting of troops are taken into account, then the peasant indeed had cause to rebel.

In west Germany conditions were often rather similar to those in France. The trend towards reduced dependence was most pronounced in Württemberg and Baden. Territorial rulers had control over all landlord rights for the whole territory, that is, supreme authority as landowners, supreme judicial authority as overlords and the right to hold serfs. Even so, peasants had wide rights of use in their tenancies. They could freely dispose of them, mortgage them and, to some extent, even divide them. There were fixed payments in cash and in kind, dues for sales and exchanges, payments on marriage, retirement and on inheritance. Labour services were extremely light and total exemption could often be purchased. In north-west Germany developments were similar. Peasants had virtually become owners of their farms, except for the fact that they still paid ground rents, tithes and land-tax to the state. Only on land sales was a landlord's permission still needed. In central Germany limited leasehold had extended to lease for life, and from there to rights of inheritance. Peasants had far-reaching rights to dispose of their holdings, which could only be overridden by decisions in state courts, for reasons such as persistent non-payment of rent, bad farming or proven crime.

In certain parts of north-west Germany a trend towards the creation of demesne or latifundia farms had become noticeable after the Thirty Years' War. This was the case in Lower Saxony and in east Westphalia, noticeably Paderborn, where great noble and ecclesiastical estates began to run their own large-scale farms. In such cases peasants were reduced to wage-serfs with no freedom of movement and subject to heavy labour services that took up several days of the week. But there were still fewer latifundia here than in areas to the east of the lower Elbe. Agriculture was, in short, conducted on a bewildering variety of tenures, legally, socially and economically rooted in firm customs and traditions. Yet conditions were generally better for peasants in west than in east Europe.

The peasant farms of Bavaria were in an intermediate position. Most peasant farms were rented from landlords, and holdings a half or a quarter the size of their medieval originals were most common. Here peasant rights of tenancy were inherited under a variety of customs. Some tenancies were for life only, and others were even at the mercy of annual review by landlords. These made up half of all Bavarian peasant holdings and were called *Freistifte*. Latifundia also increased in the eighteenth century more rapidly than elsewhere in south and west Germany. Bavarian peasants were usually serfs, lacking the personal freedoms so common elsewhere in west Germany. Peasant children were forced to offer their labour to their landlords once they had left the parental household. Rents were usually high, since landlords could revise them yearly. State taxes were only paid by commoners, and the privileged nobles and clergy usually paid token amounts. Perhaps what saved the Bavarian state from succumbing to rebellion was the more or less effective paternalism of rulers' territorial governments, as well as the confirmed independence of the Alpine peasants in the south, whose freedom was never fully crushed.

In many districts of east Europe a new serfdom was imposed during the course of the seventeenth century. Serfs could often not even call movable property their own. Landlords, like petty rulers, used serfs and wage labourers to run their own country houses and latifundia, or employed managers who sent them regular rents enabling them to live as courtiers and absentee landlords in the towns.

In Scandinavia Denmark was the most fertile state. In 1660, when absolutism was introduced, the crown owned about half the land. But it subsequently alienated much of it in a vain attempt to run the state without resort to extensive extraordinary taxes. Absolutism was based on a new court nobility, consisting mainly of immigrant Germans who soon obtained *Fideikommissen*, large entailed estates held as trusts. In this way the number of large estates rose considerably and large-scale enterprises also increased by dispossession of peasants. The fact that the total number of peasant holdings remained constant is explained by division on inheritance. In about 1688 about 90 per cent of all arable and pasture land was farmed by peasants. The number of small-holdings was at first very limited. When reforms were started in 1766 about 14 per cent of the land was under state control. A mere 1·5 per cent came under latifundia, and 8·5 per cent was farmed by peasants as tenants or even as owners. The number of peasant proprietors was, however, very small. Finally, there was also a class of landless living-in servants, *Einlieger*, often employed by more well-to-do peasants.

In Sweden the land-owning nobility still lived mainly on rents, and *säterier* or demesnes never formed more than 20 per cent of all the land owned by the nobility. It was generally recognized that peasants had extensive rights over the land they farmed. There was a sharp distinction between the *skattebonde*, who owned his own land, and the crown farmer who was only a tenant. Even so, crown tenancies tended to be purchased and turned into free peasant land. In this way the proportion of peasant-owners grew from 31·5 per cent in 1700 to 46·9 per cent in 1772. Land ownership lost its class exclusiveness. The privileges of 1723 had already permitted better-off burghers and non-nobles to purchase noble estates. The landless and rural poor or *torpare*, *backstugusittare* and *inhyseshjon* steadily increased their numbers, however. Partible inheritance drastically failed to keep pace with population increase. Among them only torpare had any land of their own. The other two groups were landless workers employed by peasants and nobles.

Latifundia had spread to Poland, Lithuania and west Ukraine by the sixteenth century. Compulsory labour services which developed into serfdom during the second half of the century seem to have been very severe, so that not infrequently duties took up six days of the week. It was frequently the smaller landlord who made the highest demands. The increasing price that the west was prepared to pay for Polish grain stimulated the growth of latifundia until the middle of the seventeenth century.

In Russia the position of the peasants deteriorated even further. The *knout* was introduced as a means of punishment. In 1667 rights of asylum in Church were taken from the peasants. In 1682 a *ukase* permitted the sale of serfs without land. Free peasants existed in areas of new settlement to the north and south, where they lived in autonomous village communities. Palace peasants lived on demesnes belonging to the princes in return for special payments in kind. Some peasants became serfs through debt and served as domestic servants or as agricultural workers. At least, officially, the great peasant law of 1649 no longer recognized slavery by contract.

The legal process of levelling down pomestia lands granted on service tenure to free, allodial property was already well under way by the middle of the seventeenth century. Pomestia lands were now frequently inherited as a matter of course, and this was made law in the ukase of 1684. In this way it also became possible to exchange, sell or give away land, although the ukase of 1685 only allowed donations of up to one-half the whole value of the estate. The distinction between pomestia and allod had almost vanished by the time of Peter the Great. The army reforms put through by Tsar Peter finally allowed connections between pomestia service and pomestia landholding to lapse. Peter the Great himself showed little interest in pomestia agriculture, although the ukase of 23 May 1717, which regulated the inheritance of movable and immovable property, was important in that it prevented the continual fragmentation of agricultural estates by limiting partible inheritance to movables. Partible inheritance increased peasant burdens on ever-shrinking demesnes, which in turn led to reduction in state revenues from taxes. After 1717 landed property was not to be divided or sold and it might only be inherited by one member of the family. Alienation by mortgage was forbidden. Thus Tsar Peter hoped to gain a firm indication of the taxable capacity of the nobility, which he could use to calculate the amount of state service they were to do. But the law was not fully applied and it met with resistance, particularly among the lesser nobility. It was repealed on the accession of Empress Anna in 1731.

The services required by the state from the nobility now steadily decreased, and in 1736 all permanent duties of state service were abolished. In 1762 all compulsory state service was done away with. It now became a free contract between the state and its official, who received a salary in cash. State service thereby ceased to be tied to any property rights. After 1762 owners of land might exploit its mineral wealth, water, fisheries and forests without state intervention. After 1785 the individual might freely dispose of land.

Land ownership became a monopoly of the nobility. In the course of the eighteenth century it became customary for them to inherit certain administrative and military posts, and they were freed from poll tax. A law of 1730 forbade Boyar serfs, monastic serfs and peasants from owning land. In 1746 this regulation was even extended to cover merchants and craftsmen. Church land was also increasingly secularized. At the beginning of the eighteenth century monasteries and bishoprics owned 14 per cent of the land. In 1701 the administration of Church properties was taken over by a state corporation, and in 1724 a new Synod was charged with this task, which was only finally achieved in 1762. In 1764 all Church lands were declared state property, which meant that the clergy became direct servants of the state.

The landed properties of the nobility were concentrated mainly in the centre and south of Russia, excepting Moscow, Vladimir and (Iver) Kalinin. The regions of Kaluga, Tula and Ryazan had the highest percentage of serfs. In Kaluga it rose to 83 per cent of the rural population, and the concentration in Smolensk, Pskov and St Petersburg was also considerable. Along the Volga, in the north, Novgorod, Perm and Kazan state peasants predominated. Noble estates were less extensive in Siberia than elsewhere in Russia. In 1777, an official survey showed that half the properties were small- or moderate-sized, measuring between 100 and 300 desiatins each, and run with fewer than twenty serfs. Latifundia of over 1500 desiatins were just 16 per cent of the total. Under Catherine II, however, these increased especially as Russian agriculture became more export orientated. By now latifundia controlled 80 per cent of all serfs.

In the Ukraine more and more peasants became serfs during the seventeenth century, and the process accelerated after the great rebellions of mid-century. At the death of Peter the Great 63 per cent were serfs. State taxation helped the spread of serfdom in that landlords were given authority as tax collectors and legal arbitrators. Serf farms were usually small, measuring about 3·8 desiatins in the districts where *obrok* was paid and only 2·5 desiatins in districts with compulsory labour services. Around Smolensk and Voronesh, holdings even averaged five desiatins.

Compulsory labour services averaged four days a week, although some areas were run at only two days. Amounts were sometimes left unspecified. In other places the peasant had to cultivate a fixed area of about 1·5 desiatins and was increasingly treated like a landless labourer. Poll tax had the effect, however, of stabilizing the community. The communal division of land under the authority of the *mir* was undertaken in close connection with the distribution of taxes. Yet the scrupulously equal division of land inside the commune according to the number of souls was gradually given up in favour of a system which was based on the work which could actually be done by a household. One *tiaglo* corresponded to the cultivated area which a married couple could work by their own labour. In sparsely populated areas in northern Russia there was no mir organization, since settlements were often far too scattered. Collective tax payment by the community as a whole was legally established in 1785, but it had already been customary for a long time. After 1731 landlords had been charged with overall responsibility for delivery of state taxes. For this the Russian peasantry was increasingly divided into two groups. The one group comprised serfs on noble estates, the other state serfs. After 1786 a third group, of Church serfs, was added. The peasant might now be described only as a person who made payment in kind and performed services for an overseer. The Manifesto of 1762 gave owners the right to punish and dispose of their serfs with practically no legal restriction or state intervention. After 1767 serfs might no longer appeal against their lords.

Serf ownership became increasingly profitable during the course of the eighteenth century in Russia. A survey of 1730 accredited five million serfs to four million petty lords. The pressure to which they were subjected made many serfs flee illegally over the Don to the Urals and on to Siberia. Others engaged in conspiracy and larceny, and this helped rebellions such as that of Pugachev in the 1770s. At a state assembly in 1767 seventy-nine deputies demanded reductions in taxes, services and rents, rights of inheritance and greater powers to engage in trade. In 1775 the procedure of manumission was eased but met effective resistance from the nobility.

At this time services and payments existed in two basic forms. One was service by labour and the other through payment of rent or *obrok*. In the far north there were still the remains of peasant farming by rent, but generally the peasant carried out compulsory services. The larger properties preferred obrok, but in central Russia labour services were predominant. Obrok levels of payment averaged two to three rubles a year in the 1760s. By the 1780s they had risen to four roubles and by 1800 to five, although devaluation lessened any real increase. On smaller properties owners demanded various services in kind. The rent of state peasants was in general 50 per cent lower than that of peasants belonging to the nobility. But even state peasants had to pay increased retaining rents of one to three roubles a year in the 1760s. Peasants paying obrok were considered more fortunate than those who did labour service. In Prussia after 1718 the king experimented with the abolition of serfdom on crown demesnes. This only served to split the peasantry even further into crown tenants, with lighter duties, and serfs of the nobility with increasingly heavier burdens. King Frederick II wished above all to preserve peasant holdings, because he thereby kept traditional land-taxes and made the state less dependent on its service nobility. This was an important fact at first too little recognized in the liberal reforms at the beginning of the nineteenth century.

Since the middle of the eighteenth century, a strong movement had made itself felt in Denmark aiming at basic reforms of existing conditions in agriculture and inspired by the ideas of the Enlightenment and of the Physiocrats. Books and periodicals publicized reform proposals, especially under the ministry of the German immigrant Struensee. Demesne lords took up his ideas and Graf Bernstorff distinguished himself as an agrarian reformer. He abolished labour services and tithes and broke up his demesne farm into peasant plots with hereditary leasehold. He also redistributed village and common lands, abolishing common grazing, fixing dates for communal sowing and regrouping farms into more manageable individual enterprises. Rents went up as productivity increased. The chief gain lay in greater social harmony.

Modern research makes it possible for us to compare the incomes of peasants in west and east Europe. In districts west of the Elbe, in the Bohemian forest and in Burgenland peasants generally paid rent for their own farms. A detailed study of the peasantry of the bishopric of Paderborn in east Westphalia shows that 23 per cent held more than ten hectares, half had two to ten hectares and 27 per cent had a half to two hectares of land. Cultivated land was taxed at an average of three talers per hectare, although small farms paid considerably more. Even so, duties were much less heavy than in east Prussia and elsewhere to the east of the lower Elbe. Rent took between 17·2 per cent and 29·6 per cent of total production in farms of up to two hectares, in the medium-sized farms between 8 and 16 per cent, and on farms over ten hectares 17·5 to 23·3 per cent.

We have less detailed figures for the rest of eighteenth-century north-west Germany outside the Paderborn area. On the whole conditions were similar, and the least heavily burdened were those in the north Ruhr area. In east Prussia, by contrast there were even serfs who paid more in taxes to the state than in rent to their landlord. Some tenants paid up to the equivalent of 15 per cent of their gross income in the form of labour and cartage services, and this figure might even rise to over 40 per cent in a number of instances. But only one in two peasant enterprises rendered labour service. The peasant holdings of eighteenth-century east Prussia can be classified as follows. There were peasant farms with real incomes of more than seventy hundredweight of rye, where holdings provided a meagre livelihood and cereals were supplemented by cabbage, beets, peas and beans. Then came plots insufficient for even subsistence agriculture, where labouring was necessary to supplement family income. The middle group of farms could produce thirty-six to seventy hundredweight of rye per harvest; the majority of peasant holdings in east Prussia were of this type.

Demesne or latifundia farms may be roughly classified as follows. In Hungary there was a transitional type of estate with small peasant holdings, where reasonable services were demanded. Then came areas with burdens of 15 to 40 per cent of gross peasant output, including parts of Saxony, Anhalt, Mark

Brandenburg, Silesia, west Prussia, parts of Russia, Bohemia and Moravia. Lastly came estates which demanded over 40 per cent of peasant production, including Pomerania, Mecklenburg, Holstein, Denmark, Poland and Galicia.

2. AGRARIAN POPULATION

An overall view of European economic development makes it clear that the greatest stimuli always came from the more densely populated west of the continent. Here technology and communications developed more rapidly. In the course of the sixteenth century the Netherlands became the greatest single centre of distribution and increasingly determined market conditions for the rest of continental Europe. An area of animal husbandry covered north-west Germany, Schleswig-Holstein and Denmark, with large-scale export of cattle, animal fats, butter and cheese based on advanced capitalistic enterprise. Behind this was a wide belt of grain production for export extending eastwards from Denmark and Holstein. In France the predominance of peasant subsistence prevented large-scale capital investment to improve yields. Land use was often very wasteful, especially in areas of poor communications. Oxen were still the predominant draught animals used in ploughing.

Traditional systems of field rotation produced low yields, and there was little experimentation to increase fertilization. Cereal yields on average seldom rose over fivefold for lack of fertilizers. In Flanders, however, they reached elevenfold with improved techniques. The main crop was still rye, and wheat remained a luxury. On poorer soils tax-free buckwheat was grown and in the warmer parts of Europe maize was introduced. Barley and oats made up the list of popular cereals. Cultivation of hemp and flax for textiles was widespread. The potato was only just being introduced. Cultivation of vegetables was usually confined to areas surrounding towns. Vineyards were still very important, although the area of viticulture shrank during the early modern era even in France. Government policies also encouraged grain cultivation over vineyards. In Brittany, then Île de France and Normandy fruit-farming was prevalent and the main area of French vine growing was restricted to lower Languedoc, Bordeaux and Burgundy. Animal husbandry played a subordinate rôle. At first only Normandy and the

Limousin were interested in raising new and better breeds. France was also backward in sheep- and horse-breeding.

There were therefore a number of reasons for the poor state of French agriculture, which was hardly helped by inadequate internal communications and numerous inland tolls and customs posts. But France was a land of great contrasts and vast distances by early modern standards. It already had a comprehensive literature of agrarian science even before the Physiocrats. Local agricultural associations already existed and bombarded the authorities with complaints and suggestions for improvements. Advice was available for growing new types of animal fodder and for introducing the potato, especially in the north-west. During the last years of the *ancien régime*, France suffered no famines as bad as that of 1709. Subsequent food crises, although severe, were restricted to individual regions.

In Germany great improvements came after the end of the Seven Years' War in 1763. The planting of clover and lupins spread from the Palatinate, as did that of tobacco and vegetables. Potatoes were grown as field crops in Prussia after 1746. Spanish merino sheep were introduced in Prussia, Saxony and Württemberg, a first sign of improvement in animal breeding. A literature of farming practice had been in existence since the sixteenth century and became increasingly scientific. A Lower Austrian country gentleman, Freiherr von Hohberg, published his *Georgica Curiosa* in 1687. Hohberg wanted nothing to do with the Cameralists but wished that absentee landlords would return to their duties as their own estate-managers.

In Prussia, where Frederick William I and Frederick II made active efforts to improve agriculture, much land, especially marsh was made arable. Immigrants from various countries were settled there. In addition, the transition to a more intensive method of cultivation was encouraged by the introduction of beets and cabbage, fruit, flax and hemp, and by cattle-breeding on the Dutch and English pattern. Rights of common pasturage and of field rotation were revised in favour of individual rather than collective farming. This was done at the expense of the weaker peasants and opened the way for capitalistic agriculture. This process was especially noticeable in Prussia, Hanover, Schleswig-Holstein and south-west Germany. The change from barter to a money economy, commutation of labour services into money rents, the luxurious existence of an aristocratic few, the increased social status of landowning, the costs to the state of war and diplomacy – all these factors made for a credit economy. The world of banking and state finance had arrived.

The export grain trade now shaped the economy of Schleswig-Holstein, which joined Denmark to form a single state and developed excellent markets in west Europe, especially during the Seven Years' War. In Prussia market conditions were subordinated to state military demands during the wars of King Frederick II. Army needs had been given priority under Frederick William I, but it was his successor who really made *Magazinwirtschaft* (military supply economy) into a virtual strategic monopoly over the Prussian grain trade.

In the Swiss Confederation grain-growing was increasingly replaced by potato-cultivation in the eighteenth century. A special school of agrarian economists prompted its culture and it certainly helped to provide minimal needs for food among a growing rural population. Animal husbandry also became more lucrative than arable farming and diversification into dairying provided opportunities to supplement incomes, as did the cottage-based textile industry where agriculture and industry came together.

The Swiss wine industry was increasingly restricted to areas where climate and soil conditions produced quality as well as quantity. Better communications with France and Germany meant that wine imports undercut home produce. For fruit-growing the question of home supply remained of great importance, and regulations by the authorities applied to planting especially in Glarus, where every homestead was ordered to grow a cherry tree in 1697.

In the Habsburg lands, nobles and clergy built up demesnes. Even so, grain-growing for export played a lesser part than in the latifundia of the Vistula region, partly because of less favourable communications with west Europe. The centres of population were Prague and Vienna. Cattle- and sheep-raising were popular in the highlands of Slovakia, from where cattle and wool could more readily be exported. In Bohemia agricultural produce was often processed further, barley into beer for instance.

Even smaller landlords tended to emulate territorial rulers in Germany by exploiting the mining and industrial potential of their property, especially from the late seventeenth century onwards. At first serfs were recruited into manufacturing, notably where this was based on the countryside. Estate records, or *Urbare*, were now kept and extended by careful land surveys. Whereas in the past only the head of the peasant household had been entered with his rents and taxes, full-scale farm inventories began to be regularly kept and revised, together with careful records of legal ownership. Progressive landlords influenced peasants to grow new types of crops, which included the new 'earth apple' imported from America into central Europe for the first time in the 1660s; tobacco had been grown since the 1640s. By the 1670s Austrian tobacco production was well under way and in 1723 it was made a Habsburg state monopoly, a policy which subsequent Austrian governments have followed right down to the present day.

Viticulture along the Danube and in Burgenland held its own in the more competitive atmosphere of the eighteenth century. Competition from Hungary in all foodstuffs, not only wine was very keen and the agrarian production of Danubian Austria had to become increasingly capitalistic. The province Ob der Enns pioneered clover production – it was already in cultivation by the 1650s – and the great gentleman farmer Freiherr von Hohberg emphasized that especially good seed could be obtained in the market at Wels. He was against byre feeding and experimented with hardy breeds of cattle. Yet the average number of cows and sheep per farm in Austria was a mere 20 and 120 respectively. Sometimes cows were still kept in their stalls during the whole summer. High pasturage on the Alm improved cattle strains wherever it was introduced. Land clearance continued vigorously, for example in the region around Wels, Ob der Enns, until the 1740s.

Great advances were made in Russian agriculture in the era of Peter the Great. Sheep-rearing was improved in order to strengthen the Russian textile industry. New strains were imported from Saxony, Poland and Silesia by government order in 1706. With the sheep came shearers who modernized techniques in Russia. In 1715 Tsar Peter began sending his sheep-farmers to west Europe to pick up new techniques. Cows from Suffolk and bulls from Tyrol were imported. Dairy farming was copied from Dutch models. But these innovations were at first limited to those enlightened farm-managers who also had enough capital resources. In agricultural techniques there were for many no advances at all, and advances usually came only when prices for exports began to rise. The growing of flax and hemp spread, which helped greatly in keeping the Russian balance of trade positive during the eighteenth century. Tsar Peter introduced the potato, and in 1717 regulations were issued to stimulate tobacco culture. Hungarian and Persian vines were planted along the Don, and the Russian forestry industry was put under state control.

There were also noticeable changes in Swedish agriculture during the eighteenth century. The cultivation of oats increased, especially in the newly cleared areas, and raised the number of cattle. Slow advances were made in potato cultivation, for which the entrepreneur and factory-owner Alström canvassed support from the highest ranks of society. The single annual crop under a three-field system still prevailed, especially in Östergötland and around Lake Mälaren near Stockholm. In Scania, Öland and Gotland a more advanced system of alternate autumn-sowing, spring-sowing and fallow prevailed. Although the great Linnaeus claimed that this method would turn Scania into Sweden's granary, it seems that yields were not greatly increased. The main increase came instead from new land clearances.

Forest clearance, especially in Värmland, was made necessary by increasing partible inheritance. New 'forest' farms, or *Torp*, mushroomed almost overnight, but a secure subsistence could never be guaranteed, so that social tension became a commonplace of Swedish rural existence. Land redistribution was now a political necessity; its most enthusiastic advocate was Jacob Faggot, who became chief inspector of the first comprehensive government land survey. In 1746 and 1755 he published his findings, and his work pioneered the system of government land reform. His approach to the problem of rural population pressure was not influenced by the enclosure movement, which came to Sweden relatively late. Until the 1740s Swedish state policy resisted partible inheritance, especially of peasant farms. But under the influence of Faggot, policy was reversed in the interest of population increase, which for strategic reasons was put above the more traditional planning of land resources. Eventually mass starvation was only really avoided by heavy Swedish emigration, especially to North America, during most of the nineteenth century.

Before the 1660s pre-absolutist Denmark had been a major

exporter of grain and cattle. With the loss of Scania to Sweden, however, exports fell, and during the eighteenth century they lay well below those of the earlier period. After 1700 Danish grain could no longer compete with Russian and Polish exports. Prices sank to such an extent that a new form of bondage called *stavnsband* was introduced in 1733, tying agricultural labour to the soil. This applied to all peasants between the ages of fourteen and forty-seven. It helped to form militias and made the process of taxation easier, especially since the Crown now tried to run the government without resort to extraordinary taxation. Tax exemptions of the nobility were also abolished. But harvest yields were still low, running at four to fivefold for oats and rye as late as the 1750s, and for barley five or six times the amount sown could usually be harvested. Production for the export market was increasingly based on large farms after the 1750s. Danish trade policy was dependent on Dutch needs, and the introduction of tariffs in Holland meant that Danish agriculture had to switch from cattle for meat production to dairy-farming. In 1725 the Dutch frontier was closed to cattle imports.

Agrarian production for home markets diversified greatly during the eighteenth century all over Europe. In the export trade, however, increased competitiveness among producers led either to increased farm size or to a switch away from traditional commodities such as cereals to dairying and market gardening. On the whole arable farming suffered, and animal husbandry became more lucrative.

3. FORESTRY

Complicated conditions of land tenure had a restrictive influence on capitalistic production of timber, just as it had on production of grain and cattle. In France, three million hectares of common woodland came under state control. At least another four million belonged to nobles, townsmen and peasants. Despite Colbert's reforms France had to import timber again for ship-building after 1700. Efforts were made to import supplies from French Canada. By 1721 it was estimated that the six hundred forges and foundries operating in France could not be supplied by home grown fuel.

Because of the development of extensive coal fields in central Europe the demand for wood dropped and supplies outran demand. Prices fell after the Thirty Years' War and only reached pre-war levels again in the 1690s, when Louis XIV's wars once again stimulated demand. In the eighteenth century population increase and rising industrial production helped to keep forestry profitable.

4. MANUFACTURING

A. *Organization*

(i) Guilds

The Guild system still dominated production, though its hold was less firm in eastern Europe. In France and England guild control was not as strong as in central Europe. In France and England guilds were mainly confined to large towns, and elsewhere free masters predominated. Cottage industries were very important. French guilds were early subjected to royal control and the state encouraged their development. In an edict of 1673 Parisian guild organization was taken as a model for the provincial towns, who were to have new guilds which would also include country craftsmen. Such plans, however, remained utopian. Too much state supervision might turn out to be a hindrance to economic progress.

In Germany guild control was greater partly because the loose federal system of the Empire allowed a great number of territorial and municipal authorities to function with high jurisdictions at very local levels. New forms of production and consumption used the guild system, although some new industries broke free. Traditional organization was granted to the Frankfurt-am-Main wig-makers, licensed as a guild in 1745. Yet other relatively new occupations, distilling, chocolate-manufacture, soap- and carpet-making, remained guild-free. Painters, printers and engravers were sometimes counted as belonging to the free arts.

Guilds came increasingly under the power of territorial state authorities, becoming instruments of absolutist control. If they failed in this task, they were dissolved. This was particularly clear in Brandenberg–Prussia. Attempts by imperial, federal assemblies and courts to gain a say in guild affairs failed as territorial states became increasingly powerful. On the other hand trades were sometimes amalgamated into one guild, as happened when the slipper, shoe- and boot-makers combined into one footwear industry in Berlin in 1734. But such amalgamation could also be exploited by journeymen and apprentices in order to withhold labour and seek better conditions. Early modern prototypes of strikes and lockouts were by no means unknown. Yet the authorities retained the upper hand.

In the first half of the eighteenth century, some co-operation between territorial rulers and the federal Empire was achieved. The permanent imperial assembly at Regensburg was urged by Prussia to issue a law in 1732 allowing specific merchants to dissolve guilds which persistently opposed government regulations. Where guilds were abolished, craftsmen tended to move into suburbs and villages to avoid urban taxation or to find employment with estate-owners and managers. The late seventeenth century was a time of general recession in the smaller towns of central Europe. The alternative was to re-impose manufacturing and trading embargoes on the countryside. By the late eighteenth century only linen handweavers, tailors, smiths and carpenters were allowed to operate outside the towns in Prussia. Strict craft regulations were imposed. Despite this a survey of 1797 in Mark Brandenburg showed that 30 per cent of all craftsmen were village based. In east Friesia over half were engaged in country crafts.

Similar conditions applied elsewhere in the German territorial states. In Schleswig-Holstein conflicts between the Danish crown and the Dukes prevented successful development towards freer trade and industry. Crown policy became increasingly mercantilist as Danish absolutism got under way after the 1660s. This favoured urban development in a traditional, guild-based manner. In 1688 a proclamation was issued forbidding the further dispersal into the countryside of economic activity belonging to the towns. Only blacksmiths, wagoners, coopers, cobblers and tailors were allowed to remain as village craftsmen. The others had to move into a town. The Ducal administration had to accept these orders from Copenhagen and by 1711 townsmen were given extensive marketing control over agrarian production. Village crafts could now be exercised outside a three-mile radius of any town.

After the Great Northern War further conflict developed between the royal government and Duke Carl Frederick of Gottorf. In 1736 he refused to renew the code of 1711 inside his Duchy. The crown had often violated the prohibition because of favouritism or so as to increase revenue. In the villages along the Elbe estuary there were so many craftsmen that it almost seemed as if the freedom to carry on a trade really existed. This was even more the case on the west coast from Dithmarschen to Eiderstedt and Tønder. Noble estates encouraged craft industries in contravention of town privileges. The crown deliberately supported the textile industry in country areas, by decrees in 1737 and 1751 which gave linen-weavers the same status as free manufacturers and the right to employ apprentices and journeymen. In north and north-east Schleswig linen soon became the most important branch of employment after farming. Weaving tended to spread more rapidly in areas of poor agriculture, particularly in the villages around eighteenth-century Hamburg.

Guild development in east Europe was influenced by western finance and central European practice. In Poland, however, town guilds attempted to extend their influence over the countryside by exporting their own craftsmen to the villages. In Lithuania and the Ukraine, where the Greek Orthodox Church predominated, religious conflicts tended to exclude a number of masters from the guilds. These outsiders formed their own groups in suburbs outside town jurisdiction, on lands belonging to nobles or clergy. Such free craftsmen were even sometimes supported by town patricians in their capacity as individual land-owners. *Territoriali*, craftsmen with crown privileges, also remained outside general guild control. But neither old nor new guild organization remained popular. The Thirty Years' War did not succeed in destroying the system. Guilds produced their own brand of paternalism and exclusiveness conducive to 'baroque' society. Yet the shortage of craftsmen was so great in east Europe that anyone with a skill could become a member. In central Europe there was much more competition and standards of work were much higher. Many guilds only accepted sons and sons-in-law of members, and the development of craft operations into capitalistic undertakings was often opposed.

In Russia the towns were often too weak to foster their own guilds. Crafts came under the control of noble, monastic and crown estates. But in Moscow there was enough demand to run several guilds, of bakers, tanners and even icon-makers. In Moscow most masters worked without journeymen. Their apprentices were usually employed for terms of five years, but to become a journeyman no examination was required. Many apprentices left early and guild standards in a central and west European sense were unknown. There were, however, much stricter regulations for gold- and silversmiths, who were carefully examined before becoming masters. Under Tsar Peter western guild standards were introduced, at least in theory.

Jewish craftsmen gained a certain importance in parts of east and south Europe. The Sephardic and Ashkenazy Jews who came to Holland during the seventeenth century were able to work as diamond-cutters, tobacco-twisters, printers and silk-weavers. The guilds generally refused them entry, with the exception of some small provincial towns. In Hamburg, Altona and other German cities Jews were excluded from guilds, and only in Glückstadt did King Christian IV of Denmark give them privileges, thereby promoting the mercantile power of the town. The Ottoman Empire operated a much more generous policy to those Jewish specialists who had been expelled from Christian Europe, above all from Spain, Portugal, Sicily and Provence. During the sixteenth century the Turkish guilds of Constantinople were multi-racial and free of religious bias. By the seventeenth century a Christian element seems to have become more predominant. In Salonica, the most important centre for textiles, a considerable division of labour under free masters using advanced workshop techniques existed. In Bohemia and Moravia many Jews had been engaged as craftsmen by the fifteenth century. At first they were not allowed to form guilds, although the Jewish butchers in Prague were able to combine sometime before 1620. A royal regulation of 1648 opened the way for the further extension of Jewish crafts. In the first half of the eighteenth century about 65,000 Jews lived in Bohemia and Moravia, and in Prague there were several independent Jewish guilds, though in Moravia they were more dependent on the local nobility.

There may have been up to three million Jews in Poland and Lithuania at the beginning of the seventeenth century. The first Jewish guilds were formed in Cracow, Lvov and Przemysl and became increasingly powerful by the second half of the century. They received extensive royal support, although the Polish nobility tended to retain substantial numbers of 'free' craftsmen as an unorganized labour force.

Jewish communities were an important part of the east

European social structure. They had their own strict organizations under control of their elders. The *Kahal* Jewish guilds tended to come under double control, from the royal government as well as from their own communal authorities. They were, however, always subjected to discrimination.

(ii) The putting-out system
Where craftsmen depended on extensive markets for obtaining raw materials as well as sales outlets, they formed alliances with merchants through trading contracts. To the latter they delivered wool, cotton, silk and metals, to be disposed of as finished or semi-finished goods over wide areas. Craftsmen now became dependent on merchants who not only supplied them with raw materials, but also gave them so much credit that they lost any economic autonomy that they formerly may have enjoyed. This was the putting-out system that already existed in the later medieval economy. Its heyday came in the early modern period and by the sixteenth century it was the most effective type of industrial and manufacturing system available. It was most widespread in textiles, but other industries such as mining or paper-making that relied on heavy investments in machinery and capital goods also depended on it. Yet where the system became too powerful, craftsmen and skilled labourers soon became economically dependent on the merchants. The latter depended on sound profits which could best be achieved by increased, rationalized production.

The putting-out system favoured the division of labour and guildsmen began to be employed alongside 'free' workers. In general, coarse work was done in the country and then finished in town. This led to social change as the system began to encourage those with 'incentive'. In the Calw textile industry managers originally started as dyers. In Solingen guilds of swordsmiths, hardeners, grinders and bladesmiths worked together, but the swordsmiths were in charge of sales. Guilds also became dependent on the putting-out system, as for example in the linen-producing areas of Saxony, Lausitz and Silesia. Basically guilds were always at a disadvantage against those who controlled the putting-out system. If they complained at profiteering, guild-free labour was employed, and the entrepreneur in charge bought a privilege from the state to protect himself further. Peasants were also cheaper than guild labourers.

(iii) Factories

Where special knowledge and technical ability were demanded, entrepreneurs tended to concentrate their concerns and increase their production by division of labour. The beginnings of such industrial activity lie in medieval Florence and Flanders. The undertaking of John Winchcombe in Newbury at the beginning of the sixteenth century typifies this early development. But the concentration of industry took centuries to form a basis for a national economy. The traditions of the guilds and the paternalistic economic policies of rising absolute states as often as not hindered as much as helped industrial development. A new phase began in the second half of the seventeenth century, for example with the factory of van Robais in Abbeville, set up under Colbert's protection as a royal manufactory. Here some thousands of male and female workers were employed, a large number of whom lived and worked in one moated district surrounded by a bank and ditch. Spinning was also concentrated in this complex. On the other hand weaving looms were located in town houses of up to 30 per overseer. In silk production up to 120 spindles were accommodated under one roof.

In Protestant territories a strict 'work ethic' did prevail, whereby the able-bodied but unemployed were put into workhouses in the belief that everyone should lead an active life. Vagabonds and prisoners were put to work, as well as those in poorhouses and orphanages, for the good of their own souls and the profit of the state. We find early examples of workshops connected with workhouses and orphanages in Hamburg, Berlin and Copenhagen. In textiles some branches of the industry were particularly suited to workshop organization: thus calico-printing, which developed at the end of the seventeenth century in Holland and spread to Switzerland, Augsburg and Saxony. A factory for *passementerie* (lace edgings and borders) was set up in Rheims in 1665 with 120 women employees. In 1729 a sail-cloth manufacturer in Moscow even claimed to employ 1,160 workers. Workshops now came into existence all over Europe in all branches of production, especially where mass production for military needs was needed, or where luxury articles such as tapestries and porcelain were demanded. The writings of Forberger, Reuter and Slawinger have popularized workshop management in many branches of production during the eighteenth century.

(iv) Machine goods

Concentration of craftwork was an essential feature of early industrial activity. It also made the supervision and servicing of machinery more economical. Naturally, central Europe fell far behind eighteenth-century England (where over half the coalmines employed over a hundred people in 1700); the largest mines had five hundred to a thousand workers.

The Polhem metal-processing works in Stiernsund in Sweden began to employ machinery in such a way as to reduce the amount of labour required. Polhem installed machines for crude routine processes, among them to cut iron bars, split iron into nails, roll tin plate, make gearwheels, forge pans, hammer out tin goods and household utensils and finish ploughshares and clock parts. Considerable technical apparatus was used in shipyards and sugar refineries and to make soap, beer, paper, gunpowder and glass. A French royal glass company was set up with two hundred workers and in the middle of the eighteenth century employed nearly a thousand in enclosed workshops. Armaments factories were also set up in all European states from Colbert's France to Czar Peter's Russia.

(v) Technology

Really imposing technological developments in continental Europe had to wait until the end of the eighteenth century, although many innovations date back to the seventeenth century. The middle of the seventeenth century was a period of scientific advance monitored by the great learned societies, which also began to take an academic interest in practical science. Yet practical application still lagged behind theoretical knowledge until well into the eighteenth century, although an international scientific community now began to emerge in Europe. In 1722 Reaumur published his experiments on turning iron into steel, and in 1738 Schlüter brought out his famous handbook of metallurgy. Cramer was one of the first to try to connect technology with chemical theory. England and Scotland developed the right type of pragmatism for scientific advance in industry during the eighteenth century, a pragmatism that Francis Bacon had already recommended a century previously. Existing centres of industry began to lose their former importance. The use of coal-fired smelting-ovens spread from England to France and the south Netherlands during the early eighteenth century, and English steam engines began pumping operations. Their use had spread to Slovakia by 1721.

New professions arose with the new techniques, and a modern engineering industry began to emerge distinct from the older crafts and guilds. The existing educational system with its religious bias now had increasingly to adapt to new forms of technology and science. In Prussia this led to the establishment of *Realschulen* under Frederick William 1. Under the stimulus of mercantilism and rationalism new schools were started to promote industry. The University of Halle led the way for future technological development, and Christoph Semler opened the first *Realschule* in Halle in 1708. In 1747 such an establishment started in Berlin under the headmastership of Johann Julius Herker, a pupil of August Hermann Francke. Children of burghers were now educated for careers in trade, industrial production and agriculture and specialized in mathematics, science, commerce, technical drawing and geography.

The Cameralists also extended the school curriculum to include politics and administration. Chairs were founded in these fields at the new Universities of Halle and Frankfurt-an-der Oder in 1721, but other universities had already developed the topic in the seventeenth century, Uppsala in Sweden for instance. Technology usually developed from pure science. The idea of science as unifying knowledge was particularly important at the new eighteenth-century university of Göttingen, where Beckmann laid the foundations of technological science in Germany. In the nineteenth century an institutional framework was created around road-, bridge- and canal-building and mining to form the first technical schools. At the time of the French Revolution the first *École Polytechnique* grew out of the mid-eighteenth century *École des ponts et chaussées* in Paris. Mining academies were created in the 1770s in Chemnitz and in 1773 in St Petersburg. Clausthal received its charter in 1775 and Freiberg in Saxony followed in 1776.

Engineers and managers needed trained merchants, accountants and bankers. Savary's *Parfait Négociant* and Marperger's numerous German publications paved the way for this. At the University of Leipzig, Ludovici developed courses in commerce and published a lexicon of trade. In 1767, Johann Georg Büsch's Hamburg school of commerce opened its doors.

(vi) Entrepreneur and worker

Relations between entrepreneur and worker were to a large extent controlled by state officials and operated according to Christian paternal and mercantilistic principles. State participation in early modern continental Europe must never be underestimated, even if theory did remain stronger than practice. Sixteenth-century mining was perhaps the first heavy industry to come under territorial state control. The industrial enterprises of rulers were increasingly in the hands of trained commercial, industrial and mining councillors, often with places in the monarch's privy council. The skills of Jewish communities were also called upon to extend state activities. Some entrepreneurs combined various types of activity, as for example Schnitzler of Berlin, who was both merchant and sugar-manufacturer. The nobility of Europe also played an increasingly important role in eighteenth-century industries. Entrepreneurs were encouraged to purchase noble status. Ennobled factory owners were especially active in east Europe, in Bohemia, Moravia, Slovakia, Hungary, Poland and Russia. Where they were also established landlords, they had complete control over land and peasant labour, and could produce extremely cheaply.

Eighteenth-century Europe experienced a mixture of old and new labour relations. Guilds and crafts continued to operate closed shops with extremely labour-intensive, high-cost production. At the same time guild-free factories and shops sprang up, competing with each other for markets by marking down the price of their goods. The managers of such undertakings were often trained in the new schools of commerce and engineering and their attitudes to workers were increasingly dominated by the laws of supply and demand. Women and children were more and more used as operatives, especially in textiles where their labour was cheaper than manpower. In calico-printing, children were used, as they were in many subsidiary jobs in mining. An important feature was the use of guildhalls, workhouses and orphanages as factories and workshops. Unskilled labour was never in such short supply as skilled or semi-skilled. Legislation to prevent the emigration of native labour was promulgated at the same time as each state tried to poach labour from abroad. In order to build up a labour force for the future, arrangements were made for shop-floor training, which was not as thoroughly organized as in the older guild and craft industries. The new Realschulen and polytechnics now took over technological training and began to spread from France across central and east Europe.

Conditions of work varied greatly. In Catholic Europe a large number of saints' days continued to be celebrated. Austrian miners for example worked 245 days a year but made up time by shiftwork. In Bleiberg there were six and a half 'shifts' a week; each shift lasted nine hours, and the working week averaged fifty-eight hours. Wage structures were often very broad, and many an industrial or craft worker had a small agricultural holding to provide supplementary income. In mining and glass-making land and housing usually accompanied wages. Many workers also received payment in kind or *Pfennwert* (cheap goods) as part of their wages. Work was carried out under a great variety of conditions, from livery and domestic service to money wages for piece-work, so-called *Accordlohn*. Serfdom was still adaptable in the eighteenth century to industrial and craft production, especially in east Europe.

B. *Production*

(i) Mining and metal processing

The production of precious metals in central Europe began to decrease as resources became more difficult to exploit and American bullion more plentiful during the sixteenth century. In the late seventeenth century Brazilian gold from the Minas Geraes reached the European market, although a new phase in native production came with gold finds in the Urals after 1745. Production of silver continued in east central Europe, with lower yields than before, based on the Harz, Saxony, Bohemia, Tyrol and the Carpathians, where production was increasingly in state hands. Even Norway had silver mines at Kongsberg, which became a Danish crown monopoly after 1661. Mining in the Harz picked up somewhat after the Thirty Years' War when prospecting was thrown open to all. As late as the Seven Years' War new foundries were being started at Eisleben, Leimbach and Mansfeld. Bohemian copper-mining at Kutna Hora continued, as did Alpine working in Tyrol and around Salzburg. There was a considerable shift in Slovakian production to the Spišska Nová Vés area. Central Slovakia produced only 60 per cent of its former capacity by the first half of the eighteenth century, whereas around Spišska Nová Vés production had reached 13,428 hundredweight in 1743.

Sweden, with its Stora Kopparberg, continued to provide considerable competition to east central European copper mines, producing no less than three thousand tons in the peak year of 1650. In the 1670s production ran at a steady two thousand tons but subsequently declined to half that amount by 1700. The report of Erik Odhelius, chief metallurgist to Charles XI in 1690, showed that despite falling production Sweden still had more copper than any other European country and that she provided half the total European consumption. Yet in the bad war years between 1716 and 1720 production sank below a thousand tons. It remained near these levels during the eighteenth century, although its superior quality found Swedish copper a good market everywhere. Copper, however, lost its importance to iron, although it took a long time to develop the technology and communications necessary to exploit Swedish iron in the Arctic.

The Danes exploited Norwegian copper near Trondheim, financed by the Hamburg banker Teixeira and Nunes Henriques from Amsterdam. In Russia copper production gained importance when four mines were opened in the Urals in the 1720s. Copper and brass processing also spread beyond the old centres of Nuremberg and Aachen. There were works in Sweden, the north and south Netherlands and the Austrian Alps. Aachen only processed 50,000 hundredweight of calamine from Altenberg in the 1670s, whereas Stolberg used double that amount in the same decade. Altenberg remained the chief supplier of calamine to west Germany. Local copper production continued to supply Aachen, where in the Herrenbergen in 1779 and 1780 twenty-five mines produced 10,500 hundredweight of calamine.

An indication of the amount of metal processed in Aachen can be gained from investigations that took place after the great town fire of 1656. In 1663 there were 20 to 25 furnaces, and by 1691 only 10 master coppersmiths seem to have been operating. Between 1667 and 1669 93 furnaces were recorded in Stolberg, owned by thirteen families. The Peltzers alone ran 34 of them, and the Lynens had 10. Stolberg now produced 28,000 hundredweight of brass a year. In Aachen there had been 15 copper masters in 1665, producing 5,000 hundredweight of brass in that year. In 1669 the coppermasters of Stolberg in the districts of Eschweiler, Wilhelmstein and Kornelimünster formed their own guild of 33 members, under the supervision of Pfalzgraf Philipp Wilhelm von Neuburg in his capacity as ruling Duke of Jülich. They formed a closed shop against outsiders and against exports, although their association had failed by 1698, when 32 individual works were competing for supplies. Among them Gotthard Schardinel was one of the most important with a single enterprise of 20 smelting furnaces working at one time. At that time about 140 furnaces and over 100 forges, calamine mills and wire-drawing works were operating, with a production of about 40,000 hundredweight of brass. The prosperity of Stolberg lasted into the 1750s, but competition from Iserlohn made itself increasingly felt, as did that of England and Sweden. By 1775 production had dropped to 30,000 hundredweight of brass. A new brass industry was formed on a corporate basis in Westphalia in 1735 at Hemer and Iserlohn. In 1704 Georg Giesche of Wroclaw received a state privilege to exploit the calamine deposits of Beuthen, which yielded a yearly production of 10,000 hundredweight.

Tin production continued to move northwards from Bohemia to the Erz mountains. This was partly a result of Protestant immigration out of Counter-Reformation Habsburg lands, and by the first half of the eighteenth century annual tin production in Saxony was over 8,000 tons, whereas that of Bohemia was about 6,300 tons. Lead was also produced in the Harz, Upper Silesia and Poland, as well as in the east Alps, but no figures are as yet available. Idria continued to produce mercury as well as Iberia and Huancavelica in South America. After 1696 stamp mills were used in Idria. The extraction of rare cobalt ore in Saxony in the second half of the seventeenth century stood at 127 tons, and between 1700 and 1720 it reached a high point of 300 to 400 tons a year.

In the eighteenth century French iron production surpassed that of Sweden in volume and was only exceeded by that of Russia. Colbert had a considerable influence in increasing production with state aid. German iron production was widely scattered from the Saar to the Hunsrück and Eifel through to the east central highlands. In the Hunsrück, the Rheinböllen foundry operated together with Stromberg installations in Nassau; these were of great importance during the Thirty

Years' War, under the management of Jean Mariot from Liège. In the Eifel works were concentrated near Schleiden, Vich and Düren. After 1667 Vich valley forges became important under Hoesch family proprietorship. They specialized in black sheet-iron but availability of fuel meant that forges often had short working lives, thus not just dependent on the availability of local ores. In 1736 the Lendersdorf foundry was shut down because of charcoal shortages and was only opened again in 1780. Thimbles and padlocks were made and exported as far as Lyons. Production of nails and bolts was also expanded with exports from Liège, and by 1775 there were three slitting-mills in the Schleiden district. Bar iron also came from the Cologne area, the Schleiden valley, Luxemburg and Jülich.

The Aachen pin industry made good some of the losses caused by the emigration of master coppersmiths. In 1615 a guild of Spanish needle-makers received its charter, on condition that products were only made from fine round steel by a method of production pioneered at Cordoba. In 1622 the town council dropped the description 'Spanish' and substituted its own name for the product. By the end of the seventeenth century this industry was partly organized on the putting-out system, distinguishing between 'rough' and 'fine' master-smiths. The latter did the polishing, sorting, packing and despatching. Chief entrepreneur was Cornelius Chorus the Elder, who in 1700 had over 50 guildmasters under him and another 50 journeymen in his factory. In about 1730 he claimed that his enterprise provided a means of livelihood for 1,000 people. Aachen needle merchants were able to sell their wares all over Europe because of the high quality of their product.

In Siegen iron-smelting depended on peasant co-operatives for charcoal. Little advance had been made here since the medieval era. The same applied in Fulda and along the Weser, although specialization in iron stoves improved profits. When resources of ferrous minerals became scarce because of a particularly steep increase in demand later in the eighteenth century, more economical methods of production had to be found. A temporary measure was to move into county Mark, Essen and Werden where there were ample supplies of coal and charcoal. There were 90 *osmund* forges in county Mark during the 1760s, 37 of them in the parish of Lüdenscheid alone, and six in Iserlohn. An osmund steel marketing association for county

Mark had existed since 1662. Wire production was carried on with waterwheels on the rivers Lenne, Ramede and Nette. Needle production spread from Cologne to Menden in Mark. As in the case of Iserlohn, a thimble industry came to the district from Utrecht.

The whole system was regulated by territorial state authorities. The steel-smiths of the Siegen area, blade-smiths from Solingen district, and wire-drawers of county Mark were tied to their workshops. Regulations issued in the name of the Great Elector resembled Colbert's *règlements*. Staples and cartels for marketing were standard in the European metal industry. In this way well established towns such as Cologne and Frankfurt, Nuremberg and Augsburg could retain control over profits from actual mining and manufacturing areas. The greatest stimulus to production came during war-time, particularly in the iron industries of Schmalkalden and Suhl, where firearms were made. There had always been a shortage of skilled labour, especially during the wars of Frederick II and Maria Theresa. In Silesia the first coalmines were opened alongside blast furnaces after 1703. After the Prussian takeover foundries for iron-casting were built in Malapane and Kreuzburg. In the 1770s Heinitz and Reden set up the modern Upper Silesian mining industry, with Königshütte as its main centre, hardly inferior to great works in Britain.

In Bohemia production in Brdy suffered temporarily during the Thirty Years' War, and by 1700 there were six blast furnaces and fourteen forges in operation. In the Spišska Nová Vés and Hron river districts iron production flourished as new methods were introduced under Habsburg state supervision, which had extended as far as Transylvania by the mid-eighteenth century. Whereas the political difficulties affecting the Polish state were also reflected in the decline of its iron industry, the Russian industry's production increased considerably. In 1628 German technicians discovered iron deposits in the Irbit district and built the first cast-iron furnaces in Tula. Four years later the Dutchman Vinius received a state monopoly on condition that he settled in Tula and taught Russians iron-processing. Further Dutch projects followed along the rivers Vaga, Kostroma and Sheksna, and at Kaluga. In 1668 the government began to operate its own furnaces at Ugoda and Pavlovsk. Total iron production for that year was about 200,000 Pud or 8,000 tons.

Iron production again increased under Peter the Great, spreading out from Tula and Olonets to the Urals and Siberia at Vierkotur and Tobolsk in 1697 and Neviansk and Kamensk after 1699. In peace-time iron was also imported from Sweden via Novgorod. In 1693 a works was set up in Kachinsky near Tula; that of Olonets was reconstructed in 1703. In 1705 an iron works was started at Sestrabesk near St Petersburg. Iron production then developed to such an extent that Russia became an exporter after 1716.

Real expansion continued after the end of war with Sweden. Under the direction of native entrepreneurs and Tsarist state officials, the Demidovs, Tatichevs and Hennins, five new works were opened in the Urals between 1722 and 1724, four of them also for copper. The Demidovs expanded activities into Siberia, and one works was built in Irkutsk by the forced labour of Swedish prisoners of war. There were now thirty-eight foundries in the province of Kazan, as many in the province of Petersburg, thirty-nine in Moscow, and seventy on the Oka. Total production of Russian pig iron was about 25,000 tons in 1718. But quantity and not quality predominated, although needles were locally made in Ryazan and Moscow. Before 1730 state initiative had been predominant, subsequently the industry was opened to private entrepreneurs. A state commission under director Schönberg reported in favour of handing over royal demesne iron works to private individuals. The Blagoletz works were run by Schönberg, Biron and Polish entrepreneurs after 1739. Other Urals iron-works were taken over by local masters or by foreigners. By 1750 there were a hundred and fifty enterprises in the Urals alone. Russian iron production had risen to about 54,000 tons by 1767.

Swedish iron production was 32,600 tons in 1720, and twenty years later had reached 51,000 tons. Sweden's share of the European export market in bar iron was about 35 per cent in the 1750s, the chief importer being England. By the 1720s nearly 40 per cent of English iron requirements were satisfied with Swedish imports. Of iron exports only about 10 per cent consisted of steel in eighteenth-century Sweden, but quality was consistently high. Not for nothing had Colbert tried to settle Swedish iron-masters in France. English master ironsmiths also tried to copy Swedish processes. The heart of the early modern Swedish iron industry was at Värmland. In 1695, 22 per cent of all iron produced came from there, 17 per cent from Närke, 16 per cent from Gästrikland. Värmland iron was mostly exported via Gothenburg. Swedish iron-works or *bruk* used the putting-out system. Export-orientated merchants in Stockholm and Gothenburg paid for production in advance and thereby pre-empted price levels. *Bruk* managers also gave credit to their workers as well controlling the pay of charcoal-burners and carriers. Swedish arms manufacture became world famous, but domestic and agricultural tools were also important items, especially in the workshops of Christopher Polhem at Stjärnsund. Even the mystic Emanuel Swedenborg was interested in making improvements to mining and metal-processing.

(ii) Glass, stone and clays

Murano was the main centre of Italian glass-making. However, the new French technique of casting rather than blowing mirrors caused serious competition there, and in 1727 a number of furnaces was closed. Nehou's invention had first been used in 1688. Up to 1665 the Paris suburb of Saint-Antoine had its own factory blowing mirrors, staffed with a number of Italian workers. A further factory was built in Tour-la-Ville near Cherbourg. Both works were then combined in a privileged Companie Royale. After Colbert's death this privilege was withdrawn, but his successor Louvois selected rival entrepreneurs for state support. The mirror-casting factory at Saint-Gobain was soon especially successful.

German glass production was widespread in the central highlands. As well as table and hollow glassware, glass gems, rings and mirror glass were made. Ruby glass became a speciality in Potsdam in 1680, and Nuremberg remained one of the most important glass-making centres. During the eighteenth century cutting and polishing factories spread from the Nuremberg area to the Upper Palatinate and into the territories of Ansbach and Bayreuth. Mirrors were also made at Fürth, Schleichbach near Würzburg, Lohr on the Main, Neustadt on the Dosse and Grünenplan near Münden. In 1710 the first mirror-casting factory was built in Neuhaus which was taken over by the Austrian state in 1728. In Franconia glass-making was encouraged by Italian and French immigrants in Schleichbach. In Thuringia glass-making suffered from fuel shortages. There were glass works in the Bavarian Forest, Black Forest,

Rhine uplands, Lippe and Paderborn in east Westphalia. Wood shortages usually shut down the workshops, which then had to move to new localities. The first coal-fired glass manufactory in Germany was set up at Königstelle in county Mark in 1723.

Most famous of all glass north of the Alps was undoubtedly that of Bohemia. Hollow and crystal glass and vitreous pigment glass were developed, even to make beads and false jewels. This industry was concentrated on Reichenberg, Gablons, Frankenau and Turnau as well as Haida, Langenau, Böhmisch-Kamnitz, Burgstein and Kreibitz. With the decline of Murano, Bohemian glass came to dominate the European market. Bohemian glass was being exported to the whole of Europe by the seventeenth century. In 1752 strict government regulations were issued to exclude foreigners and protect trade secrets in Bohemian glass manufacture. Commercial travellers were the main glass-dealers, sometimes organized in co-operative companies: they obtained their glass-ware on credit.

Glass-making was one branch of industry where the principle of guild-free, state-planned workshops could best be used. There was increasing division of labour in painting, engraving and cutting of glass. Independent trade corporations of glass polishers had existed in the Riesengebirge since the eighteenth century. In Silesia glass engraving by water power was started in 1690. Glass furnaces were also increased in size to accommodate the need for cheaper glass bottles. The glass container industry got under way in central Europe during the late seventeenth century. This forced master glass-makers to join together in co-operatives to provide greater capital outlay and increase their competitiveness.

Important advances were made in the manufacture of pottery after the second half of the seventeenth century. In the fifteenth century majolicas and faience had been made in Italy. In the sixteenth century this manufacture spread to France, Germany and the Netherlands. Faience was made in Hamburg and Hanau after the 1620s. Between 1660 and 1750 no less than 116 such works were set up in Germany. Thereafter porcelains and china-ware, which had been imported to Holland and England by the East India Companies, began to be imitated in Europe. In 1707 the physicist Walter von Tschirnhaus together with the Saxon chemist Johann Friedrich Böttger succeeded in producing a paste for Dresden porcelain manufacture. Böttger soon discovered the real white or hard porcelain by using local kaolin. The territorial ruler adopted the process and financed a factory in the Albrechtsburg at Meissen which became an important source of income for Saxony. Soon other territorial rulers purchased the secret of porcelain manufacture and built their own industries. In 1718 the Emperor followed suit in Vienna. Real porcelain was first made in Neudeck in 1747, in Berlin in 1750, in Frankenthal in 1751, in Fürstenberg in 1753, in Nymphenburg in 1754, in Sèvres in France in 1756 and in Copenhagen in 1760. In Italy Meissen workers were imported to make hard paste in Venice using kaolin from Saxony. But the works closed in 1727 for lack of access to the necessary kaolin. In 1744 a specialist from Meissen helped to set up the St Petersburg porcelain industry. Porcelain was soon valued as a household article and the home market became insatiable in the eighteenth century. Each state thus developed its own products, Delft in Holland, Sèvres in France, Copenhagen in Denmark, Nymphenberg and KPM in Prussia and Germany.

(iii) Chemical industry

The chemical industry was only in its beginnings, but the manufacture of dyes, soap and gunpowder was already important in the eighteenth century. Larger-scale production of dyes was first carried out in Saxony. Potash was important for dye-works. Full use of it was made in Danzig and Riga, and alum was extracted in Bohemia.

(iv) Wood and coal

The rise of coal-mining in the eighteenth century came just soon enough to save the forests of central and east Europe from being destroyed to provide wood for strategic industries such as minerals and shipping, as had already happened in large parts of west and Mediterranean Europe. Baltic forest products alongside Norwegian timber remained crucial to west Europe. The forests of Finland and Sweden around the Gulf of Bothnia were also increasingly exploited for exports.

Increased coal production came with steam hydraulics, invented and used for the first time in Britain, and soon copied in the Wurmrevier mines near Aachen, where 800 workers were employed after 1735. Ruhr coal-mining became increasingly effective, especially with the introduction of British hydraulics

in 1734. Progress here was by state-controlled mining regulations, such as those of Cleves and Mark in 1766. In county Mark
128 pits produced 32,000 tons of coal in 1739, and in 1754 688
miners produced 43,000 tons from 110 pits.

(v) Textiles

In France the increase in manufactured cotton cloth and printed
textiles was considerable, often because of the initiative of foreigners, especially the Swiss. Rouen, Bolbec and Mulhouse were
centres of these branches of the textile industry. The same is true
for the silk industry in Lyons. New textile industries developed
in most urban centres with enough capital to exploit an insatiable market for fabrics. There were centres at Monschau, Düren,
Burtscheid, Kornelimünster, Vaals, down to Limburg and Stolberg, all organized on a widely scattered putting-out system.
Rough carding and finishing remained town-based. In 1719
Mahias von Asten built the first cloth factory in the copper
works centre of Stolberg, where the Peltzers also diversified production by introducing textiles. The greatest activity developed
in Monschau and Jülich, which had access to the soft lime-free
water of the river Rur and to the wood and the peat of the
Venn. After the end of the seventeenth century Monschau cloth
producers faced increasing competition from weavers in the
Duchy of Berg, especially in Lennep. To overcome this, fine
Spanish work techniques were introduced after 1730 by the son
of a clergyman from Velbert. Scheibler cloths were sold all over
Europe and the Near East. In about 1760 Scheibler was
employing over 4,000 workers.

Cloth production in Düren was run by the Schoeller family
after 1718. In 1753 Anton Lejeune from Verviers was domiciled in Düren to make Verviers cloth, known for its excellence.
He drew in further immigrants and rose to become mayor. On
the lower Rhine cotton and silk industries flourished, especially
when Protestant entrepreneurs from Cologne moved out to
Mülheim, on the opposite bank of the Rhine. Krefeld also had
to thank Protestant immigrants for its prosperity. The situation
was much the same in Wuppertal, which set up a varied
industry in braids and allied haberdashery.

In Westphalia woollens and linen were produced in cottage
industry alongside thread, knitting and stocking-making.
Despite a general decline in textiles as metal industries deve-

loped, Westphalia, east central Germany, Silesia and Bohemia remained the main areas of German linen production, with a flourishing export trade. The Westphalian flax harvest was one of the largest in Europe. Linen was concentrated locally on the northern uplands and along their slopes in Ravensberg, Minden, Lippe, Osnabrück, Diepholz, Hoya, Münster and the whole Teutoburg forest from Hellweg district as far as east Frisia. Hemp production was especially encouraged for the shipping industries that needed strong sail-cloth and ropes. Tecklenburg was an important centre for hemp.

In hemp and linen production spinning was important and people of all ages, including children, took part in production. Large families became desirable for production and additional work was increasingly available to landless rural workers. Cottage industry was especially advanced in an area such as Westphalia where *Anerbenrecht* (the process of farm inheritance by the youngest) prevailed. Yarn exports from the region between Elbe and Weser, the Harz, Thuringian forests and the Lüneburg heath were even more lucrative than linen. Bleaching also became increasingly important for the export market.

In the Black Forest area linen was an important cottage industry, although most production was for home use. Durlach linen was exported as far as Norway in the seventeenth century, however. In the southern districts of the Black Forest cotton developed with Swiss capital, and in the Austrian lands of Alsace and Swabia entrepreneurs provided the capital. After the 1750s embroidery work became as important as spinning. The linen-weaving carried out on the Swabian Alb around Urach is of interest in this period, as is the putting-out system of the *Zeuhandlungscompanie* of Calw. In Augsburg entrepreneur Johann Heinrich Schüle from Künzelsau combined the printing-press with the printing of cottons. Imperial intervention, however, led to an embargo on lighter cottons in the interests of more traditional cloth manufacture. Bavarian textile manufacture was priced out of the market, despite state subsidy. With a population of about one million, eighteenth-century Bavaria could not make crude cloth production for the home market pay against more sophisticated imports. Its strict Catholicism also prevented an enlightened immigration policy, so that neighbouring Protestant Franconia soon outstripped Bavarian production, especially in Erlangen, Roth and Schwabach.

In Brandenburg-Prussia, the centre of gravity lay in the wool industry. The Berlin warehouses were model state enterprises for supplying the Prussian army, and after 1763 they even supplied the Russian army for a time. Frederick II also took the linen industry of Silesia from Austria and added it to that of Prussian Westphalia based on Bielefeld in county Ravensberg. Silesian linen production was mainly export-orientated. Mixed cloth was popular and was first introduced by Huguenot immigrants. The same is true for cotton and silk manufacture, introduced in Berlin after 1744. Like the porcelain industry it was strictly controlled by state mercantilism. Although silk production was not as valuable as other textiles, it was still of special social importance, and was supervised by Frederick II as a showpiece of state enterprise, drawing its inspiration from Lyons and Geneva and exercising a strong influence on the future development of Prussian state planning. Something similar occurred in Saxony. The state took the initiative and numerous workshops grew up after the middle of the seventeenth century. After 1697 Saxony also obtained favourable trading rights in Poland when the two countries came under the same ruling dynasty. The Austro-Prussian wars over Silesia after 1740 seriously disrupted economic growth in east central Europe. But after 1763 a reconstruction programme under administrator Xaver began to form the basis of nineteenth-century Saxon industrialization.

Cottage industries were particularly export-orientated in the mountainous areas of the Swiss Confederation. In the St Gallen region at the beginning of the eighteenth century cottage industries far outstripped those of the towns. New centres arose outside town, often in places of ecclesiastical seigneurs, especially those of the Abbot of St Gallen in Herisau, Trogen, Rorschach, Arbon and Hauptwil, where the 'shows' competed with St Gallen for trade. These fairs undersold the more traditional, guild-regulated markets. In the St Gallen region of a total population of about 100,000 in the last quarter of the eighteenth century no less than 80,000 men, women and children are thought to have been employed in the textile industry, at least a third of these in embroidery works. The putting-out system predominated. Many weavers also employed spinners as out-workers. Weaving and spinning was generally done on a part-time basis on the poorer farms by women, children and old people. Winding was usually carried out by weavers' children and old people.

Knitting and embroidery were also entirely under the control of the putting-out system after 1750. Another linen-producing area in central Switzerland, Aargau and Lucerne, expanded alongside Emmenthal. In 1760 the Swiss linen industry stretched from Berne to Lucerne. Around Zürich a woollen industry was important, backed by cottage industry, with town council controls that provided the best jobs for its own craftsmen.

The Swiss cotton industry grew substantially where it was free of guild regulation. Although there were opportunities for developing the putting-out system even in the towns, the craft system was often preferred, especially by small country manufacturers (*Tüchler*). After 1662 Zürich town council attempted to restrict access to its markets by *Tüchler*, who now had to resort to middlemen. Among rural spinners and weavers there were two groups, those with farming land and those without. Only the latter were wholly dependent on the putting-out system. Weaving was usually a valley industry, but spinning also took place in the mountains. After Zürich the next largest Swiss centre for textiles was Winterthur. Canton Glarus also became increasingly important for textiles in the eighteenth century, especially new, lighter 'Indian' materials. Zürich tried in vain to prevent this development by passing monopolistic laws. Cotton was soon the most valuable branch of the Swiss textile industry. After 1750 cotton production extended from Lausanne far into the German Black Forest, to Swabia and the valleys of Graubünden, from the Ajoie region to the Gotthard pass.

In the second half of the seventeenth century linen-weaving became more competitive in Upper Austria than in neighbouring Bavaria. In all there were by 1713 83 linen masters' guilds in the province, as well as its cottage industry, but quality was poor. In the eighteenth century superior-quality Bavarian linen was marketed in an attempt to outsell the Austrian product. The Austrians retaliated after 1730 with tariffs and embargoes.

The problem of raw material shortages was especially acute in the Linz woollen industry, although this was partly overcome by skilful centralization under town councillor Christian Sind in 1672. Technical direction was in the hands of foreign specialists using local labour for routine jobs. Habsburg mercantilism increased the variety of finished goods that Linz had to produce. By 1730 thirty different kinds of woollens were listed. Many factories of this type changed ownership frequently. In 1717 the

Sind enterprise in Linz was taken over by the Vienna town almshouse, and in 1724 the Levant company of Vienna took on the factory. Under Maria Theresa the enterprise flourished, and in 1754 it was made into a state enterprise. It was now a model for future Austrian textile development. The Linz enterprise used factors who acted as minor entrepreneurs, had spinning done in various Austrian provinces and even across the border in Bohemia. At its peak in 1762 46,309 spinners worked for the factory; 28,604 in Upper Austria and 5,541 in Lower Austria, 1,550 in Styria and 10,516 in Bohemia. The Bohemian contingent even increased to 16,720 in 1786. Total numbers employed in spinning for the Linz textile industry were thus very large indeed, and to support this number cottage industry was essential. In 1748 11,763 woollen cloths were finished and by 1764 the number was 26,042.

The Abbot of Kremsmünster set up a business for making woollens in 1749 and soon employed 600 spinners. In 1710 the Bohemian board of trade encouraged the development of a school of commerce, headed by Count Waldstein, who had textile factories in Horni Litvinov. In the Habsburg lands industrial enterprise increasingly became merely a question of capital finance. Magnates were therefore in the best position to become investors. They often combined with foreign dealers such as Allason von Rumberg, Wingfield, Franchin, Nurse and Coulston. Other native noblemen apart from Count Waldstein who became industrialists included the Kaunitz of Slavkov and Krisanov, Gallas in Hradek, Harrach in Namest on the Han and in Ganoricit, Haugwitz in Namest on the Oslau, Franz von Lothringen in Kladrub and Potstejn, Schmidtgabner in Resolanec, Baron Neffes in Heralc, and the Kaunitz of Hatzfeld. They also controlled cottage industries as well as textile workshops. A large part of production still came from home industry, and often only finishing was done in the factory itself. The Leitenberger enterprise employed only 100 people in the workshop and over 2,000 in cottage industry attached to the firm. Horni Litvinov textiles were among the first in the Habsburg territories to concentrate all the processes of cloth production into one factory complex. There were forty-five different operations, and in 1728 391 persons were employed there.

Stimulated by the examples of Italy and Switzerland, silk began to be processed in Habsburg Austria at Graz and Ljubljana, and by the Becher enterprise on Count Sinzendorf's Lower Austrian estates at Walpersdorf, which used specialist labour from France and the Netherlands. The enterprise lapsed, however, and had to be restarted with new capital by Karl Bertalotti and Ludwig Mittermayer. The same thing happened with the other Sinzendorf enterprise which made silk stockings in Walpersdorf and silk ribbons in Traismauer. A *Kunst-und Werkhaus* was started with state support in 1676 on the Tabor to deal with silk processing and design as well as woollens and porcelain production. It was a very early type of craft and design school. The school was under the rule of Bishop Rojas and the brothers Geyer of Edelbach, but when the Turks besieged Vienna it was burnt down.

Under Becher's influence, Vienna in 1702 had no less than twenty silk manufacturers who paid taxes. The Bratti firm operated silk looms in the Schottentor poorhouse under the direction of foreign master-weavers. This enterprise was taken over by Passardi, Bussi and Hengstenberger with imperial Habsburg privileges. The other master silk-weavers in Vienna combined in 1710 to form a brotherhood of satin, gold, silver, silk and half-silk cloth-makers, limited to a membership of between twenty-four and thirty. In 1717 François Dunant, a manufacturer of taffeta from Geneva, bought the right to settle in Vienna with sixteen workers. This firm was taken over by Viscont after 1725 and began to flourish. In 1727 Hengstenberger was licensed to produce gold and silver brocades for thirty years in Lower Austria. In the same way Geramb obtained silk monopolies, although at this time there were already about thirty manufacturers in Vienna. In Prague 11 noblemen formed a company in 1725 to build a silk factory run by French masters, who were to teach the native workers. In 1729 this enterprise had forty-two looms, but this number was down to twenty-five in 1732. The enterprise failed to fulfil government hopes that it would supplant imports of foreign silk. Lack of capital, poor quality and high costs of production hindered it. The situation was similar in Vienna, although it improved there after the 1750s. Silk ribbon making was successful and by 1736 there were 22 workshops. Gabriel Garlipp exported silk braid worth many thousand Gulden a year from his Habsburg patented factory in the poor Josephstadt district of Vienna.

Textile industries in Hungary, Slovakia and Poland also grew up with the support of the nobility. In Russia Tsar Alexis began imports of cotton plants and mulberry trees. In 1681 satin manufacture was started but without success. The Dutch started cloth manufacture in Moscow in 1684. Tsar Peter was mainly interested in promoting large-scale production in metals and, above all, textiles. In 1702 Moscow received its first sail-cloth factory. Russian enterprises began to employ a massive labour force long before this became customary in central and west Europe. Some of the first textile factories had between 100 and 500 looms each. War, as in the years between 1705 and 1715, tended to bring many difficulties with it but the new Russian textile industry always had plenty of work in supplying its army and navy. Success could only be achieved by the use of forced labour. Compulsion also applied to manufactures, as happened to textile managers who were forced to amalgamate by the ukase of 1712. This was not very effective, however. On the death of Tsar Peter there were 26 different textile factory centres in Russia, the most important of which were in Moscow and St Petersburg. There were also works in Voronetz, Kazan and Azov making *passementerie*, stockings, hats and tapestries, and often based on foreign expertise.

Russian light industries tended to suffer lack of capital and only heavy industry and textiles received the necessary state support. Specialists, tools and equipment were often sadly lacking, despite an over-abundance of unskilled labour. Russian textiles did not achieve the same quality as west European products, although English middlemen were increasingly prepared to trade them in Asia during the later eighteenth century. Large-scale domestic production in Russia was hampered by the lack of purchasing power among consumers, and so official bodies, the army and civil service, became the largest buyers.

In Scandinavia the textile industry was not important, despite efforts by the Danish crown to encourage a home industry. In the 1680s and 1690s the state helped to finance lace and cloth works by bringing in Jewish and Protestant immigrants. It was hoped to increase home production by forcing the army and navy to buy only Danish textiles. By 1706 the crown had begun to set up linen and hemp factories. Silk came under Copenhagen guild control in 1705, and the linen-weavers were also organized in guilds. In 1737 textiles were sold from a state-supported central warehouse and guild restrictions were imposed so as to increase the profitability of the putting-out system. Textile merchants now had to have two years practical experience abroad, notably in branch offices in Holland and England. Each merchant had to finance at least two looms on the putting-out system and to buy a fixed minimum from the weavers. In this way production spread beyond the guild crafts to the countryside while the Danish state retained supervision over both.

Swedish absolutism under Charles XI helped to finance textile workshops, and production increased in Stockholm and Norrköping, which became the centre for wool-processing in Sweden. Among the chief entrepreneurs was Peter Speet from Lübeck. The Barnängen works of Per Gavelius near Stockholm earned its founder a noble title. The Alströmers also made Alingsås into the third largest Swedish textile centre in the eighteenth century.

State initiative had a considerable part in developing the European textile industry, especially in the north and east during the later seventeenth and eighteenth centuries. In Alsace, the Rhineland, Westphalia and Switzerland private initiative was also important. A strong mercantilist impetus from the state improved textile production in most of the German territories, especially in Prussia and the Habsburg lands, but also in Russia and Denmark. Despite the fact that east European textile manufacture was less competitive than western products, protection ensured home markets in most absolutist states. Specialists and equipment imported from the west soon taught native workers and technicians to run their own industries with support from state capital and guaranteed markets. Where the state went over to a system of free trade and lower tariffs, native industries tended to wither, for they were not able to compete on open markets.

(vi) Production for the transport industry

In the seventeenth century the most prosperous ship-building industries were in the United Provinces and England. France's shipyards on the Atlantic and Mediterranean coasts also became important. German yards were on the North Sea and Baltic coasts, most importantly at Emden, Bremen, Hamburg, Altona, Lübeck, Rostock, Wismar and Danzig in Royal Poland.

Emden's heyday as a centre for freighting came in the second half of the eighteenth century, when the town provided an outlet for Brandenburg–Prussian colonial ambition. Actual ship-building was confined to smaller coasters and fishing smacks. After the Prussian takeover in east Frisia an Asiatic Company was floated in 1751, opening trading with two boats bought in England. Later on one boat was built in Emden, and the rest came from shipyards in Amsterdam and Norrköping in Sweden.

Shipyards were to be found on the main rivers, at Oldenburg on the Weser and at Stade on the Elbe (which the Swedes lost to Hanover in the Great Northern war), and also on the island of Wilhelmsburg between Hamburg and Harburg. Elbe ship-yards became important after the 1690s when saw-mills were constructed to form the basis of the industry. In Hamburg the Roosen yard opened and on the Hanoverian bank of the Weser the enterprises at Vegesack became important. In Bremen 66 native ships were built in 1678, the largest being 125 *Last* (250 tons). But ships of greater capacity were also owned although they were usually made outside Germany. In 1696 Bremen ship-building still only employed a labour force of about 60. Wharves for servicing and repairs were non-existent. In the eighteenth century Bremen's ships were usually built at Lübeck.

Hamburg showed considerable interest in ship-building, for its port had much sea trade and yards were needed especially for repairs. The Portuguese had various ships built there in 1648 to fight the Dutch East India Company for the Portuguese Asian trade. Hamburg started building convoy escort ships in the 1660s using the skills of Dutch master ship-builders. During Louis xiv's wars Hamburg's ships often sailed as neutrals and were prepared to sail for any small enterprise such as the Scottish Darien scheme. Hamburg and its neighbour Altona competed in ship-building. The permanent imperial assembly at Regensburg even issued laws in 1712 to settle disputes between masters and workers in the ship-building industry, though they were a dead letter. Hamburg yards were still too new to build all types of sea-going craft, as was shown when the Ostend Company removed its orders from Hamburg to Holland in 1705. Hamburg also had no forge for heavy ships' anchors until the 1720s. Hamburg's ship-building declined in the eighteenth century because of guild restrictions which meant that new large-scale works were built away from the old yards outside the town's jurisdiction. After 1744 the town council tried to protect local ship-building by means of subsidies and a number of new ships were built in the years that followed.

The ship-building industry of Altona gained in importance during the eighteenth century. The first large order was completed in 1704, when Admiral Paulsen of the Danish navy took delivery of a warship with fifty guns. In 1743 the Altona journeymen carpenters guild of shipwrights numbered over 100 members. Altona sub-contracted work to smaller yards such as those at Neustadt, which were also used by Lübeck. Ship-building brought in high profits, and most sea-ports tried to foster their own industry. Such a case was Kiel with its Seekamp yards on property belonging to the Counts of Schack. Smaller vessels were built at Eckernförde, Kappeln on the Schlei and larger ones at Flensburg, Sønderborg and Åbenrå.

Lübeck was, however, the most important ship-building centre in Germany, and it is the only place for which statistics are available. During the Thirty Years' War trade was brisk. In 1637 Lübeck built and sold 29 boats, totalling 2,500 *Last* (5,000 tons). Between 1618 and 1648 a total of 642 boats was constructed. These good times never returned and the highest figures for the eighteenth century were 22 boats (totalling 2,460 tons) in 1727 and 18 (2,520 tons) in 1743. Average ship size was 90 Last (180 tons). Surprisingly, construction of large ships of over 100 Last became rarer. Chief shipper and builder was Thomas Fredenhagen, who between 1655 and 1679 part-owned 28 newly built ships from Lübeck. In the 1690s he had two great hulks built of 270 (540 tons) and 295 Last (590). Lübeck continued to build ships for export, however, receiving commissions for substantial-sized hulks, mostly from Bremen and Amsterdam.

Ship-building at Wismar suffered from Swedish occupation and control during and after the Thirty Years' War. The Swedish government tended to give preferential treatment to its own industry, especially that of Norrköping. By 1710 only one master shipwright was left in Wismar. Rostock fared slightly better. The Swedes also accorded better conditions to its oldest ally in Germany, the town and port of Stralsund. The Stralsund fleet ran to 300 ships in 1629 but was down to 100 with two large vessels for trade with Spain of 120 and 180 Last at the time of the great siege in early 1630. In 1685 the town had only

38 ships, totalling 1,028 Last, the largest of which was a mere 60 Last. In about 1696 the town had 50 ships, totalling 1,256 Last, and the largest ship was now 80 Last. Average ship size was only 25 Last. Some Stralsund ships were from other yards such as Eckernförde, Kappeln and various shipyards on the Mecklenburg and Pomeranian coasts. Ships were also bought from the Darss, Carlshaven, Barth, Anklam, Damgarten and the Swedish yards at Kalmar and Västervik. On the other hand a series of ships was built at Stralsund for use in Stockholm.

Many ships were built in the vicinity of Barth and Demmin on the island of Rügen and at Prerow. Some master shipwrights from towns like Stralsund and Lübeck broke guild discipline to work in these yards. After 1708 regular orders came from the Swedish Admiralty, which subsequently slumped when the Swedes began to lose the war under Charles XII. In 1691 there had been twenty-eight master ship-builders but by 1721 there were only sixteen, and two of them had diversified into merchant shipping. With peace in the early 1720s, Rügen's yards once again produced about ten ships a year. Between 1740 and 1756 sixty-six ships were built by twenty-two master-builders. There were also 11 ships' carpenters, who were outside guild control, working on the island.

Barth, Greifswald and Wolgast were the most important Pomeranian shipyards. At Barth ship-building began to provide serious competition for Stralsund by 1700. It also developed its own trade in the 1720s, which then further stimulated its ship-building. In the 1770s Barth ran 35 cargo vessels of 30 to 60 Last (90 to 120 tons). Ship-building in Greifswald was never very considerable and the town had no guild of carpenters, although it ran six ships of 50 Last in the later 1720s. Shipyards at Wolgast were important until the town was destroyed in 1713. By 1758 it still only had six master carpenters. Ship-building in Uckermünde entailed competition for Stettin, which also came from Warp and Stepenitz. Foreign masters from Holland and Denmark worked in Stettin itself, where ships were built for the Swedish Admiralty in Karlskrona in the early eighteenth century. In 1708 a ship of 180 Last was constructed there. Under the Brandenburg-Prussians Stettin ship-building lapsed, but in 1754 the port still had 70 sea-going ships.

Under the Great Elector of Brandenburg, Benjamin Raule was commissioned to establish a ship-building industry in

Kolberg, and a Dutchman, Viktor de Port, was active as chief ships' carpenter for the Elector. Yet as late as 1741 Kolberg ran only 19 ships. Its own ship-building was still minimal and its ships' carpenters were in the same guild as ordinary carpenters. Elsewhere in eastern Pomerania, Darlowo, Trzebiatów and Slupsk had ship-building industries. During the Thirty Years' War, Darlowo had 17 ships which sailed to Spain, Holland, and England and Norway to fish for herring. These ports provided a certain amount of competition for Danzig, acting as alternatives at times of war and trade embargo.

Surprisingly, Danzig only had nine master ship-builders in 1695, and the figure never went much above 10 in the eighteenth century. They ran fair-sized yards, however, for the number of journeymen often reached 200. Danzig also took on apprentices from all over the North Sea and Baltic, for Danzig boats were quality-built. Shipyards were directly controlled by the town council without guild influence, and production was competitive and export-orientated. Experts from abroad were especially welcome. Compared with Danzig, the yards at Elbing were puny. In 1641 a Dutch Mennonite, Heinrich Goverssen, had founded a shipyard there, making use of the temporary prosperity of Elbing which occurred whenever Danzig was closed because of war. Guild control over ships' carpenters also decreased the town's competitiveness after 1714. Elbing now only built coasters and row-boats.

In East Prussia Königsberg (Kaliningrad), Pillau (Baltiysk) and Memel (Klaijpeda) were the most important ship-building centres. The people of Königsberg were shipowners themselves, and in 1622 owned 77 smacks of 12 to 70 Last with a total burden of 2,500 Last (5,000 tons). Swedish naval activity in the seventeenth century subsequently destroyed much of this prosperity. Riga, Reval (Tallinn) and Narva were now more favourably placed for east Baltic ship-building.

The Great Elector had tried to entice ships' carpenters from Holland to Königsberg on especially favourable terms and as a result Benjamin Raule had a number of warships built in Königsberg and Pillau. The Brandenburg state then employed an agent in Holland to recruit shipyard specialists, and under Van Worckum ships built in Königsberg were sold to the government. After 1690 Königsberg ships' carpenters were granted a state charter, but in spite of these efforts few really large ships were built. Even so in 1695 the port had a fleet of 76 ships totalling nearly 3000 Last (6000 tons), with an average size of 38 Last. They were mostly coasters or smacks sailing as far as Danzig and Stockholm. Some reached 80 Last in size. Sailings out of the Baltic were not usually attempted in Königsberg-built hulks; those of Danzig were preferred. Attempts by the Portuguese to finance shipyards of their own in the east Baltic came to nothing after 1713. In 1725 total shipping out of Königsberg, Pillau and Memel had sunk to 22 at 1451 Last. One grand exception was in 1732, when the brothers Saturgis ran a ship of 250 Last, the *Prinz August Wilhelm* which had been locally built in Königsberg by shipping-inspector Eigel. In 1753, Königsberg once again ran coasters of a total tonnage of about 2700 Last.

The south-east Baltic hinterland provided some of the finest ships' timber in the world during the eighteenth century. Raw materials were especially sought after by Dutch, Swedish, German, Danish, Russian, Polish and English yards. In Russia under Peter the Great ship-building entered a new and important phase. Tsar Peter himself had studied ship-building in Holland and England and now had ships built at his new town of St Petersburg. Good supplies of wood, pitch, tar, iron, copper and hemp made west and east coast Sweden also very suitable for quality ship-building. Gothenburg and Stockholm, Västervik, Norrköping, Kalmar and Karlskrona were the main centres. In Finland ship-building was mainly in Dutch and Swedish hands and during the eighteenth century Åbo (Turku) and Hamina Fredrikshamn became important.

Certain lines of development can also be observed in the production of vehicles for land transport. As the four-wheeled coach became more popular, its production began to be streamlined and labour divided. Yet carriages were still only for the ostentatious, rich and powerful, and they were often heavily carved, brocaded products. As towns began to be paved in about 1700, new, lighter types of coaches developed, suited for travel in narrow streets of populated towns, or conversely out to country seats along good turnpike roads. Examples of these new wagons were the Berline and the Landau. Paris workshops pioneered the fashion in vehicle production during the reign of Louis xiv, and the other capitals and commercial centres of Europe soon followed suit.

(vii) Printing and papermaking
The techniques of printing and publishing were all pioneered during the fifteenth and sixteenth centuries. During the seventeenth century printing spread to even the most remote parts of the continent and a newspaper industry began to develop. Paris and Lyons, Frankfurt, Nuremberg and Leipzig were the main publishing centres, and Cracow, Copenhagen, Stockholm and St Petersburg had officially sponsored printing-presses. Papermaking spread out from Italy and the south, so that by the eighteenth century cheaper types were being developed in Germany using more wood pulp and fewer rags. Quality paper usually came from south and west Europe, but Saxony had as many as 32 paper mills in 1767. Mercantilist governments usually encouraged their own paper industries and then used the product in government and bureaucracy. Peter the Great had paper mills built in Moscow, St Petersburg and Duderov.

(viii) Building and furniture
After the Thirty Years' War the central European building industry went into a boom period of which as yet too little is known. New public buildings used increasing quantities of bricks and stone. Architects and engineers received better training and more attention was paid to matching artistic design with technical function, especially in military architecture. Standards of living among the well-off also became more luxurious. Castles became palaces and bare interiors became Aladdin's caves of delight and comfort. Furniture became a large-scale industry based on Nuremberg, Augsburg, Hamburg and Danzig, each of which specialized in the manufacture of particular types of furniture – cupboards, secretaires, tables, trunks and chairs. Style and make became important and were imitated. During the Renaissance Nuremberg became famous as a centre of Peter Flötner's furniture. Soon Augsburg began to take over. Influenced by Philipp Hainhofer whole groups of artists and craftsmen worked together. Some, such as Baumgartner, David Altenstetter and Matthäus Wallbaum, became well known.

In north Germany Hamburg and Danzig produced the best-known tables and cupboards in the Baroque style. After the reign of Louis xiv French furniture production dominated the European market, especially the Paris cabinet-makers, Boulle,

Oppenord, Cotte, Cressent, Caffieri and Meissonier. From craft origins a branch of furniture making had now arrived in the world of art and culture, but it was all still a long way from the revolution in mass-produced furniture of the earlier nineteenth century. The homes of the majority of continental Europeans were still very bare in the eighteenth century. Craftsmen in this branch of industry still worked individually, producing quality goods for the wealthier sections of the community. Large contracts, for church pews, for instance, did allow for enterprises such as Roentgen in Neuwied which employed ten bronze workers, ten locksmiths, ten mechanics, one clockmaker, and a hundred saw bench operatives in the 1720s.

(ix) Food and drink, sugar and tobacco

Brewing, baking, slaughtering and fleshing remained guild-controlled. Town and country differed greatly from each other. Farms baked, brewed and slaughtered according to their own and their village neighbours' needs, though mass production in food processing did get under way during the seventeenth century, as standing armies and navies grew. Most sea-ports had undertakings for making ships' biscuits. Large-scale operations developed in fishing, brewing, sugar-refining and tobacco-processing.

The fishing industry had hardly changed from earlier times. Stockfish, herring and cod were still needed to supplement basic diets all over the European mainland. Whaling was a newer industry that expanded greatly after the 1650s. The German North Sea ports extended their activities from Frisia, Bremen and Hamburg, and the Danes of Jutland were also active in this dangerous work. The first Frisian and Schleswig-Holstein whalers were manned by experienced native sailors who had seen service on Dutch and French whaleboats in the 1630s. Blubber and whalebone found increasing domestic and farming uses for lighting, oils and fertilizers as well as foodstuffs.

A new feature of the seventeenth century was the wide production and sale of strong spirits distilled from grain. Production spread from the United Provinces to Westphalia, Schleswig and East Prussia. Scandinavia became especially active in the production and consumption of crude spirits, *brännvin* and aquavit, and Russia produced vodka. In Denmark Ålborg held a similarly important position. The beer-brewing industry became one of the most technologically and socially advanced of all major production industries in this period. North German and Danish beers had now reached perfection as export products. But the brews of Franconia, Bavaria, Upper and Lower Austria were, and still are, very fine. Outside Vienna there were 86 breweries in the Mühlviertel and Machland, 37 in the Traunviertel, 96 in the Hausruckviertel, and production had reached 220,000 *Eimer* or firkins by 1700. Brewing was usually guild-controlled and held high status in all the small towns of central Europe. Perhaps the finest ales of all were made in Pilsen (Plzen) in Bohemia. The royal breweries at Copenhagen also developed into a large industrial undertaking. In about 1640, 35 brewers were producing 20,000 barrels of beer a year, but there was continual friction with the Copenhagen brewer's guild; this was finally settled in 1739 when the guild rented the royal brewery.

Sea salt also held its own with mined salt as a result of cheaper sea transport. But mined salt was of finer quality and remained essential in central Europe, where important mines existed from Lüneburg down to Salzburg and from Halle to Wieliczke and Olkusz in Poland.

After 1650, Europe imported sugar not only from Brazil but also increasingly from the West Indies. The French led the way with mercantile policies whereby molasses were refined in west and south France. Marseilles, Nantes, Angers, Orléans, Saumur and Rouen soon developed as centres of sugar-refining. In 1728 there were 4 refineries in Marseilles and by 1755 the number had increased to 14. French home consumption increased from 100,000 pounds in 1700 to 230,000 in 1789, but the greater part of French sugar production was exported. Hamburg also installed its own sugar refineries, and had 30 factories going after 1650. By 1690 nearly 8,000 people were employed in the sugar industry and in 1750 there were several hundred refineries (on small-scale production). A few refineries ran to a workforce of 40, but the majority had only about 5 workers. A large refinery would produce 6,000 hundredweight of fine sugar and 600 hundredweight of syrup per year.

Sugar-refining was especially attractive to mercantilist governments. Brandenburg–Prussia established three refineries in Berlin between 1660 and 1673, but such projects failed to gain steady access to cheap raw materials, the so-called colonial goods market. It was cheaper to buy the finished product from west Europe. The Hohenzollerns attempted to set up refineries in Berlin at regular intervals all through the late seventeenth and eighteenth centuries. In Habsburg Austria sugar-refining was introduced after 1719 in connection with the Ostend Company, but it failed because of English and Dutch pressure after 1733. A new phase began in the 1750s when state privileges were granted to the Arnold Company to build a refinery at Fiume (Rijeka).

Tsar Peter's Russia also ran sugar refineries as state monopolies. The Kremlin had its own works before 1701, when it was moved to make room for the arsenal. After the war years in the 1720s a licence was granted to Pavel Westor to build a refinery in Moscow, although it was eventually set up in St Petersburg. In the first year only ten tons of refined sugar were produced, but production was artificially increased when the import of sugar was banned in 1723. In the same year Westor built two more refineries at Moscow and Kaluga, and the Moscow refinery soon became one of the largest industrial enterprises Russia had ever known. In 1762 there were only four refineries in Russia but they were all on a large scale.

Denmark became a significant sugar producer after gaining the island of St Croix from the French in 1733, and in the same year a Danish West India Company started a refinery in Copenhagen which became the greatest sugar market in north Europe. In Sweden privileges were given in 1648, 1661 and 1662 for refineries but production was never large and only developed after a ban on imports of sugar and syrup in 1738.

With increasing tobacco imports from North America during the seventeenth century a new industry of tobacco-twisting began, producing goods to smoke, snuff and chew. The United Provinces produced, then as now, the finest tobacco goods in Europe. Native European tobacco was also grown, manufactured and consumed. The market for both sorts spread from Hamburg, Bremen and Lübeck inland to Cologne, Westphalia and the Palatinate, to Strasbourg, Hanau, Hanover and Brandenburg. From the 1750s Ukrainian tobacco was imported via Lübeck and distributed for further processing. The Habsburg lands also processed their own produce under state control and acted as middlemen for Balkan and Turkish produce.

Service Industries

I. COMMUNICATIONS

A Technological development

The Atlantic coast of Europe clearly led the world in shipping technology in the seventeenth and eighteenth centuries. The Baltic took second place. French canal construction was also well developed for inland trade. A typical example was the Orléans canal built in 1692 to link the Seine and Loire. The Languedoc canal in southern France was also of crucial commercial importance. It was built by Pierre Paul Riquet at Colbert's instigation between 1666 and 1681 to link the Garonne at Toulouse with the Mediterranean via the Aude. Late seventeenth-century French canal-building reached a high standard which was not surpassed, even with later technological improvements. In central Europe the most important canals for heavy transit trade were the Havel-Spree canal, and the Kiel canal built in the later eighteenth century. In Russia access to the Baltic was also obtained by linking the Volga and the Don.

There was little improvement in road building, however, although hard surfaces began to appear on increasing numbers of French *chaussées*. These were kept in repair by resort to *corvé*, or compulsory labour, especially after 1738. In 1747 an *École des ponts et chaussées* was opened and a corps of bridge and road engineers established in 1750. Road construction was above all of military and strategic value to absolutist governments in central and east Europe. Frederick II of Prussia even allowed roads on his borders to fall into disrepair in order to hinder foreign invasions.

In shipping the activity of the Hanseatic and Scandinavian Baltic ports fell far behind that of the English and Dutch, although neutrals were always more active during times of war, especially in the Mediterranean. At such times there were cargo carriers who managed to come to arrangements with the Barbary pirates, an especial nuisance to weaker naval powers such as the German Hansards. Central European sailings to ports outside Europe were still rare in the eighteenth century. The occasional Hamburg ship sailed across the Atlantic using the ports of Portugal and north-west Africa. The slave trade with the West Indies via the west African coast had its attractions, especially to the Brandenburgers, but they failed to compete with the Portuguese, Dutch and British. In the 1770s Hamburg ships plied the French Antilles, as well as Danish St Thomas and Dutch islands.

B   *Land routes*

(i) Transit between Atlantic, North Sea and Mediterranean
Transit trade in the region between Rouen and Hamburg was much influenced by political events. In peacetime sea routes were preferred because transport costs were cheaper. Merchants in Cologne and Frankfurt usually received goods by sea via Amsterdam and then along canals and rivers. Economic, colonial and dynastic rivalries between states were particularly acute in this period, and communications were often temporarily disrupted. Frankfurt's trade with the Netherlands was disrupted in 1652–4 and even had to go via Venice and the sea-route. One way round these difficulties was to cancel customs and excises for the duration of the emergency. Early modern governments thought growth in trade possible only if a neighbouring state was deprived of some of its trade. Bilateral trade agreements were popular, thus one reached between Austria and Venice in 1656 which mutually reduced tariffs by a quarter. High taxes at Rovereto diverted Alpine traffic from there to Graubünden. In 1658 Bavaria signed a treaty with Austria to encourage the transit of goods from Bavaria to Venice and on to Turkey. Taxation of transit goods was an extremely important government weapon in the later seventeenth century and no export-orientated industry anywhere in Europe could afford to ignore it. The traditional world of dynastic politics also became one of mercantile diplomacy.

Louis XIV's war against the Dutch Republic in 1672, which was followed by the Habsburg Emperor's war against France, led to the re-routing of sea trade through Germany. In 1675 Tyrol transit rates were reduced and Venice responded by giving more favourable conditions to the German trading community. The Palatinate war after 1688 again encouraged re-directed transit trade over the Alps. War increased smuggling and blockade-running, especially by neutrals such as the Swiss and Venetians. Similarly, in the Spanish Wars of Succession, Bavaria was in alliance with France, so that Silesian iron goods had to be re-directed via Venice. Receipts from customs for imports into Venice increased 600 per cent between 1702 and 1707.

(ii) Transit through Schleswig-Holstein

The transit trade through Schleswig-Holstein increased in importance when war, trade embargoes and increased tariffs affected passage through the Sound, especially in the 1670s. At that time the route between Eckernförde, Husum or Tönning became crucial. During the wars at the beginning of the eighteenth century customs dues were reduced for Schleswig-Holstein transit trade, although the Danish crown put on pressure so that its interests in Sound trade were not prejudiced. Transit across the land bridge between North Sea and Baltic was also made more difficult by the monopolistic policies of Lübeck, which refused to allow intermediate towns a share of profits in its trade with Hamburg.

(iii) Routes in central and south-east Europe

After the upheavals of the Thirty Years' War Leipzig again became the chief entrepôt of central Europe, linking the heavily populated and heavy-production regions of central Germany with east Europe. Its communications went to the sea via Bremen, Hamburg and Danzig, to the west via Frankfurt-am-Main, to the south via Prague and Nuremberg, and to the east via Berlin and Breslau (Wroclaw). But some important routes also by-passed Leipzig, such as the direct Elbe river line via Magdeburg, Dresden and Pirna. From the 1680s linen from Saxony, Lausitz, Bohemia and Silesia was stapled in Dresden and taken directly to Hamburg by water. Spanish wines, Russian hides, fish and other staple commodities were carried to the Saxon Elbe towns on the return journey, and from there they were sent on to Bohemia, Moravia and Austria. Hamburg and the North Sea routes were now linked to Bohemia, Poland and Hungary via the Saxon staple towns. The Habsburgs tried to control profits from their end of this route by making Prague a staple town. East-west traffic also increased along the road from Frankfurt-an-der-Oder via Königsbrück to Dresden and from there to Freiberg, Chemnitz (Karl Marx Stadt), Zwickau and Reichenbach. This road linked Poland with Nuremberg and also by-passed Leipzig via Sagan, Jüterbog and Magdeburg to reach Lüneburg and on to Hamburg and Lübeck, or went by the shorter route across Brandenburg via Krossen, Frankfurt-an-der-Oder and Berlin to reach Hamburg and Lübeck through Mark Brandenburg. The latter route became even more attractive with the building of a canal between Oder and Spree under the Great Elector. There was now direct inland waterway traffic between Hamburg and Wroclaw. After 1669 Silesian yarn sold at Hamburg was decidedly cheaper when shipped by water than when sent by land via Leipzig, Magdeburg or Frankfurt-an-der-Oder.

This was a shorter route than the *Grosse Heerstrasse* via Leipzig and faster than the *Kleine Heerstrasse* via Magdeburg or Frankfurt-an-der-Oder. From the late 1660s about a quarter of the Polish and Silesian trade that had formerly travelled via Leipzig went directly by water to Hamburg, and this trade route began to expand. By 1710 goods from Poland, Silesia and even from Austria and Bohemia, such as yarn, linen, dyes, wool, wax, skins, Austrian and Hungarian wines, travelled overland to Breslau (Wroclaw) and from there by water to Hamburg. The return trade upriver was in fishmeal, oil, sugar, dry goods, spices, tobacco, sweet wines and dyewoods. From now on Berlin became an important business centre and together with Leipzig controlled the economy of the north-east German hinterland. Despite the rise of Berlin, Leipzig continued to dominate the chief internal trade routes of east-central Europe in the eighteenth century, and its staple continued to link with that of Nuremberg and Regensburg. In 1699 carriers from Regensburg took tin, dyes, steel, copper, vitriol, Styrian iron, potash, butter and millet via Gera, Zeitz, Naumburg, Freiberg, Eisleben, Aschersleben, Magdeburg and Brunswick to Bremen and Hamburg, bringing back wines, spices and colonial goods.

In the eighteenth century the ancient route which crossed the Thuringian forest at Oberhof and which linked south

Germany directly with the sea via Erfurt also became active again. Potash and iron goods went to Erfurt, to Wanfried on the Werra, from there by the river Weser to the North Sea and on to Holland, or via Magdeburg to Hamburg and then by sea as far as Spain. Although Leipzig retained its chief position in east central European trade, this position was no longer a monopolistic one in the eighteenth century, especially when dynastic links with Poland involved the territory in wars with Sweden and Prussia. Yet recovery was swift, and the Leipzig fairs remained indispensable for the free flow of trade between central, east and south-east Europe.

Construction of the Oder-Spree canal destroyed the prosperity of Stettin as a transit port on the lower stretches of the Oder after 1668. It then had to rely on trade within the Swedish Empire but was subject to redevelopment by the Prussians after 1770. Its river trade to the Baltic was now freed from the remaining Swedish customs tolls at Wolgast. The Silesian trade increased along the Oder with the development of Odermünde. There was also a very lively trade between Frankfurt-an-der-Oder and Breslau after its incorporation into the Prussian state during the 1740s.

Central European trade routes all made use of important rivers to the north. The one exception was the Danube route via Regensburg, Linz and Vienna and from there overland to Venice or Trieste. Regensburg was the bridgehead for important routes going the other way into Germany. It was an alternative for trade between Germany and the south-east during times of war, such as the Seven Years' War. The Danube route also became crucial for the expanding Habsburg Empire as the Turks were pushed out of Hungary after the 1680s. This expansion provided the Habsburg state with alternative area for industrial development after the loss in the 1740s of its most industrial province, Silesia. Great efforts were made to develop the industries of Bohemia, Moravia and Austria and to seek new trade outlets for exports via the south and south-east, using the Danube and the Adriatic. After the destruction of Poland the Habsburg lands were able to develop trade with east Europe via Galicia, thus by-passing Prussian Silesia. This route went through Brody, Cracow and Lvov and became very important for the export of iron goods from the Habsburg provinces. The port of Trieste was also developed under direct Habsburg control in order to provide an alternative to Venice and became increasingly prosperous.

(iv) Routes in eastern Europe

During the first half of the seventeenth century Russia was in no state to conduct effective international alliances and trade agreements. The situation improved after 1650 as the Romanovs began to combat the Turks and Tartars on the fringes of south-east Europe. To some extent these problem zones could be by-passed by direct trade with Persia farther to the east. Russia and Poland were even prepared to combine in a transit trade alliance with Persia after 1667 in order to circumvent the Turkish hold on the Black Sea and Moldavian lands. This agreement was renewed in 1686. The Swedes also achieved some success in Russian trade relations, although the Prussians failed to obtain any favoured state treatment. Under the Dutchman Fabricius, the Russians granted favoured treatment to Armenian transit trade via Novgorod to Narva in peace years after the 1680s. When the Swedes took up relations with the Turks against the Russians this potentially prosperous trade route disappeared.

The political situation brought Russia and Persia closer together after the 1660s, and the Armenian trading community tended to benefit from this. Trade in silk products was interrupted by the revolt of Stenka Razin but was re-established in the 1670s, based on the centres of Astrakhan, Smolensk, Novgorod and Archangel. Distances were so vast that it was only profitable to trade in luxury goods, which gained in mystique and rarity value when sold in central, north and west Europe. An Armenian trading company was established by the negotiating skill of a Dutch envoy, von Klenk. Yet Armenian merchants themselves never got beyond Moscow before 1676. Thereafter they were allowed as far as Archangel, and from 1686 they were allowed to use the short route via Novgorod. From there they began to trade with the other countries of Europe. They were keen to import Scandinavian quality metal goods and were prepared to offer staple rights for oriental silks and furnishings in return. Swedish hostilities with Russia and Poland destroyed this potentially excellent plan. Fabricius nevertheless refused to admit defeat, and as late as 1700 he was still trying to connect Swedish–Persian trade via Russia from his base in

Persia. From a mercantile point of view it would have been advisable for Sweden under Charles XII to make peaceful arrangements with Russia and Poland. After 1685 Armenian–Russian trade links had been developed with Baltic Courland, and with the growth of St Petersburg Courland trade faced increasingly to the east. While Mitau (Jelgava) rapidly lost importance, Liebau (Liepaya) gained a vital place on the route to Moscow via Bauska and Polotsk. In 1696 Russian–Persian trade in textiles and spices was regulated by the states and conducted by Armenians. Ultimate trading points were envisaged in Holland, England, France and Portugal.

In 1697 Tsar Peter signed a trade treaty with Brandenburg–Prussia, giving mutual access to Königsberg and to various Russian markets such as Moscow and Astrakhan, with forwarding trade to Persia and China. Armenian traders came to Königsberg and links with the region east of the Black Sea were also established via Poland and Russia. The trouble with this trade was that it was far too vulnerable. Such overland Asian routes depended above all on relations between Persia, Turkey and Russia. Some security was however achieved when St Petersburg was opened and the Russian state began to expand into the Baltic. The 1717 Russo-Persian agreement for bilateral trade stabilized the exchange of goods in east Europe and central Asia, although Turkish and Levantine trade continued to outflank it as regards access to west European markets. Even so, by 1722–3 Tsar Peter had extended his power to the Caspian, driving the Persians from the western and eastern shores of the sea. The silk centre of Ghilan now came under Russian control, though the south shore was only temporarily in Russian hands (1724–6). By 1737 the Russian advance had continued farther west with the capture of Azov. From now on the Ottoman Empire was under pressure on its northern frontiers.

2. TRADE

In France some improvements in internal trade were achieved by canal, bridge- and road-building programmes under state supervision, although local and provincial customs barriers still proliferated, except in those peripheral provinces which were *d'effectif étranger*, such as Alsace, Lorraine and Roussillon, which had more foreign than internal trade. The turnover of trade of the Beaucaire fairs in south France increased rapidly, as did the annual fairs in Normandy and Brittany, where colonial produce began to play an increasingly lucrative role. In addition the large urban centres of Paris, Rouen, Dijon, Lyons, Orléans and Toulouse acted as magnets for trade and business in surrounding towns. The ports of the Atlantic and the Mediterranean had a closely delineated hinterland. The Seine became a crucial route for supplying Paris with basic food and fuel.

French foreign trade was almost totally government-controlled. But in Colbert's lifetime, and even more after his death, strong liberalizing tendencies showed themselves, for instance in the trade centres of Rouen, Nantes, Lyons and Lille. Yet mercantilism reigned supreme, and found its expression in bilateral state trading treaties with Holland, Prussia, Denmark, the south Netherlands and the Hanseatic towns towards the end of Louis XIV's reign. France developed a trade surplus that was the envy of continental European states that also operated mercantilist absolutism. French charter companies dealt with all forms of colonial and inter-continental trade, although during the eighteenth century freer enterprises also obtained their chance of profit, including those trading with French North America and the West Indies. There was very active trade with the French Caribbean, Martinique, Guadalupe, Haiti and the Lesser Antilles, carried out from French Atlantic ports such as Rouen, Dunkirk and Bordeaux. Ships of the Senegal-Guinea Company did the round trip with slaves to French West Indies.

In the 1720s the real French weakness of primitive banking and credit facilities was exposed by the failure of John Law's speculation in stocks and shares. Government control was re-imposed and French foreign trade increased greatly during the reign of Louis XV, especially with the rise of the Atlantic ports from Calais to Bordeaux and of Marseilles in the south-east. The French East India Company traded in Africa and North America as well as in the Far East. The first demands for liberalization of overseas trade in Europe came from French publicists such as Cournay, Morellat and Raynal, who called for a system of *laissez faire-laissez aller* after the 1750s. This retreat from protectionism achieved its first great success in 1769, when the privileges of the French East India Company were cancelled; French trade with India now increased. Turgot was a pupil of Cournay and continued trade liberalization by his famous edict of 1776 which opened a new era in French economic thought.

Conditions in central Europe were still determined by the loose federalism of the German Empire, which fell into a member of economic regions. Small-state territorial autonomy was also a barrier to any proto-national and monolithic economic planning. Small territories followed their own economic policy according to their own mercantilist and absolutist dictates. Protectionism ruled supreme. The result was a myriad of customs barriers within the Empire. Rivers and roads were all riddled with tolls. Prussian customs policy favoured imported goods from the west, although separate internal tolls were kept between all the Hohenzollern provinces. Despite the drastic increase in the price of most merchandise that this entailed, internal central European trade continued to grow during the eighteenth century. The great rivers, the Rhine, Weser, Elbe and Oder, were used to the full, and although trade in this region did not grow as spectacularly as in the Atlantic seaboard region, it did remain buoyant. The same applied to the Danube basin.

Inside Germany small-state autonomy led to the predominance of small-town trade. Even so, established market towns competed with the new administrative centres of princely absolutism – thus Brunswick and Lüneburg came into competition with Hanover and Wolfenbüttel. The traditional imperial towns of west and south Germany retained their importance, although their independence was threatened by increasingly powerful territorial states such as Prussia, Bavaria, Hesse, Baden and Württemberg. Most German foreign trade went through the ports of the North Sea and Baltic. Unlike the earlier period trade had been based on the Rhine and on the south, travelling to Italy, the main outlets in the eighteenth century were in the north, at Emden, Hamburg, Bremen and Lübeck. Contact with the Netherlands and Italy of course remained relatively important, and new links with the Balkans and Adriatic were also opened as the Habsburg Empire expanded into south-east Europe. In the first half of the eighteenth century Hamburg began a policy of freer trade by opening its port facilities to foreign merchants, and after 1748 grain had free transit in the harbour. Turnover increased accordingly and Hamburg began to warehouse basic goods such as fish, livestock, and cereals. Its trade began to increase at the expense even of Danzig and Amsterdam, especially in the boom years after the Seven Years' War had ended in 1763. Hamburg benefited from the new colonial liberalism of the French, Spaniards and Danes in the era before the Napoleonic Wars. Even the German textile industry gained through this freeing of foreign trade.

There were considerable internal barriers to freer movement of trade. Thus Bremen's interior trade on the Weser suffered because of high tolls imposed in Oldenburg after the Thirty Years' War. Yet Bremen's own industries were stimulated by the arrival of French refugees. In about 1700 sailings to Greenland also increased, and both transport trade and textile manufacture in the town benefited from the Seven Years' War. In 1769 a maritime insurance company opened in Bremen for the first time.

Unlike Bremen and Hamburg, Lübeck really did decline in the eighteenth century. Its restrictive guild policies closed the town to skilled foreign labour, although Lübeck trade and produce kept their reputation for high quality. The town retained a lead in the production of high-quality starch, tobacco and sugar products such as marzipan. After 1673 it also ran its own exchange bank, the function of which was to facilitate transit trade between the North Sea and the Baltic. In this way the Lübeck partriciate retained its prosperity.

Emden, which came under the Hohenzollerns after 1740, was also important as a rival port to Bremen. The Prussian government tried to build up its own chain of ports from Emden through to Stettin, Kolberg, Königsberg and Memel. State support was given to found a herring company, a marine insurance company and, belatedly, a Levant company in 1765. But the Prussian home market was still too poor to make these ventures a success.

Coastal trade was particularly well developed along the south Baltic coast where the economies of many small German states interwove with those of Denmark, Sweden, Poland and Prussia. Without this the great international bulk trade of the Baltic could not have flourished. For example Rostock had a rich grain growing hinterland in Mecklenburg. Later Stettin developed waterway trade with Berlin, Frankfurt-an-der-Oder and Silesia, all under Prussian state supervision. Memel in particular had a rich hinterland in the first-class hard-pine forests of Lithuania.

The remaining imperial towns of Germany were affected differently. Cologne declined because of territorial rivalry and Counter-Reformation policies, unlike Frankfurt-am-Main, which welcomed foreign skills, especially in banking. Augsburg just retained its manufacturing industries, whereas Nuremberg tended to diversify to survive, rather like Frankfurt. Few of the old imperial towns did as well as the newer centres at Hamburg, Leipzig, Munich, Hanover, Karlsruhe, Darmstadt and Stuttgart, and only Frankfurt really retained its international position. Leipzig trade fairs in the eighteenth century outdid even those of Frankfurt-am-Main. Leipzig controlled the Levant overland trade between central Europe and the Near East. Jews, Armenians, Greeks, Walachians, Serbs and Courlanders were all to be found at the fairs there. Eighteenth-century trade figures indicate that on average each Leipzig trade fair transacted between five and eight million talers of business in actual goods. Attendance at one of these fairs by three thousand merchants was considered low.

Because of the Guelph's dynastic links with Britain, trade fairs for English manufacture also became important in Brunswick and Hanover during the eighteenth century. A number of towns specialized in transport and communications, especially the new production centres of the Ruhr. Mainz and Regensburg were also important centres for transit trade. Territorial state capitals such as Munich, Hanover, Berlin, Kassel and Dresden all ultimately owed their prosperity to the rise of eighteenth-century state mercantilism and absolutist bureaucracy.

Dutch trade and above all capital finance remained of crucial importance to the further development of the eighteenth-century central European economy. The Dutch controlled not only bulk trade but also the trade in quality colonial goods. Dutch exports to the German territories are estimated to have been about three times more valuable than German imports to Holland in this period. German workers were employed in Holland and helped to redress an unfavourable balance of trade, as did Dutch investment in production, above all of raw materials such as iron, copper and silver ores. Most German territorial governments survived by borrowing on the Amsterdam money market whose bills of exchange often saved central

European states from bankruptcy. Regional trade between the United Provinces and the Rhineland–Westphalian hinterland was especially lucrative. The north German market, however, could be serviced more readily from Bremen and Hamburg than from Amsterdam. Yet most large-scale transactions in international trade with German territories tended to go via middlemen in the Exchange at Amsterdam in the later seventeenth and eighteenth century.

The south Netherlands (most of modern Belgium) remained in Austrian Habsburg hands after the end of the Spanish War of Succession. They experienced a considerable industrial growth, stimulated by the presence of coal, iron and native capital resources. Liège textiles were important exports to west Germany, as were high-quality Belgian metal goods. Political pressure from the Dutch and English, however, meant the continued closure of Antwerp and the Scheld, whose natural potential as an international entrepôt was greater than either London or Amsterdam.

France's most important exports were colonial products, such as coffee and sugar, as well as native luxury goods, such as wine, brandy and agricultural products. In return France received timber, grain and other bulk raw materials from Hamburg and the Baltic. Most French trade with central Europe went via the Hanseatic ports. Overland trade also went via Lorraine and Alsace or by transit through Luxemburg and Switzerland. Strasbourg was the centre of this land-based exchange of goods. There were also the old trade routes from south Germany to Lyons and Marseilles, from where Levant trade became increasingly profitable. The Swiss played an important rôle in Franco-German trade especially at times of hostilities and war, when direct trade became too hazardous. Trade between Swabia and Switzerland was dependent on textiles and raw produce such as linen thread. St Gallen's manufactures were made up partly of raw materials from Swabia and the Allgäu. For this purpose there was a special thread market in Lindau. Rorschach, Ausserrhoden, Speicher and Wald were transit trade centres for Swabian and Silesian linen cloth. The floss silk industry of central Switzerland supplied German manufacturers via Frankfurt to Krefeld, Elberfeld, Nuremberg and Magdeburg.

Italy's trade with Germany also used both sea and land routes. Venice was no longer as important as in previous centuries, especially as there was now competition from Trieste, but it continued to attract merchants especially from south Germany until the 1790s. German exports to Italy included textiles and manufactures from Franconia, Saxony and Silesia. Trade was dominated by south Germans and reached into Lombardy, to the fairs of Sinigaglia, using Genoa as entrepôt for Spanish and South American markets. Trade agreements between Venice and Saxony were renewed in 1769. Direct sea links were also occasionally used between Hamburg and Venice. In the north European Levantine trade Swedish and Danish ships used Ancona; south Italian ports also traded with Hamburg, especially in vegetable oils and fats. Of the Italian ports, however, Leghorn and Genoa were the chief centres of sea trade with Hamburg.

In the Habsburg Empire after 1740 Bohemia produced textiles, glass, manufactured metal goods and processed food and drink. Its chief trading outlet was Saxony. In return it imported goods from Hamburg and Leipzig for the rest of the Habsburg hinterland. The textiles of Linz also went north via Bohemia. The real expansion of Habsburg trade came in Vienna, however, which now dominated the Danube basin and linked German trade with the Balkans.

Eighteenth-century Inner Austria could still compete with Germany in the production and export of quality iron goods. Tyrol retained a certain prosperity through its Alpine transit trade. The markets of Hall near Innsbruck and of Bolzano were especially important for German textile exports to north Italy. The Hungarian plain with Slovakia, Galicia, Slavonia and Transylvania became increasingly agricultural and concentrated on cattle and wine exports into north and central Europe. The port of Trieste became the most important port in the Adriatic after Venice as a result of Maria Theresa's policies of state support. Trieste was built to lessen the dependence of Habsburg trade, especially Bohemian trade, on Saxony and Prussia. Industrial raw materials such as potash now went from Trieste to Hamburg by sea and avoided the Elbe river route. Trieste operated as a gateway to the Levant, and the Balkans and Ottoman Empire grew in importance as trading partners during the course of the eighteenth century. Three important trade-routes were now via the Leipzig fairs, via the Danube and via the Mediterranean. Yet land-routes within the Ottoman

Empire were unfavourable to bulk trade. The Leipzig fairs overshadowed all others in trade between the Balkans and central Europe.

There was little direct German sea trade with the Levant, although a few firms were established in Smyrna and Constantinople. But the Turkish mint also bought Austrian silver talers for its Arabian and north-east African trade. These coins were struck in Günzburg and handled by firms from Augsburg. In the eighteenth century English traders were the chief middlemen in the Levant trade, but goods were also shipped via Marseilles, Leghorn and Trieste. The partition of Poland destroyed the internal cohesion of east-central European trade in the second half of the eighteenth century. The Vistula with its outlet at Danzig became increasingly dominant. Prussian attempts to circumvent Leipzig's eastern trade by halting it at Breslau and Frankfurt-an-der-Oder and redirecting it through Berlin and Stettin failed. The industrial economic power of Saxony was still too strong for Brandenburg, traditionally Germany's poorest electoral principality.

In the east Baltic St Petersburg now overshadowed Riga, Reval and Dorpat. Chief buyers of Russian goods were the Dutch and English, but Lübeck, Hamburg and Bremen were also involved. In return they delivered colonial and manufactured goods. Russian, Jewish and Courland Baltic merchants were very active at the Leipzig fairs. Swedish and Finnish iron goods and forest products were still handled by Lübeck merchants for the central European market. There were even slight increases in the Hanseatic share of Scandinavian iron exports, although the lion's share stayed with British traders. Imports into Scandinavia were much more strictly government-controlled. Sweden's own shipping industry was favoured by the state. Trade with distant countries was handled by the East India company based on Gothenburg. Swedish dependence on grain imports grew steadily during the century. Whenever the political and military situation permitted Sweden imported cereals under short-term favourable bilateral trade agreements with Russia, Danzig, Poland and East Prussia. Swedish trade with the west centred mainly on Amsterdam, Hamburg and, increasingly, London. In the eighteenth century tar became the main export of Finland, most of it going to England, and the German ports receiving only a limited amount. Finnish timber boards went to Schleswig-Holstein. In return the chief import was grain (95 per cent of it rye) and also malt.

The united kingdom of Denmark–Norway supplied north Germany with fish and forest products, in return for grain and manufactures. Copenhagen also became a miniature Amsterdam, distributing colonial goods in the Baltic region. Danish trade flourished as a result of the government's skilful policies of neutrality during much of the eighteenth century. The Danes also handled the trades of the Faroes, Iceland and Greenland as crown monopolies, often to the detriment of the islanders and natives. Norway's exports of tar, copper, iron and dried fish went mainly to Schleswig-Holstein, who in return supplied much of Norway's intake of grain. Flensburg took a leading part in this trade. Bergen's fishing trade was however closely linked to the Dutch market by this time. Gone were the days of Hanseatic monopolies on Norwegian trade.

Anglo-German trade was more indirect, although it was dependent on the supply of grain and forest products out of the Baltic. Yet sales of English manufactured goods to central Europe increasingly went via Hamburg and the Elbe route to the Leipzig fairs. Imports of English coal even started to arrive in north German ports.

Although England dominated Portugal's European trade, Hamburg supplied Portugal directly with manufactured goods, textiles, materials for ship-building, copper and grain. Danzig, Bremen, Memel and Stettin exported grain in return for vegetable oil, cotton, rice, coffee, cocoa, hides, Brazil wood and tobacco from Oporto and Lisbon. East Indian goods such as tea, cinnamon, pepper and nutmeg also came via Lisbon. Setubal provided salt, the Algarve cork, figs and other fruit and Oporto vegetable oil, cork, sumac and port wine. Voana exported fruit and fortified wine. In Spain Cadiz was important for exports to America; returning goods came mostly via Malaya.

The German export trade was mainly confined to Europe until the end of the eighteenth century. Inter-continental trade became increasingly limited to colonial powers and their companies, who held a monopoly of trade. German ships did use the Mediterranean and Adriatic, but only the occasional boat reached the West African coast, usually under a Dutch flag. German trading expeditions set out to West Africa financed by the Great Elector, who inspired a slaving expedition to St

Thomas following the example of the Danish West India Company. Brandenburg colonies on the West African coast were too expensive and had been sold again by the time of King Frederick William I. Frederick II took up the idea of overseas expeditions again and from 1752 onwards he financed sailings from Emden to China. In the following year a Bengal company was formed, but then came the difficulties of the Seven Years' War.

The dynastic union of England and Hanover brought English colonial trade from North America up the Elbe to Harburg. But German shipping to North America only really increased after the Declaration of Independence by the United States of America in 1776. The Danes acquired the West Indian islands of St Croix in 1733, and the sugar trade was so buoyant that there were complaints of insufficient merchants and boats to cope with it. West Indian molasses sugar had to be diverted to Flensburg. Strict *asiento* regulations for trade between Spain and its American colonies were only relaxed after 1765 as regards central Europe.

Swiss colonial trade was hampered for lack of access to the sea and the mercantilist policies of its neighbours – France in particular long refused direct access to Swiss merchants. Swiss exports overseas were also too heavily laden with duties to be worthwhile. But skilful investment enabled Swiss entrepreneurs to participate in the financing of Dutch and French colonial trade. The Faesch and Hoffmann families traded in the West Indies under Dutch flags. The Diodati from Geneva traded in Hamburg and belonged to the Dutch East India company. The Saladins from Geneva were active in the English East India company. In the 1720s there was a large colony of Genevans in Constantinople and a branch in Smyrna. Merchants from Zürich had colonies in Bergamo and Leghorn, in Milan, Vienna and Trieste, and also had active trade relations with Germany and the Netherlands. Merchants from St Gallen were to be found in Lyons and Marseilles, in Paris and Le Havre as well as in Nantes and Bordeaux. The firm of Pourtalès from Neuchâtel had settlements and warehouses in Paris, Lyons, London, the East Indies, Africa and America. The inhabitants of Glarus, who had begun by dealing in cheese, also handled dried fruit, herbs and slate, building up trade in Italy, England, Norway and Russia based on textile imports and exports. Firms from Appenzell and Herisau were equally successful.

The Habsburg monarchy attempted to cut tariffs. In 1775 a customs area was created for the patrimonial lands with the exception of Tyrol and the Vorlande provinces. In 1784 Galicia was added, but Hungary formed a separate customs area. There were clearly defined trading areas within the Habsburg monarchy which encouraged the exchange of goods between individual provinces, such as between Carinthia via Salzburg to Upper Austria, and between Lower Austria, Moravia and Styria. Salzburg gave special concessions to Habsburg trade between Upper and Lower Austria. From 1749 onwards trade statistics were kept and these show that Lower Austria had the greater export trade. Vienna became the largest single market on the Danube, acting as entrepôt for trade between Germany and Hungary and also as middleman for the Adriatic and Balkans. Linen and woollen goods came down river from Linz. Salt and iron goods came from Salzburg. Grain, textiles and glass came from Bohemia. Half of Vienna's export trade was in textiles. Agrarian produce made up another third, although grain exports from Lower Austria decreased as the town grew in population. Later in the eighteenth century Bohemian glass began to make up 15 per cent of the kingdom's export total. Moravia produced mainly for export. Its flax went to the textile industries of Bohemia and Silesia and its grain to Vienna. Moravia linked the export trades of Bohemia, Silesia and Hungary especially via yearly trade fairs at Opava (Troppau).

Inner Austria's export of iron goods led to a favourable balance of trade. In Styria about 320,000 hundredweight of pig-iron was produced annually in the later eighteenth century, 30 per cent of it for export, mainly to Hungary and the Levant. On top of this about 1,200,000 scythes, sickles and knife blades were sold annually. Carinthia's production of iron was about 155,000 hundredweight a year, which went mainly to Italy and the Levant. Carniola produced barely 20,000 hundredweight, mainly for export to Italy. Carinthia also exported non-ferrous metals, cattle and coarse linen to Italy, while the Carniolans' most lucrative export was mercury.

Tyrol's greatest source of income was from transit trade across its Alpine passes. Salt from Hall was the only bulk export and it played a similar rôle to that of Hallein salt in the

Salzburg area. South Tirol engaged in the production of silk for export. Certain routes began to prosper at the expense of others once Trieste was opened. The Pustertal and Brenner routes grew at the expense of the Tauern. Vorarlberg, however, remained landlocked and backward. The total value of officially registered Habsburg imports rose from 24,200,000 Gulden in 1776 to 32,100,000 Gulden in 1788. Exports were worth 27,200,000 and 32,700,000 Gulden in the same years. Austrian trade with Hungary and Transylvania in 1783 was worth 12,800,000 Gulden in imports and 9,700,000 Gulden in exports, and with Galicia the totals were 1,300,000 and 360,000 Gulden.

Hungarian trade statistics were first recorded in 1748. The main exports were agricultural produce and there was an important transit trade between Austria and Transylvania. Despite its favourable balance of trade, Hungary had a very high proportion of nobility, a small urban population and a peasantry with low purchasing power. Between 1748 and 1782 Hungarian imports more than doubled to 9,200,000 Gulden, whereas exports increased by 125 per cent to 13,500,000 Gulden. The main export was cattle and in 1748 61,200 oxen (including 37,000 from Transylvania) were imported into Banat and Turkey alone. In 1782 about 80,000 Hungarian oxen were exported. Hungarian grain production was stimulated by the increasing needs of Vienna. Poland took more than half of Hungarian wine exports while export of sheep's wool to Moravia also increased. Transylvanian trade with foreign countries had a total value of less than 3,000,000 Gulden, with a negative balance of trade. Here cattle was the only important item for export to the west. Imports from the Ottoman Empire were three times as valuable as corresponding exports. But the urban communities in Transylvania helped to produce a favourable balance of trade in finished goods. Industrial exports went almost exclusively to the Turkish lands.

When Poland was dismembered, the Habsburgs took Galicia and also Bukovina. These provinces were incorporated into the Habsburg state customs union founded in 1775. Galicia had a considerable export trade in manufactured goods and especially in cheap textiles. In 1783 imports were valued at 5,450,000 Gulden and exports at 4,440,000. By 1787 exports were worth 5,550,000 Gulden. Galicia's foreign trade was still mainly in a north–south direction, but transit trade from west to east increased.

Habsburg foreign trade continued to expand all through the eighteenth century despite the loss of Silesia. Imports increased from 29,000,000 Gulden in 1790 to nearly 52,000,000 Gulden in 1804; exports from 18,000,000 Gulden in 1789 to 34,900,000 in 1804. But the balance of trade became increasingly negative. In 1797–8 Austrian trade was valued at 5⅔ Gulden *per capita* in urban areas, and only at 1½ Gulden *per capita* in rural districts, making an overall average of 2⅔ Gulden *per capita*. The Polish territories taken over by the Habsburg Empire increased this negative balance considerably.

Habsburg–Russian trade developed once the two powers began to share common frontiers. Export goods such as grain, hemp and linen were made state monopolies, and in 1662 monopoly trade already covered sable, hides, potash, pitch, tallow and hemp, controlled by Tsarist customs policies. After 1667 customs dues were introduced favouring the *Gosti*, who formed a commercial patriciate for the Tsars. They now monopolized Russia's foreign trade. Foreigners paid on average two and a half times more in taxes than native town dwellers. Dutch traders in particular received favoured treatment in Russia from the 1640s to the 1660s. But there were also connections with German ports such as Lübeck and Hamburg. French contacts with Russia had almost completely ceased, however, and the Compagnie du Nord, created by Colbert in 1669, had no direct trade with Russia.

To some extent fiscalism hindered the expansion of Russian foreign trade. In 1680 53 per cent of state income came from consumer taxes and town excises. High prices, however, had an inhibiting effect on consumption, especially during the financial crisis of 1654. Liquid capital was always scarce in the second half of the seventeenth century, yet under Tsar Peter Russian businesses and manufactures developed on an increasingly large scale. The Voronin shops, factories and smithies in Moscow alone took up 82 buildings, in which considerable numbers of foreign experts were also employed. Voronin diversified into fisheries in Samara on the Volga, also taking a large part in supplying the Russian army with grain. Ukharov had a distillery in Moscow, a salt works in Siberia, ten shops in Yenisseisk and six in Irkutsk. The Stroganovs were one of the great merchant houses with offices in Moscow, Kaluga, Ryazan and Ustjiny in 1670 and representatives in Doordrecht and Antwerp. During Tsar Peter's reign Russian military and naval strength was used to open the Baltic to direct export trade. Chief products were flax, grain, leather and silk after 1710. After 1722 two-thirds of all Russian exports went via St Petersburg. There was, however, considerable opposition to this from English and Dutch merchants, who had colonies in Archangel, as well as from Russian merchants using the Dvina. Most of Peter's early merchant naval enterprises were conducted with captured Swedish boats.

Ambitious wars and foreign policy delayed the development of internal Russian trade. After 1721 Tsar Peter attempted to stimulate the home market; he issued sumptuary laws and handed out monopolies on trade to certain urban centres, but with little effect. Traditional trade fairs still predominated, especially those at Makariev, which was started in 1524, and at Irbit, started in 1643.

Foreign trade, the most lucrative item of treasury income, was strictly controlled by Tsarist legislation. Monopolies were sold by the state to the highest bidders; thus for example the fisheries were transferred to the Menshikovs in 1704, the linseed trade to merchants from Vologda and the rhubarb trade to Germans. But state control of foreign trade eventually brought diminishing returns, for it was over-exploited to pay for increasing military and naval costs. Liberalized trade was increasingly demanded by Russia's top economists such as Luberas, Pososhkov, Ragusinski, Kurbatov and Saltykov.

In 1711 the Tsar leased the China trade to three Moscow merchants, Philatev, Gregoriev and Maiev, for an annual rent of 260,000 roubles. In 1717 the grain trade was declared free to all. In 1719 all monopolies except potash and resin were revoked. The China company only lasted one year, as did subsequent companies formed in 1723 for trade with Spain and with the Caspian Sea. The Russians still lacked sufficient capital as well as men experienced in international business. The trading house run on a family basis was the usual form of enterprise. Peter never gave up the task of developing foreign outlets for Russian trade. In 1715 he appointed trade representatives in Paris and Antwerp and in the following years others in Vienna, Cadiz, Liège and Bordeaux. In 1717 an agreement was signed between Russia and France, but the details were not given. An agreement with Persia in the same year was followed by another in 1722, ratified in 1729. Russian merchants also had access to China after 1698 by a regular caravan trade, which was disrupted by political differences for a time after 1722.

The volume of Russian foreign trade was still limited. Between 1700 and 1726 imports rose by 50 per cent from 1,000,000 to 1,500,000 roubles, and exports even more impressively from 1,300,000 to 2,400,000 roubles. Russia had a very positive balance of trade. However, the overland part of this export trade had a negative balance. Among exported goods grain was important, although in the south Russia still lacked a good harbour with access to the Black Sea. Swedish iron provided stiff competition for Russian iron exports. Russia still depended on imports of manufactures from west Europe, and especially England, colonial goods from Holland, wines from France and silk goods from China.

Much Russian trade continued to be carried out on a barter basis; although Peter tried to introduce cash payment after 1723, this failed because of lack of bullion to cover internal monetary needs. After Peter's death the forced pace of change was relaxed. Russian internal trade could not make much progress while the mass of the population were still serfs, who were tied to the land. The only possible areas of growth in consumption were in the expanding populations of the towns. But in 1724 there were only 328,000 town dwellers – possibly 3 per cent of the total population. In 1786 there were 1,300,000 – 4 per cent of the total. Yet there was increasing consumption by the upper class of nobles, state servants and merchants. Their demands for luxury goods dominated import trade. After 1742 the state attempted to enforce laws to limit ostentatious living, but with little success.

A further increase in foreign trade occurred after the liberalization policy of 1726, when all merchant monopolies held since 1685 were withdrawn. From now on landowners might trade in their own agricultural produce although some monopolies on trade were reintroduced after 1730. In 1750 Shuvalov bought a monopoly of trade in grain, stock-fish and hides and after 1755 in the export of hemp, alcohol, leather and tallow. Inland trade was improved by the systematic abolition of internal tolls after 1733. State interest rates went down to 6 per cent in 1734, and the first effective merchant bank appeared in Moscow, followed by an exchange bank in 1756. Companies for Persian trade were re-established in 1755. The Kamchatka Company of 1764 traded in Siberian furs. These firms were small, however – Kamchatka started with a capital of 10,000 roubles, rising to 60,000 in 1772.

The Russian state continued its policy of bilateral trade agreements with a new treaty with Britain in 1734, granting 'most favoured nation' treatment in St Petersburg, Moscow, Astrakhan and Archangel. An agreement with France gave Russian trade access to the Mediterranean. Russo-Persian trade was strictly regulated after 1717. Trade with China was regularized after 1728, although the Russians tended to abuse their privileges by increasing quotas. A great step forward in tariff policy came in 1731 when wool was freed from import duty. In 1757 taxes on luxury imports were increased while those on basic raw materials such as hemp and flax were reduced. In general the structure of Russian foreign trade remained unchanged in the eighteenth century. England, Holland, Germany and France were Russia's main trade partners. Russian trade by sea had a favourable balance, but land trade was always in deficit. Grain exports increased noticeably, reaching 172,000 hectolitres in 1720 with some fluctuation thereafter. A great increase came after the building of the southern Russian ports; until then textiles and allied raw materials were the most important agricultural exports. Iron was the main industrial export, and in 1767 the amount exported was nearly 2,000,000 *Pud*, of which 90 per cent went to England. Russia had taken the place of Sweden as chief supplier of crude iron to the west.

Swedish export-import trade was mainly controlled by Stockholm and Gothenburg. But a number of other ports such as Gävle were increasingly active in export trade. South Finland also began to flourish via its ports of Turku (Åbo), Helsinki and Lovisa. Vyborg declined after the Russian takeover, because of monopolistic policies favouring St Petersburg. A mercantilist shipping policy in the state of Sweden–Finland restricted the Dutch carrying trade. The *Produktplakat* of 1724 forbade the Dutch from directly supplying salt and colonial goods, and was later extended to exports of food and wood products. The immediate result was shortages and price increases which hit especially the salt-fish industry of Bohuslän. Copper, iron and timber remained the chief exports of Sweden and Finland. A peak in copper production had already been reached in 1650 but even in the 1690s Sweden still produced half Europe's copper. Iron now took over from copper as chief export, however, especially as British demands increased. Swedish bar iron exports exceeded 40,000 tons a year in the 1740s, half of which went to Britain. But after about 1770 Britain bought more iron from Russia than from Sweden. Germany, Holland, France and the Mediterranean were also supplied, and Sweden still led marginally in the world market, ahead of Russia. The areas around Stockholm, Gothenburg and Helsinki also became important for the export of sawn timber in the eighteenth century. Gothenburg in particular supplied the British market. Stockholm, however, lost its leading position in tar exports after the Northern war, when Britain began to buy tar products from its North American colonies. Russia also exported tar via Archangel to west Europe.

Swedish imports from the south and west of Europe were headed by salt and textiles throughout the eighteenth century. Grain imports were also increasingly paid for by exports of fish and liver oil from Bohuslän. In addition colonial products such as raw sugar and tobacco were imported. The Swedish East India company was very successful in the years between 1734 and 1806. It supplied tropical and oriental products to Gothenburg and Stockholm in direct competition with Amsterdam, Hamburg and Copenhagen.

The Danish export-import trade was very lively because of its excellent geographical position. Copenhagen was Scandinavia's most important trade centre. The town benefited from crown protectionist policies which kept rivals such as Ålborg insignificant. The Danes also held their own islands and trading ports in the East and West Indies after the later seventeenth century. The company that traded with the East was refounded in 1670 with a capital of 163,000 Riksdalers, and was granted a monopoly for forty years. The Danes as neutrals benefited from war, and during the Palatinate war (1688–97) the company's profits were nearly 218,000 Riksdalers.

The Danish West Indies company was also successful after occupying the islands of St Thomas and St John in the 1660s. In 1671 the Danes began to operate in the Atlantic slave trade alongside the British, Dutch and Portuguese. The Danes even allowed Brandenburg some trade concessions on St Thomas and along the Guinea coast where forts were erected. Real progress was made when the island of St Croix was bought from the French in 1733.

In the later seventeenth century many boats from Holland and Hamburg attempted to avoid trade embargoes by sailing under the neutral flag of Denmark. The Danes imposed strict regulations on the passage of belligerent powers' shipping through the Sound. Copenhagen became a staple for the west Baltic and a centre of the grain trade. By the Treaty of Travental the Dutch for a time regained their trading ascendency in the Baltic. Denmark's next chance to benefit came during the Northern war. By 1726 Copenhagen's right of staple had been extended to include wine, salt, tobacco and brandy. Now its only rival was Aalborg, which had a salt depôt, although Copenhagen did not have sufficient boats to supply all the Danish towns and the Dutch were invited to smuggle via the Jutland ports. By 1730 Copenhagen's strict shipping monopoly had broken down. Lübeck also continued to supply numerous Danish ports from Århus to Ålborg. The ports of Schleswig-Holstein also dealt in manufactured and colonial goods as well as flax, tow and hemp for Denmark. As yet west European interest in Danish grain was still slight, since Poland produced more cheaply for export and England still had export surpluses. The main buyer of Danish grain was Norway, in return for iron, timber and fish.

In the 1730s the Danes reorganized their colonial trade. The East India company was dissolved and an Asiatic company was formed, with wide-ranging privileges, based on Tranquebar. For a while Copenhagen became more important for Far Eastern produce than Hamburg. Danish West Indian trade depended on raw sugar imports to the refineries of Copenhagen. The company was most successful after the 1730s when it leased out its monopolies piecemeal to private shippers. During the 1730s Danish currency kept a steady value and its *Kurantbank* (deposit bank) loaned large sums to the state and to the monopoly companies engaged in colonial trade. Shipowners and wholesalers were organized into one society in 1742 and agreements were signed with foreign powers to gain protection for all Danish trade, including pacts with North African Barbary pirates and the Ottoman Empire. In 1749 there was an agreement with France by which Denmark acquired the status of most favoured nation.

The outbreak of the Seven Years' War brought Denmark renewed opportunities for business as a neutral. She refused to support France or England in the war but did agree to supply French shipping. In 1756 Denmark concluded a pact of armed neutrality with Sweden. Transit and cargo trade now flourished in a kind of temporary Nordic trading union between Denmark–Norway and Sweden–Finland. Main exports to the west were fish and timber, in return for salt and wine. As English and French boats temporarily disappeared from the Baltic, Danish shipping took on the rôle of major carrier, with sailings to the Mediterranean as well. But not much came of the 1747 General Trading Company, which was to have made Copenhagen a staple for the export of all Baltic produce and to have supplied the Baltic with Mediterranean and colonial produce. In 1754 the Danes opened St Croix in the West Indies as a free port and traders were encouraged by state premiums to use its facilities. In the 1760s St Thomas was also made a free port and now the islands became important for trade to and from the French West Indies.

During the Thirty Years' War east–west trade in Europe was intensified and strengthened. Demand for basic raw materials rose, especially for metals and textiles. Yet sea-trade was greater in volume and also cheaper than overland or river trade throughout the seventeenth and eighteenth century. East Europe tended to lag behind west Europe in manufactures; dependent on credit and technology from the west, the east supplied the west with increasing amounts of raw materials, in return for manufactured goods. Great international centres of trade and finance grew up at Leipzig, Vienna, Hamburg, Copenhagen, Amsterdam and London. Poland, Russia, Austria and Prussia became increasingly dependent on western finance.

A clearly defined central European trade area now began to emerge alongside an Atlantic and a traditional Mediterranean world, encouraged above all by mercantilist policies of absolutist, dynastic states. The trading companies, especially the large charter companies of Holland and England, were emulated in north Europe after the middle of the seventeenth century. They also found their counterpart in overland trade, such as the Russia company in Berlin and those founded by Peter the Great for trade with China. Most of these state-backed enterprises were short lived and subject to political pressures, but they were usually as quickly refounded as they were swiftly dissolved. They did, however, tend to lack capital and adequate markets at home and abroad, which no state in north, east and central Europe was able artificially to create merely by mercantilist legislation.

On the whole the era of great trade fairs was now over in the west, but in east and central Europe they retained their importance, from Frankfurt to Leipzig in Germany, to Mankariev and Irbit in Russia. Fairs were replaced by capital cities with exchanges, banks and commodity markets and by centres with lively sea trade. In the European interior fairs with roving merchants of all nationalities were, however, still predominant. Merchants from the various German territories were to be found along the Mediterranean in Venice, Genoa and Marseilles, in the Iberian peninsula at Lisbon, Cadiz and Malaga, in the west at Bordeaux, Le Havre, London and Amsterdam, and also in north and east Europe. Each European court and government had its accredited merchants as well as diplomats with overseas connections, and in this mixture of politics, finance and trade the Venetians were pioneers. The Germans, Dutch, Swiss, French and English soon followed. In north Europe the British ousted the Dutch as the main foreign traders during the eighteenth century, and in Sweden in particular large firms were founded, such as John Hall and Co., Tottie, and Arfwedsson in Stockholm. Dutch-founded firms predominated in Danzig, while British firms were important in Königsberg. Pedlars were also important piecemeal traders. They sold large quantities of manufactured goods such as farm tools, cooking utensils, glassware and textiles at all the villages and local markets of Europe.

The eighteenth century also saw the beginning of national trade statistics. A crude comparison could now be made between the various countries that were emerging as modern states. Britain and Spain took first and second place in turnover of foreign trade. But German, Russian and French trade was also buoyant. It is estimated that in 1700 Europe conducted inter-state trade worth £62,000,000 a year. By 1800 the total had increased to £228,000,000. World trade in the same years was £88,000,000 and £302,000,000. These crude figures are unreliable, however, and are only intended to give some rough guide to the volume of international trade before the nineteenth century, when the real expansion came.

VI *Money, Credit and Insurance*

The volume of bullion in circulation in Europe as coinage increased dramatically in the sixteenth century as a result of continued silver and gold rushes. In the eighteenth century Mexico and Brazil produced most but older mining regions such as central Europe and Peru continued to supply significant amounts. The Brazilian gold mines of Minas Geraes helped to double gold production from 10,000 to 19,000 kilogrammes per year in the eighteenth century. European gold came from Salzburg, Transylvania and the Urals. Easier extraction of silver led to its cheapening against the value of gold, from the ratio of 1:11 to 1:15. More gold was actually minted in eighteenth-century Europe than ever before. Yet the majority of coins circulating remained of copper and silver alloys. In France the Louis d'argent or écu blanc of 60 sous, equivalent to the German Taler piece, had been introduced in 1641. French coinage regularly fell in value, especially during Louis xiv's wars. This led to John Law's paper-money experiment in Paris in the early eighteenth century. When the crash came it destroyed any advance in French banking for the rest of the century. French minting of gold coinage, the famous *Louis d'or*, continued for prestige reasons.

In Germany the large silver Taler remained remarkably stable, although small silver coins regularly depreciated in value after the end of the Thirty Years' War. Over-spending by territorial courts, armies and bureaucracies, as well as falling production of silver from central European mines, led to debased silver coins being struck in the second half of the eighteenth century on a scale reminiscent of the early 1620s.

Saxony led the way in coinage regulation after the 1660s.

The Zinna agreement between Saxony and Brandenburg in 1667 opened the path towards stable coinage rates that eventually began to operate in all the German territories. Yet even though large silver coins were now strictly controlled in quality and quantity of precious metal, small coins with copper alloys continued to be minted in badly debased form in all territories. After 1687 Brandenburg introduced another devalued Taler standard (from 10½ to 12 to the silver bullion Mark), although the old gold standard of 1559–66 was kept in the Spezietaler. The new silver Taler remained money of account and was usually only minted in ⅓ pieces. It was called the *Kuranttaler*. First Sweden and then the Rhineland adopted the new standard, but it only became the standard for the whole of Germany in 1738.

Austria was the first to adopt lighter money with a 20 Gulden standard in 1748, worth 13½ Kuranttaler. By 1754 the Bavarians had also set up their own standard which was even more debased than the Austrian at 24 Gulden to the silver bullion Mark. This standard became established in the south and west of the Empire during the 1760s, when Saxony and Brunswick also adopted it. Only Prussia, Lübeck and Bremen stuck to the Kuranttaler, while the rest of the Empire was on the devalued Konventionstaler. Leading coins were now the Maria Theresa Taler and the Bavarian Marientaler. Not to be outdone in this, Frederick II of Prussia also attempted to debase his coinage and to mint a prestigious *Friedrichsdor* in 1750, in emulation of the French monarchy. His silver standard reduced the Taler to 14 to the silver bullion Mark. This Taler was minted out at 24 Gutegroschen. The Austrians now had a better standard than the Prussians since the Austrian silver unit was worth 90 Kreuzer, and the Prussian 80 Kreuzer. The Konventionstaler of 1753 was worth 120 Kreuzer.

Special monetary arrangements prevailed in the German seaports, where there was a complicated relationship between Taler, Gulden and Mark. Traditionally a Reichstaler (silver coin) was worth 3 Lübeck Marks (money of account). One Gulden (gold coin) was worth 2 Lübeck Marks or ⅔ Reichstaler. In 1725 Hamburg introduced a currency standard of 34 Marks, equal to 11⅓ Talers. Lübeck followed in 1728 and Mecklenburg in 1765. In Bremen there was a gold Taler worth 72 Groten.

Minting and circulation of copper coins became widespread

during the sixteenth century and reached a peak in the money crises of the seventeenth century. By the eighteenth century all currencies had standard small change of copper alloy. Wars tended to increase the amount of debased face-value coinage in circulation. The import of foreign coins was often forbidden by state governments, as happened in Poland under King Ladislas IV. King Sigismund forbade the minting of coins smaller than a Taler in 1627. Ladislas restricted coins to ducats and whole and half Talers. After 1659 copper pennies were minted in large amounts, called *boratinki*, after money lender Boratini. The Polish Gulden with a nominal value of 30 groszy now made its appearance.

In Russia Alexei Mihailovich allowed his mints to cut foreign Talers into halves and quarters and to over-stamp them with his own equestrian effigy and signature. These coins were called *Jefinki*. Russian copper coins of one to five kopecks were also issued. All these coins had greater face-value than intrinsic value. In 1663 when the silver rouble was decreed by the government to be worth only 15 copper roubles, opposition to the measure led to bloodshed. After 1701 Tsar Peter allowed the minting of gold coins as a prestige measure. They had the same value as the German ducat. But a more practical silver rouble was added, as well as the griwna, worth 10 and 5 kopeks. These coins kept their value, whereas copper coins worth one, half and quarter kopeks, which Peter had minted in large amounts after 1704, were rapidly debased. After 1768 Catherine II issued the first Russian paper money.

In Sweden Gustavus Adolphus had a wide range of coins struck from 5 ducats down to the $\frac{1}{4}$ Taler. He attempted to introduce a copper standard and had coins of intrinsic copper value stamped weighing up to 11 kilogrammes. In the 1630s and 1640s the Swedes in Germany also minted copper coins. Under Charles XII war-time copper coins of up to 20 kilogrammes were issued. In the seventeenth century the Royal Bank at Stockholm had begun to issue paper money and during the Great Northern War more was issued under the direction of Görtz, Charles XII's minister, in 1715. Swedish experiments in paper and copper currencies were perhaps the most interesting of all early modern monetary developments.

In Denmark Christian IV introduced the silver Krone worth 8 Marks or 16 Schillings at the beginning of the Thirty Years'

War. The silver Krone was now worth 1¾ ducats. King Christian had *Portugals* minted, valued from 2½ to 20 ducats, gold Klipps worth up to 8 Talers and silver coins up to 6 Talers. In the second half of the century much copper money was minted in the Danish ports of Schleswig-Holstein and after 1713 Frederick IV issued the first Danish paper money.

All merchant communities were accustomed to using monies of account settled by bills of exchange drawn on the Girobanks of large centres such as Amsterdam, Hamburg and Nuremberg. In Hamburg the *Mark Banko* was used; in Nuremberg it was the *Goldgulden*. Most German territories opened their own state-supported exchange or Girobanks in the eighteenth century. From 1703 there was an imperial Girobank in Vienna and in the following year a Vienna town bank was formed. The Habsburg state *Bankalität* controlled banking from 1714 to 1745. With the increase in banking came a corresponding rise in the handling of paper money. In 1750 it is thought that nearly 2,000,000 Reichstalers of paper money were in circulation in the German Empire.

Public banking began in Sweden with the Stockholm *Banco*, opened in 1657 by Johan Palmstruch, descendant of a Dutch immigrant to Riga; he had copied the bank from the merchant and deposit banks of Amsterdam and Hamburg. Its main office was in Stockholm and there were branches in the most important provincial towns. In 1660 after two devaluations of copper money used since 1644, the bank felt compelled to issue promissory notes to prevent customers from demanding repayment of deposits. In 1688 the bank and its paper money were given the backing of the Swedish Estates in parliament. From now on the bank funded the Swedish national debt. Other institutions of a more public character were added during the course of the eighteenth century, for instance the *Järnkentoret* in 1747, whose object was to protect the interests of Swedish iron producers dealing with foreign as well as native buyers. A similar bank for manufacturers was also established. Discount facilities were introduced in the 1770s for most Swedish industries.

In Russia it was not until 1750 that a number of credit institutions were founded. In 1754 the aristocracy formed banks in Moscow and St Petersburg to help to finance large farms and estates on a mortgage system. Capital for this came from monopolies on alcohol distilling. In the same year St Petersburg merchants also opened their first trade bank. Private banking remained indispensable no matter how much the state supported giro, exchange and loan banks in the eighteenth century.

Some towns developed a sound reputation in banking, among them Hamburg, Geneva and Augsburg. Others, Frankfurt and Leipzig for instance, extended credit by the traditional method of trade fairs. France was dominated by Protestant bankers from Switzerland and south Germany. When France officially entered the Thirty Years' War in the 1630s, the Hervarts became leading bankers in Paris by financing the war effort. Genevan bankers helped Louis xiv through his wars. Many others, such as Lullin, Marcel, Saladin, Turrettini, Mallet, Debay, Cramer and Richard, soon followed. In 1700 Paris banking was led by Samuel Bernard together with others – Deneuve, Hébert and Tourton. French private banks were notoriously unreliable as the system of paper credit under John Law was to show. Credit was re-established by a unified *Banque Protestante* in the first half of the eighteenth century, as well as by the *Comandite Tourton et Baur* headed by the son of an inn-keeper from Ulm. Swiss bankers in France were able to beat all English and Dutch competition by the 1730s, and Genevans began to dominate Parisian banking until the French Revolution. In the eighteenth century Geneva, alongside Amsterdam and London, played a significant role as a centre where European states might raise government loans. The firms of Boner, Delon et Cie, and Urbain Roger raised money for Austria and Denmark, and in addition funds from Berne, Zürich and St Gallen were drawn upon. In 1755 a bank supported by the town council, that of J. J. Leu et Cie., was founded, while at Berne the activities of firms such as Zeerleder and Morel et Marcuard went into the international field.

Paris banking circles were not only connected with Geneva and other Swiss centres of trade but also with south Germany, Frankfurt, Augsburg and Vienna. In Frankfurt merchant banks developed from the wine and spice trade, among them d'Orville and Stedel, the brothers Bethmann, de Neufville, B. Metzler sel. Sohn & Co., L. L. Willemer & Gontard. In Augsburg exchange banks developed out of the gold- and silversmiths' trade, led by the firms of Johann-Thomas Rauner, Samuel Bertermann and Gerhard Greiff in the early seventeenth century. Bertermann went bankrupt in 1696 with 600,000 Gulden of debts. This led to mergers among the survivors, such as Münch and Rauner. Firms such as Rad & Hösslin also survived for a time by diversifying into the wine trade. In Vienna Johann Fries from Mulhouse succeeded in getting a foothold. Away from the big centres of trade a few bankers established themselves, especially in territorial state capitals – in Munich Johann Baptista Ruffini, in Berlin Splitgerber and Daum. The latter combined banking and trade with manufacturing. In Hamburg the Sephardic Jews lost their importance when the Teixeira firm moved to Amsterdam, and their place was taken by Ashkenazy Jewish and foreign firms, such as the Parish concern. Cologne, Leipzig and Breslau were less important in pure banking, although many of their firms did engage in it alongside trade and manufacture, such as the Cologne businesses of Meinertzhagen, Hack, Peltzer and Recklingshausen. In Kassel the territorial rulers themselves acted as bankers, lending money to other ruling princes and states in the German Empire. In Schleswig-Holstein Kiel kept its position as a money market for the Holstein and Danish aristocracy. After the middle of the seventeenth century nearly all the administrative capitals of the German Empire employed Jewish court factors to provide credit and supplies. In 1700 Samuel Oppenheimer, banker of the Habsburg court at Vienna, was owed seven million Gulden. Similar firms operated in Stuttgart and Berlin. Hanover had Leffman Behrens, and Wolfenbüttel the Davids. Seligmann served the court in Münich, and in Frankfurt-am-Main the chief Jewish bankers were the Rothschilds. Hamburg had the firms of Fürst and Goldschmidt. Yet the development of lending by state banks turned German private banks more and more into stock exchanges.

Eighteenth-century Germany was slow to develop its own stock exchanges, although Frankfurt-am-Main became predominant. There were other exchanges at Leipzig, Augsburg, Nuremberg, Cologne, Hamburg, Lübeck, Königsberg and Danzig. The Berlin exchange, dating from 1739, became a stock exchange dealing with produce from Prussian sea trade, and Habsburg Trieste began operating an exchange in 1755. Connections between dynastic rulers and private banking concerns were well developed. The Leipzig banks went with the Saxon dynasty to Poland and established themselves in Warsaw. When the Hanoverians came to the English throne, English banks and credit houses were soon operating in Lower Saxony. The private banks of Amsterdam, London and Hamburg also predominated in Scandinavia and the Baltic, their connections reaching as far as St Petersburg.

In France where the legal system was well developed, even licensed notaries engaged in banking and credit services. French iron-masters especially depended on such credit facilities. The *courtiers de commerce* (commercial agents) also made financial deals from monies readily raised by legally established *sociétés*. The state, however, remained a chief source of finance, granting subsidies to trade and industry.

In Denmark industry and trade were subsidized by a state financed *Kommercefond* and *Generalmagazin*. But the importance of these state credit institutions was slight compared with the private banks, especially those of Hamburg. The Swedish iron and copper industries provided the backing for state and private credit banking centred on Stockholm and Gothenburg. Many *bruk* or industrial and manufacturing concerns were managed with advance credit to pay their workers. This system applied throughout the eighteenth-century Swedish metal and textile industry.

In the Habsburg lands and in east Europe manufacturing companies usually had their own capital. The great industries of Bohemia grew up on this basis. Since the time of Tsar Alexis there had been a special type of merchant capitalism in Russia which developed further under Tsar Peter. Capital was raised by borrowing from the government, which in turn raised funds by the sale of monopolies. Great nobles also invested in industry, such as the Tolstoi who put in 20,000 roubles and Tomikin, who invested 33,000 roubles in needle workshops. Undertakings obtained government advances, such as the 45,000 roubles granted to the Apraxin silk workshops, and the 20,000 roubles to the Dokuchaiev cloth workshops. Nearly all the Russian undertakings in mining and metal processing were financed by the state and only later did private firms take over. Foreign investment was insignificant at the time of Tsar Peter and increased little during the eighteenth century. The concentration of means of production in the hands of a small aristocratic circle was very striking. Many entrepreneurs were also great landowners.

Merchant banking was well established in early modern

Europe, especially in Hamburg, Amsterdam and London, and was essential to the economies of the Scandinavian countries. No Stockholm firm could last for long without capital support from abroad. The way was either to go through state bank finance or to approach a merchant bank lending at market rates. Long-term loans from abroad were still rare. Trade fair credit was still widely used, and petty credit was still given to individual customers; wholesalers supported their retailers. Merchants often forwarded goods to customers on short- or medium-term credit. Much internal trade was conducted in this way. Merchants preferred to lend to their wholesalers and retailers rather than to the aristocracy and princes, because they had better legal recourse against the former, whereas the latter dragged out repayment over years and decades.

The bill of exchange continued to be the chief method of organizing credit. By the seventeenth century bills of exchange had become transferable and negotiable. A branch of commercial law developed to deal with conflict arising out of the difficulties that this caused. The way round was for banks regularly to discount bills of exchange; this could be conducted in such a way as to control brokerage. This meant that payment of the sum stated on a bill could be made by a banker before it became due on deduction of a certain percentage, and the bill continued to circulate in the name of the bankers. The state usually attempted to fix maximum rates of interest on loans. In the eighteenth century borrowing was mostly quite cheap, at bank rates of 5 per cent and on bills of exchange at 4 per cent.

Landowners lived on credit even more frequently than merchants. This was partly because of their ostentatious lifestyle, including the ruinous institution of court-life which became so fashionable all over Europe at the end of the seventeenth century. Most tenant farmers and peasants were also in debt, often to ecclesiastical creditors. In Brandenburg the territorial Estates ran their own mortgage service to rescue landlords from ruin after the end of the seventeenth century. In Silesia, Schweidnitz and Jauer began issuing mortgage bonds before 1740, and in Bremen land rents became negotiable interest bonds. The first German mortgage bank grew up in Brunswick and later became the territorial state bank.

In the eighteenth century most capital investment still went into land. Even the concept of national debt took a long time to spread, and many absolutist states still talked of rulers' debts. In Bavaria as late as the 1760s whether landlords were responsible for the debts of their predecessors was still disputed. Many territorial rulers used a wasteful system of alienating regular revenue and frequently had to be rescued from bankruptcy by committees of their Estates and territorial assemblies. Forced loans or *dons gratuits* were also used by rulers to obtain money from the wealthier nobles, clergy and burghers in their territorial state. These means had already been employed by Emperor Charles v and King Philip II in the sixteenth century, and were still customary in Austria as late as the eighteenth century. In war especially the aristocracy received demand notes from the Emperor. State bankruptcy was the last resort of territorial rulers, and was used quite regularly after the sixteenth century; creditors were deprived of their assigned state revenues and given fixed-interest bonds by way of compensation. Old debts were repudiated and a new bank rate was fixed to attract new credit. Bankruptcy badly shook business confidence and could not be used too often.

In France royal *intendants* began to supervise taxation more and more in the provinces during the seventeenth century. Under Louis XIV these arrangements took final shape. *Taille* was paid by peasants and commoners, whereas nobles and clergy obtained exemption in return for state service and *dons gratuits*. Indirect taxes such as *aides* and *gabelles* were very unevenly imposed and varied greatly from region to region, mainly in the north and centre of France. In areas of *grande gabelle* commoners were forced to buy a certain quota of salt each year. A sales tax of 5 per cent was fairly standard on all transactions of cattle, timber and sea fish. On small sales one-eighth to one-quarter was even taken as value-added-tax. Wine merchants had to pay a *droit annuel*, and there were numerous customs duties. France was divided into five large lease areas, each with their own company which had bought a monopoly from the crown. These were limited in 1661. There were also areas of designated foreign trade such as *Franche-Comté*. A third group were the truly foreign areas such as Alsace and the three bishoprics of Metz, Toul and Verdun. Then there were special taxes such as the *trépas de Loire*, the *comptabilité de Bordeaux* and the *douane de Valence*. These levies hindered internal trade and trade between provincial zones.

Even so, under Richelieu state income increased from 43,000,000 to 80,000,000 livres a year; state debt however also rose from 27,000,000 to 47,000,000 livres a year. Many of the uprisings in France in the first half of the seventeenth century were caused by rigorous and unfair new tax measures. Under Mazarin the clever but unscrupulous financial administration of Particelli d'Emeris (1643–8) did much to cause rebellion. In 1661 income was 84,000,000 livres, but *rentes* and debt servicing took all but 32,000,000. By introducing economies Fouquet's successor Colbert brought order into Bourbon financial administration for the first time since Sully. He reduced taille but raised excise rates, or aides, from 5,000,000 to 22,000,000 livres. Thus Colbert hit the poorer sections of Bourbon France by decreasing direct and increasing indirect taxation. He only managed to reduce customs dues for a short while though in 1670 he did manage to balance the budget. On the outbreak of war with the Dutch in 1672 military expenditure increased again, as did court luxury. Colbert resorted to any measures he could to raise short-term credit for Louis XIV. In 1683 gross income was 119,000,000 livres, which cost 22,000,000 livres to collect, against expenditure of 99,000,000 livres, including short-term debts of 27,000,000 livres.

Colbert's successors found more and more difficulty in managing royal debts. Deficits increased as war expenditure rose. Taille was alienated and fell to 30,000,000 livres by 1712. Excises worth 70,000,000 livres in 1690 were only worth 47,000,000 livres by 1715. But yields on new kinds of produce increased, such as those on paper, postal services and tobacco.

The *rentes* system remained the backbone of French state finance. State lotteries were also introduced to attract loans from petty gamblers. Promissory notes on state funds were given and after 1701 *billets de monnaie* were printed. New offices were created and sold. Coinage was recalled and reissued in a debased form, while taxes were fixed in terms of the older currency. The loan market came increasingly under the control of court bankers during the last years of Louis XIV; among these Samuel Bernard was the most outstanding. In 1715 the Bourbon French national debt was 2,936,000,000 livres, and annual regular income was a mere 160,000,000. In 1695 a new poll tax was introduced. This was to be raised from the whole population, from the princes of the blood down to the common man, in proportion to their assumed income. This was abolished in 1698 but reintroduced in 1701 in a modified form. In 1710 an income tax of 10 per cent was introduced as a war measure on all social groups. But no matter how fiscal administration was improved, social inequalities in taxation remained. The main obstacle to fair collection was the rentes system which gave permanent, individual exemptions, and which the crown was too spendthrift to redeem. By the 1750s the 10 per cent income tax had been reduced to 5 per cent.

Various phases of French fiscal administration can be discerned. First came the Duke of Noailles, who improved matters and did not shrink from severe measures such as reduction of paper money value against coinage and punishment of creditors lending at exorbitant rates. Law's credit bank also led to improvements at first, but he issued too much paper money against non-existent taxes and securities and crashed when he failed to honour the stock of the Compagnie d'Occident in 1720. Yet Law had clarified the rôle that credit could play in private and state finance, although reaction against excessive use of credit was so strong after his failure that the establishment of public credit institutions in France was retarded for almost a century. The brothers Paris had the task of disposing of Law's paper money, which had a face value of 2,500,000,000 livres. They reduced it to 1,700,000 livres. The state also reduced creditors' annuities to 51,000,000 livres. Paris-Duverney, who was the leading figure in fiscal administration up to 1726, managed to raise the yield of indirect taxes from 61,000,000 livres in 1721 to 92,000,000 in 1726. A more orderly system of state finance was introduced under Cardinal Fleury during the minority of Louis xv. But after 1729 the wasteful system of tax-farming was reintroduced. The currency reform of that year fixed the marc d'or at 740 livres, 9 sols; the marc d'argent at 51 livres, 3 sols, and the livre Tournois at 1·02 gold francs. After 1745 Marchault d'Arnouville began to tax church property held in mortemain, and every citizen, including the clergy, at 5 per cent on their incomes. These measures led to opposition from those previously exempt. Louis xv's ostentation and French participation in the Seven Years' War once again put state finances out of order.

In Germany federal, imperial finance was dependent on grants from territorial rulers acting as Estates in the imperial assembly. Taxes were assessed according to the *Römermonat* schedule originally standardized by the imperial assembly of 1521 and regularly modified according to temporary needs. As they became impoverished, many of the former imperial towns had their federal tax quotas reduced. Federal tax quotas were still impressive, however. During the Polish War of Succession (1733–5) the Imperial Knights and Hanseatic towns alone were assessed at 400,000 Gulden. Imperial federal taxes were paid by most territories up to the end of the Empire in 1806.

During the Spanish War of Succession the Habsburg imperial treasury had debts of 61,000,000 Gulden. Charles VI attempted to reduce this debt, using the Viennese *banco di giro* of 1703 and the Viennese town bank of 1706. A new *Universal-Bancalität* was also set up to amortize debts; it amalgamated with the town bank seven years later. Finances improved a little during the period of peace after the Turkish wars, but were again burdened by the war with Prussia.

The Seven Years' War cost the Habsburg treasury 260,000,000 Gulden. In 1763 total Habsburg debt was 275,000,000 Gulden and net income in 1768 was only 42,000,000. In 1768 42 per cent of net income came from extraordinary tax grants of provincial Estates. The military establishment demanded 42 per cent of income and debt servicing 34 per cent. Administration cost $15\frac{1}{2}$ per cent and the court 8 per cent. The Habsburgs could never balance their income and expenditure, and this was done for them by court bankers. Indeed the Habsburgs won their Turkish wars because of the credit advanced to them by the private banks of Oppenheimer and Wertheimer. Augsburg bankers were also used; their experience and connections in exchange business and their activities as goldsmiths and jewellers made them suitable middlemen in subsidy and army payments.

In Brandenburg-Prussia Elector Frederick William had an exchequer income of 440,000 Talers in 1640. After he had acquired Mark, Cleves, Ravensberg, Minden, part of Pomerania, Halberstadt and Magdeburg his net income increased by one-third. In the 1680s his net income had risen to 1,600,000 Talers, demesne income making up two-thirds of this. Most of this income went towards paying for the court and an army of 30,000 men. Brandenburg-Prussia had a higher ratio of soldiers per head of population than any other European power.

They could only be financed through heavy taxation. By 1740 Prussian royal demesnes made up a quarter of the total land area of the state. Without demesne revenue the army could not have been paid for. The Great Elector changed many direct taxes into excises, using as a model excises customary in the Netherlands. In 1616 an attempt had been made to introduce excise in Cleves and Mark, and in 1660 in the towns of Brandenburg the Great Elector followed this precedent. By 1720 all the towns of the Prussian state paid excise taxes. Skilful, peaceful administration under King Frederick William I meant that his son, Frederick II, inherited a state free of debts and credit of 10,000,000 Talers in 1740. But even so 80 per cent of all state income and expenditure went to the army.

The Silesian wars under Frederick II placed severe strains on this well ordered state of affairs. By the end of the second Silesian war the Prussian state was in the red, although its acquisition of industrial Silesia was potentially very advantageous. In the years of armed peace before the Seven Years' War Prussian state treasury reserves rose to 13,000,000 Talers. Other reserves were added so that Frederick II started war in 1756 with 20,000,000 Talers. This reserve had gone by 1758, and British subsidies kept him going for a time. The Seven Years' War cost Prussia 40,000,000 Talers. Systematic debasement of the Prussian currency became essential, as well as heavy war contributions from Silesia and occupied Saxony, both industrially developed and perhaps the richest parts of central Europe. Saxony alone bore about a third of total Prussian war costs.

When the ravages of war had been put right the finances of Prussia were developed on more rational peace-time principles, although the army still consumed the lion's share of state finance. In the 1780s gross income was about 24,000,000 Talers a year, with administrative costs of 4,000,000 Talers. No less than 30 per cent of gross income came from royal demesnes. Military expenditure had decreased slightly but was still about 70 per cent of total net income. Court and administrative costs increased to include subsidies to industry, trade and agriculture. Agriculture alone received 5,000,000 Talers in state subsidies in 1785-6. Between 1763 and 1786 this sector received 40,000,000 Talers in all. By 1786 the royal treasury had reserves of 51,000,000 Talers.

In the Electorate of Bavaria the territorial Estates had been deprived of their political powers since the time of Maximilian I during the Thirty Years' War. But the Estates still played an executive role in tax collecting, especially in the collection of excise on wine and beer. They also continued to underwrite rulers' debts. Bavarian Maximilian I had succeeded in increasing income by imposing salt-tax and other excises. In 1618 he had 4,000,000 Gulden surplus in his treasury. War and ostentation quickly brought state finances into the red; they reached a nadir in the pomp and circumstance of Maximilian Joseph III's reign (1745–77). It was essential for the Estates to regularly take over rulers' debts to stave off bankruptcy. This occurred for example in 1722 when Maximilian Emanuel's debts of 22,000,000 Gulden were taken on by the Bavarian territorial Estates. By 1749 the ruler again had new debts of 34,000,000 Gulden. By 1760 Bavaria was paying 1,000,000 Gulden a year in interest on existing rulers' debts. A quarter of state income came from customs on foreign trade, 20 per cent from beer excise, and the rest from foreign trade; there were also other excises such as those from salt and from demesnes. Agriculture brought in about 45 per cent of total income. Analysis of accounts is complicated by the fact that most treasuries made piecemeal budgets that were seldom audited as a whole during the late seventeenth and early eighteenth centuries. Some improvement took place, however, in town council administration, where budgets were increasingly open to scrutiny by the citizens. Accountancy was now rationalized and linked with politics and law in state administration. National debts funded on low interest rates backed by state banks began to take over from Estates' and private or municipal loan banks, which had charged much higher rates. The accounts of eighteenth-century Frankfurt-am-Main were a model of efficient administration.

Nonetheless Frankfurt never managed to get rid of heavy debts accumulated during the sixteenth century, in spite of higher income from taxes. In the seventeenth century excises on merchants were increased. During the Thirty Years' War forced loans to the Swedes and to the imperialists had to be paid, let alone the cost of fortifications. In the fiscal year 1633–4 this alone came to 275,000 Gulden. Three years earlier the Swedes had even demanded 100,000 Gulden as an extraordinary levy. When the Treaty of Westphalia was signed in 1648 a large sum still had to be found to pay off the Swedish and imperial armies of occupation. But records in Frankfurt covering this and earlier periods were partly destroyed by bombing during the Second World War, so that it is now best to study the archives there for the fiscal period after 1733. Between 1733 and 1800 town income rose from 348,940 to 852,057 Gulden. Most taxes were indirect and came from the wholesale and retail trade in town. On the whole income tax was under 10 per cent, although town officials and councillors paid up to 25 per cent in 1733.

Hamburg's buoyant trade and shipping enabled it to increase town council income greatly during the seventeenth and eighteenth centuries, to an extent unparalleled in any other town in Germany. In 1716 income was 3,000,000 Marks, and by 1800 it was nearly double that amount. Income from direct taxation steadily became a smaller proportion of the total. By 1659 it was only 28 per cent, although it rose again during the eighteenth century to over 40 per cent of total tax revenue. The main tendency was therefore towards a fairer distribution of the tax burden, with fewer taxes on consumer goods, which relieved the common man, and more direct taxes on the propertied, who could well afford them. Yet one should not over-estimate the Hamburg town council's willingness to tax its own ruling class. In 1686 the two rich parishes of St Nikolai and St Peter provided 59 per cent of all the taxes collected and 52 per cent of all fortification and dyke money. Resident foreigners were always more heavily taxed than native citizens. Hamburg town expenditure increased nearly twenty times between 1600 and 1800. Buildings costs rose most, as social and medical needs increased. Whereas salaries just kept pace, debt-servicing became cheaper, although military and naval costs rose almost thirty times. Hamburg's finances closed regularly with surpluses to guard against political and military-naval insecurity.

In Russia finance tended to suffer from relatively loose organization and also from some degree of official corruption. The sokha was only 14 roubles, but it was raised regularly after 1600. Traditional taxes were relatively low. During the uprisings of the seventeenth century many land registers were lost, and instead of careful resurveys rushed and superficial inspections were made. It soon became apparent that the number of sokhi had decreased drastically, and after 1647 land registers were abandoned in favour of taxes on annual produce and profits. New excise taxes were also levied in seventeenth-century Russia, on salt in 1646 and a general tax in 1657 when wars with Poland required a series of special war-taxes. There was also a sales tax of 10 per cent on all transactions as well as taxes on house ownership. An extraordinary income tax of 5 per cent in 1634 made 300,000 roubles, to which Moscow alone contributed 90,000. The Moscow *gosti*, their allied guilds and all textile merchant corporations provided 46,000 roubles. Land-tax reform finally came in 1678 when new hearth-tax registers were drawn up. After 1710, taxes were assessed according to local population. Hearth-tax was increased for the first time by ½ rouble per hearth. In 1680 direct taxes represented only 25 per cent of state revenue. Sales taxes were important as well as excises on public houses, mills, baths and weighbridges. There were also taxes on buildings, cellars, cattle-troughs and even chimneys. Stamp duty on paper and print was introduced in 1699. The most lucrative taxes were customs and excise. Increased taxation on the church came after 1707 when serious attempts were at last made to secularize monastic lands. The state in return took over upkeep of hospitals and schools.

In 1717 the Russian system of taxation was completely changed. A tax of ½ rouble per head per annum on the whole population was to replace all direct taxes. Clergy and nobles were also to pay 10 per cent income tax. To cover administrative costs the basic rate was raised to 80 kopecks, and the simplification that this entailed even led to reductions in indirect taxes. Tsar Peter's budget finally balanced. War-time expenditure had risen significantly, and army and navy had taken between 76 and 96 per cent of the total. Treasury income in 1680 was 700,000 roubles, in 1725 5,000,000. Peace-time costs for the new Russian navy were 1,400,000 roubles. Shortages of coin outside Moscow and St Petersburg were so acute that officials and soldiers often only received pay intermittently. A new ministry took charge of indirect tax receipts after 1710 and new areas of financial administration were set up.

Inadequate circulation of money made public credit difficult but in spite of this Tsar Peter managed to carry out several substantial credit operations. In 1709 he raised loans from the monasteries of the Holy Trinity and Saint Sergius, from the merchant community through Filatev, and from the service nobility through 'Lieutenant' Menshikov. He was still a long way from establishing Giro, exchange and credit banks on the western model, however. The greatest increase in Russian state finances during the eighteenth century came because of an enormous increase in the taxable population. This was sufficient to pay for the mounting costs of army and navy administration, foreign policy and luxury at court, despite the fact that poll tax was reduced several times. Biron had reduced it by 17 kopecs and under Tsarina Elisabeth a further reduction of ten kopecs came, and in 1752 of yet another three kopecs. But tax arrears continued to accumulate. In 1747 these were cancelled as a measure of realism entered fiscal policy. When the situation became acute, as it did during the war against Sweden in 1742, special measures were used. Officials' salaries were cut and some indirect taxes were reintroduced. The state salt monopoly came back in 1751 and the sale of spirits came under state control. By 1750 the yearly state deficit was a mere 100,000 roubles, though by 1761 the government had 8,000,000 roubles of unfunded debt. The Russian banking system was still undeveloped.

Seventeenth-century Swedish credit finance depended on Dutch expertise, such as that provided by the Spierinck brothers during Gustavus Adolphus' reign. One of them was ennobled under the name of Silvercroon, and between 1629 and 1635 he directed the Swedish customs administration in Prussia. There were also the brothers Wewetzer, one of whom was superintendent of customs and excise and ennobled under the name of Rosenstierna. Louis de Geer worked closely with his Dutch kinsman Trip in metal products, as did Marselis with his relations in Holland. Up to the time of Charles xi there were more foreigners who lent money to the Crown than native Swedes, among whom only the de la Gardies and Oxenstiernas were prominent. Swedish colonial expansion during the seventeenth century could only be financed by utilizing taxation from the natural and barter economy as well as from the monetary sector. This could be seen in the ransom paid for Älvsborg at the end of the Kalmar war after the peace of 1613. The sum was to be paid to Denmark in imperial Talers. Payment of troops had increasingly to be made by living off the land, both at home and abroad, in the many wars Sweden fought in Denmark, Poland, Russia and Germany. Subsidy policies modelled on France were also used. The Bärwalde alliance with France in 1631 provided 400,000 Talers per annum for Swedish troops in Germany. These monies were eventually paid via Amsterdam and Hamburg. French payments were erratic, for the independence of Swedish war policies made the two powers very uneasy allies. After 1648 the Swedes had great difficulties in paying off their surplus mercenaries, and it was thus a major object of Swedish diplomacy that peace terms should include demobilization payments from Germany.

Under Queen Christina Swedish court expenditure and ostentation rose as never before, and much crown property was alienated. Regent Oxenstierna and the nobility in the Royal Council held the view that crown finances must be consolidated by imposing new indirect taxes by customs and excise. But instead of this a wasteful system of alienating crown lands was instituted. The same thing was done in Denmark to the profit of the nobility. The burghers on the other hand insisted on increased taxes on landed property. In the Swedish financial crisis after peace was signed in 1679, the question of reduction or contribution was keenly disputed. Charles XI used the method of reduction, that is, recovery of alienated crown property. Yet he also used the contribution method by increasing taxation. The Northern war nearly ruined Sweden's finances. Thereafter Swedish revenue was seriously affected by loss of German and Baltic provinces. Until 1709 desperate attempts were made to raise money by forced loans as Charles XII tried to save his empire beyond the Baltic. After 1716 Görtz issued state security bonds funded by the Swedish government as national debt. Smaller sums circulated as state bank-notes within the country, and nominal value coins or *mynttecken* were also used. Swedish state finance and banking were highly advanced by the standards of the late seventeenth and early eighteenth centuries in Europe. Yet emergency coinage was already being redeemed and abolished by 1719 as the era of absolutism gave way once more to traditional oligarchy. Once more a system of Estates' extraordinary tax grants, sale of crown property, forced loans or contributions and farming of major customs revenues provided the bulk of state revenue. Despite the strictest economy measures, costs still came to over half the total expenditure. However, administration of the national debt was now placed in the hands of a special Estates' treasury. Under the régime of the 'Hat' party oligarchy war against Russia was financed by increasing national debt and borrowing from the state bank, which was forced to issue considerable quantities of paper money. In the mid-1740s Sweden went over to paper money as the state bank was no longer in a position to exchange the paper notes for coin.

Denmark was occupied with monetary problems during the 1650s and soon introduced copper coinage, which was especially useful in times of war, when money was readily needed for paying mercenaries and equipment. Until 1638 the Danish nobility had hardly been affected by state taxation, but thereafter they began to contribute, although on condition that they administered their own tax assessment, levy and payment. Land-taxes from tenant farmers and peasants continued to fall, so that the crown became increasingly interested in imposing excises on the towns. However, the crown still received considerable tax income from the Sound tolls. In the peak year of 1639 Sound dues amounted to 616,000 Riksdalers. King Christian IV himself advanced money to the state from his own private business operations, and in 1650 the national debt was kept down to 4,000,000 Riksdalers. Most of the credit for the Danish crown had come from the Holstein nobility and was negotiated at annual fairs at Kiel; by the mid-seventeenth century this source began to dry up. Great merchants and private bankers such as Diego Teixeira and Marselis from Hamburg and Amsterdam now had to be approached, as the Danish national debt reached its crisis point as considerable amounts of land were lost to Sweden. Debt finance was temporarily eased by sales of crown property. Then the introduction of absolutism brought reforms in the organization of government under the direction of Hannibal Sehested. He became finance minister and President of the Treasury Board under which the whole financial administration was united, except the Sound tolls, which still came under the Privy Purse. These reforms did not last, and Denmark financed its part in the Great Northern war by short-term and expensive loans, many of them from the Holstein nobility. Yet Denmark had started the war well with a debt of only 500,000 Riksdalers, and this was soon backed by clever subsidy treaties with the Netherlands and the Habsburgs, although all administrative reform ceased. By 1710 the national debt had risen to 1,500,000 Riksdalers and was funded by increased Estates' extraordinary taxes, alienation of crown lands especially in

Dithmarschen, and imposition of forced loans. Nominal value coinage and paper notes were issued. One million Riksdalers of paper money was circulating by 1715, but the state was able to buy back all paper notes at full value thereafter. During this time the Danish crown kept levels of Estates' extraordinary taxation low in Norway in a policy designed to retain loyalty.

Denmark entered the era of peace after 1715 with unfavourable balances of trade, manufacturing and agrarian production. Court and military expenditure remained high and so did taxes. The Danish crown once again needed subsidies, this time from Britain and France, although it did finally remove all traces of paper money by 1728, and from then on the high quality German Kuranttaler of account dominated Danish exchange. The state opened an all-purpose *Kurantbank* for exchange, mortgages and subsidies to industry in 1736, although it tended to lend too much at too low a rate of interest and suspended operations temporarily between 1745 and 1770.

VII Conclusion

In the previous chapters we have studied various sectors of the economy, looking at demography, agriculture and forestry, trade, transport, banking and finance in the early modern era. But what of the economy of continental Europe as a whole. What trends and changes were taking place? Until well into the eighteenth century, agriculture was still the most important sector of the economy. By far the greater part of Europe lived on the land and a large number of people were engaged in subsistence agriculture. For continental Europe this was even more the case than in the Atlantic or the Mediterranean regions. Yet the eighteenth century also saw the rise of industry based on existing and new urban centres, gradually spreading out from north-west to central Europe. Most research into pre-industrial early modern Europe economic history has tended to concentrate on the history of prices and to work out trends from them. The pattern that emerges is that there was overall economic growth in Europe from the later fifteenth century until the early seventeenth century, when a period of stagnation set in. After the 1620s it seems that the economies of England, Spain and the Italian states were in recession.

In other parts of Europe this change is more difficult to trace. In the Netherlands particularly the economic position remained favourable up to 1650. Chaunu has tried to interpret the world economic situation on the basis of statistical information from the sixteenth century onwards, including the Far East, which began to be influenced by European economic factors. In agriculture he has emphasized that the price rise of the sixteenth century was followed by price stagnation in the later seventeenth and earlier eighteenth century. Yet other sectors of the economy did not altogether follow this pattern and colonial trade especially fluctuated widely. In coinage there was an ever-increasing volume of bullion from about 1510 to the 1620s, which often exceeded the amount of goods and services that were in supply. Europe in this period had about 25,000 to 30,000 tons of bullion in circulation, as against an increase of only 15,000 to 20,000 tons between 1620 and 1750. Trade seemed to level off between 1590 and 1620, and only became buoyant again at the end of the seventeenth century.

Frederic Mauro's macro-economic picture on the whole agrees with that of Chaunu. He has divided the long recession of the seventeenth century into cycles. Between 1595 and 1620 there is an intermediate, healthy stage, based mainly on Spain, Germany and the Baltic, where economics were still buoyant, with a certain revival even between 1620 and 1635. But there were counter-trends in the latter period with crises of war, plague and bad harvests in Italy, Germany, east-central Europe and even Spain especially between 1619 and 1623. Only north-west Europe continued its 'pre-industrial' boom, above all Holland and the great colonial charter companies.

Wheat prices rose between 1615 and 1635, and thereafter fell steadily until the mid-1680s. A rise in the 1690s was followed by a fall until 1705, then a short rise, and a sudden fall from 1715 to 1725, with fresh rises thereafter. Price levels also tended to move in unison in the various states of Europe, although the figures for early modern Poland, especially for Lvov, are consistently the lowest that we have. Altogether the spread between the highest and lowest prices at the beginning of the seventeenth century was much greater than at the beginning of the eighteenth century, which is a good indication of the increasing tempo of communications, banking and exchange. By the mid-eighteenth century prices were consistently higher in the Atlantic and Mediterranean regions of Europe than in central and east Europe. There were of course great local variations within each of these large regions.

Increasing prosperity was postponed in Poland until after the 1660s, whereas in Germany it came in the 1650s immediately after the Thirty Years' War. Yet in Frankfurt-am-Main Leipzig and Berlin prosperity came late in the 1680s. France followed at about the same time despite the horrors of war, bad harvests and high taxation at the end of Louis xiv's reign, and a real boom eventually came in the 1720s. The price of farinaceous products continued to increase even at times of overall price stagnation in comparison with prices of other products, such as meat and beer, which remained stable. Between 1600 and 1750 wheat rose on average about four times as much as the price of beer.

A fuller impression cannot be gained merely on the *basis* of bullion and price studies. Other statistics must be taken into account – from trade, industry and above all from demography. For Scandinavia and the Baltic the Sound tolls are essential records for calculating the total volume of officially recognized trade passing out of the Baltic until the end of the eighteenth century. Taking 125 tons as the average size of the early modern boats passing the Sound, we find that in 1620 the volume of Baltic shipping reached a peak, with nearly 5,250 sailings. Subsequent low-points were in 1628 and 1630 when the Dutch were at war with Spain and when the Swedes entered the Thirty Years' War. Further fluctuations continued until a low-point in 1645 when war again, this time between Sweden and Denmark, meant that only 874 boats officially passed the Sound. By 1649 trade had reached another peak, to be followed by a recession up to 1665. Once again war brought decline as Louis XIV fought the Dutch after 1672. Thereafter peace tended to lead to increased sailings. The Northern war and the Spanish Wars of Succession had a catastrophic effect on Baltic shipping. Thereafter numbers of sailings went up again, to 5,370, only to be halted once again by the Silesian Wars and the Seven Years' War.

Conditions in the great port of Danzig were prosperous in the 1610s, though severe economic crisis followed between 1626 and 1629, because of war between Sweden and Poland which led to a Swedish blockade of Danzig. Thereafter Danzig gained through increased demands for grain and timber made on its hinterland by war-time Europe. The second half of the seventeenth century was less prosperous for exports fell as Danzig was more directly involved in hostilities. The best trading years seem to have been those of relative peace in 1668/9, 1679 to 1687, 1698/9, and after 1713 and 1721. There was a serious depression after 1734 because of the Polish War of Succession, followed by the Silesian wars in the 1740s.

The trade and prosperity of Hamburg increased at the expense of the Dutch after resumption of hostilities with Spain in 1621/2. Between 1586 and 1622 Hamburg's port customs entries doubled, although recessions came briefly at the end of the 1620s because of Danish involvement in the Thirty Years' War. The Elbe was blockaded then, although Hamburg soon sought and found a *modus vivendi* with the Danes. A brief boom after the peace of 1648 was consolidated when Hamburg gained trade as a result of the Anglo-Dutch wars in the 1650s, 1660s and 1670s. But in the 1680s there were counter-trends, especially after the Danish blockade of 1686. The wars at the beginning of the eighteenth century probably led to a decrease in the volume of merchant shipping, especially because of piracy in the Channel. Surprisingly the Silesian wars in the 1740s led to increased business with a slump in the peace years before the Seven Years' War broke out in 1756.

The fluctuations in trade at the Sound and in the ports of Hamburg and Danzig on the whole follow the same general trends, which were dominated above all by the Dutch Republic and the power first of its shipping trade and then of its finance. Dutch dominance was most marked in the first half of the seventeenth century, and thereafter British, Swedish and other Scandinavian shipping grew in importance. All the same as late as 1660 three-quarters of Amsterdam's floating capital was tied up in Baltic trade. The Dutch still charged the lowest freight rates and had the highest investment in ship-building. Their exchange and commodity markets were still predominant.

This western trading activity stimulated producers on a large scale in east, central and north Europe, the Polish nobility of the Vistula region for instance. Whether this international trade retarded the growth of internal trade and society, preventing the development of more lively peasant and burgher economies in countries like Poland is still disputed by the experts. Certainly contacts with ports such as Amsterdam, Lübeck, Copenhagen and Hamburg brought increased wealth to the east and south-east Baltic hinterlands, but it is questionable how far down the social scale this prosperity spread. Most states tried to obtain favourable balances of trade in the Baltic region by imposing mercantile navigation acts, although those of the Dutch, Danes, British and Swedes tended to cancel each other out.

The Baltic was early modern Europe's main source of grain, timber products and raw material for textiles such as hemp. Scandinavia also led in copper and iron production, and Russian bulk trade became increasingly important in all these commodities after the opening of St Petersburg in the early eighteenth century. With its well-developed riverways and canals, the south and south-east Baltic had a supply base stretching into the heart of Poland, Silesia and the Carpathians. The main routes opening up the heart of Europe to sea trade went along the rivers Rhine, Weser and Elbe. Together with the waterways of the Oder, Vistula and Duna they interlocked and united sea and land routes. It is more difficult to quantify the volume of land-trade than that of sea-trade in this period. We have figures for turnover at the Nuremberg bank, for attendance at Leipzig fairs and for head of cattle passing Hungarian toll houses or *Dreissigstämter*. But on the whole bulk goods such as grain, timber and common metals were too expensive to transport over long distances by land. Lighter goods of greater individual value such as leather and furs and expensive textiles such as silk were, however, readily transported overland. On the whole manufactured goods travelled east and raw materials west, although this does not apply to oriental and Far East Asian goods. In Hungary, along the Black Sea and in the Balkans the continental region interwove with the Mediterranean world. The Balkan region of early modern Europe came partly under the political domination of the Turks, and its economic history has still to be studied in depth. Altogether the early modern era was one of dominance of sea-routes and shipping.

The task of quantification has only just begun. Once the problem of trade is more closely known, industrial production must also be more closely studied. Gaps in the records are particularly great, but we can establish certain crude phases of expansion, recession and stagnation. Difficulties were above all experienced as a result of war, often trade wars, and religious persecution. Industrial production, especially of textiles, moved all over Europe from the main late medieval centres in the south Netherlands and north Italy. Population movements during the Reformation and Counter-Reformation stimulated the textile industry in England, north Holland, parts of Germany and Switzerland, all of which became leading textile producers. In the metal and mining industries there was a similar diffusion from central Europe and the south Netherlands to the states of the north, west and east. Religious emigration from provinces such as Styria and Salzburg also helped to spread pre-industrial technological skills and manufactures.

We have gained some insight into the economic history of early modern continental Europe and how its component state systems developed, conflicted and co-operated with each other and with neighbouring regions of the Atlantic and Mediterranean. It is hoped that the background has been provided for more detailed studies in the quantification of early modern trade and industry, and for the necessary task of providing sound demographical studies to reinforce our understanding of economic history in the heart of Europe between the fifteenth and the eighteenth centuries.

WEIGHTS AND MEASURES

Metric standard	British standard
1 Klafter *or* 3·3 cubic metres	4·3 cubic yards
1 Festmeter	
1 Ster } *or* 1 cubic metre	1·3 cubic yards
1 Raummeter	
1 Hektar *or* 10,000 square metres	2·4 acres
1 Kilometer	0·6 miles
1 Liter	0·2 gallons
1 Kilogram	2·2 pounds
1 Zentner *or* 50 kilogrammes	110·2 pounds
1 Tonne *or* 1,000 kilogrammes	0·98 tons
1 Last *or* 2,000 kilogrammes	1·97 tons
Russian standard	
1 Dessiatin	2·8 acres
1 Pud	36 pounds

Select Bibliography

W. Abel, *Massenarmut und Hungerkrisen im vorindustriellen Europa* (Hamburg and Göttingen, 1974)

W. Abel, *Agrarkrisen und Agrarkonjunktur in Mitteleuropa, 13. bis 19. Jahrhundert* (2nd ed., Hamburg, 1966)

W. Abel, *Geschichte der deutschen Landwirtschaft* (2nd ed., Stuttgart, 1967)

W. Achilles, 'Getreidepreise und Getreidehandelsbeziehungen', *Zeitschrift für Agrargeschichte und Agrarsoziologie*, 7, 1959

Georg Agricola (1494–1555), *De re metallica* (Basle, 1530, 1561)

T. Aston (ed.), *Crisis in Europe, 1560–1660* (London, 1965)

E. Åström, *From cloth to iron. The Anglo-Baltic trade in the late seventeenth century* (Helsinki, 1963–6)

A. Attman, *The Russian and Polish markets in international trade, 1500–1650* (Gothenburg, 1973)

E. Baasch, *Holländische Wirtschaftsgeschichte* (Jena, 1927)

V. Barbour, *Capitalism in Amsterdam in the 17th century* (Baltimore, 1950)

J. J. Becher, *Psychosophia oder Seelenweisheit* (Vienna, 1678)

G. Benecke, *Society and politics in Germany, 1500–1750* (London, 1974)

G. Benecke, 'Labour relations and peasant society in northwest Germany c. 1600', *History*, 58, 1973

L. K. Berkner, 'The stem family and the developmental cycle of the peasant household; an 18th century example', *American Historical Review*, 77, 1972

F. Blaich, *Die Wirtschaftspolitik des Reichstags im Heiligen Römischen Reich* (Stuttgart, 1970)

P. Blickle, *Landschaften im Alten Reich* (Munich, 1973)

Jerome Blum, *Lord and peasant in Russia* (Princeton, 1961)

B. Boëthius, *Gruvornas, Hyttornas och Hamrarnas Folk* (Stockholm, 1951)

I. Bog, *Die bäuerliche Wirtschaft im dreissigjährigen Krieg* (Coburg, 1952)

I. Bog (ed.), *Der Aussenhandel Ostmitteleuropas, 1450–1650* (Cologne, 1971)

C. R. Boxer, *The Dutch Seaborne Empire* (London, 1965)

F. Braudel, *Capitalism and material life, 1400–1800* (London, 1973)

F. Braudel, *The Mediterranean and the Mediterranean world in the age of Philip II*, 2 volumes (London, 1972–3)

O. Brunner, *Adeliges Landleben und Europaeischer Geist* (Salzburg, 1949)

D. Buisseret, *Sully* (London, 1968)

P. Burke, *Venice and Amsterdam* (London, 1974)

P. Burke (ed.), *Economy and society in early modern Europe. Essays from Annales E.S.C.* (London, 1972)

Cambridge Economic History of Europe, volume 4 (Cambridge, 1967)

F. L. Carsten, *Origins of Prussia* (London, 1954)

F. L. Carsten, *Princes and Parliaments in Germany* (Oxford, 1959)

P. Chaunu, *Conquête et exploitation des nouveaux mondes. XVIe siècle,* (Paris, 1969)

A. E. Chistensen, *Dutch trade to the Baltic around 1600* (Copenhagen, 1941)

C. M. Cipolla, *Guns and sails, 1400–1700* (London, 1965)

C. M. Cipolla (ed.), *The Fontana Economic History of Europe*, volume 2 (London, 1974)

D. C. Coleman (et al), *Revisions in mercantilism* (London, 1969)

P. Coles, *The Ottoman impact on Europe* (London, 1968)

Ralph Davis, *The rise of the Atlantic economies* (London, 1973)

Ralph Davis, *A commercial revolution* (Historical Association pamphlet, London, 1967)

M. Devèze, 'Climat et récoltes aux 17e et 18e siècles', *Annales E.S.C.*, 15, 1960

A. G. Dickens, *The German nation and Martin Luther* (London, 1974)

J. G. van Dillen (ed.), *History of the principal public banks* (Hague, 1934)

B. Dmytryshyn (ed.), *Medieval Russia. A source book, 900–1700* (2nd ed., Illinois, 1972)

P. Dollinger, *The German Hansa* (London, 1970)

P. Earle (ed.), *Essays in European economic history* (Oxford, 1974)

R. Ehrenberg, *Capital and finance in the age of the Renaissance* (London, 1928)

M. J. Elsas, *Umriss einer Geschichte der Preise und Löhne in Deutschland*, 2 volumes (Leiden, 1936–49)

J. Faber, 'The decline of the Baltic grain trade', *Acta Historiae Neerlandica*, 1, 1966

S. Fischer-Galati (ed.), *Man, state and society in east European history* (New York, 1970)

G. Franz, *Der dreissigjährige Krieg und das deutsche Volk* (3rd ed., Stuttgart, 1961)

G. Franz (ed.), *Quellen zur Geschichte des deutschen Bauernstandes in der Neuzeit* (Munich, 1963)

A. Friis, *Alderman Cockayne's project and the cloth trade* (New York, 1927)

D. V. Glass and D. E. C. Eversley, *Population in History, Essays in historical demography* (London, 1965)

P. Goubert, *Louis XIV and twenty million Frenchmen* (Harmondsworth, 1970)

P. Goubert, *Beauvais et le beauvaisis de 1600 à 1730* (Paris, 1960)

G. Grüll, *Bauer, Herr und Landesfürst* (Graz, 1963)

Ingrid Hammarström, 'The price revolution of the sixteenth century: some Swedish evidence', in P. H. Ramsey (ed.), *The price revolution in sixteenth century England* (London, 1971)

E. F. Heckscher, *Mercantilism*, 2 volumes (London, 1935)

E. F. Heckscher, *An economic history of Sweden* (Harvard, 1954)

F. W. Henning, *Herrschaft und Bauernuntertänigkeit . . . Ostpreussen – Paderborn vor 1800* (Würzburg, 1964)

S. von Herberstein, *Description of Moscow and Muscovy* (London, 1969)

V. Husa (et al), *Traditional crafts and skills* (London, 1967)

H. Inalcik, *The Ottoman Empire, the classical age, 1300–1600* (London, 1973)

P. Jeannin, 'Les comptes du Sund', *Révue Historique*, 231, 1964

J. H. C. von Justi, *Gesammelte Politische- und Finanzschriften*, 3 volumes (Leipzig, 1761–4)

H. Kamen, *The iron century. Social change in Europe, 1550–1660* (London, 1971)

H. Kellenbenz, 'Les industries dans l'Europe moderne, 1500–1700' in P. Léon (ed.), *L'industrialisation et typologie* (Paris, 1972)

H. Kellenbenz, 'Les industries rurales en Occident de la fin du Moyen Age au XVIIIe siècle', *Annales E.S.C.*, 1963

H. Kellenbenz, 'Der Pfeffermarkt um 1600 und die Hansestädte', *Hansische Geschichtsblätter*, 74, 1956

H. Kellenbenz, *Unternehmerkräfte im Hamburger Portugal- und Spanien-handel, 1590–1625* (1954)

H. Kellenbenz, *Sephardim an der unteren Elbe* (1958)

H. Kellenbenz, *Probleme einer deutschen Sozialgeschichte der neueren Zeit (1500–1800)* (Nuremberg, 1960)

H. Kellenbenz, 'The economic significance of the Archangel route (from the late sixteenth to the late eighteenth century)', *Journal of Economic History*, Vol. 2, No. 3 (Rome), 1973

E. Keyser, *Bevölkerungsgeschichte Deutschlands* (Leipzig, 1943)

E. Keyser (ed.), *Deutsches Städtebuch* (various volumes since 1939)

W. Kirchner, *Commercial relations between Russia and Europe, 1400–1800* (Bloomington, 1966)

V. von Klarwill (ed.), *The Fugger News-Letters* (London, 1924)

F. Klemm, *A history of western technology* (London, 1959)

C. Koeman, *Joan Blaeu and his Grand Atlas* (London and Amsterdam, 1970)

T. S. Kuhn, *The structure of scientific revolutions* (2nd ed., Chicago, 1970)

B. Kuske, *Köln, der Rhein und das Reich* (Cologne, 1956)

E. Le Roy Ladurie, *Les paysans de Languedoc, XVe-XVIIe siècles,* 2 volumes (Paris, 1966)

C. D. Ley (ed.), *Portuguese voyages, 1498-1663* (London, 1947)

F. Luetge, *Geschichte der deutschen Agrarverfassung* (2nd ed., Berlin, 1966)

F. Luetge, *Deutsche Sozial- und Wirtschaftsgeschichte* (3rd ed., Berlin, 1966)

M. Luther, 'On trade and usury (June 1524)', in *Collected Works,* Philadelphia Edition, 45, pp. 245-73

M. Malowist, 'Les produits des pays de la Baltique dans le commerce international au XVIe siècle', *Révue du Nord,* 42, 1960

F. Mauro, *L'expansion européenne, 1600-1870* (Paris, 1964)

F. Mauro, *Le XVIe siècle européen: aspects économiques* (Paris, 1970)

R. Mousnier, *Les hiérarchies sociales* (Paris, 1969)

R. Mousnier, *Peasant uprisings in 17th century France, Russia and China* (London, 1971)

Thomas Mun, *England's treasure by forraign trade (1664)* (reprinted, Oxford, 1928)

J. U. Nef, *The conquest of the material world* (London, 1964)

Axel Nielsen, *Dänische Wirtschaftsgeschichte* (Jena, 1933)

F. L. Nussbaum, *A history of the economic institutions of modern Europe* (New York, 1937)

J. Ochmanski, 'La grande réforme agraire en Lithuanie et en Ruthénie Blanche au XVIe siècle', *Ergon,* 2, 1960

Adam Olearius (1600-71), *Offt begehrte Beschreibung der Newen Orientalischen Reise* (2nd ed., Slesvig, 1656)

I. Origo, *The merchant of Prato* (London, 1957)

Z. P. Pach, *Die ungarische Agrarentwicklung im 16. und 17. Jahrhundert* (1964)

G. Parker, *The army of Flanders and the Spanish road, 1567-1659* (Cambridge, 1972)

J. H. Parry, *The age of reconnaissance* (2nd ed., London, 1966)

A. F. Pribram (et al.), *Materialien zur Geschichte der Preise und Löhne in Österreich* (Vienna, 1938)

B. Pullan, *Rich and poor in Renaissance Venice* (Oxford, 1971)

B. Pullan (ed.), *Crisis and change in the Venetian economy* (London, 1968)

T. K. Rabb, 'The effects of the Thirty Years' War on the German economy', *Journal of Modern History,* 1962

G. D. Ramsay, *English foreign trade during the centuries of emergence* (London, 1957)

F. Redlich, *The German military enterpriser and his work force*, 2 volumes (Wiesbaden, 1964–5)

M. Roberts (ed.), *Sweden's age of greatness, 1632–1718* (London, 1973)

R. de Roover, *Business, banking and economic thought in late medieval and early modern Europe* (ed. J. Kirchner) (Chicago, 1974)

R. Rörig, *Die europaeische Stadt und die Kultur des Bürgertums im Mittelalter* (3rd ed., Göttingen, 1964)

H. H. Rowan (ed.), *The Low Countries in early modern times* (New York, 1972)

J. Rutkowski, *Histoire économique de la Pologne* (Paris, 1927)

G. K. Schmelzeisen, *Polizeiordnungen und Privatrecht* (Münster, 1955)

H. Schreiber, *Teuton and Slav* (London, 1965)

V. L. von Seckendorff, *Teutscher Fürsten-Staat* (Frankfurt-am-Main, 1656, 5th ed., 1678)

Charles Singer (et al), *A history of technology*, volume 3 (Oxford, 1957)

J. Sirol, *Le rôle de l'agriculture dans les fluctuations économiques* (Paris, 1942)

B. H. Slicher, *The agrarian history of western Europe, 500–1800* (London, 1963)

C. T. Smith, *A historical geography of western Europe before 1800* (London, 1967)

R. E. F. Smith (ed.), *The enserfment of the Russian peasantry* (Cambridge, 1968)

W. Sombart, *Der moderne Kapitalismus*, 2 volumes (Munich, 1922)

J. Sonnenfels, *Grundsätze der Polizey, Handlung und Finanz-wissenschaft* (2nd ed., 3 parts, Vienna, 1768–76)

S. H. Steinberg, *Five hundred years of printing* (London, 1959)

G. Strauss, *Nuremberg in the sixteenth century* (New York, 1966)

G. Strauss (ed.), *Manifestations of Discontent in Germany on the Eve of the Reformation* (Indiana, 1971)

J. Strieder, *Studien zur Geschichte kapitalistischer Organisationsformen* (Munich, 1914)

J. Strieder, *Jacob Fugger der Reiche* (Leipzig, 1926)

V. L. Tapié, *The rise and fall of the Habsburg monarchy* (London, 1971)

J. Topolski, 'La régression économique en Pologne du XVIe au XVIIIe siècle', *Acta Poloniae Historica*, 7, 1962

G. Utterström, 'Climatic fluctuations and population in early modern history', *Scandinavian Economic History Review*, 3, 1955

Joseph de la Vega, *Confusion de confusiones (1688)* (English version edited by H. Kellenbenz, Boston, 1957)

F. van der Ven, *Sozialgeschichte der Arbeit*, volume 2 (Munich, 1972)

Max Weber, *The Protestant ethic and the spirit of capitalism* (9th impression, London, 1968)

H. van der Wee, *The growth of the Antwerp market and the European economy*, 3 volumes (Louvain, 1963)

H. Wiese and J. Bölts, *Rinderhandel und Rinderhaltung im nordwesteuropäischen Küstengebiet, 15. bis 19. Jahrhundert* (1966)

C. H. Wilson, *The Dutch Republic* (London, 1969)

C. H. Wilson, *Profit and Power* (London, 1957)

C. H. Wilson, 'Cloth production and international competition in the 17th century', *Economic History Review*, 1960

C. H. Wilson, *Mercantilism* (Historical Association pamphlet, London, 1958)

T. Wilson (with introduction by R. H. Tawney), *A discourse upon usury (1572)* (London, 1925)

R. Wohlfeil (ed.), *Reformation oder frühbürgerliche Revolution?* (Munich, 1972)

I. Woloch (ed.), *The peasantry in the Old Régime* (New York, 1970)

A. Wyczański, 'Le niveau de la récolte des céréales en Pologne du XVIe au XVIIIe siècle', *First International Economic History Conference* (Stockholm, 1960)

A. Wyczański, 'En Pologne: l'économie du domaine nobiliaire moyen, 1500–1800', in *Annales E.S.C.*, 18, 1963

A. Wyczański, 'Agricultural production and its significance in 16th century Poland', *Studia Historiae Oeconomicae*, 4, 1969

Index